Rebellious Civil Society

Rebellious Civil Society

Popular Protest and Democratic Consolidation
in Poland, 1989–1993

Grzegorz Ekiert and Jan Kubik

Ann Arbor
THE UNIVERSITY OF MICHIGAN PRESS

First paperback edition 2001

Copyright © by the University of Michigan 1999
All rights reserved
Published in the United States of America by
The University of Michigan Press
Manufactured in the United States of America
♾ Printed on acid-free paper

2004   2003   2002   2001   5   4   3   2

A CIP catalog record for this book is available from the British Library.

Library of Congress Cataloging-in-Publication Data

Ekiert, Grzegorz, 1956–
    Rebellious civil society : popular protest and democratic
consolidation in Poland, 1989–1993 / Grzegorz Ekiert and Jan Kubik.
        p.   cm.
    Includes bibliographical references (p.   ) and index.
    ISBN 0-472-11027-6 (alk. paper)
    1. Protest movements—Poland.   2. Political culture—Poland.
3. Poland—Politics and government—1989–   4. Democracy—Poland.
5. Post-communism—Poland.   6. Civil society—Poland.   I. Kubik,
Jan, 1953–   .   II. Title.
HN538.5.E39   1999
303.48′4′09438—dc21
                                                                99-36478
                                                                CIP

ISBN 0-472-08830-0 (pbk. : alk. paper)

For Ela and Martha

Contents

Figures

Tables

Acknowledgments

Data collection for this study was a collaborative effort, and a number of colleagues from all four countries participated in this endeavor. Event analysis is a time-consuming and laborious process, requiring endless hours of checking, interpreting, and verifying hundreds of pieces of information. Krzysztof Gorlach and Kazimierz Kloc supervised two research teams in Poland that scanned selected newspapers and weeklies. Without their efforts and painstaking work, the database would never have been constructed. Jason Wittenberg designed the computerized database, helped train research assistants, and supervised data inputting and coding procedures. He also offered invaluable help in solving many problems that emerged during the data analysis. Anna Grzymala-Busse spent countless days analyzing data, creating tables, and rechecking data. We are grateful for her enthusiasm and help. Jacek Stefanski, an independent historian from Krakow, compiled the chronology of events. The full version of his work was published in Poland (Stefanski 1995).

A project of this magnitude required significant financial resources as well. Our research was generously sponsored by the Program for the Study of Germany and Europe at the Center for European Studies, Harvard University; the National Council for Soviet and East European Research; the Elfride Drager Memorial Foundation; and the American Council of Learned Societies. We also benefited from the opportunity to spend a few weeks as Sawyer Fellows at the Advanced Study Center of the International Institute, University of Michigan, Ann Arbor.

Parts of this study appeared as working papers, articles in professional journals, and chapters in edited volumes. We also presented findings of the project at several conferences and invited lectures. Initial findings of our Polish research were discussed during the conference at the Center for European Studies at Harvard in December 1993. Our special thanks go to the participants of this conference. Many colleagues served as reviewers for our papers and discussants on conference panels. They offered encouragement and helped enormously to shape various parts of the manuscript and improve our thinking and interpretations. In particular, we would like to acknowledge our intellectual debt to Sidney Tarrow, whose work whetted our appetite for protest and movement studies and who shared with us his research materials and helped to launch the project. Our special thanks go to Martha Kubik, Ela Ekiert, Myron Aronoff, Mark Beissinger, Nancy Bermeo, Michael Bernhard, Valerie Bunce, Ellen Comisso, Susan Eckstein, Michal Federowicz, Bela Greskovits, Jan Gross, Peter Hall, Krzysztof Jasiewicz, Robert R. Kaufman, Michael Kennedy, Sergiusz Kowalski, Ireneusz Krzeminski, Christiane Lemke, Darina Malova, John Markoff, Susan Olzak, Maryjane Osa, Dieter Rucht, Andrzej Rychard, Anna Seleny, David Stark, Mate Szabo, Carol Timko, John Waterbury, and Mayer Zald.

CHAPTER 1

Introduction

What is the role of popular protest in the consolidation of new democracy? This is the key question of our study. By answering it, we hope to illuminate a range of empirical and analytical issues critical for understanding the complexity of postcommunist transformations in Poland and elsewhere in East Central Europe.

The bulk of empirical evidence presented in this book comes from our research project on protest politics in four postcommunist countries: East Germany, Hungary, Poland, and Slovakia. The idea for this project evolved during a casual conversation at a conference where the first stages of postcommunist transformations in Eastern Europe were hotly debated. A year earlier, Poland had begun the implementation of its difficult macroeconomic adjustment program. Initial commentaries on the possible effects and outcomes of Poland's bold reforms were either triumphant or alarmist. While some observers marveled over the boldness of the Balcerowicz Plan, others immediately focused on its negative consequences, including a sharp decline in the national product, a meteoric rise in unemployment, a dramatic decline in social spending, and a rapid emergence of social inequalities. For critics of the new economic policies, Poland and other East European countries implementing fast transitions to a market economy were destined to replicate the Third World's predicament of underdevelopment, underinvestment, and chronic social problems. They expected mass outbursts of social discontent engendered by uneven distribution of the economic transformations' costs.

Meanwhile, many scholars struggled to make sense out of the rapid changes spawned by the collapse of state socialism in Eastern Europe. They grappled with new theoretical problems and analytical issues involved in studying the multidimensional (political, economic, cultural, and social) transition process taking place across the region. Faced with an array of challenges, they focused by necessity on a few topics considered to be especially important and consequential: the formation of political parties and party systems, elections, constitutional choices and constitution making, and above all economic transformations, including macroeconomic adjustment programs, privatization strategies, the creation of markets, and the restructuring of firms and sectors of the economy. In brief, most of the literature on regime transitions in Poland,

Eastern Europe, and the former Soviet Union centered around the "classical" themes of institutional politics or economic transformations; often their interdependence was discussed.

While the high/elite-level politics of parties, parliaments, and governments was carefully dissected, its low/popular-level counterparts such as regional/local politics or, most importantly to us, protest politics was largely overlooked. We were familiar with several journalistic accounts of protests against the initial costs and consequences of the postcommunist transformations. But the existing studies and reports did not provide enough information to understand the role of unconventional politics vis-à-vis other, more thoroughly investigated types of politics. The only abundant and systematic source of information was public opinion polls conducted by both old and new research institutes. They tracked the sentiments and attitudes of the population. Yet we still did not know exactly how the public's disappointment with the early results of the transition and their criticism of government policies registered by opinion polls were translated into action. And we understood well that the study of perceptions and attitudes alone cannot produce any reliable knowledge on protest activities. We accepted Tarrow's dictum that

> protest is, first and foremost, a form of action—not a set of dispositions towards, or reports of participants in collective action. Without carrying out systematic studies of collective action itself, it is difficult to know when, against whom, and in what context people decide to engage in protest activities. (1991, 13)

The initial perusal of the Polish press revealed that protest actions were quite common, but it was difficult to assess the scope, depth, and causes of this phenomenon. Moreover, to explain the magnitude and other features of protest in Poland, we had to place the country in a comparative perspective. We needed to know whether there were differences among postcommunist countries in the level of active opposition to elite-guided policies and how different policy choices regarding the speed and sequencing of transformations affected the behavior of popular collective actors. Our early conversations generated a number of more specific questions as well. They included: Were Poles more prone to protest than their neighbors, given the tradition of Solidarity strikes and demonstrations? Which social groups were challenging the new governments' policies or the new sociopolitical order through unconventional political actions? Which organizations were most active in organizing protest? What strategies of protest were most commonly used? What social cleavages were most visible in protest politics? What were the targets of protest? What types of rhetoric and symbols were used by protestors? How effective was protest in shaping policies of the new democratic state? Except for anecdotal evidence, there was nothing that would provide answers to such questions. At the same time, we realized that these questions were usually overlooked by students of democratic transitions in other regions.

Thus, we began the tedious and uninspiring task of collecting systematic information on protest activities in postcommunist countries. In order to explore cross-country variations, we decided that data collection must be conducted in several East European states. We limited our choice to Hungary, the former East Germany (the German Democratic Republic, or GDR), Poland, and Slovakia. Although these four countries shared some similarities, their post-1989 trajectories varied significantly. We assumed that our selection should allow us to control for critical differences in the type of challenges faced by each country and the major choices made by their elites at the outset of transition. In short, we have in our sample two fast reformers (GDR and Poland) and two slow reformers (Hungary and Slovakia). Moreover, we have two countries where the continuity of the state was not questioned (Hungary and Poland) and two countries where the state underwent a fundamental transformation. Slovakia, following the "velvet divorce," acquired independent statehood in 1993. It faced the task of building new state institutions and developing new domestic and foreign policies. The GDR lost its state institutions following the reunification of Germany in 1991. The entire institutional order of the country was thoroughly transformed and the West German federal state structure was imposed, creating five new Länder.

This book, however, will focus exclusively on Poland; other cases will be used only selectively to highlight specific features of Poland's developments. We decided that the Polish case warrants separate treatment and provides an excellent starting point for the future four-country analysis. Poland, after all, was the first country that entered the regime transition, as well as a country with a rich history of collective struggles under state socialism. Moreover, since Polish economic reforms were initiated amidst a debilitating economic crisis and the reform strategy was radical, one could expect strong popular reactions. In addition, Poland's transformations were thoroughly examined by scholars who developed a range of theoretical arguments and collected a considerable amount of empirical evidence. In a sense, Poland has acquired a paradigmatic status in studies of postcommunist transitions the same way Spain became the example of South European democratizations.

The Polish transition began in 1980 with the emergence of the Solidarity movement and was characterized by rapid mass mobilization and open political struggle between the newly constituted independent organizations and the entrenched forces of the party-state. This early effort of democratization was aborted by the imposition of martial law and the de-legalization of Solidarity. Its legacies, however, shaped Polish politics through the 1980s. By the end of the decade democratization was back on the agenda, this time leading to the orderly transfer of power to new political elites. But this long process of deconstruction of the Polish party-state left a visible imprint on the mode of power transfer (roundtable negotiations) and on the consolidation of the new democratic system after 1989.

The most important social legacy of the pre-1989 system was a specific structure of social cleavages. Due to the ontological uniqueness of state socialism, the main protagonists in the struggle between "the state" and "society" (the main collective actors in this system) were constituted through cultural-political rather than economic-political processes (Staniszkis 1989; Ekiert 1991; Kubik 1994a and 1994c; Linz and Stepan 1996, 269–74). As Staniszkis (1992, 10) argued, collective actors were formed at least partially due to the "exploitation of 'value-added' myth rather than interest-led politics." Elsewhere she wrote:

> The weakness of horizontal links and the underdevelopment of civil society typical of state economies, or the development of civil society around different moral visions and value systems, as is happening in Poland today, give rise to artificiality and theatricality in public life, even at those rare moments when society wins an opportunity to speak about itself. (1987, 74)

Solidarity came into existence in August 1980 as the culmination of a long and complex social process initiated at least as far back as the mid-1970s. Because of the geopolitical situation, the state's control over the means of production, and its political control, the struggle in Poland of the late 1970s was not for political power, but for authority and legitimacy, that is, for public predominance among the competing discourses defining social and political order. The fundamental distinction was drawn between those who controlled political and economic resources and attempted to legitimize their authority, and those who had little power but struggled to make "their" discourse visible, audible, and, eventually, hegemonic. The emergence of such a "cultural" cleavage prior to a regime transition is not without historical parallels (see Hunt 1984 or Schama 1989 on the French Revolution).

What happened in Poland in the late 1970s and early 1980s can, then, be construed as a confrontation between the entrenched *political-economic-cultural* class and an emergent social entity that may be labeled the *cultural-political class in statu nascendi*. This cultural-political class was made up not of workers or intellectuals but of all those who subscribed to a system of principles and values, usually referred to as counterhegemonic, unofficial, independent, or alternative—who visualized the social structure as strongly polarized between "us" ("society," "people," etc.) and "them" ("authorities," "communists," etc.). Thus the founding of Solidarity in August 1980, a revolutionary *political* act, was the culmination of a basically *cultural* process. Before they transformed the institutional map of their country, the people who engaged in oppositional activities and later in Solidarity revised their thinking in a process that can be construed as the creation of an a- or anti-communist counterculture, built around a highly articulate set of symbols. The mobilizing power of these symbols was demonstrated throughout the 1980s. During that period, millions of Poles participated in massive protest campaigns, acquiring familiarity with various protest strategies. Thousands of grassroots activists developed organizational skills and built clandestine networks, which became the backbone of the resurrected mass movement at the end of the decade. In 1988, another massive wave of strikes swept the country and resulted in bringing the Solidarity leadership and communist authorities to the negotiating table.

As a result of the "roundtable" negotiations that began in Warsaw on February 6, 1989, Poland became the first country in the Soviet bloc to initiate a peaceful transfer of political power. The semi-democratic elections in June 1989 led to the political triumph of the re-legalized Solidarity movement, the first postwar, noncommunist government was in office by the end of the summer, and the communist party dismantled itself by January 1990. The transfer of power was followed by comprehensive transformations of the national political institutions and local administration and by radical economic reform. The new political elites that emerged from the Solidarity movement set Poland firmly on the course toward liberal democracy and a market economy.

The transformation policies, however, had to be forged and implemented amidst a deepening economic crisis and regional political chaos, as well as disintegrating regional economic and political institutions. These external adversities, combined with radical macroeconomic stabilization measures, contributed to a sharp decline in real incomes, a dramatic rise in unemployment, new social inequalities, and growing insecurity. Few people anticipated such harsh realities; professional and social groups responded with strikes and protests of increasing intensity during the period from 1989 through 1993.

At the same time, the political consensus concerning the extent, speed, and sequencing of institutional reforms, which initially unified the new elites, unraveled. The post-Solidarity political bloc, united for the 1989 elections and initially constituting a single caucus in the parliament, split into several fiercely competing parties with contrasting programs and political agendas. Consequently, during the 1989–93 period, Poland experienced a turbulent political evolution. It had three parliamentary, two local, and two presidential elections, as well as eight consecutive prime ministers and six governments. Not long after its political triumph in 1989, the Solidarity-based political movement disintegrated, and descendant political parties were unable to form effective electoral coalitions. Ironically, the ex-communist parties were returned to power as a result of the 1993 elections.

To summarize, the Polish case stands out among all East Central European transitions due to at least five unique features. They include:

1. Pioneerism. The whole East Central European "revolution" began in Poland in 1980 with the rise of Solidarity, or arguably even earlier, during the rebellions of 1956, 1968, 1970, and 1976. Poland was also the first country to experience a negotiated transfer of power and to introduce major institutional reforms.
2. Relative oversymbolization. The symbolic and cultural aspects of this revolution were far more pronounced and articulate than in other countries of the region.
3. Formation and disintegration of a massive social movement. The rise of Solidarity in 1980, its mass character, and its disintegration in 1989–91 had a decisive formative impact on the shape of Polish postcommunist politics, inhibiting, for example, the development of a Western-type party system.
4. Shift of the organizing principle in the middle of the transition. Solidarity, a mass movement organized according to the *place of work,* was complemented/partially replaced by Citizens' Committees and budding political parties, organized according to the *place of residence.*
5. Administrative reform. Poland carried out the most comprehensive administrative reform in East Central Europe during the early years of democratic consolidation. As a result, local communities were burdened/blessed with a number of administrative prerogatives and responsibilities. Local political arenas acquired some autonomy from national-level politics.

In this book we will try to determine how the combination of these five features influenced the early consolidation phase of the Polish transition (1989–93). It could be expected that three features of the pre-1989 deconstruction phase—(1) early mobilization, (2) oversymbolization of the central political discourse, and (3) mass character of the movement—would have a strong, *adverse* impact on the consolidation phase, since they delayed the development of pragmatic, issue-oriented politics. Two other features—(4) the reactivation of local elites (through Citizens' Committees) and (5) the decentralizing administrative reform—should have a *positive* impact, for their combination should lead to the *decoupling* of national and local/regional politics. This, in turn, would shield local social, political, and—most importantly—economic processes from the volatility of central politics. Vice versa, state policies would be at least partially insulated from local challenges.

Yet such a decoupling may also produce serious problems for the new state if the *linkages* among its various institutional domains are poorly developed.[1] As we will demonstrate, Poland did indeed suffer from the disjointed development of political realms and intense political competition among collective actors representing each of them. In particular, the poor institutionalization of the relationship between the state and its citizens seems to be a reason for the high intensity of collective protest during the analyzed period. There can be no doubt that collective protest and other unconventional forms of behavior emerged as a dominant form of public participation. This further delayed the development of formal representative institutions, weakened the capacity of the state to implement policies, and increased the involvement of civil society's organizations in politics.

Empirical data presented in this book suggest that between 1989 and 1993 in Poland, the fragmentation and weakness of the party system and legislative bodies, as well as an institutional frailty of the state, were accompanied by the growing size and contentiousness of civil society. All of these factors need to be taken into account if we want to understand the logic of postcommunist transformations in Poland and other countries of the region. It is not evident that in and by themselves electoral reforms and constitutional engineering are sufficient to produce democratic consolidation (Hagopian 1993, 466); crafting a democracy by political elites has its limits (Di Palma 1990). If there is such a thing as "democracy by design," many non-elite actors were among the designers. In brief, democratic consolidation appears to be a complicated process, in which historical legacies and popular actors play a significant role.

Theoretical Concerns

The aim of this book is to offer a rich narrative on the post-1989 political developments in Poland and at the same time address important theoretical issues of contemporary comparative politics. We strive to bridge a gap between two important subfields: the study of democratic transition and consolidation and the study of protest and social movements. Transition from communism to postcommunism (or any regime transition) consists of three *logically* distinct, though *empirically* overlapping, phases: the deconstruction of the old regime, the transfer of power, and the consolidation of the new regime. The duration and outcomes of these phases vary from country to country, producing distinctive national trajectories of regime transitions. Our analysis is designed to elucidate a specific pattern of democratic consolidation that occurred in Poland, a pattern in which protest played a prominent role.

Scholars developed two basic approaches to explain variation between cases of regime transition: structural, which emphasizes "variables of context" (or legacies); and processual, which stresses variables of "process" (or agency).[2] Since classical research paradigms in social sciences are not easily applicable to studying a rapid and fundamental political change, many researchers abandoned structural approaches and adopted the processual, elite-centered perspective. O'Donnell and Schmitter and their collaborators, who made the elite transaction model prominent, argued that "elite pacts" are a crucial element in the successful transition from authoritarian rule (1986, 37–39). Similarly, Diamond and Linz claimed that "the skills, values, strategies, and choices of political leaders figure prominently in our explanation of the enormously varied experiences with democracy in Latin America" (1989, 14). Higley and Gunther contended that "in independent states with long records of political instability and authoritarian rule, distinctive elite transformations, carried out by the elites themselves, constitute the main and possibly the only route to democratic consolidation" (1992, xi).

Methodological emphasis on rational choice explanations and on modeling political processes in the image of game theory (Kitschelt 1992a; Geddes 1994a) further reinforced the already dominant elite-centered focus of democratic transitions research. Additionally, the greater availability of "elite" data fortified the dominance of the elite-centered perspective. Party programs, public speeches and interviews of leaders, reports on electoral campaigns, election results, journalistic commentaries, etc., are all easily accessible in the public domain. Such sources of data enable one to reconstruct the political positions of elite actors and the bargaining processes taking place among them and to trace their compromises, coalitions, and policy choices. By contrast, data on the political activities of non-elite actors are not readily available, and public opinion polls are usually used as the sole source of empirical knowledge on the politics of the populace at large.

Nevertheless, a number of recent contributions to transition literature emphasize the need for a synthesis between the two classical approaches. The synthetic model of regime transitions, which incorporates variables (dimensions) of both structure and agency, has been revised in an illuminating fashion by the revival of the institutional approach (Powell and DiMaggio 1991; Steinmo, Thelen, and Longstreth 1992; Hall and Taylor 1996). By bringing institutions back into the analysis, various authors were able to demonstrate how the political choices of elite actors are shaped, mediated, and channeled by institutional arrangements, which they inherited from the old regime or established as preliminary solutions during the first stages of transition (Crawford and Lijphart 1995; Haggard and Kaufman 1995; Karl and Schmitter 1991; Stark and Bruszt 1998).

The institutional approach, however, accords more prominence to certain dimensions of consolidation and neglects others: the formation of party systems is usually viewed as the most important element in the stabilization and consolidation of democracy. Such a view is well expressed by Haggard and Kaufman (1995, 370), who emphasize that "the capacity to organize stable political rule—whether authoritarian or democratic—in the modern context of broad social mobilization and complex economic system ultimately rests on organized systems of accountability, and these in turn rest on political parties."[3] Works on Eastern Europe also focus on the complex interactions between economic and political institutions (Przeworski 1991; Bresser Pereira, Maravall, and Przeworski 1993; Ekiert 1993). This problem has come to be known as the "dilemma of simultaneity" or "transitional incompatibility thesis" (Offe 1991; Sztompka 1992; Armijo, Biersteker, and Lowenthal 1994).

This preoccupation with (1) elites, (2) party systems, and (3) the relationship between political and economic changes has resulted in a considerable gap in democratization literature.[4] Little is known about activities of non-elite actors and the ways in which their activities shape the process of democratization. There are, however, students of democratic transitions who are beginning to emphasize the importance of the resurrection of civil society and its political role both during the decomposition of authoritarian rule and in its aftermath.[5] It is often noted, for example, that the greatest challenge to the policies of the newly democratized states may come from various organizations of civil society (labor movements, interest groups, etc.). Yet the development of such organizations and their political role have not been systematically documented and analyzed. The study of civil society's role in democratic consolidations has often been reduced to the study of political attitudes, conducted on representative samples of the population. The "third wave" of democratizations makes possible, often for the first time in the history of a given society, administering unconstrained public opinion polls. Understandably, many scholars capitalized on this opportunity and studied public attitudes and their changes during the transition process.[6] Such studies contribute to our knowledge of public reactions to regime change and are very useful as long as public opinion poll results are not accepted as a substitute for data on actual political behavior. As Tarrow (1989, 7–8) emphasizes, "unless we trace the forms of activity people use, how these reflect their demands, and their interaction with opponents and elites, we cannot understand either the magnitude or the dynamics of change in politics and society."

Our research project was based on the assumption that event analysis and, in particular, the systematic collection of data on collective action from newspapers can shed new light on the political behavior of non-elite actors during democratization. Newspaper-based event analysis becomes a highly effective tool for studying civil society's activities, especially when combined with other empirical evidence collected through case studies of organizations, public opinion polls, and governmental censuses, yearbooks, reports, etc. We also agree with Neidhardt and Rucht (1991, 459), who conclude that "social movement research should concentrate more on the interactions of movements with other agents." For us in this project, "other agents" include associations and organizations of civil society, political parties, and state agencies.

Thus, while we applaud the institutional approach for providing a welcome correction to both the voluntarism of the processual, elite transaction model and the determinism of the structural approaches, we want to go a step further and emphasize the role of the dynamic interaction between elites and popular movements/protests in transition politics and in the process of postcommunist institution building.

Our analysis is founded on an assumption that democratic consolidation is a highly contingent and complex process taking place in several spheres of the sociopolitical organization of society, including the state, economy, political society, and civil society. Developments within each sphere and the relationship between them produce often confusing outcomes and increasing uncertainty. During transitions, when institutional orders of societies undergo major reformulation, protest actions may become the principal tools of institution building and an important mechanism through which the public sphere and the domain of the political are being reconstituted and new boundaries between the state and society established. Due to the highly indeterminate and amorphous situation produced by the collapse of communist regimes and uncertainties generated by the institutional transformations in the polity and economy, protest actions may become a major factor contributing to the emergence of new organizations and collective identities.

We expected that in the postcommunist countries, protest actions would emerge spontaneously and often express only rudimentary grievances or fears. They would be launched because (1) a pool of legitimate procedures for airing grievances is not yet defined; (2) routine mechanisms of conflict mediation are not yet fully developed or are viewed as illegitimate by some actors; and (3) political constraints on protest activities are lifted and law enforcement agencies are not decisive in persecuting actions that stretch the limits of legality. Yet these spontaneous and poorly structured protest actions could produce social organizations that, in turn, would attempt to establish alliances and mobilize resources, begin to construct new collective identities, and work to establish issues areas that would become the ground for future struggles. For such organizations, an escalation of conflict would often be the only way to assert themselves publicly as "serious" political players. Defining anew both the state and the repertoire of contention directed against it should resemble the nineteenth-century processes analyzed by Tilly, who writes:

> As parties, unions, and other associations specializing in the struggle for power grew in importance, so did the idea—and the reality—of parallel

streams of people, guided by shared interests and beliefs, which over-flowed the narrow channels of elections or labor-management negotiations which were being dug at the same time. (1984, 310)

Thus, within the relatively open political space created by the old regime's collapse, popular protests should contribute to the process of defining the public domain and remaking the boundaries between the state and society. Contentious politics should become a tool of negotiating and defining new relations and distribution of influence and authority among old and new political and social actors. In brief, we expected popular protest to be a crucial element of the state making and remaking process occurring in postcommunist countries. In making this assumption we followed Bright and Harding, who wrote:

As contests over state activities, boundaries, and structures, popular protests, social movements, and ultimately revolutions must be included as statemaking processes. . . . they are all mechanisms through which politicians and state managers, social and economic elites, and popular groups contest—and in contesting, alter—what the state is, what it shall do, and who shall have access to its resources. (1984, 5)

Analyzing the role of protest in postcommunist transformations, we will emphasize strongly the cultural dimension of this process. During the last several years, many students of collective action and social protest focused their analytical lenses on this dimension of protest actions. Klandermans characterized this new trend most succinctly: "In the literature on social protest, the insight is winning ground that one's interpretations, rather than reality itself, guide political actions. . . . Interpreting grievances and raising expectations of success are the core of the social construction of protest" (1989a, 121–22).[7]

This insight has been confirmed by a number of empirical works. Eckstein observed in her summary of an extensive study of Latin American popular protest that

The impact of cultural values and norms on defiance can thus be very different from what Kornhauser (1959) and other 'mass society' theorists posited. Kornhauser argued that the breakdown of norms stirred unrest. Yet we have stressed the opposite: that cultural traditions may spark protest. In the absence of cultural (and group) bonds, disgruntled individuals are likely to accept their lot, however grudgingly, or turn to individual, not collective, efforts to address their plight. (1989a, 36–37)

The emphasis on the cultural dimension of collective action is highly relevant for our work, since cultural (symbolic) factors played a particularly pronounced role in the deconstruction of Polish state socialism (Kubik 1994a); they have also emerged as crucial components of postcommunist transformations.[8]

The results of the research project presented in this book expand our understanding of democratization and draw attention to the relatively neglected dimensions of democratic consolidation. We focus specifically on an institutional domain that is critical for the progress of democratic consolidation: civil society. We adopted a broad concept of civil society in order to take into consideration organizations embedded in economic relations (trade unions, employers' organizations), voluntary associations, and other organizations of the public sphere. We decided to trace the activities of these non-elite collective actors and their impact on the process of consolidation to counter the existing pro-elite bias in the literature. Furthermore, we focused on protest activities, which are the most spectacular mode of public participation within the realm of civil society.[9]

Our efforts to analyze the role of bottom-up mobilization during the regime transition and consolidation would be impossible without the help of contemporary research and theorizing on social movements and collective action. This innovative and dynamic field of research has one feature that poses difficulties in applying its concepts and findings to cases of regime change. Most empirical research and theoretical reflection focused on stable Western democracies. American researchers always treated more fundamental parameters of the political system as given and stable. As a result, they were mostly concerned with the question of how collective actors marshal their resources to respond to more transient changes in national- or local-level politics. European scholars were more sensitive to the variety of states both in their institutional architecture and in their capacities. They, however, also studied stable political systems and consolidated democracies.[10] In contrast, regime transitions are periods "between states" during which most characteristics of the political context are undergoing rapid transformations. Thus the notion of political opportunity structure that informed the bulk of recent research and theorizing in the field of social movements has to be reconsidered (see Ekiert and Kubik 1998). We accept, however, a significant portion of the analytical apparatus developed by the students of collective action. We find concepts of repertoires of collective action, collective action frames, and mobilizing structures, as well as broader theoretical approaches emphasizing identities and resources, to be extremely useful in analyzing consolidating polities.

In sum, the originality of our study has two sources. First, we approach postcommunist transformations from a specific analytical angle: our focus is on the behavior of non-elite actors constituting civil society. Second, we attempt to synthesize two separate literatures (on social movements and democratic consolidation) to provide an effective analytical framework for the understanding of a specific pattern of institutionalization of democracy in Poland and elsewhere in East Central Europe.

Research Strategy

Our quest for information on protest activities quickly showed that data collected by governmental agencies (for example, strike statistics that provide only the number of strikes, strikers, and hours lost) were not sufficient for our purpose. Thus, guided by recent research advances in the field of social movements and collective action, we decided to use protest event analysis as a method for data collection. Following the pioneering work of Charles Tilly and his associates, event analysis has become an accepted and often indispensable research method in the study of collective action, protest, and social movements. Despite its imperfections and limitations, acknowledged by those who use it, event analysis is uniquely capable of providing researchers with the most extensive and systematic sets of data on protest activities and their different components and dimensions.[11] It allows for the study of both qualitative and quantitative aspects of protest actions over time and in large geographical areas. It may also be used in several different research designs, either focusing on a single case or employing a comparative perspective. It can be applied to answer a variety of questions concerning collective action, its forms and outcomes, its organizers and participants, responses of the state, and broader political issues. This method allowed us to create comparable data sets for protest events that took place in four former communist countries during the first five years of democratic consolidation.

Newspapers provide the most complete account of protest events and are virtually the only source of information on many important dimensions of protest activities. However, in the case of democratizing societies, the validity and reliability of newspaper accounts as the data source presents a special problem.[12] In principle, the existence of freedom of the press is a fundamental precondition for any application of protest event analysis based on press sources. In addition, the quality of the press coverage may have a critical impact on the quality of data. For these reasons, protest event analysis has usually been used for analyzing protest activities in North America and Western Europe, and Western newspapers (especially the *New York Times*) were used as a data source even if information was collected for other countries. The media in developed Western democracies are characterized by a robust liberal tradition, institutional stability, independence, and high standards of journalism. Moreover, the state's involvement in media activities is highly restricted and their freedom guaranteed.

The media in newly democratized societies have to deal with the legacies of censorship, state manipulations, and political subservience (Curry 1984 and 1990). Following the collapse of the old regime, however, the state's control over the content, personnel, and institutional survival of the media is usually abolished or at least significantly restricted. Typically, the print media are able to secure more freedom and independence than electronic media, such as radio and TV, which are seen as particularly useful weapons in post-breakthrough political struggles. Economic criteria and market viability become important factors in shaping the content and securing the institutional survival of newspapers and journals. This new situation stimulates a rapid growth of the print media. New journals and newspapers appear, old newspapers disappear, there are new owners and employees and new editorial boards. In sum, institutional instability, inexperienced newcomers, and "old-timers" committed to the old ways are the problems facing Eastern Europe's postcommunist media. Researchers from Radio Free Europe were highly critical in their evaluation of East European media in 1993. They argued that

> the media in Eastern Europe still suffer from a variety of ills related to dire economic problems, a lack of experience with democracy, low journalistic standards, and the fact that the political systems of many countries are in flux. . . . Although independent periodicals have proliferated in virtually all East European countries, a number of leading newspapers . . . are either closely associated with the government or are the organs of major political parties. Censorship has all but disappeared in most countries; but some media laws as well as the policies of some governments have arguably restricted the latitude of journalists. . . . The standards of journalism in most countries are still low. With a few exceptions, periodicals in the postcommunist countries of Eastern Europe have a clear ideological bent; journalists are often closely associated with particular political philosophies and frequently tend to combine factual descriptions of events with commentary.[13]

While this harsh judgment applies more to some countries and less to others (such as Poland), the reliability of the press as sources for data collection in democratizing countries must be seriously considered. Our experience indicates that data collection should be based on several different sources that are carefully selected in order to control for possible biases. Moreover, our data show that quality of press coverage improves significantly over time, which is a welcome development but one that creates an additional problem for a quantitative analysis.

The print media sector in communist countries was highly developed and at the same time tightly controlled through a variety of overt and covert means and practices. The post-1989 political and economic changes included the cre-

TABLE 1. Number of Daily Newspapers
and Periodicals in Poland, 1980–93

	Dailies	Periodicals
1980	88	2,482
1985	97	2,846
1990	130	3,007
1991	122	2,968
1992	129	2,950
1993	124	3,139

ation of guarantees of substantial freedom of the press and an increase in the number of dailies and periodicals. In terms of the number and variety of available newspapers and periodicals, communist countries were comparable to developed democracies. For example, the number of newspapers and periodicals in Poland between 1980 and 1993 (see table 1) was similar to the number of publications available in developed democratic countries such as Spain or France. Although the overall number of newspapers and periodicals did not change significantly following the collapse of the communist regime, there was a major shift in the importance and quality among existing and newly funded publications. Therefore, an extensive preliminary study of several publications had to be conducted before a final selection of sources was made.

As a source for our database, we selected two national "prestige" newspapers—*Rzeczpospolita* and *Gazeta Wyborcza*.[14] Our coders read every issue of each paper published during the analyzed period (1989–93). In so doing, we avoided the problems associated with selecting (sampling) a subset of issues to be analyzed (Kriesi et al. 1995, 259–63; Rucht, Koopmans, and Neidhardt 1998). The papers we selected are the largest (in terms of readership) and the most comprehensive dailies in Poland. Before 1989, *Rzeczpospolita* had been a governmental daily, but after a change in personnel, it emerged as the country's most reliable and objective paper. Despite its formal status as a state-owned newspaper, it has ceased to be the government's mouthpiece and retained its independence even before it was partially privatized. *Gazeta Wyborcza* was founded in the spring of 1989 as an organ of the Solidarity movement. The paper quickly distanced itself from any explicit affiliation with political parties that succeeded Solidarity and has become the most popular daily in the country, with a circulation higher than that of any other paper in Eastern Europe. Its bias is clear: it sympathizes with the liberal-democratic option, most prominently represented by the Union of Freedom (formerly Democratic Union). Both newspapers have extended networks of regional offices and cover both national and local events. These two dailies were supplemented by four

TABLE 2.   Distribution of Press Reporting on Protest Events

Reporting distribution	1989	1990	1991	1992	1993
Gazeta Wyborcza only	94	85	77	90	73
	29.9%	27.8%	26.4%	28.7%	29.2%
Rzeczpospolita only	114	85	61	90	53
	36.3%	27.8%	20.9%	28.7%	21.2%
Weeklies only	6	42	15	24	21
	1.9%	13.7%	5.1%	8.2%	8.4%

Note: The percentages represent the proportion of protest events that would have been missed if one of these sources had been eliminated from the sample of publications that were coded.

weeklies: *Tygodnik Solidarnosc* (the official organ of the Solidarity trade union), *Wiesci* (a weekly focusing on agriculture and peasant issues), *Polityka* (a prominent political weekly), and *Zycie Gospodarcze* (a major business weekly). Again, the coders were asked to read every issue printed during the analyzed period. By selecting these four weeklies, we gained access to both national and regional news as well as to specific sectoral reporting. The reliance on several sources greatly increased the amount of information on protest events recorded in our database. Table 2 illustrates the number of protest events that were covered by one daily only or exclusively by one or more of the four weeklies.

The data indicate that our reliance on the two dailies improved our "coverage" by 21–36 percent of events yearly. While coding weeklies added only a small percentage of protest events to the database, they provided additional information about events that were sometimes sketchily covered by the dailies. We agree with Beissinger that "in a transitional society the best strategy available to a researcher is likely to be a 'blanketing' strategy, utilizing multiple sources and multiple types of information whenever they are available" (1998, 290).

The increasing accuracy (and presumably validity) of press coverage of protest events is easily detectable in our database. As time passed, descriptions of protest events found in newspapers were increasingly detailed and comprehensive. Table 3 illustrates the percentage of events for which we do not have

TABLE 3.   News Articles Missing Information on Aspects of Protest Events (in percentages)

	1989	1990	1991	1992	1993
Duration of protest	35.4	28.4	21.6	15.3	7.6
Number of participants	70.7	56.9	41.8	40.1	26.0
Sponsoring organizations	50.3	28.8	16.4	15.0	5.6

information on the duration of protest, the number of participants,[15] or organizations leading or sponsoring protest events, over the studied period.

We have to acknowledge that the quality of our data is uneven. For many protest events, we have detailed information regarding all dimensions of the protest action; for others, a number of important pieces of information are missing. This high and variable amount of missing data poses serious problems for a statistical analysis of our results. For example, the duration of protest events and the number of participants are the critical elements in calculating protest magnitude, a potentially very useful, synthetic variable. But various methods of estimating missing values produced divergent results. Bearing this in mind, we decided to present our findings in as simple a form as possible.

For the entire period of 1989–93, we were able to collect information on 1,476 protest events. In our research project, we adopted a broad definition of "protest event" to cover all types of noninstitutionalized and unconventional collective public action. Our definition includes the following elements: (1) "public" is understood to mean an action that is reported in at least one newspaper; (2) collective action is an action undertaken by at least three people, although extreme acts such as self-immolation, hunger strikes, or acts of terror—carried out by individuals as a form of political protest—are also counted as "collective acts"; (3) a collective public action is an act of protest if it is undertaken to articulate certain specific demands, it is not a routine or legally prescribed behavior of a social or political organization, and its form deviates from the routinely accepted way of voicing demands. We considered the demand to be "articulated" when the participants (whether organized or not) turn to institutions, organizations, and enterprises, both public and private, and

1. demand that specific decisions, laws, or policies be changed;
2. demand the removal of individuals responsible for such decisions and policies;
3. demand the right to participate in the decision-making process;
4. demand the abolition of existing or creation of new institutions or laws;
5. make financial claims against the institutions or organizations;
6. express general opposition to the policies of institutions, leaders, or organizations; and/or
7. demand recognition of their identity and rights.

We distinguished three types of protest events. If separate protest actions are officially directed or coordinated by one decision-making center, they constitute together a protest campaign, which we count as one protest event. We also use the notion of "series of protests," which denotes a number of different protest actions undertaken by various collective actors at approximately the same time that articulate the same or similar demands. For such events, however, we could not identify a coordinating center. All other protests were counted as simple protest events.

Protest events were coded if at least one of the following bits of information was recorded in the source(s): (1) the date the protest event began or ended, (2) the form of protest (e.g., strike, demonstration), (3) organizers and/or participants in events, (4) demand(s) or postulate(s) put forth by the protestors. Protest events were coded using the extended coding scheme reproduced in appendix A, which included 77 variables. This scheme was designed to expand the scope for potential analyses that would include the internal dynamic of protest events and their cultural dimension (collective action frames, discourses, symbolic resources, etc.).

We do not claim that our research registered the entire universe of protest activities in Poland. Newspaper sources are not perfect. Media reporting is known to focus more on bigger events and controversial issues and ignore smaller and noncontroversial events (see McCarthy et al. 1995). It can be argued, however, that protest events that did not find their way into public space through media reporting have little impact beyond their immediate local context. In addition, it is questionable whether an extra effort (such as a study of police records) could change the general picture of protest activities in any meaningful way. At the present moment, the data we collected represent the most complete and detailed information on protest activities gathered in postcommunist countries of East Central Europe. In this book, however, we will rely on other sources as well. Taking the view that research is best pursued through adopting multiple strategies of inquiry, we use other primary and secondary sources, abundant existing survey data, media content analysis, and findings of other research projects on postcommunist politics.

Plan of the Book

The book is divided into eight chapters. Chapters 2 and 3 serve as a general background for our analysis. The purpose of these chapters is to provide a succinct overview of developments in Poland before and after 1989. Such a background is indispensable for the more detailed analysis of protest politics presented in the subsequent chapters.

Chapter 2 traces the development of the relationship between the state and society in Poland under state socialism. It focuses on political crises and collective protest, analyzing their impact on institutions and policies of the Polish regime. Among all state-socialist regimes, Poland was the most crisis prone and unstable. Party-state policies were often challenged from below by different groups and organizations. A significant number of the country's citizens took part in various kinds of protest actions before 1989. Through a series of public political confrontations, specific repertoires of protest were developed, and unconventional protest activities were broadly legitimized as a way of opposing government policies. As a result, Poland not only displayed a number of institutional and political peculiarities, but also had distinctive traditions of protest that predated 1989. We argue that these legacies have a powerful impact on regime transition and consolidation.

In chapter 3 we offer a brief overview of the country's developments since 1989. We focus on three critical dimensions: (1) major political developments in both national and regional/local politics, including elections and government changes; (2) economic transformations and their outcomes; and (3) social developments and popular evaluations of the political and economic changes.

Chapter 4 introduces our conceptual model. We begin by laying out the distinction between three political realms—the state, political society, and civil society. We analyze the relationship among these institutional realms and their transformations during the regime transition and consolidation. We also enumerate conditions for judging the progress of consolidation. In the second part of this chapter, we describe the development and institutionalization of these three realms in post-1989 Poland, arguing that during the first years of post-communist transformations the Polish polity was characterized by governmental instability, a weak and fragmented political society (party system), and a rapidly expanding civil society. In this context, protest activities sponsored by organizations of civil society became a routine mode of public participation and interaction between the state and society.

Chapter 5 focuses on general dimensions of protest, describing (1) the nature of protest events (number, scope, size, duration, magnitude); (2) protest participants and organizers (social categories, organizations); (3) their strategies and repertoires of protest; and (4) targets and outcomes of protest events.

Chapter 6 presents a case study of a critically important but grossly misunderstood political event: the fall of the Suchocka government in May 1993. The successful no-confidence vote followed by the dissolution of the parliament ended the reign of political forces descendant from the Solidarity-based opposition and opened the way for parties associated with the old regime to return to power. In this chapter we show that the linear causal pattern of objective costs of economic reforms→ subjective grievances/perceptions→ protest actions is not unambiguously supported by our data. We also argue that protest actions are most likely to succeed in their objectives when the activities of actors within civil society are combined with the actions of political actors in the parliamentary arena. In short, protest politics is bound to have a direct impact on government policies when alliances and links are established across the institutional domains of the polity.

Chapter 7 focuses on a cultural dimension of protest politics, analyzing collective action frames and political discourses shaping protest activities. The evidence presented and analyzed here supports one of the major findings reported in chapter 5: while protest magnitude intensified and its symbolism became more radical, the predominant tenor of protest's rhetoric remained moderate and reformist.

In chapters 6 and 7 we investigate the relationship between economic factors, political perceptions, and protest activities. Using three sets of data (economic indicators, public opinion surveys, and protest data), we note that protest actions have a strong impact on popular perception of the political and economic situation. In other words, it is not the growing perception of political and economic ills that spawns protest activities; rather, the emergence of protest activities directly influences popular perceptions. Widespread protest generates a decline in popular confidence in state institutions and policies and a more critical evaluation of the country's situation.

In the concluding chapter we summarize two sets of contributions offered by this study. First, we recapitulate what we have learned about contentious collective actions in Poland. Second, we recount how collective protest shaped the first phase of democratic consolidation and how it shaped the type of democratic regime that emerged in postcommunist Poland.

CHAPTER 2

Political Crises and Popular Protest
under State Socialism → Poland

In this chapter we analyze the political crises and cycles of protest that took place in Poland from 1945 to 1989. A historical overview of contentious politics under communist rule is necessary for two reasons. First, we want to show that popular protest and political activities of non-elite actors were a recurrent feature of political development and had a significant impact on institutions and policies of the Polish communist regime. Second, we are convinced that without out a clear understanding of past resistance strategies and patterns of political mobilization, crucial facets of the current social, political, and economic transformations can be easily misapprehended or misjudged (see Bunce 1999, 155).

Poland's post–World War II political developments were distinctive in comparison to other parts of the region. The country experienced five major political crises (in 1956, 1968, 1970, 1976, and 1980–81), involving massive mobilizations of various social and professional groups, that provoked coercive responses by the state. It has often been argued that communist Poland was an extreme example of both the institutional weakness of the party-state and the strength of various groups within society who were able to openly challenge state policies. It was the only country where mass protests became a frequent way of exerting political pressure and defending collective interests. This unique feature of Polish politics was a legacy of the de-Stalinization crisis of the 1950s (Ekiert 1996). Paradoxically, Poland's successful and relatively peaceful dismantling of Stalinist rule, culminating in October 1956, became a serious liability for the country's post-Stalinist ruling elite. The de-Stalinization process engendered institutional, political, and cultural legacies that coalesced into a unique political opportunity structure that set Poland apart from other East Central European regimes. After 1956, the Polish communist regime became institutionally more diverse, culturally more tolerant, and economically more constrained than most of its East European neighbors. As a result, it was more vulnerable to collective action from below, and its policy choices were constrained by real or anticipated opposition by various social groups. The Polish ruling elite frequently resorted to state corporatist practices, buying the quiescence of strategic social and professional groups or regions. Such policies imposed additional burdens on an inefficient economic system and magnified

21

economic difficulties. In addition, Polish workers, students, and intellectuals became more defiant and more willing to air their grievances and defend their interests through contentious actions. As we will show in subsequent chapters, the legacy of this contentiousness under state socialism had a significant impact on the early phase of democratic consolidation (1989–93).

Resistance and Protest under State Socialism

There were two common misconceptions concerning state-socialist regimes: the belief that communist party-states were strong, characterized by a high level of institutional stability and a sufficient measure of citizens' compliance; and the view that due to their highly repressive nature, any organized opposition was impossible. In fact, these states were cumbersome but ineffective bureaucracies[1] and faced critical challenges in maintaining political stability, especially in their declining years. Despite their highly repressive nature, waves of popular mobilization and various forms of collective protest occurred repeatedly. The threat of protest became an important element of every policy decision made by the ruling elites. In addition, all cases of contentious action demonstrated considerable protest potential and the actual ability of social actors under state socialism to organize large-scale protests that these regimes were not able to prevent, despite their enormous repressive capacity. Such actions reflected the institutional and political weaknesses of these regimes and effectively challenged the image of a homogenized and atomized citizenry, incapable of exercising any effective political pressures and skillfully manipulated by the rulers, that was suggested by the concept of totalitarianism and other "one-actor" models. The persistence and impact of these protests also questioned the validity of "state-centered" explanatory models, according to which only state elites or the hegemonic power in the region were accorded an active role in shaping political processes.[2]

Popular protest in East Central Europe displayed a number of peculiarities. First, the distinction between routine and unconventional forms of protest can hardly apply to state-socialist regimes. Political terror during the Stalinist period effectively eradicated all routine forms of dissent and protest. In a highly repressive social environment, even simple disagreement over minor economic or local issues was considered politically subversive and invited severe repression. Havel (1985, 49) emphasizes this point, arguing that "in societies under the post-totalitarian system, all political life in the traditional sense has been eliminated. People have no opportunity to express themselves politically in public, let alone to organize politically." Second, under such conditions, open defiance indicated strong, preexisting undercurrents of resistance to communist rule. As many studies of protest in various social and political systems demonstrate, under conditions of social and political oppression open acts of defiance

simple disagreements become "subversive" "everything politicized"

2 misconceptions:
① state parties strong, states stable, citizens compliant
② organized opposition impossible

may be infrequent, but they are founded on widespread discontent and everyday resistance (Scott 1986 and 1990; Weller and Guggenheim 1989; Colburn 1989; Kershaw 1983; Eckstein 1989a; Kopstein 1996; O'Brien 1996). In Eckstein's words, "what passes for apathy may reflect quiet dissatisfaction with, and defiance of, existing political options" (1989a, 27). Similarly, Scott argues that "most of the political life of subordinate groups is to be found neither in overt collective defiance of powerholders nor in complete hegemonic compliance, but in the vast territory between those two polar opposites" (1990, 195).

In state-socialist regimes, as in other repressive regimes, "resistance . . . was less to be found in the open protests, petitions, riots, and revolts that did occasionally erupt but rather in a quiet but massive pattern of evasion" (Scott 1990, 136).[3] For many decades these undercurrents of political resistance and their extent and importance were overlooked by the scholars. Most of the existing studies focused on rare acts of open rebellion or on oppositional activities by members of the political and intellectual elites. This was, no doubt, the result of highly restricted access to information, a lack of independent public opinion, and the difficulties in conducting research. However, it was also the result of an elite-centered theoretical optics of scholarly research.

A systematic account of patterns and forms of everyday resistance under state socialism has yet to be written. It is certainly difficult to establish clear-cut boundaries between various forms of insubordination and resistance and even more difficult to assign political intentions and significance to such actions.[4] There is, however, enough evidence to conclude that the scope of defiance and resistance was much greater than instances of open protest actions would indicate. Moreover, such forms of resistance formed a crucial dimension of the relationship between the state and society under state socialism. Several obvious examples come to mind. There was extensive peasant resistance against collectivization, which delayed the state's takeover of land for many years and in Poland obstructed collectivization policies altogether (cf. Gorlach 1989; Lewis 1979; Rev 1987; Dobieszewski 1992). Churches and religious communities resisted the state's forced secularization and atheization policies (cf. Manticone 1986; Micewski 1994; Osa 1989; Ramet 1987). There was pervasive dissent among intellectuals (cf. Skilling 1981; Karpinski 1987; Haraszti 1987; Bugajski 1987; Goldfarb 1989; Frentzel-Zagorska and Zagorski 1989; Smolar 1991; Bernhard 1993), while cultural defiance among the youth and students was reflected in their fashion, music, and art as well as in the emergence of new social movements in the 1980s (cf. Bozoki 1988; Misztal 1990; Ryback 1990; Tismaneanu 1990; Kurti 1991; Wertenstein-Zulawski and Peczak 1991; Glinski 1996). Working-class resistance on the shop floor was a widespread phenomenon (cf. Haraszti 1977; Pravda 1979 and 1983; Sable and Stark 1982; Burawoy 1985; Burawoy and Lukacs 1992, 35–58). And, finally, illegal and semilegal economic activities were common and undermined the institutional and ideological foundations of state socialism (cf. Kenedi 1982; Aslund 1985; Wedel 1986; Szelenyi 1988; Gabor 1989; Los 1990; Seleny 1991). If the defiance was so wide ranging, however, the question arises why major protests were relatively few, and why they occurred more frequently in Poland than in any other country of the region.

Political Crises and Protest in Poland

Scholars have explained the extraordinary frequency of popular protest and political instability in post-1945 Poland in two ways. Some interpretations pointed to a number of peculiar factors that characterized Polish society and the party-state (Schopflin 1983). These factors reflected both Poland's past historical experiences and the peculiarities of the imposition and consolidation of the communist regime. Among these factors, the following seven have been listed most often: the existence of the institutionally strong and politically independent Catholic Church, the survival of private ownership of land and noncollectivized agriculture, a long history of strong anti-Soviet sentiments and uprisings against foreign domination, the strength and intransigence of the intelligentsia, the rebellious nature of the working class,[5] the institutional weakness of the Polish party-state, and its dismal economic performance. The second approach was based on systemic interpretations that emphasized the internal logic common to all state-socialist regimes. According to these interpretations, state-socialist institutional systems produced self-destructive tendencies and were highly crisis prone. By their nature, such regimes not only were highly repressive but also generated economic inefficiency, policy inflexibility, and underlying political instability. For a variety of unique historical factors, Poland was seen as the clearest example of such logic.[6]

We argue that neither social and historical factors peculiar to Poland nor a self-destructive logic of state socialism alone can explain the specificity of Poland's political developments under communist rule. In order to explain Poland's distinctive developments, one must focus on the country's particular political experiences, the dynamics and outcomes of political struggles and conflicts, and their cumulative political and institutional as well as cultural consequences. In this sequence of events, the specific resolution of the de-Stalinization crisis in 1956 created institutional and cultural foundations for Poland's subsequent turbulent political history. Peculiarities of Polish state socialism should be seen as resulting from a series of open confrontations between party-state elites and various forces within society that produced each time only temporary accommodations. From this perspective, Poland's postwar history presents itself as a long political learning process in which both sides of the confrontation developed new strategies of resistance and protest absorption, produced new institutional, political, and cultural resources, and traded concessions and defeats.[7]

Resistance to Imposition of a Communist Regime

The imposition of a communist regime in Poland was accompanied by a period of open and intense resistance and political struggle. Organized forms of opposition and protest reached their peak in 1946 but quickly subsided in the face of relentless and brutal repressive actions conducted by the Soviet forces, the communist-controlled security police, and the army. Following the rigged elections in January 1947, the victorious communists declared amnesty for members of the political and military underground. However, political repressions only intensified, lasting well into the 1950s. This cycle of protests displayed the most varied repertoire of collective action in Poland's postwar history. According to Kersten (1984, 1987), forms of opposition against the communist takeover during this period included (1) everyday resistance and symbolic defiance; (2) public demonstrations and strikes; (3) political struggle of legal opposition forces; (4) underground political organizations; and (5) armed resistance. Our knowledge about the strength and influence of antiregime movements and organizations as well as about the extent, forms, and intensity of protests is still relatively limited. Official communist data show that the number of illegal political and military organizations dropped from 1,057 in 1945 and 1,064 in 1946 to 721 in 1947 and 566 in 1948. The membership of these organizations was estimated at 80,296 in 1945, then 61,264 in 1946, then 46,084 in 1947, and 13,166 in 1948 (cf. Jakubowski 1988, 157; Wozniczka 1992, 16–18; Hemmerling and Nadolski 1990; Szpakowski 1996; Otwinowska and Zaryn 1996). Between 1944 and 1948, the security police recorded 45,800 so-called terrorist acts against state authorities. During the same period, as a result of repressive actions against the opposition, 8,668 people were killed, some 150,000 arrested, and 22,797 sentenced by military tribunals (cf. Turlejska 1987, 42–43, and 1990; Marat and Snopkiewicz 1990; Paczkowski 1994).

  The cornerstone of legal opposition against the communists was the Polish Peasant Party (PSL), led by Stanislaw Mikolajczyk. Other political forces such as the Labor Party, independent socialists, or nationalists also attempted to organize legal political activities. Their efforts were quickly subverted by security forces. Leaders and activists of these parties were harassed and arrested. Communist agents infiltrated the leadership of such parties in order to destroy them from within. As a result, all legally existing noncommunist parties were destroyed or forcibly merged with the communist party and its satellites. Mikolajczyk escaped from Poland after the communist-declared victory in the falsified elections of 1947 and the wave of repression against independent politicians that followed. Remnants of the PSL were merged into the communist-controlled United Peasant Party, and the Polish Socialist Party was merged with the Polish Workers Party in 1948. The period of legal political opposition was over (cf. Zaryn 1996; Kostewicz 1996; Paczkowski 1991).

Armed resistance and legal opposition activities were also paralleled by other forms of collective protest. In May 1946, mass antiregime demonstrations in several cities were brutally dispersed by the security police, followed by student strikes. During these events some protesters were killed, others wounded and arrested (cf. Brzoza 1996; Mazowiecki 1989). The country also experienced waves of workers' strikes, mostly caused by economic problems (low wages, excessive production quotas, lack of food, repression against workers' representatives, etc.). According to partial data collected by the Ministry of Labor and Social Welfare, during the last quarter of 1945, there were 42 strikes in 56 enterprises. In 1946, there were 136 strikes in several hundred factories (cf. Gnatowska 1985; Kenney 1993; Kloc 1989; Kersten 1990, 222–23). It is clear that existing analyses of protest and resistance in Poland have focused on post-1956 events and have not paid sufficient attention to this early period of struggle. With the information currently available, one can argue plausibly that specific features of Polish Stalinism, such as its notable self-limitation in comparison to other East European regimes, should be linked to the widespread and intense resistance and protest activities occurring during the formative stages of the communist regime. Despite the fact that by 1948 organized resistance and open protests were eradicated by political repression and consolidation of the party-state's institutional structures, there were important legacies of this period that shaped the nature of Polish Stalinism as well as the de-Stalinization crisis in 1956. But the reemergence of collective protest in Poland after 1953 was a direct consequence of the political crisis that affected all Stalinist regimes in the mid-1950s.

The October 1956 Crisis

The period between 1953 and 1956 was crucial for subsequent events that shook Poland in 1956. This was a time of great uncertainties stemming from the gradual dissolution of the political order constructed by Stalin and his clones in East Central Europe. Stalin's death in March 1953 roused vague expectations and hopes for change. The dismal economic situation caused frequent outbursts of social unrest. Some groups, such as intellectuals and young party activists, benefited more from the new situation than others. Reformist and more pragmatic factions inside the communist parties were able, for the first time, to challenge effectively the Stalinist establishment. Internal debates and struggles that split elites of state-socialist regimes during that time focused on three general issues:

1. the problem of political and economic relations between the Soviet Union and its satellite regimes that arose after dissolution of a main tool of Stalinist policies in the region, the Information Bureau of the Communist and Workers Parties (Cominform), in April 1956 as well as the formal normalization of relations between the USSR and Yugoslavia in June 1956;
2. reassessment of domestic Stalinist policies, resulting in a complete reshuffling of political elites, reorganization of the political police, rehabilitation and readmission to the party of former leaders accused of rightist deviations, posthumous rehabilitation of some victims of Stalinist terror,[8] and the dismissal and indictment of some security force functionaries responsible for the most glaring abuses of power during the Stalinist years;
3. the reevaluation of Stalinist forced industrialization policies, which resulted in a debate on ways of correcting and rationalizing the distorted economic system. In the center of these debates were collectivization policies, principles of investment and resource allocation, and the idea of a limited market. In general, this period of transition produced a highly chaotic political situation that was characterized by deep intraelite cleavages and conflicts, a disastrous economic situation, continued Stalinist rhetoric in the media, abrupt shifts between old Stalinist and "new course" policies, and increasing social discontent and pressures for change. Poland was in the forefront of these developments.

On June 28, 1956, a peaceful workers' demonstration in Poznan was transformed into a bloody revolt after security police fired into the crowd.[9] The situation in Poznan—Poland's fourth major industrial city—had been tense for quite some time before the demonstrations and strikes erupted. Already in 1954 and 1955, workers were bitterly complaining about acute housing and food shortages, excessive production quotas and taxes, and inadequate supplies of components and raw materials, which prevented them from fulfilling production norms. The revolt began with a huge demonstration of workers from all the city's factories in front of the town hall in response to rumors concerning the arrest of a workers' delegation from Poznan sent to Warsaw to present their complaints and demands. Within hours, after the security police fired upon the crowd approaching police headquarters, thousands of demonstrators were battling the regime's security forces, destroying police stations, seizing arms, and releasing prisoners. The omnipresent slogans "We want bread," "We want freedom," and "Down with false communism" aptly reflected workers' grievances and feelings. The Polish regime immediately mobilized massive armed forces of more than 10,000 troops and 360 tanks to quell the revolt and began repressive actions against workers who participated in demonstrations. During the revolt some 100 people were killed, 900 wounded, and 750 arrested. Among those arrested, 58 were later indicted and 27 were sentenced to prison terms.

Despite the brutality of this action, the general political situation deteriorated even further. During this time, almost the entire country was already in a state of ferment. Public cultural life was blooming, some journalists and newspapers were becoming less subservient to the party's instructions, debating clubs of the intelligentsia were formed throughout the country, and student cabarets, theaters, and jazz clubs were established. Peasants began dismantling collective farms, and workers demanded higher wages and benefits as well as industrial self-government. Growing tensions and pressures for reform were coming from many quarters of society but first of all from inside the communist party and its proxy organizations. The party and mass organizations were split by internal conflicts; pressures for internal democratization and a change of leadership mounted. The transition process culminated in two plenary meetings of the Central Committee in July and October that set the stage for a gradual and controlled turnover within the ruling elite. The October meeting, occurring within the context of Soviet pressure and great political activation in the country, made a symbolic break with the past and constituted the beginning of Poland's post-Stalinist regime.[10]

The political and institutional changes in Poland produced by the 1956 crisis were not only a reflection of intraparty struggles. They also indicated fears of the communist elites that the growing popular discontent and mobilization of society were generating closer links between intellectuals, students, radical party activists, and workers. The election of Wladyslaw Gomulka as the new party leader was greeted by enthusiastic mass rallies and demonstrations across the country. At the same time, thousands of meetings in factories, universities, and state institutions produced an avalanche of resolutions and demands that were sent to the party's Central Committee. Mass mobilization had its climax on October 24, when several hundred thousand Poles gathered in front of the Palace of Culture in Warsaw to listen to the speech of the newly elected party leader. The concluding passage of Gomulka's speech was an appeal for a return to work and a show of support for political change by increased productive effort. "Today," he said, "we appeal to the working people of Warsaw and to the whole country: enough of demonstrations, enough of gatherings. It is time to return to our daily work, animated with faith and awareness that the party united with the working class and the whole nation, will lead Poland on a new road to socialism." The period of social activation, however, was far from over. In November and December, there were street demonstrations in several cities. In 1957 and 1958, there were frequent industrial strikes. In October 1957, street demonstrations against the liquidation of the liberal weekly *Po Prostu* were dispersed by the police.

The 1956 crisis brought great changes to Polish society; it also altered the composition and policies of the party-state's elites. In order to defuse political tension, significant economic concessions were offered. Military expenditures were reduced, investment increased in sectors producing consumer goods, and the discrimination and harassment of the private sector eased. Real wages in Poland increased by an average of 20 percent as a result of the crisis. Improvement of living standards was followed by political concessions. The security apparatus was reorganized, and amnesty was granted to political prisoners. Entire groups repressed under the Stalinist regime, including fighters of the noncommunist underground (Home Army), officers of the Polish prewar army, soldiers of the Polish armed forces in the West, and activists of the Polish Socialist and Polish Peasant parties, were rehabilitated. As a result of the October transition, the political leadership of the country was thoroughly changed, and a relatively open political discussion was carried out inside the party. Polish economists designed far-reaching reform proposals to improve the effectiveness of the economic system. New organizations emerged, while existing institutions and organizations elected new leaders. More autonomy was granted to many traditional "transmission belts," such as trade unions or student and youth organizations, as well as to the two communist-controlled political parties (United Peasant Party and Democratic Party). Spontaneously organized workers' councils in factories were legalized and traditional forms of cooperatives reestablished. Collectivization policies were halted, and the majority of collective farms were dismantled (out of 9,975 collective farms in June 1956, only 1,934 remained).

The institutional structure of the Polish party-state became more pluralistic than in any other state-socialist country. The new parliamentary elections were prepared for 1957 with a new electoral law allowing for a secret ballot and more candidates than the number of available seats. Also, a symbolic representation of independent Catholics in the parliament was permitted. Censorship was drastically limited, and Polish culture and intellectual life experienced a period of remarkable revival. The media discarded militant Stalinist language and experienced unprecedented programmatic changes (cf. Eisler 1993; Wladyka 1989; Jarocki 1990). In the education system, curricula were changed in all types of schools, and a new legal framework for the functioning of universities, giving them a large measure of internal autonomy, was enacted. The Polish primate, Stefan Cardinal Wyszynski, was released from prison and promised significant concessions. Shortly, other imprisoned priests were released, expelled bishops and priests assumed their former duties, lay Catholic organizations were formed, Catholic papers and publications were allowed to be published, and religious instruction returned to public schools.

Responding to strong anti-Soviet sentiments, relations with the USSR were altered. Military advisers left Poland. The Soviet Marshal Konstantin

Rokossowski was relieved of his duties as Poland's minister of defense. The Polish debt to the USSR was canceled on the basis of unfair pricing practices, and new credits were granted by the Soviet state. An official agreement was signed concerning the "legal status of Soviet troops stationed temporarily on Polish territory," which stipulated that such presence "cannot infringe in any way on the sovereignty of the Polish state or allow any interference in Polish People's Republic internal affairs." Finally, an agreement was signed concerning the repatriation of Polish citizens who remained in Soviet territories after the war. By March 1959, about 224,000 Poles were allowed to return to Poland. Promises of the new regime included economic reforms, decentralization and workers' self-government, freedom of expression in art and science, a halt to jamming of foreign broadcasts, and guarantees of a secure existence to individual peasants and small private enterprises. The new party leadership and its policies were accepted with great enthusiasm by large segments of the population. This seems to have been the only moment in the history of communist Poland when the regime could claim a substantial measure of genuine popular support.

The liquidation of these achievements and the retreat from promises began already in the fall of 1957 and lasted for several years. Revisionist forces within the party were marginalized. The economic reforms were never implemented, and workers' self-government had been rendered meaningless by the end of 1958. The media's newly acquired freedoms were rescinded. Religious instruction was banned from public schools, and the relationship between the state and the Church deteriorated. Polish society was not able to defend the concessions granted to it by the regime in an hour of weakness. As Karpinski points out, "after October 1956, the program of the intelligentsia was quite often limited to simple trust and hope. Gradually these feelings turned to disappointments" (1982, 105). It can be argued that, besides the weakness and fragmentation of reformist forces in Polish society, the tragedy of the Hungarian revolution contributed to a reversal of policies by the new regime in Warsaw. These two 1956 events were closely interwoven and for years represented an example of the hopes, perils, and limits of the liberalization attempts in the region. In the long run only the Polish Church seems to have been an undeniable beneficiary of the Polish October. However, intellectual elites also secured some limited autonomy, and the peasants were saved from forced collectivization. During the 1956 crisis, as in all other cases of de-Stalinization, the principal political actors were the anti-Stalinist forces within the party, intellectual elites, and students. The Church and Catholic circles played a very limited role, open anticommunist forces were absent, and neither workers nor peasants were able to organize and exert a visible impact on the political scene (cf. Kersten 1993, 142–43). Thus, intellectuals and the intelligentsia were the winners of the transition to a post-Stalinist environment. They extracted the most tangible concessions from the party-state. Their living standards, freedoms, and opportunities were greater than those of other groups in Polish society.

Despite the reversal of the October policies and promises made in 1957, from the beginning of the 1960s Poland remained the most liberal and open country in the Soviet bloc (cf. Brus 1978). The institutional, political, and cultural consequences of the Polish October can hardly be overestimated, especially if we compare them to the outcomes of two other major de-Stalinization crises—Hungary in 1956 and Czechoslovakia in 1968—as well as to the other state-socialist countries that survived de-Stalinization without an open political crisis. Kersten argues that

> in 1956, the change in power relations between the state and society took place. After "October," the communists relinquished their ideological domination step by step. They focused on controlling only those actions which were significant from a political point of view. They accepted some elements of pluralism in culture, expanded freedom to pursue research in sciences, accepted the existence of private agriculture, . . . approved (despite some harassment and repressions) the existence of the Catholic Church as an independent and powerful organization. Gradually, these forced concessions diminished the dependency of society, making it possible for different social groups to articulate their aspirations. (1993, 145)

Similarly, Holzer points out that "Polish experiences in 1956 produced, on the one hand, the belief in the power of society (the regime can be forced to make concessions). On the other hand, they produced self-assurance among the power elite (masses can be relatively easily pacified if one can wait long enough for political energy to burn down)" (1991, 40).

In sum, as a result of the post-October transition, Poland became a country with semi-autonomous public spaces, an independent Catholic Church, a modicum of intellectual freedoms, a limited freedom of travel, an openness to the West in culture and sciences, and a degree of institutional independence within the universities, media, and professional organizations. These "uncontrolled spaces" became laboratories of experience that nurtured political dissent and opposition. In 1956, the new repertoire of collective protest emerged, and the culture of resistance among educated classes was symbolically validated. Certain elements of the noncommunist national tradition were resurrected and tolerated by the party-state. This situation differed radically from the outcomes of the 1956 de-Stalinization crisis in Hungary and in 1968 Czechoslovakia.

Student Revolt—March 1968

In March 1968, a student revolt brought into sharp relief Poland's internal problems—growing economic stagnation, increasing intra-elite conflicts, a determined retreat from the promises of October 1956, and an intensifying campaign against the intellectual elites.[11] The revolt was a desperate effort by groups of intellectuals and students to defend the remnants of the concessions achieved in 1956 and an attempt to force the authorities to keep alive the legacies of 1956. It was also the political culmination of the escalating conflict between the increasingly conservative regime and the increasingly "revisionist" intellectuals.

In February 1962, a debating society founded by Poland's leading intellectuals during 1956, the Club of a Crooked Circle, was banned. The following year, two influential cultural weeklies were liquidated, censorship was tightened, and certain liberal writers, artists, and scholars were sharply criticized by the party leaders. In response, in March of 1964 a group of thirty-four writers and scholars sent a letter of protest to Premier Jozef Cyrankiewicz, criticizing censorship and restrictions on artistic freedom and cultural production, as well as demanding changes in the state's cultural and educational policies. The letter caused a considerable stir. In March 1965, two young revisionist intellectuals—Jacek Kuron and Karol Modzelewski—wrote an open letter to party members that contained a critical analysis of party-state policies. In both cases, the regime responded with repressive actions against the signatories of the letters. Their books and articles were banned, contracts canceled, and passports confiscated, and official police investigations were begun. Kuron and Modzelewski were arrested and sentenced to prison terms, as was Melchior Wankowicz, one of the signatories to the "Letter of 34." In 1965 state-church relations, which had become increasingly strained after 1958, deteriorated rapidly following a letter sent by the Polish Episcopate to West German bishops. The letter was an official invitation for the latter to participate in the celebration of a thousand years of Polish Catholicism and declared "we forgive you and ask for your forgiveness." The communist authorities responded with a smear campaign against the Church, playing on the anti-German sentiments dormant in Polish society. It also refused to allow Pope Paul VI to visit Poland, causing an international sensation. In 1966, intellectuals criticizing the regime policies during meetings organized to commemorate the 1956 events were expelled from the party. Many others gave up their party membership in a gesture of solidarity. Following the Arab-Israeli war in 1967, the conservative and nationalistic faction within the party elite embarked on an ugly antisemitic campaign, so as to display their solidarity with the Soviet-supported Arab countries. This served to aggravate further political tensions throughout the country; the greatest impact was felt, however, in major academic centers.

During the 1967/68 academic year, political tensions at Warsaw University were high. The catalyst for open confrontation was the decision to close production of a patriotic nineteenth-century Polish play, "Forefathers' Eve" by Adam Mickiewicz, at the National Theater in Warsaw. The play's final performance on January 30 turned into a patriotic manifestation, after which a small student demonstration was dispersed by the police. Two of the demonstration leaders, Adam Michnik and Henryk Szlajfer, were expelled from the university.

Some 3,145 people in Warsaw and 1,098 in Wroclaw signed a petition protesting the banning of the play and addressed it to the authorities. The Warsaw branch of the Union of Polish Writers criticized the regime's cultural policies at one of their meetings and demanded that the production of "Forefathers' Eve" be allowed to continue unhampered. When a peaceful assembly of students at Warsaw University protesting the expulsion of Michnik and Szlajfer was attacked by the plainclothes security police forces on March 8, 1968, a full-scale confrontation erupted. During the next several days, students organized rallies and street demonstrations; all of them turned into battles with the militarized police (ZOMO). In the space of a few days, the wave of student demonstrations spread to all major Polish academic centers. In several cities, students launched street demonstrations and fought with ZOMO. During street confrontations, students were brutally attacked with water cannons, tear gas, and truncheons. Faculty members were often beaten together with students, whenever police invaded university buildings while pursuing demonstrators. In other university towns, there were rallies, meetings, and occupation strikes. Students everywhere condemned police brutality and demanded formation of an independent student organization, abolition of censorship, introduction of economic reforms, and observance of the constitution and political rights.

The regime responded to the rebellion of students and intellectuals with a fury. Hundreds of students were expelled from universities, sentenced and jailed, or drafted into military service. Intellectuals who sympathized with students were viciously attacked in the press; universities were purged and the vestiges of their autonomy abolished. The authorities closed down the departments of economics, philosophy, sociology, and psychology at Warsaw University. A propaganda campaign in the mass media portrayed students and intellectuals as agents of Zionism, revisionism, German revanchism, and American imperialism. The anti-intelligentsia campaign was paralleled by an escalating anti-semitic campaign. Hundreds of people lost their party membership and jobs because of their Jewish roots. As a result, following the March events, some 20,000 people (mostly of Jewish descent) were forced to leave Poland. The party also attempted to create mistrust and division between workers and the intelligentsia. Party organizations mobilized groups of workers to stage protest meetings against "troublemakers" and "ungrateful" students and intellectuals who lived at the expense of the working class while shamelessly slandering the workers' state. Consequently, in December 1970, when workers of the Polish coastal region went on strike to protest drastic price increases, students and intellectuals did not join their struggle.

The events of 1968 signaled the final defeat of those groups and forces that secured the most tangible concessions in 1956—that is, the intellectuals and reformist factions within the party. Bielasiak argues that a major consequence of the 1968 upheaval was that the liberal and revisionist elements within the PZPR [Polish United Workers' Party] were virtually eliminated from significant positions. More important, the revisionists, disillusioned by the wholesale attack on the intellectual community, ceased to believe that one could reform the system from within. They saw the 1968 attacks as evidence that the party cared exclusively about power, and that no meaningful political change was possible. Initially, and for some time, they therefore retreated into political passivity. (1983, 15)

The merciless Soviet destruction of the Czechoslovak reform movement in the summer of 1968 was the final proof for what many saw as the impossibility of reforms from within.

While the March events, with their antisemitic and anti-intellectual campaigns, represented a setback for the Polish intelligentsia and Polish culture in general, they also left important legacies that became evident only during the late 1970s. First of all, the defeat of the revisionist opposition changed the ideological orientation of intellectuals. According to Kolakowski, "March 1968, despite all prosecutions and repressions, finally liberated Polish culture from ties with the Communist system and its ideology. There was nothing left to 're-vise' anymore, and nobody was ready to expect any improvement from one or another party faction" (1983, 62). Moreover, following a dramatic protest by independent Catholic deputies in parliament against police actions in March, left-wing and revisionist opposition groups began to recognize independent Catholic circles as their natural allies. It was Michnik who emphasized this legacy of the 1968 events: "Bridging the artificial boundaries which separated a Pole-radical from a Pole-Catholic is, in my view, one of the most precious values of the March legacy" (1981, 34; see also Michnik 1993). Finally, the March events became a formative political experience for the young Polish intellectuals who, for the first time, faced head-on the repressive reality of state socialism. Tens of thousands of students participated in street demonstrations and strikes and were beaten by the police. Thousands were expelled from universities and hundreds arrested. All experienced firsthand the "organized lie frame-up" used by the authorities and the media to discredit protest participants. As Holzer argues:

> the entire generation of young intelligentsia—students and young intellectuals—inherited from the March events the awareness of their own weakness and the feeling of bitterness against the rest of society which refused to support them. But they also inherited the hatred against the regime which responded to a timid protest with violence and tear gas, with lies in the media, with expulsion from universities and jobs, with arrest and trials. (1984, 19)

It was this generation that returned to politics during the days of the Solidarity movement and rose to power after 1989. Therefore, Eisler is absolutely right when he states that "formation of the '68 generation was the most important and enduring value of the March events" (1991, 411). However, before defeated intellectuals and students mounted a new challenge to the regime, another collective actor entered the Polish political scene.

Workers' Revolts of 1970 and 1976

After the government announcement of substantial price increases in basic foodstuffs on December 12, 1970, workers in the coastal cities of Gdansk, Gdynia, Elblag, and Szczecin held mass meetings, elected strike committees, drew up lists of demands, organized marches to local party headquarters, and inevitably clashed with the police and military forces.[12] These events constituted the largest and most violent working-class uprising in the history of statesocialist regimes. The first protests and confrontations with police broke out in Gdansk and Gdynia on December 14. During street riots, the party, trade union, and government buildings were burned down. Protesting workers were killed and wounded when the police forces opened fire. Strikes and violent street clashes continued the next day, and by December 16, violent protests had spread to other coastal cities. The following day, workers in Szczecin (the second major industrial center of the coast) joined the rebellion with strikes and violent street demonstrations. In the course of the next few days, there were strikes in hundreds of factories throughout the region, repeated demonstrations, and street battles between thousands of workers armed with bottles of gasoline and the police and military forces equipped with armored vehicles, tanks, and helicopters. In many instances, the police and military fired at unarmed crowds, killing and wounding protestors. According to official data, between December 14 and 20, 45 people were killed, 1,165 wounded, and 3,161 arrested.[13]

As a result of street riots, 19 public buildings were burned down, including the regional party headquarters in Gdansk and Szczecin; and 10 tanks, 18 armored personnel carriers, and some 60 police cars were destroyed. At the same time, massive forces of police and soldiers were concentrated in coastal cities, curfews were imposed, and the region's communication with the rest of the country was cut off in an effort to prevent any further escalation of strikes and demonstrations.[14] On December 19, however, when the coastal region was already effectively pacified, strikes broke out in other parts of the country. That day, there were about 100 strikes throughout Poland, but they all remained localized and ended by December 22. There were also small street demonstrations in several cities, dispersed promptly by the police. The brutality of police action, the military occupation of factories, and arrests of strike committees' members, as well as a dramatic change in the country's leadership, contributed to the rapid decline of protests and the regime's recovery of political control in the region. During this crisis the Polish intelligentsia, students, and the Church did not join with the workers and remained remarkably silent. Thus, the workers lacked any influential allies, and their protests were easily suppressed and political tensions promptly and skillfully defused. While sporadic strikes occurred during the first months of 1971, workers were effectively demobilized by the end of March.

The December 1970 revolt was a turning point in the tradition of workers' protest. The events created a historical memory of heroic struggle against the regime and became a symbolic reference point in working-class resistance in a similar way that the 1956 and 1968 events had become a reference point for dissenting intelligentsia (see Kubik 1994a, 163–68; Laba 1991; and Goodwyn 1991). For an entire generation of workers, especially those living in coastal cities who participated in strikes and demonstrations, the brutal and repressive nature of the regime was revealed. The revolt also signified the political awakening of the Polish working class. Workers' demands were not exclusively economic but covered an entire range of other issues pertaining to Poland's political situation. Such demands were heavily influenced by concepts of social justice and equality and focused on the functioning of public institutions, including trade unions and the media; economic reforms; management and organization of production in enterprises; and broader social issues such as health care, housing conditions, or public transportation (Chmiel and Kaczynska 1988). Moreover, the events produced a new repertoire of protest, a new collective action frame, and an experience of collective action that shaped patterns of workers' protest in years following 1970.

The differences between the workers' demands and actions in 1970 and in 1980 should not, however, be disregarded. The 1980 demands were articulated in the clear language of political rights—this was absent in 1970. Ten years later, the strikers demanded not only credible and truthful information in the media but above all the abolition of censorship and constitutionally guaranteed freedom of expression. Similarly, they demanded not only the democratization of existing trade unions but the right to form new, independent unions.[15] This difference was not a reflection of any "linguistic incompetence" among the 1970 strikers but indicated a fundamental change in the political imagination and the emergence of a new political discourse in 1980; this discourse was forged through complex interactions, involving workers, dissident groups, and the Church.[16]

The workers' rebellion sealed the fate of Gomulka's regime and closed a distinct period in Polish postwar history. The party's divided leadership used the occasion to accomplish a long-overdue transition of power within the ruling elite. On December 20, at the extraordinary Seventh Plenary Party Meeting, Gomulka was demoted and his four closest associates removed from the

Politburo. The new party leader, Edward Gierek, promised a two-year freeze on food prices and unspecified economic reforms. In spite of these pledges, there was a resurgence of strikes and protests that continued for another several weeks. Without a further response in other parts of the country, they slowly subsided. Gierek's regime skillfully restored order by blaming the use of force on the departing leaders, by offering economic concessions, and by reintroducing into the public discourse elements of nationalism/patriotism (Kubik 1994a, 31–74). The original Five-Year Plan for 1971–75 was redrafted and revised to satisfy more of the people's social and economic needs rather than to fulfill quantitative production targets. Also, a new agricultural policy was announced that abolished compulsory delivery quotas for private farmers. Real wages increased by 22 percent as an immediate result of the crisis (Staniszkis 1984, 257). On February 15, the government, responding to lingering strikes and workers' demands, canceled all price increases and lowered food prices to the levels of before December 13, 1970. The promises of the Gierek regime, however, soon collapsed.

Gierek based his new economic policies and political promises on a massive influx of Western loans and an opening of the global market to Polish goods. He made no real effort, however, to reform Poland's economic institutions and practices. In the middle of the 1970s, it all backfired. An economic crisis that had already begun in 1974 took center stage in 1976. On June 24, 1976, the regime attempted to deal with the crisis by restructuring the prices of food and consumer goods, and in so doing effectively cut real wages. On June 25, workers responded with mass revolts in two industrial cities in central Poland and short-lived strikes in many other locations. The strikes that took place in 130 factories across the country were generally peaceful. They lasted only one day; that evening the price increases were revoked by the country's prime minister. In two cities, however, events turned violent and had lasting repercussions. In Radom during the street demonstrations, party buildings were attacked and set on fire, and in Ursus workers blocked the main railroad tracks in the country and fought with the police.[17]

As in 1970, the regime acted decisively. Street demonstrations were brutally dispersed by militarized police, and hundreds of workers were arrested, beaten, and dismissed from their jobs. In Radom two people were killed during the riots, 121 wounded, and more than 2,000 arrested. Also, 75 policemen were injured. Throughout the entire country, several thousand people lost their jobs as a direct consequence of their participation in the protests, and 500 were indicted. The events ended with a series of trials in which 25 workers were sentenced to prison terms ranging from two to 10 years. The repressions were followed by a propaganda campaign and orchestrated political rallies against "troublemakers" and "vandals." This time, however, the intellectual elites, already mobilized to prevent changes to the Polish constitution, saw that real strength lay in cooperating with and supporting the workers. In September 1976, a group of intellectuals founded the Committee for Workers' Defense (KOR) and demanded amnesty for all workers arrested and tried as well as an end to repressions (Lipski 1985). They began publishing information on political persecution in Poland and collected funds to assist the victims of state repression. Also, the Catholic Church officially called for an end to repression against the workers involved in protests.

In the aftermath of the June 1976 events, an alliance among workers, intellectuals, students, and the Church began to emerge. The formation of KOR stimulated the rapid development of independent groups, organizations, and initiatives across the country. Intellectuals, students, workers, and peasants formed their own organizations to monitor state repression and offer help and protection to the victims. Opposition activists began funding political organizations. Underground publications flourished, and clandestine publishing houses and distribution networks were established. Independent self-education groups were formed, and unofficial "underground" universities were organized. The newly formed opposition groups secured their existence and consolidated the independent democratic space; they brought together committed groups of leaders and supporters who reevaluated past experiences and designed new strategies.[18] Meanwhile, the economic crisis engulfed all branches of the economy and began eroding official power structures. The Marxist-Leninist project that for years had supplied political imagination and self-justification to the party's elite was crumbling to pieces. Pope John Paul II's visit to Poland in 1979 became an open symbolic confrontation with the regime, setting the stage for a new round of political struggle between the party-state and society.[19]

The Rise and Suppression of Solidarity

In the summer of 1980, when a huge wave of social unrest shook the country, the collective actors who entered the political stage this time were only nominally the same. For the first time in Poland's postwar history, the social and political conflict transcended the ideological categories developed in intraparty struggles and the symbolic cleavage between revisionists and dogmatists. It went beyond all traditional limitations, divisions, political visions, strategies, and concepts.[20] Moreover, the political and social gap between workers and intellectuals was bridged as a result of the post-1976 developments and opposition activities. In August 1980 society, unified and organized in an all-new national movement, was ready to sign a genuine contract with the party-state. The new workers' organization "Solidarity," led by its own grassroots leaders and supported by the Church, by the intellectuals, and by the majority of the nation, gained strength from day to day. With some 10 million members, Solidarity was a mighty political force that was able to threaten not only the domestic order but the political stability of the entire region. In contrast to earlier protests, many demands of the organized populace were distinctly political: freedom of association, freedom of conscience, freedom of the press, social autonomy and self-government, equality of rights and duties.

Pravda wrote that "1980 brought an unprecedented expansion and politization of workers' demands. Instead of pressing only for material security . . . strikers asked for institutional change [and were] in the forefront of the struggle for civil liberties" (1983, 68).[21] The crisis in Poland was primarily a political crisis. It foreshadowed the collapse of a specific concept of social and political order, a concept that found its manifestation in the system of power established in Poland in 1944–45. The August Agreements that followed the nationwide strike action announced the formation of the first free trade unions in the communist world and established a completely new model of state organization. This model combined an authoritarian state that controlled national politics with vibrant, democratic politics in spaces where the state's control was rapidly waning.

The successful conclusion and unexpected concessions forced upon the Polish party-state by the strikers set this political conflict apart from all earlier state-society confrontations. The summer of 1980 produced a rapid mass mobilization and unprecedented wave of strikes that involved all social strata and every region of the country. According to Marciniak, these strikes were characterized by

1. the absence of preexisting organizational resources on the level of enterprises, such as independent employees' organizations; 2. a countrywide territorial scope and local universality; 3. long duration and the tendency for the expansion and escalation of protests; 4. strong bonds of solidarity between strikers that bridged factory, industry, and social divisions; 5. dignified character of protest actions and absence of violence; 6. a strong impact on significant segments of the establishment (local authorities, management, enterprise party and union organizations); 7. rapid development of strong organizational structures and a common identity that quickly led to the formation of a nationwide movement. (1990, 7)[22]

But perhaps even more important was the fact that the movement won significant political concessions and the time necessary to secure and consolidate the achievements of the successful countrywide collective action. Thus, by the end of the summer, Polish society had new organizational structures that emerged during the strikes and a network of old embryonic opposition organizations that were formed at the end of the 1970s. For the first time, a state-socialist regime was facing a highly organized, independent opposition movement with independent resources, experienced grassroots leaders, and the capacity to mobilize millions.

The institutionalization of Solidarity also provided the impetus for the independent organization of other social groups that were unable to join the union, because they were not employees of state enterprises or public institutions. University students were the first group to start their own independent organization and to press for reforms of the education system (Anusz 1991; Kowalczyk 1992; Wejnert 1988). Establishing independent farmers' unions proved to be more difficult. Polish farmers did not represent a cohesive social group due to four decades of exploitation, cultural and political mistreatment, and abuse by the state. Deep-seated grievances among farmers, however, very soon resulted in a campaign of protests in the countryside that ranged from localized hunger strikes to spectacular demonstrations and occupation of public buildings (Halamska 1988; "Farmers' 'Solidarity'" 1988; Blasiak 1989). Artisans, craftsmen, and small businessmen also organized their own independent union.

Even the existing state-controlled organizations—the professional associations and youth organizations, the two existing political parties (United Peasant Party and Democratic Party), and the communist party itself—were transformed by the explosion of popular participation following August 1980. They underwent a rapid process of internal democratization and a change in their leadership. As a result, organizations that served as "transmission belts" between the party-state and society and controlled the political space now acquired a significant degree of autonomy and often challenged the state's policies. Among independent organizations that existed prior to the summer of 1980, those affiliated with the Catholic Church grew rapidly. The Catholic intelligentsia and many individual priests were deeply involved in the Solidarity movement, although the Church hierarchy attempted to position itself as the mediator of conflicts between society and the state. Thus, the civic fever sparked by Solidarity spread to all groups, cities, and villages, and to all organizations and institutions of the Polish party-state. The self-governing spirit even affected the police and the military, as their members attempted to organize independent trade unions.

In a country of 35.5 million, one-third of the population became members of independent professional, social, and political organizations. Moreover, the level of mass participation in various forms of collective action was phenomenal. By the end of the first Solidarity period (1980–81), one in five Poles had participated at least once in a collective protest. Predictably, only one in 10 people living in the countryside participated in protest actions, while in cities the ratio was one in four. Twice as many men as women (more than 30 percent of whom were younger than 25) participated in protest actions (Adamski 1989,

175). To sum up, Polish society experienced an unprecedented cultural and political revolution that altered all institutional structures, political attitudes, and modes of participation.[23] The emergence of multidimensional, self-organized, active, and democratic civil society became the most striking characteristic of the Solidarity period.

Solidarity was not just an organized social force and a vehicle for alternative political participation. It represented an intellectual and symbolic formation that provided a multitude of groups and actors with a distinct collective identity. This identity was built on concepts and ideas developed by the democratic opposition in the 1970s combined with some elements of the social and ethical doctrine of the Catholic Church (Kubik 1994a; Osa 1997). Solidarity's distinctive alternative political discourse was based first of all on the notion of inalienable human and political rights; the movement also appropriated important segments of national and patriotic values and traditions (Kowalski 1990). In brief, Solidarity's identity was created around symbols and values that set the movement apart from the official political language, official values, and ideology. Thus the insurmountable division between the alien communist state ("Them") and society ("Us") was amplified and elaborated.

Pitted against each other were two distinct and well-defined political forces representing the state and society and two separate cultural and political idioms that appealed to different values and traditions and used different political calendars and symbols.[24] Solidarity emerged as a powerful re-creator of the noncommunist national traditions and values and as an exponent of a powerful vision of reform and political change based on the self-organization of a democratic society against the post-totalitarian state. It easily defeated the party-state in the battle for national symbols and legitimation claims and pushed the communist elites into a position of guarantor for foreign political domination, the guarantor indispensable only as long as the geopolitical balance of power in Europe remained unaltered.

The regime's ability to survive and adjust to an unprecedented challenge from below was due in part to the pragmatism and flexibility of those in power. It was also the result of Solidarity's self-imposed limitations.[25] Walicki emphasized this paradox when he pointed out that

> if Poland were not part and parcel of the Soviet empire, one would ask only why a powerful, all-national movement demanded so little, and how it would be possible to combine a fully-fledged participatory democracy on the local level with communist-dominated government and, more important, with full communist control over the coercive powers. (1984, 5)

On December 13, 1981, martial law was imposed in the most extensive internal military operation in the history of state-socialist regimes. Poland's borders were sealed, communication systems cut off, a national curfew imposed, extraordinary repressive legal regulations introduced, all organizations suspended, and tens of thousands of Solidarity activists detained. Literally overnight, Poland changed from the most liberal to the most repressive regime in the Soviet bloc. Despite its startling short-term success, the imposition of martial law did not break the political stalemate between the state and society that emerged during the Solidarity period, as had happened in Hungary after 1956 and in Czechoslovakia after 1968. While Solidarity's legal organizational structures were destroyed and its resources dispersed, the movement soon emerged as a loose network of groups organized around territorial, institutional, professional, and personal bases, unified by a set of common goals, values, and symbols.

These underground organizations formed the backbone of opposition and resistance against the post–martial law regime. During this period, public opinion polls consistently showed a significant segment of the population (approximately 25 percent) in strong opposition to the regime. Jasiewicz concluded:

> one of the most important results of the "Polacy '84" survey was the confirmation of the hypotheses that the political conflict that most sharply emerged in Poland in 1980–1981 was not resolved as a result of martial law and political events that followed its imposition. Quite to the contrary, it persisted, although in less visible and spectacular forms. (1986, 9)

The most visible forms of oppositional activities were street demonstrations and protests organized on the thirteenth of every month (the imposition of martial law) and other noncommunist national holidays. Street protests were most frequent and dramatic in 1982 and 1983, although they were usually confined to Solidarity strongholds in several big cities. The most important component of underground Solidarity's activities, however, was the formation of independent educational institutions as well as countrywide underground publishing and distribution networks.

While the extent and intensity of oppositional activities and public support for underground Solidarity declined as the decade wore on, groups of hard-core activists continued to bring a broad range of clandestine activities to all regions of the country. When martial law was lifted in 1984, legally existing groups and organizations gradually extended the limits of permissible activities. By the end of the decade, Poland was again the most politically liberal country of the Soviet bloc.

Although the imposition of martial law destroyed legal opposition and liberated the ruling elites from constant political pressures and threats, it did nothing to improve the party-state's capacity to deal with Poland's economic crisis. Also, with the passage of time, it became increasingly clear that their initial success in crushing independent organizations was not followed by any consistent demobilization strategies through which the Polish party-state elites could again emerge as the unchallenged political force in the country and regain the political initiative. For a variety of reasons, the ruling elites refrained from massive political repression and searched for some sort of accommodation with representatives of the defeated opposition. This inconsistent demobilization process, during which both sides of the conflict frequently changed their strategies and failed to achieve convincing success, stretched over the entire decade, prolonging the political and economic difficulties that began in the 1970s.

In the spring of 1988, after several years of simmering tensions within the population, strikes and protests again erupted in factories and universities across the country. Students organized demonstrations on the anniversary of the March 1968 events and occupation strikes at several universities in May. Independent street demonstrations were held in many cities on May 1. In April and May, the former Solidarity strongholds—the Lenin Shipyard and the Nowa Huta and Stalowa Wola steelworks—and a number of other factories went on strike. During these strikes, the restoration of the Solidarity union and the reinstatement of Solidarity activists fired during and after martial law became major demands. These political demands were, however, eclipsed by a large number of specific demands concerning wages and benefits as well as shop-floor issues particular to a given enterprise. As a result of these actions, former leaders and activists of the Solidarity movement regained their positions in the country's political life. These strikes, however, failed to stimulate mass political mobilization and revive the spirit of 1980. According to Marciniak (1990), they resembled "normal" strike waves taking place in many societies. Protests were territorially limited and failed to achieve local universality. They were shorter in duration and diminishing in scope rather than expanding. Bridging the social boundaries became difficult. Strikes sharpened existing divisions and were not supported by any social elites of the country. Finally, they did not produce new organizational structures and collective identities.[26]

While the first wave of strikes did not bring any tangible political concessions, the second wave during the summer of 1988 was far more successful (Tabako 1992). This time, the strikes spread to the Silesian coal mines and Solidarity strongholds in the regions of Szczecin and Gdansk. Party-state authorities saw it as another potential political earthquake. Despite resistance from important segments of the ruling elite, party leaders finally agreed to meet with several representatives of the opposition, granting them thereby a quasi-legal status. In the fall of 1988, long preparations for the famous "roundtable" negotiations began, negotiations that changed the history of East Central Europe. Both the ruling elite and the Solidarity-based opposition had to reach an internal consensus for entering the talks. They finally began in Warsaw on February 6, 1989, and were held in a climate of growing social tensions and multiplying protest actions. For example, in February 1989 there were 214 strikes, including 81 occupation strikes. In the first two weeks of March, work stoppages took place in 223 enterprises and strikes in 341, affecting all regions and all industries in the country.[27] During the same time, there were street demonstrations organized by students and ecological movements. Public opinion polls revealed that 4.4 percent of adult Poles participated at least once in strikes and demonstrations in 1988 and 8.4 percent in 1989 (CBOS 1989). Among 314 protest events recorded by the Polish press in 1989, about 80 occurred before the signing of the roundtable agreements.

There is a widely shared belief in the existing literature that the surrender of power by communist regimes during 1989 represented in essence a pacted transition accomplished through peaceful negotiations between the reformists within the ruling elite and representatives of independent democratic groups; sustained mass mobilization supposedly did not occur and therefore had no significant impact on the transfer of power. While this may have been the case in some countries, for example in Hungary, such a view should be definitely revised when it comes to Poland. The roundtable negotiations and their final outcome were to a large extent shaped by the wave of popular mobilization that began in the spring of 1988, peaked in the summer of 1988, and lasted well into 1989. In general, the 1989 transfer of power was forced by a mass political movement that emerged in 1980, regrouped and went underground after the imposition of martial law, survived the 1980s through a myriad of clandestine activities, and resumed its overt pressure on the authorities in 1988. Thus, Polish political developments reflected a powerful challenge from below that lasted over a decade, involved millions of people, and celebrated its final triumph in the events of 1989.

The roundtable agreements were signed on April 5 and provided for relegalization of Solidarity, Rural Solidarity, and the Independent Student Union. The opposition also gained limited access to the official political process through semidemocratic elections that were scheduled for June 1989. The results of the roundtable negotiations set in motion a rapid process of liberalization, and the party-state elites very soon lost any control over events. The parliamentary elections represented a clear moral and political victory for the restored Solidarity movement. By the fall of 1989, Poles had established the first noncommunist government in the region since the 1940s, and by January 1990, the Polish United Workers' Party ceased to exist. The country embarked on the arduous road of postcommunist transformations.

Political Crises and Protest in Poland: Conclusions

This chapter examined Poland's experiences under communist rule from a specific theoretical angle. We demonstrated that political crises and collective protests shaped a distinct type of state-socialist regime, one that was more tolerant, institutionally more pluralized, and at the same time relatively weak and susceptible to challenges from below and political upheavals. The high incidence of political conflict and popular protest cannot be attributed exclusively either to social, political, or historical factors specific to Poland or to general contradictions present in the communist organization of the economy and politics. Instead, the source of Polish exceptionalism can be found in the country's unique political dynamics and its crisis-driven political development.

The event that set Poland on its unique political trajectory was the de-Stalinization crisis of 1956 and its immediate aftermath. The transition to the post-Stalinist regime produced distinctive institutional, political, and cultural arrangements, amounting to a modicum of institutional and cultural pluralism, setting Poland apart from other state-socialist regimes in the region. Eventually, it made Poland's regime more vulnerable to various forms of popular mobilization and protest and provided political actors outside the party-state with necessary resources. As a result, different groups within Polish society periodically challenged the policies of the regime through mass political protest. Such struggles were important generation-defining events and provided symbolic, intellectual, and organizational resources for future confrontations. Over time, various oppositional milieus developed their specific repertoires of contention and collective action frames, enhancing the opposition potential of society. This potential was activated in subsequent political crises in which challenging groups, despite their ultimate failures, were able to influence institutions and policies of the Polish regime and win tangible political and economic concessions. Thus, even though the process of deconstruction of the state-socialist regime in Poland began in earnest during the 1980–81 crisis, its beginnings go back to the 1956 de-Stalinization crisis.

Different, group-specific repertoires of protest coalesced during the political crisis of 1980, producing a sharp polarization between the state and society and uniting various groups in Polish society into a powerful revolutionary movement. During the 1980s, the political situation of the country was to a large extent shaped by the rise, the legalization, and de-legalization of the ten-million-strong independent trade union movement, the self-organization of other social and political actors, and the revival of the Polish national and democratic traditions.

Following the rise of Solidarity, Poland's political trajectory departed even further from the developments in other Soviet-bloc countries. It was the only country where a broadly based political counterelite emerged and large segments of the population were independently organized and politically active. Despite Solidarity's defeat in December of 1981 and the imposition of a highly repressive regime, the party-state elites were never able to recover political initiative and introduce effective economic and political reforms. In 1989, the nine-year political struggle culminated in another wave of oppositional activities and mass protests. This forced the authorities to enter a controlled political transition that proved to be their ultimate demise. The essence of democratization in Poland was not an elite transaction with "weak society facing the weak state" (Stark and Bruszt 1998, 16). It was a strong, organized, and mobilized society that forced the communist elites to negotiate their exit from state socialism and relinquish their control over the country.

The post-1989 experiences of Poland's new democracy, analyzed in the following chapters, are shaped by these legacies of popular struggles. As we will show, following the 1989 transfer of power, collective protest in Poland was intense. Our comparative study indicates that Poland had the highest incidence of protest among the East Central European postcommunist countries (Ekiert and Kubik 1998). The high level of collective protest is not an exclusive result of costly economic and social policies introduced by Poland's postcommunist governments. Other countries have been implementing similar measures to facilitate the transition to a market economy with much less opposition from groups and organizations within society. In Poland, various groups had developed considerable resources and expertise necessary for mounting successful contentious collective action well before the fall of communism. These resources were used and developed further in the new democratic environment. This is one of the reasons why early post-1989 Polish politics was more turbulent and contentious than in other postcommunist countries.

CHAPTER 3

Post-1989 Poland: Basic Trends in Politics, Economy, and Society

As we suggested in the introduction, regime transitions should be seen as complex, multilayered processes. In this chapter we will present a brief history of Polish postcommunist transformations, concentrating on national-level politics with a short synopsis of the major developments in regional and local politics. Protest politics and their links to conventional politics on both national and local levels are analyzed in detail in the remainder of the book.

The main conclusion of the second chapter was that in no other country was popular protest more important in bringing down state socialism than in Poland. This is not to say that the elite negotiations were insignificant; they were critical in assuring a smooth transfer of power and in hammering out the technicalities of transition. But these negotiations were conducted against the background of heightened social mobilization, which produced a revolutionary aura around the whole process.

The Polish roundtable negotiations were more comprehensive than similar talks in other East European countries. The initial preparations began already in the summer of 1988. The actual negotiations lasted for two months (February 6–April 5, 1989) and were conducted at the main "roundtable" (twice), three major "tables," eleven "subtables," and, informally, at the government's retreat, called Magdalenka. Each table and subtable dealt with a separate set of issues.[1] The main accomplishment of these negotiations was "a simple horse trade: opposition participation in rigged elections in return for the relegalization of Solidarity" (Castle 1996, 234).

It is clear, therefore, that the middle stage of postcommunist transition, transfer of power, was not an intra-elite affair. One of the final acts of the dying regime was to authorize compartmentalized elections.[2] The upcoming elections reenergized society and resulted in yet another wave of popular mobilization. As many Poles savored a euphoric mood engendered by the political gains wrested from the party-state, thousands of activists began preparations for the first semidemocratic elections since World War II.

According to the roundtable agreement, Solidarity and other organizations were allowed to compete for 161 (35 percent) of the seats in the Sejm and 100 (100 percent) of the seats in the newly formed Senate. During the two-month campaign, Solidarity was supposed to have access to 23 percent of air time on television, and more air time on the radio, as well as to promote its program and candidates in several independent papers. In practice, its access to the media was minimal, and the "Coalition" (as the communists and their allies labeled themselves for the elections) enjoyed a tremendous advantage in being able to present its views without any restrictions. Yet they did not conduct an orchestrated, uniform official election campaign.

The party-state's electoral nom de guerre, "Coalition," was deliberately evasive to avoid any association with communism/socialism. It also indicated that the satellite parties, the SD (Democratic Party) and ZSL (United Peasant Party), were now defined as full-fledged and serious partners of the PZPR (Polish United Workers' Party). This labeling technique exemplifies what seems to have been the fundamental election commandment of the party-state: do not reveal who you are unless you are asked. An SD chairman of a regional election commission observed: "Those who thus far emphasized their party membership and carried the PZPR badges in their lapels suddenly prefer not to make a display of it."[3] According to the rules agreed upon during the roundtable negotiations, the political affiliation of candidates on the voting cards and possibly on other documents was not to be specified.[4]

Coalition candidates did not want to be associated with their party, yet they had to sell themselves through concrete political images; so they portrayed themselves as, for example, "patriots," "people of strong religious convictions," "efficient and successful managers," or "supporters of private enterprise." It is clear that the party-state's primary electoral strategy was mimicry: the Coalition candidates ran without revealing or emphasizing their political identity and, first of all, tried to avoid any association with "socialism." They understood very well that in June 1989 such an association was a political liability and did their best to come up with public images that were definitely a- or non-socialist.

The elections of June 4 and 18 (runoffs) were an astonishing success of the newly re-legalized Solidarity movement and the unanticipated, thorough defeat of the communist bloc: Solidarity candidates won all of the mandates they were allowed to contest, except for one. The scope of the Coalition's defeat stunned both sides; it became evident that the communists had no democratic mandate to rule and that some arrangement would have to be made to include Solidarity in governing. As a spokesman for the PZPR put it: "As the consequence of electoral results the opposition must assume co-responsibility for the state."

The first major issue to be decided by the new parliament was who should be elected to the newly created office of president and how to go about it. On July 3, Adam Michnik, editor in chief of Solidarity's daily, *Gazeta Wyborcza*, published an article entitled "Your President, Our Prime Minister." It was an ingenious, though controversial, actualization of a vaguer concept of power sharing, so essential for the Polish version of pacted transition. On July 19, the joint session of the Sejm and Senate, acting as the National Assembly, elected Wojciech Jaruzelski to be the first president of postcommunist Poland. He received 270 votes, while the required minimum was 269. Many Solidarity deputies abstained to make this election possible. General Czeslaw Kiszczak, the former minister of the interior and Jaruzelski's main ally, began his unsuccessful efforts to form a government based on a wide coalition.

On August 7, Lech Walesa proposed that the former allies of the Polish United Workers' Party, the Democratic Party (SD) and the United Peasant Party (ZSL), join the Solidarity's Citizens Parliamentary Club to form a governing coalition. On August 17 the three partners signed an agreement, Kiszczak gave up his mission, and the way was opened for the realization of Michnik's idea. A week later the Sejm asked Tadeusz Mazowiecki, one of the intellectual leaders of the opposition and Walesa's close adviser, to form a government. His cabinet was ratified on September 12: the communist era in Poland was over and the stage was set for the consolidation of democracy.

The primary task of the new government was to jump-start the economy, hanging dangerously over the abyss of hyperinflation, and to begin redesigning the institutional structure of the state. The team led by Leszek Balcerowicz, deputy prime minister, immediately set out to develop a package of economic reforms. On December 27–29 the Sejm passed a package of legislative acts amounting to the (in)famous "shock therapy" for the Polish economy. On December 29 a constitutional amendment was adopted changing the name of the country from the Polish People's Republic to the Republic of Poland, and the passage guaranteeing the PZPR "the leading role in the country" was deleted.

For the Mazowiecki government, 1990 began as a nail-biting thriller: on January 1 the Balcerowicz Plan went into effect, and nobody was sure whether and how soon the economic reforms were going to produce results. After several months, clear signs of success appeared (dramatically reduced inflation, tremendous reinvigoration of the consumer goods market), but at the same time both industrial and agricultural production began their dangerous downward course.

During this early period of democratic consolidation, the principal features of the "Polish road from socialism" were taking shape. The main task of postcommunist governments was to build and maintain a protective "political umbrella" over the economic reforms. Building this umbrella was not an easy task, however, for political and economic life were dominated by six trends or processes that often worked against each other. They included:

1. emergence of the postcommunist political field, that is, the formation of political parties out of both the communist mono-party and the Solidarity movement;
2. electoral and governmental volatility;

3. building of the new institutional order, including redesigning the state architecture (for example, the decentralization of state administration);
4. dynamic growth of civil society;
5. implementation of the radical economic reform, which changed people's material situation and challenged their thinking about economic issues;
6. formation of new political attitudes and definitions of sociopolitical reality.

Emergence of the Postcommunist Political Field

In January 1990, the PZPR (Polish United Workers' Party) dissolved itself, and two new parties were formed on its ruins: SdRP (Social Democracy of the Polish Republic) and PUS (Polish Social Democratic Union). The latter disappeared from public life in July of 1991 after an undistinguished existence. The former, led by several influential, younger PZPR activists, remodeled its identity through an aggressive media campaign and defined itself as a modern social democratic party. It nevertheless did not manage to shed a label of "ex-communist" and had a hard time convincing the electorate that it was no longer "them." In fact, this first major political cleavage of the post-1989 era—"us—Solidarity" versus "them—former communists"—had a profound impact on political competition, voting patterns, and electoral outcomes.

At the same time, Solidarity's leadership faced the dilemma of transforming a massive, complex movement, bifurcated into a trade union and Citizens' Committees, into a more durable political organization or set of organizations. Citizens' Committees (CCs) were a unique feature of Polish postcommunism. Through them, hundreds of thousands of people channeled their energy to defeat communist candidates during the compartmentalized founding elections of 1989. In 1990, two momentous political questions had to be answered: What is the relationship between CCs and Solidarity? and What is the role of CCs within the newly emerging field of political parties?

The history of CCs began on December 18, 1988, when Walesa officially convened the Citizens' Committee of the Chairman of Solidarity. It was an elite group of intellectuals and activists conceived mostly as an advisory board to the chairman but also as a "shadow cabinet" of sorts (Borkowski and Bukowski 1993, 196). On April 8, 1989, after deciding to form a united electoral front, Solidarity leaders called for the formation of regional and local Citizens' Committees. Thousands of such committees were formed during the next two months. Their aim was to organize Solidarity's electoral campaign, but most of them attracted local activists who wanted to work on a variety of local problems, ranging from pollution and environmental degradation to redesigning school systems.

After the electoral victory of June 4, Walesa authorized a very controversial move: the dissolution of the CC at the provincial level. "The CCs at the local level were allowed to continue, but without the Solidarity logo and union financing" (Grabowski 1996, 225). This not only severed the links between the CCs and Solidarity but also led to a tremendous diversification of local patterns of civic activization, which by now constituted a full-fledged civil society. The "golden age" of local CCs came between September 1989 and May 1990, when they took part in the preparations for the free election to local self-governments and became foci of spontaneous social and political activities. "They led the mobilization against the old power apparatus. . . . At the same time they performed . . . the function that in the Western democracies are the domain of specialized voluntary associations, elected local authorities, and political parties" (Grabowski 1996, 228). And once again the CCs achieved spectacular electoral success. Their candidates came in first among all the organized forces participating in the elections.

Almost as soon as the days of glorious electoral victories were over, CCs entered a terminal identity crisis. From June 1989 on, they were organizationally fragmented; after May 1990 a serious "philosophical" dilemma came to the fore. As a diversified set of independent and varied groups, CCs constituted a classical civil society; but the tension between this organizational diversity and their specific self-identity and their sense of mission led to rapid (self-)destruction. The CCs were localized and diversified, yet many activists subscribed to a common symbolic frame that was supposed to forge out of this fragmented set of organizations a unified movement. Among the principal features of this frame, one can find the following elements:

1. CCs embodied the dream of "the third way" between capitalism and socialism, as well as between the suffocating uniformity of state socialism and the "empty" procedural diversity of Western democracy.
2. CCs were striving toward unity yet without any centralized coordinating center (understandable after Walesa's "treacherous" dissolution of the CCs' regional structures).
3. CCs were *civic* but not *political*. The Krakow CC wrote in its manifesto: "We are a citizens' movement. This means that in the center of our attention are citizens' problems, regardless of their political views, profession, or material status. Our activity is to facilitate social integration" (Borkowski and Bukowski 1993, 58).
4. CCs were the culmination of a specific historical trajectory, including the "symbolic organicism" of Solidarity. An individualistic philosophy of liberal civil society was almost nonexistent in CCs' programs.

This common symbolic frame proved too weak to hold the movement of CCs together once the major split occurred. Some activists opted for a single, unified organization, for they believed that only unity could provide sufficient political "protection" for the economic reforms. Others believed that a plural field of political parties should be created as soon as possible to jump-start "true" democracy. As the slowly emerging political parties began building their own organizations on the basis of CCs, some activists joined them and became "politicians"; others accepted time-consuming positions in the newly created local administrations; still others grew discouraged by the growing politicization and professionalization of the movement and left politics altogether. In sum, what eventually destroyed the CCs was an unresolved tension between their apolitical and organic philosophy and the pragmatic demands of local politics as well as the pressure coming from various political forces, which wanted to co-opt CCs as their local base and component. Citizens' Committees were among the first casualties of "the war at the top" and the emergence of political parties.

"The war at the top" was a phrase Walesa coined to capture the essence of the political philosophy that emphasized the need for early pluralization of the Solidarity movement and the emergence of a well-structured party system. On May 10, after several months of increasing criticism of Mazowiecki's government, Walesa announced that he intended a full-fledged confrontation with his former ally and in so doing proclaimed the beginning of "a permanent political war." On May 12 the Center Alliance was formed. It criticized the Mazowiecki team for reforming the country too slowly and called for an *acceleration*. Both economic and political reforms were to be "accelerated" to prevent former members of the nomenclature from profiting from the legal and social chaos engendered by the slow pace of reforms. The Center Alliance called for early parliamentary and presidential elections, announcing its support for Lech Walesa. Supporters of the Mazowiecki cabinet responded by forming the Alliance for Democracy (June 10), which soon evolved into a political party called Civic Movement—Democractic Action, or ROAD (July 16). Thus ended the first stage of Solidarity's fragmentation, and the second major political cleavage of Polish postcommunist politics, separating "reformists" from "revolutionaries," was opened.

On the surface, this cleavage separated Mazowiecki's supporters from the Walesa camp. But the divisions went deeper, for they were founded on different political visions. This duality can be best construed as an opposition between *the logic of the rule of law* and *the revolutionary logic*. The former was based on an axiom that held that social (political) life during the transition should be regulated, as much as possible, by the existing (though obviously evolving) system of laws. Otherwise, it was argued, the peaceful and gradual revolution would inevitably enter its Jacobin/Robespierreian phase and would "devour its children." The latter was founded on the belief that it was impossible to carry out meaningful reforms without a prior "cleansing" of the political realm of all the remnants or vestiges of the previous system (for example, former communists still occupying positions of influence).

There are two basic problems with the "rule of law" position. First, it is difficult to be "legalistic" in the middle of transition, with rapidly changing (domestic and international) pressures and institutional settings. Second, the position is paradoxical, because most of the existing laws were written by the communists and the new system is supposed to be anything but communist. The best example of the application of the rule of law was Mazowiecki's policy of a "thick line," which was immediately portrayed by revolutionaries as being soft on communists and contributed to his defeat. "Thick line" came to symbolize a policy of leniency and forgiveness toward the former party-state officials. According to reformists, it meant, first of all, a rejection of the notion of collective responsibility; each case of abuse of power and each crime committed by the communists was to be adjudicated separately in a court of law. Many people believed, however, that such a "legalistic" approach could not and would not bring justice, for the existing legal framework was constructed by the communists, who now were to be judged according to their own rules. As a result, the populace was strongly divided over this policy (Ekiert 1992, 345; Kaminski 1991b).

Politics based on the rule of law (above other principles) tended to correlate with (1) a conviction that the post-1989 Poland was discontinuous with the Polish People's Republic and (2) an emphasis on (democratic) *procedures* over (any) political *substance*. Politics based on the revolutionary logic tended to go together with (1) a belief that a decisive break with the Polish People's Republic had not yet occurred and (2) defining politics more in terms of cultural/ political substance than procedures. Thus, often at their heart lie questions of identity: "Who is the majority?" and "Who is not a legitimate participant in the political community?" In contrast to the logic of the rule of law, which is usually inclusive and formalist in its definition of citizens, the "revolutionary" logic tends to be exclusive and substantive in its definition of the true members. There was a tendency to define "true members" as "Poles-Catholics," thereby excluding members of religious and ethnic minorities, who were concerned that they might become second-class citizens.[5]

Beyond this basic dichotomy, separating reformists from revolutionaries, the process of political fragmentation and pluralization continued, although the field of political parties achieved a more transparent articulation only in 1991.[6] Significantly, these early divisions, both the "hidden" bipolarity and the slowly emerging fragmentation, were an elite affair. The self-government elections of May 27, 1990, demonstrated that most Poles did not think about politics in terms of political parties. The biggest winners among the parties were the PSL, which received 4.8 percent of the valid votes, and the SdRP, with 2.7 percent. And as public opinion polls revealed, between August and December of 1990 (1) CCs lost 25 percent of their popular support; (2) political parties emerging from Solidarity gained during the same period almost 20 percent; but (3) the distrust of political parties was growing. The number of respondents who admitted they would not vote for any party or could not decide which to choose increased from 35 percent in August to 51 percent in December (Gebethner 1992b, 12). It is obvious, therefore, that the game of political parties was limited to a narrow elite and that the oligarchization of political life was very pronounced (Wesolowski 1995, 9; Ekiert 1992, 352; Spiewak 1993, 37–38; Tworzecki 1996, 193).

During 1991, as the calls for fully democratic parliamentary elections grew persistent, the process of crystallization of various political options accelerated. A certain peculiarity of this process was that it was not based on bottom-up coalition building and the coalescence of small groups emerging within the wider public. Rather, it was the fragmentation of the political elite. Many parties were formed as a result of elite conflicts, divisions, and maneuvering, often within the Sejm. At the beginning of its term, the contractual parliament was composed of seven clubs; by October 1991 their number increased to nineteen (Slodkowska 1995, xv). Even the former communists, conventionally perceived as a united group, split into four clubs (Gebethner 1996, 60).

Several authors attempted to identify the emerging political options and classify political parties, invariably concluding that Western categories corresponded to the Polish situation only approximately. Given this correction, Krzysztof Jasiewicz (1993b) identified *five* political options: (1) Liberal-democratic (Democratic Union and Liberal-Democratic Congress); (2) Conservative (Christian National Union, Agrarian Alliance, and Solidarity); (3) Populist (Polish Peasant Party); (4) Socialist (Alliance of the Democratic Left); and (5) "the center," occupied by nonvoters and the Confederation for an Independent Poland, both "leaning toward populism."

To summarize, the party system was fragmented and fluctuating (parties were frequently formed and dissolved), and yet the crystallization of political options was progressing. At the same time, however, two basic political cleavages emerged and from then on would dominate the country's politics with fluctuating intensity. The first divided ex-communists and the post-Solidarity camp; the second separated reformists and revolutionaries. Nonetheless, the most striking feature of the party system was its weak mooring in society. Tworzecki summarized the situation very aptly: "In the words of one critic, [political parties] remind one of over-grown children, too strong and too weak at the same time: they are too strong in the . . . structures of the state, too weak in terms of links with their social base" (1996, 193).[7]

Electoral and Governmental Volatility

Electoral and governmental politics from 1989 to 1993 were stormy. During this period Poles went to the polls seven times, including two rounds during the founding elections of 1989, two parliamentary elections in 1991 and 1993, two rounds of the presidential elections in 1990, and local elections in 1990. From June 1989 through December 1993, the country had two presidents and seven prime ministers. Mazowiecki's tenure was the longest; his government lasted 16 months. Two of the prime ministers did not manage to form cabinets.

Elections of 1989

The founding election of 1989 was designed as a key mechanism of the peaceful dissolution of state socialism. On the one hand, the ruling Polish United Workers' Party did not intend to relinquish its power completely; on the other hand, Solidarity leaders at that time believed that free, unconstrained elections were not yet possible. The compartmentalized election system emerged from the roundtable negotiations as a compromise solution. The system was envisioned as "one early step within a longer transitional process. . . . It was a means to initiate rather than to confirm the regime transition process" (Olson 1993, 417–18).

The total pool of 460 seats in the lower house, the Sejm, was divided into six compartments, five of which (65 percent of the seats) were reserved for the governing coalition. The sixth compartment, comprising 35 percent of the seats, was opened for unconstrained competition, and the communists hoped to capture a significant number of these seats. The election for the newly created upper chamber of parliament, the Senate, was to be free. Solidarity won all but one of the seats it was allowed to contest (99 out of 100 in the Senate and 161 in the Sejm). The elections brought about an unexpected triumph of Solidarity. But they also produced the so-called contractual parliament, which was compromised by the existence of the reserved "communist" compartments and had, therefore, a limited democratic mandate. This political defect became especially pronounced when other countries of the region acquired their legislatures through founding elections conducted according to fully democratic procedures.

Local Elections

As early as January 14, 1990, both Mazowiecki and Walesa issued statements calling for local government elections. They took place on May 27, 1990, as part and parcel of the wider reform of the state administration and were designed to transfer a considerable amount of power to local communities. But they generated relatively weak public interest: the turnout was 42 percent of registered voters. The candidates of Citizens' Committees won 42 percent of the seats, while the "independents" took almost 51 percent. ("Independents" were not formally running on party tickets. It was widely believed that many of them represented the old establishment.) The CCs' candidates won 74 percent of the seats in multiseat constituencies (voting for "party" lists) and 38 percent of the seats in the single-seat constituencies (first-past-the-post). By contrast, candidates running explicitly as representatives of Social Democracy of the Polish Republic (the ex-communists) won respectively 1 percent and 0.14 percent of the seats. As a result, in many locations Solidarity/Citizens' Committees took power.

Presidential Elections, 1990

A dominant theme of Polish politics in 1990 was the presidency (see Grabowska and Krzeminski 1991 and Gebethner and Jasiewicz 1993). The debate was over the definition of this office and the person who should occupy it. There was a growing sentiment that General Jaruzelski should be replaced by a person representing Solidarity, elected in popular elections. On April 7, Jaroslaw Kaczynski, Walesa's closest associate and the leader of the Center Alliance, stated in an interview: "I believe that a change in the president's office is unavoidable, and Walesa is really the only candidate for the office." Solidarity's chairman announced on May 13 that he was returning to politics after a brief "vacation." The war at the top, the split within the movement of Citizens' Committees, and the pre-electoral campaign began.

On September 27 the Sejm passed a new law according to which the president was to be chosen in a popular election to take place on November 25. Initially, 16 candidates sought the 100,000 signatures required for registration. Lech Walesa and Tadeusz Mazowiecki were the candidates of the two main camps that emerged from Solidarity. Wlodzimierz Cimoszewicz was the candidate of the ex-communist coalition. Other major contenders included Roman Bartoszcze from the PSL and Leszek Moczulski from the KPN (Confederation for an Independent Poland). Walesa was the front-runner by late October, though his popularity was declining. Mazowiecki, the early leader in several polls, was losing support rapidly. For both of these contenders, an unexpected threat was looming on the horizon in the form of one Stanislaw Tyminski, a Polish businessman from Canada. By the second half of November, Tyminski edged in front of Mazowiecki, promising a major upset.

On November 25, this upset, inconceivable a few months earlier, became reality. With a 60.63 percent turnout of registered voters, Walesa won with 40 percent of the vote. But it was Tyminski who came in second with 23.1 percent, upstaging the governing prime minister Mazowiecki, who received 18.1 percent. The post-Solidarity camp reunited its forces before the second round of elections. On December 7, Lech Walesa won by a huge margin, receiving 74.3 percent of the vote to Tyminski's 25.7. Prime Minister Mazowiecki immediately submitted his resignation. On December 29, President Walesa approved Jan Krzysztof Bielecki's candidacy for prime minister; he was confirmed by the parliament on January 4, 1991, and stayed in office until December 6, 1991.

The electoral campaign and the results of the elections solidified the split within the Solidarity camp; the cleavage between Walesa and the revolutionaries on the one hand and Mazowiecki and the reformists on the other was now clearly articulated and was to dominate Polish political life for some time to come.

Parliamentary Elections, 1991

Demands for the end of the transitional system based on the roundtable formula and the dissolution of the contractual-compartmentalized parliament appeared already in early 1990. During the first half of 1991, several parties and politicians began calling for new parliamentary elections, as the formation of the political scene accelerated. After a protracted battle between the president, parliamentary clubs, and political parties over the shape of the electoral law, the date for the parliamentary elections was set for October 27, 1991. During this battle, "a rule of the thumb was: the stronger the party and the more popular its leaders, the less likely it was to opt for a pure proportional representation. Eventually, the considerations stemming from the uncertainty of the election outcome prevailed in the deputies' minds, and for the Sejm (lower house) election a PR system was adopted" (Jasiewicz 1996, 7). Finally, the Sejm adopted the Hare version of the PR system without thresholds. The Senate was to be elected through a plurality system with a single ballot.

The electoral campaign was fought across a number of cleavages, but the two most pronounced were ex-communists versus post-Solidarity organizations, and revolutionaries (mostly POC [Porozumienie Obywateleskie Centrum, Civic Alliance Center], a coalition organized by the Porozumienie Centrum [PC] Center Alliance) versus reformists (mostly the Democratic Union and the Liberal-Democratic Congress). The main issue was the pace and structure of economic reforms: both the ex-communists and the nongoverning post-Solidarity parties criticized the Mazowiecki and Bielecki cabinets for misguided economic policies and promised substantial corrections to the Balcerowicz Plan. Another significant issue was decommunization: the revolutionaries attempted to discredit the reformists, by portraying them as actual allies of the ex-communists (see chapter 7 for an analysis of this strategy). The Church supported Catholic Electoral Action (WAK), organized by the ZChN (Christian National Union), though its support was usually "unofficial."

One hundred eleven electoral committees participated in the election to the lower house (Sejm); 27 among them were registered on the national lists. Voter turnout was 43.2 percent. The elections produced a highly fragmented Sejm with 29 parties, none of which controlled more than 13.5 percent of the seats. The winner was the Democratic Union (12.3 percent of the valid vote), with the Alliance of the Democratic Left coming in second (12.0 percent of the vote). The new Senate had 10 major political groups; the Democratic Union had the largest club, composed of 21 senators. The parliament's composition reflected the extensive fragmentation within the electorate; it did not result primarily from "erroneous" institutional choices. After all, the Senate elections, conducted on the basis of a plurality system, also produced a highly fragmented chamber (Gebethner 1992a; 1996, 71).

On November 25, a coalition of five post-Solidarity parties began working to form a government; eventually Jan Olszewski, leading three of them (ZChN/PC/PL [Porozumienie Ludowe]) and having support from the post-communist PSL, managed to form a minority government, which survived only several months and was replaced by the Pawlak (June 5–July 10, 1992) and Suchocka (July 11, 1992–October 25, 1993) cabinets.[8]

Parliamentary Elections, 1993

After a vote of no confidence in the Suchocka government in May 1993, President Walesa chose to dissolve the parliament. As one of its final acts, the outgoing parliament created a new electoral system, designed to curtail parliamentary fragmentation. Three specific measures were introduced: a nationwide threshold of 5 percent for parties and 8 percent for coalitions; raising the number of districts from 37 to 52; and the D'Hondt system, favoring bigger parties. The new system was supported by the parties who believed themselves to be stronger. The election produced a less fragmented Sejm, with one coalition, five parties, and a representation of the German minority. But 34 percent of all valid votes were cast for parties and coalitions that did not pass the required threshold. As a result, a large segment of the electorate was not going to be represented in the parliament. Two postcommunist groups, the Alliance of the Democratic Left and the Polish Peasant Party (PSL), achieved a tremendous success. The former won 20.4 percent of all valid votes, which translated into 37.2 percent of the seats in the Sejm; the latter received 15.4 percent of valid votes, winning almost 29 percent of the seats. Waldemar Pawlak of the PSL formed a government, supported by both postcommunist parties, which together enjoyed a comfortable parliamentary majority. The first stage of democratic transition in Poland, during which politicians representing the Solidarity camp labored to restructure the country's political and economic system, was now over.

Evidence of political instability, clearly reflected in the exorbitant frequency of elections, was also manifest in the unusually high rate of cabinet turnovers. From the beginning of democratic consolidation until the end of 1993, Poland had seven prime ministers, four of which represented the Solidarity movement. The Olszewski government survived only five months. The next Solidarity cabinet, led by Hanna Suchocka, was forced from office after eight months, by a vote of no confidence. Such high electoral and governmental instability cannot be interpreted solely as an expected feature of transitory politics; no other Central European country had as many elections and government turnovers during the same period.

Formation of the New Institutional Order

All postcommunist governments faced the monumental task of rewriting their countries' basic laws and redesigning their basic institutional architecture. The first Polish postcommunist government of Tadeusz Mazowiecki and the "contractual" parliament produced a series of legislative acts that introduced new institutions and reformed most of the existing ones.

The communist constitution was amended in April 1989, allowing for the formation of the Senate and the office of president. Other amendments provided a framework for democratic elections and an independent judiciary and introduced guarantees of freedom of association. Liberal procedures for the registration of political parties were introduced. In December 1989, the constitution was amended again. The name of the country was changed from the Polish People's Republic to the Republic of Poland, and the country's symbol, the White Eagle, was recrowned. Also, the equality of various forms of property was guaranteed and freedom of economic activities assured. During this session, the parliament passed the acts necessary to initiate economic reforms (Zmigrodzki 1997; Rapaczynski 1993).

The formation of the new legal and institutional order proceeded slowly, creating institutional and legal chaos and engendering uncertainty. For example, industrial relations were institutionalized fairly late. Laws on collective bargaining and trade unions were created in May 1991, but they left many aspects of industrial relations unregulated. In the fall of 1992, the Suchocka government introduced a package of 12 laws to clarify the status of state-owned enterprises (Kramer 1995, 99–102; Vinton 1993). The long and arduous negotiations with trade unions that followed did not produce results before the fall of the Suchocka cabinet in May 1993. Thus, throughout the period from 1989 to 1993, the relationship between labor and the government remained largely unregulated. The tripartite commission institutionalizing the relationships among the government, employers, and labor, which would be empowered to negotiate minimum and maximum wage increases, pensions, and the procedure of wage indexation, was established only in February 1994. Similarly, several proposals on the reorganization of government and the introduction of civil service were discussed, but the appropriate laws were enacted only in 1995.

By April 1990, the new government abolished formal censorship of the press and established a commission to oversee the dismantling of the old state-controlled media system. The most important Polish dailies and weeklies were privatized. The state's regulatory power over the radio and television was regulated only in October 1992, when the parliament passed a bill making public broadcasting independent of political interference and permitting the operation of private radio and television stations. It went into effect in March 1993. The nine-person National Broadcasting Committee (four were nominated by the Sejm, two by the Senate, and three, including the chairman, by the president) was established to regulate radio and television.

The most glaring gap in the legal architecture of the new order was the lack of a constitution. The so-called Little Constitution, a provisional act, was passed by the Sejm on August 1, 1992, and signed by the president in November. It clarified many contentious issues that had plagued relations among the government, the parliament, and the president. But it was not designed to provide the country with a completely new legal blueprint and therefore was often less than adequate in solving institutional tensions (Howard 1993).

Among all legal actions, a series of constitutional amendments and legislative acts on local self-government adopted in March 1990 had the most revolutionary consequences for the structure of the state. These acts amounted to an administrative reform, which was the most extensive among the East European countries and provided local self-governments with broad prerogatives (Grochowski 1991; Regulska 1998; Swianiewicz n.d.). The creation of about 2,380 *self-governing* communes amounted to the decentralization of the state administration and the actual devolution of power from the center. The proper allocation of duties and responsibilities among the communes, the central administration, and the slowly emerging and controversial *intermediary* structures was constantly being tried and discussed. But such areas of communal life as the creation and implementation of the budget, the collection of certain taxes, the collection and disposal of solid waste, sewage collection and treatment, or maintenance of local roads (and many others) became the exclusive responsibility of local governments and were subjected to the sovereign decisions of local councils and mayors.[9]

Thus, one of the main features of Polish political life after May 1990 was a partial decoupling of the central and local political and administrative arenas. The postcommunist consolidation from then on would transpire on two, only partially coordinated levels: central and local. The dynamics (or rhythms) of postcommunist change on these two levels were different and often contradictory. The radical administrative reform opened up new possibilities for local communities, particularly their elites; some of them capitalized on these possibilities to the maximum, some did not. By and large, however, many "central" political conflicts became irrelevant from the point of view of local political and public life. This allowed local elites to concentrate on local affairs, including economic development, and in some regions of the country fostered significant economic successes. This phenomenon was noted by the architects of Polish reforms. For example, Balcerowicz observed that "one of the anchors of stability [as one of the most important preconditions of a successful economic reform] is local government—which should be, I believe, protected from the instability on the state's level" (1993, 30–31). The relative autonomy of local administrators and politicians was further enhanced through local elections, described earlier.

Dynamic Growth of Civil Society

Public passivity of large segments of the populace has been sometimes pointed out as a key feature of postcommunism. It must be emphasized, however, that this passivity was much more prevalent in politics (electoral turnout and membership in parties) than in civic activities. Early public opinion polls and sociological surveys revealed that initially (1989–92) civic activism was weak. During that time, only 1–3 percent of the respondents declared membership in cultural or local associations and social movements; 3 percent belonged to religious organizations; 4.5 percent belonged to professional associations; and 22 percent belonged to trade unions. Glinski (1993), after reviewing these studies, concluded that social activity was limited. He noted, however, that 44 percent of the respondents *declared* a readiness to join or actively participate in organizations and associations representing their interests "if such organizations or associations were created." As Glinski observed:

> There exists a considerable "declared," though unutilized, potential of civic activism, blocked by economic and cultural-historical factors, but primarily connected with the negative assessment of the functioning of the Polish political scene . . . 76% of respondents claim that people who want to engage in social affairs [public life] can achieve little or simply nothing. (1993, 103–4)

This picture emerging from public opinion surveys must be, however, compared with a quite different image, originating in studies on organizational activities of the NGO (nongovernmental organizations) sector and the Citizens' Committees as well as in our own study of protest politics. This is an altogether different story, of a vibrant and growing associational life, intense mobilization, and skillful organizing. We present and analyze this phenomenon in chapter 4.

The Main Elements of the Economic Reforms

Post-1989 economic reforms in Poland have become one of the most debated aspects of the postcommunist transformations in the region. The "shock therapy" strategy adopted by the Mazowiecki government, its costs, and its initial outcomes have been the subject of many controversies and have already generated a sizable body of analyses (Balcerowicz 1995; Kolodko 1992; Poznanski 1993 and 1996; Sachs 1993; Slay 1994). It is not our goal to evaluate these complex issues; economists are better equipped to offer a sound judgment on the strengths and weaknesses of Poland's efforts to move from a planned to a market economy. We want to emphasize a few general issues that provide reference points for our analysis of contentious politics and democratic consolidation. In particular, we will demonstrate that after a sharp and relatively short recession, the Polish economy experienced the fastest and most dynamic recovery in the region.

The situation of the Polish economy at the outset of democratic consolidation was dismal, even by East European standards. The Mazowiecki government inherited a stagnant economic system, plagued by structural imbalances, resource misallocation, pervasive shortages, and an unresolved foreign debt problem. Moreover, it was a system on the verge of hyperinflation and economic chaos. The last communist government of Mieczyslaw Rakowski, in its efforts to revive economic performance and dismantle the system of state planning and public ownership, relinquished state command over the economy, unleashed inflation, and lost control of the state budget and the money supply (Poznanski 1996, 106–13). On August 1, 1989, Rakowski's cabinet freed food prices, without however doing anything to restrain wage increases. At the same time, a highly inflationary indexation mechanism went into effect.[10] In August, inflation was 34 percent a month; in October it reached a hyperinflation rate of 54 percent a month, and the crisis reached astounding proportions. Such a dire crisis called for prompt and drastic measures.

Mazowiecki's economic team was led by Leszek Balcerowicz, deputy prime minister and the minister of finance, who, over the years, developed a reputation as one of the country's most accomplished and daring economists. Balcerowicz and his team began working on the strategies of radical economic reforms already in 1978. By 1989, they abandoned any hope that the socialist economy could be reformed and focused on another task: the transition to an open market economy. They defined the economic system they wanted to create in the following terms:

1. various private enterprises are in the majority;
2. it is based on competition;
3. economy is open to the outside world;
4. there is a strong and convertible currency;
5. the state does not stifle enterprises with a multitude of bureaucratic regulations but provides a stable framework for their activities. Additionally, the state is strong enough to resist pressures from various interest groups, including the trade unions. (Balcerowicz 1992, 39)

Mazowiecki's government was sworn in on September 12. As Balcerowicz was taking over the reins of the Polish economy, he quickly realized he had no time to indulge in testing various policy options and fine-tuning reform measures. The dramatic economic situation, as he saw it, necessitated the choice of priorities. Since inflation was by far the most devastating problem at the moment, the macrostabilization program had to be introduced as quickly as possible. "An extreme case of inherited macroeconomic instability," Balcerowicz argued, "calls for the rapid implementation of a tough stabilization program" (1994, 81). After only several weeks of discussions, analyses, and intense lobbying to secure necessary international support, a reform strategy was developed. By December 17, the packet of reform bills instituting the program was before the parliament. Eleven legislative proposals were submitted to the Sejm and Senate, and on December 27, 10 bills were passed. One of the most daring economic reform programs in history was instituted on January 1, 1990. It had five major components:[11]

1. Macroeconomic stabilization, involving tight monetary and fiscal policies and limitation of the state budget deficit; deep reduction of subsidies to producers and consumers; reduction of credit availability for state-owned enterprises; sharp increase in interest rates and holding it above the rate of inflation (to encourage savings, slow down the flight from the zloty to Western currencies, and make credit less accessible and more prudently given and spent); limitation of the growth of wages (introduction of the tax on excessive increases of wages in state enterprises [*popiwek*]).
2. Liberalization (deregulation), involving abolition of central planning; elimination of remaining administratively set prices; discontinuation of import protections and restrictions on free domestic and foreign trade.
3. Sharp devaluation of domestic currency and introduction of convertibility.
4. Institutional reforms, involving large-scale privatization and demonopolization; restructuring of firms in the state sector; reform of the social security system; creation of the safety net for the unemployed; banking reform; creation of the taxation system; introduction of local self-government.
5. Mobilization of international financial assistance.

In the Polish case, such a shock therapy strategy was necessary and possible due to a specific combination of factors. The inherited economic crisis was much worse than in other countries, the new government was highly autonomous and insulated from entrenched interests, and it enjoyed a high level of public trust and confidence.

According to Poznanski, this "bold deflationary package, through aggregate demand contraction, stabilized the economy quite quickly" (1996, 177). The inflation rate had diminished drastically already by March 1990.[12] Also, thanks to the abolition of trade restrictions, consumer goods shortages were swiftly eliminated. By lowering inflation and strengthening the domestic currency, the program laid the foundations for the subsequent economic recovery.

In the short run, however, the political and economic price for the success of the stabilization program was high. Unemployment grew rapidly, industrial output and real wages declined dramatically, and the poverty rate increased. Balcerowicz and his "shock therapy" were often blamed for all these negative phenomena by opposition politicians and trade union activists. But the transformational recession had at least two other causes: (1) the liberalization of prices led to "the 'creative destruction' of productive capacity that had previously been employed in value-subtracting activities" (Slay 1994, 5); and (2) the collapse of the CMEA (Council for Mutual Economic Assistance)—particularly Soviet—markets, higher oil prices, and the loss of Middle Eastern export markets.

Despite mounting criticism, throughout the entire 1989–93 period, the main contours of economic policies remained remarkably constant. Subsequent governments kept relaxing and modifying various elements of the program, but major departures from the initial policies were rare. Poznanski argues that only "the formation of Pawlak's government marked a true end to radical reforming initiated by the Balcerowicz programme of 1990. A vivid symbol of this reversal was the nomination of Kolodko, a chief critic of the shock therapy, to the job once held by Balcerowicz" (1996, 208).

Initial Outcomes of Poland's Shock Therapy

In recent years, a consensus has emerged among the observers of East European transitions to a market economy that countries that implemented the most radical stabilization programs and did it as early as possible have been most successful. Poland is considered to be a prime example of fast, radical, and successful reforms (*From Plan to Market* 1996; Zucchini 1997). In fact, some basic economic indicators confirm this proposition. For our study, we need to describe only some major trends of the Polish postcommunist economy. Later we will determine whether the patterns we reconstruct in this section correlate with the patterns of protest behavior we observe in our own materials. There were five major trends in the Polish economy that need to be emphasized.

First, as a result of the "shock therapy," the Polish GDP growth rate declined during the first two years of the reform program more steeply than in any other country of Central Europe. But Poland also had the fastest and most robust recovery, beginning already during the third year (see table 4). Similarly,

TABLE 4.   GDP Growth Rates in Selected Central European Countries
(in percentages)

	Poland	Slovakia	Czech Republic	Hungary
1990	−11.6	−2.5	−1.2	−2.5
1991	−7.0	−14.6	−14.2	−7.7
1992	2.6	−6.2	−6.4	−4.3
1993	3.8	−4.1	−0.5	−2.3
1994	5.5	4.8	2.6	2.0

Source: From Plan to Market 1996, 173.

industrial production declined during the first two years, but growth resumed in 1992.[13] According to Sachs and Warner (1996), there is a strong positive correlation between the scope and comprehensiveness of economic reforms and the robustness of economic growth after a period of initial decline, caused by the dramatic reorientation and restructuring of the economic system. The Polish case conforms to this regularity: the radical reform produced the fastest-growing economy in the former Soviet bloc, with growth rates well above the OECD (Organization for Economic Cooperation and Development) average.

Second, the tight monetary and fiscal policies did not eliminate the problem of inflation. Although the hyperinflation was quickly curtailed, the level of inflation remained relatively high (see table 5). Thus the effort to further reduce the level of inflation was one of the most important tasks of subsequent governments.

Third, while the major elements of the macrostabilization program were swiftly instituted, the Polish privatization program was slow, both in design and in implementation. It also produced mixed results. The private sector expanded rapidly: by the end of 1992, 45 percent of the Polish GDP was produced in the private sector, and by April 1993, this sector employed 59 percent of the labor force.[14] Much of this growth, however, came from the rapidly developing in-

TABLE 5.   Inflation in Selected Central European Countries (in percentages)

	Poland	Slovakia	Czech Republic	Hungary
1989	243.8			
1990	586.0	10.8	10.8	29.0
1991	70.3	61.2	56.7	34.2
1992	43.0	10.1	11.1	22.9
1993	35.3	23.0	20.8	22.5
1994	32.2	14.0	10.2	19.0

Source: From Plan to Market 1996, 174.

digenous private sector and privatization of small firms and services. At the same time, the privatization of large state enterprises was slow. Until the end of 1993, Poland did not institute the mass voucher privatization program, nor did it pass legislation regulating the restitution of, or compensation for, private property confiscated by the communists. A mass privatization program was announced in June 1991 and the necessary legislation was passed in April 1993, but the implementation began only in July 1995. By September 1994, of 8,441 state enterprises, 2,974 were privatized or had begun the process of privatization.[15] Almost two-fifths of all privatizations occurred during Bielecki's term in office (1991); the "slowest" years were 1990 and 1993.

Fourth, perhaps the most painful and undesired by-product of the rapid economic reforms was unemployment, which was the highest among all the countries of Central Europe (see table 6). It is important to note, however, that the decline of total employment was much smaller than the contraction of total output. "Through 1991 most of the unemployment was the result of not hiring newcomers rather than terminating existing contracts with workers. . . . Among those let go, a majority were part-time workers, white-collar personnel, and persons who combined their industrial jobs with farming" (Poznanski 1996, 180). The essence of this process was that the newly introduced hard budget constraints and competition within many branches of the economy forced restructuring and layoffs. This phenomenon is particularly relevant for any study of protest politics, since one expects heavy union involvement in opposing restructuring and defending employees facing layoffs.

Fifth, in order to understand the economic reforms' impact on the populace's standard of living and people's political actions and reactions, we need to look at the dynamic of real wages during the period under study. This is not an easy task, mostly because during the transitory periods, the difficulty of measuring people's real incomes (thus including black- or shadow-market transactions) increases. We have tried to collect information on real wages from several sources, each of which used different methods of data collecting.

As measured by official statistics, the decline in real wages in Poland was more precipitous than in Hungary and as steep as in Slovakia (see table 7). It is, however, important to remember that the decline appears to be particularly

TABLE 6.   End-of-Year Unemployment (in percentages)

	Poland	Slovakia	Czech Republic	Hungary
1990	6.1	1.5	0.7	2.5
1991	11.8	11.8	4.1	8.0
1992	13.6	10.3	2.6	12.3
1993	15.7	14.4	3.5	12.1

Source: EBRD, World Bank, IMF; compiled by Svejnar (1995).

TABLE 7. Real Wages, 1990–93 (Previous Year = 100)

	Poland	Slovakia	Czech Republic	Hungary
1990	−24.4	−5.9	−5.4	−3.5
1991	−0.3	−25.6	−23.7	−6.8
1992	−2.7	8.9	10.1	−1.5
1993	−1.8	−3.9	4.1	−4.0
1993 as percentage of 1989	72.0	73.3	82.7	85.0

Source: Kornai 1996, 13.

Note: The figures for 1990 refer only to the category of workers and employees, excluding workers in agricultural cooperatives; for 1991 and later, the data include these.

dramatic if the inflated wages of 1989 are taken as the base of comparison. If the figures for, say, 1987 are used, the decline is far less drastic: 10 percent, instead of almost 30 percent.[16] This picture changes again when, instead of looking at real net wages, one observes real incomes, which include net wages, incomes from agricultural work, and real value of social transfers. The decline is still considerable, though less dramatic.[17]

Another set of measures used to assess the economic situation of the people deals with the gap between the rich and the poor. By all accounts, during the early postcommunist years in Poland, this gap opened much wider than before 1989. Ferge (1995) reports that in Poland the ratio of the incomes of people belonging to the top percentile of the population to the incomes of the people belonging to the bottom percentile was 3.31 in 1989. In 1994, it rose to 6.57 and was then much higher than in any other Central European country.[18]

Another important change in the income distribution is associated with the reversal of "class positions" and as such is significant for our study of protest. Rutkowski demonstrated that the ratio of white-collar wages to blue-collar wages in 1992 was a reverse of the same ratio measured in 1987. Before the transition, blue-collar workers earned more than white-collar workers; in 1992 the median white-collar wage was 18 percent higher than the median blue-collar wage (Rutkowski 1996, 8).

Finally, while considering the "material" situation of the Polish populace, we need to try to assess the size of undeclared incomes from the "black" economy. In June 1994, the Institute for the Study of the Market Economy determined that 30 percent of the people surveyed had "undeclared" additional employment and that "wages" from such jobs constituted about one-seventh of the average person's income (Grabowski 1994). Not everybody had access to such jobs; the most likely participants in this black economy were young men with a secondary education.

Multiple sources of income were also analyzed by Richard Rose and his associates, who studied families' coping strategies during the transition. They found out, for example, that most families in Eastern Europe relied on complex portfolios of varied strategies of survival. For many families, wages from "official" jobs were only a part of such portfolios. Among the Central European societies, Poles were most likely to declare having "second jobs to earn some money,"[19] and by the end of 1993 their complex portfolios of coping strategies seemed to have allowed them to get by at least as well as, if not better than, Slovaks and Hungarians.

Formation of New Political Attitudes and Definitions of Sociopolitical Reality

Given these complex political, economic, and social realities, how did Poles evaluate the post-1989 changes? Two data sets provide answers to this question. First, there is an extensive data set collected by the Polish Center for Public Opinion Research (CBOS), which conducted monthly surveys of public opinion beginning in April 1990. Second, there is a series of studies conducted by the Center for the Study of Public Policy (CSPP) in Glasgow, under the direction of Richard Rose (see Rose and Haerpfer 1996a and 1996b). The CBOS studies provide a much more detailed picture, while the strength of the Glasgow studies is their comparative dimension, since identical surveys were conducted in several countries.

The CBOS and CSPP studies are complementary, for they ask different questions. While the former asked people to evaluate their present economic and political *situation* and assess the general direction of change, the latter inquired about people's approval "of the present system of governing" and "the present economic system." According to the CBOS polls, the populace's assessment of the general direction of change and of the political and economic situation from early 1990 to May 1992 was increasingly negative. Then it improved a little, but it never reached the level of positive assessment, characteristic for almost all of 1990. The CSPP yearly surveys, however, caught a different trend. While in the fall of 1991 only slightly more than half of Poles approved of their political regime, after that time their approval systematically increased. Also, the approval of the post-1989 economic system increased considerably from 1991 to 1993. The CSPP studies revealed additionally that the approval of the postcommunist political and economic regimes was stronger in Poland than in Hungary and Slovakia, though weaker than in the Czech Republic.

The discrepancy between the CBOS and CSPP results confirms a phenomenon observed by other researchers: in some postcommunist countries the approval of the new political and economic regimes was rising, while the respondents' assessments of their everyday situation either were declining or sta-

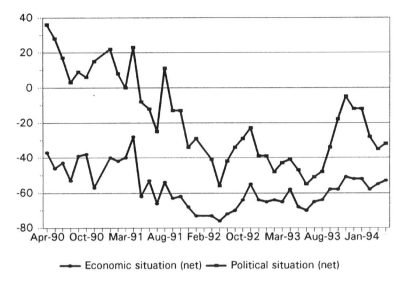

Fig. 1.   Public assessment of the political and economic situation, 1990–
94. (Data from CBOS, various reports.)

bilized at a low level. In brief, the new political and economic systems and the
principles they were based on were assessed more positively than their performance. This, of course, brings to mind Lipset's celebrated observation that the
regime's legitimacy and efficiency are different phenomena and are often assessed separately from one another (1960, 77–83). Linz and Stepan noted this
phenomenon in postcommunist East Central Europe and concluded that

> For at least a medium range time horizon, people can make independent
> and even opposite assessments about political and economic trends. We
> further believe that, if assessments about politics are positive, they can
> provide a valuable cushion against painful economic restructuring. (1996,
> 439)

It needs to be emphasized that in Poland positive assessments of politics referred to the systemic principles of the post-1989 order; assessments of actual
functioning of such political institutions as the parliament or parties were by
and large negative and much more critical than in other countries of Central Europe.[20] This finding constitutes one of the cornerstones of our argument: in
Poland, the low assessment of the "routine" political institutions correlated with
the exceptionally high magnitude of protest, which in turn was the main factor
shaping the early stages of democratic consolidation.

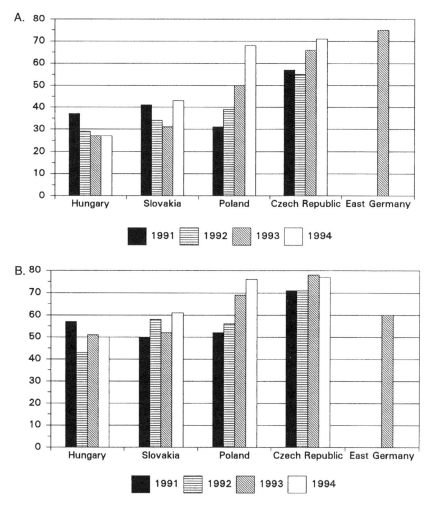

Fig. 2.   Public approval of the current economic system and the current
political regime. (Data from Rose and Haerpfer 1996a, 25, 47.)
A.   Economic system
B.   Political regime

The low and declining assessment of the sociopolitical situation by the majority of Poles was confirmed by a number of studies conducted by Polish sociologists, who investigated postcommunism from a variety of analytical perspectives. Their findings can be summarized in the following five points.

1. *Cultural chaos*

Postcommunism, as a general condition in which people found themselves after 1989, did not offer any clearly articulated cultural scheme that would allow them to interpret the new reality. As many people began their own individual quests for meanings, a process of cultural diversifications or increasing cultural chaos ensued (Tarkowska 1993). According to Tarkowska, cultural chaos is associated with the climate of emotional instability and the dominance of short-term interests and values, somewhat paradoxically combined with axiological polarization. In her own words, "Our reality seems to be—for participants as well as for observers of the changes underway—somewhat unclear, opaque, unpredictable" (1994, 270). Such a chaotic situation facilitates the development of an "apocalyptic mentality," increases people's vulnerability to symbolic and emotional manipulation, and leads to the intensification of mythical, magical, and religious forms of action.

The situation of cultural chaos has a negative effect on political participation, particularly, it seems, on conventional political participation such as voting or joining political parties. Kolarska-Bobinska, noting the emergence of "disturbances in the cognitive sphere," theorizes their political significance:

> The lack of an orderly picture of the world, of social statuses and behavioral norms is, as mentioned, one of the causes of social anomy. *It can result in an unwillingness to participate in political life as it creates more confusion and ambiguity than do economic activities* (emphasis added). (1994, 78)

2. *Uncertainty and stereotypes*

Cultural chaos exacerbated the uncertainty brought about by the rapid collapse of the old regime. For many people, the world around them changed rapidly, and they faced an uneasy task of reconceptualizing it. In their search for new interpretive schemas, they came across relatively simple stereotypes that helped them to grasp and explain new situations. Social psychologists discovered the rising popularity of such constructs as blaming "others" or scapegoating some mystical "evil persons." The cultural constructs people found handy included a "Jewish conspiracy" or "a plot of international secret agents" (see Swida-Ziemba 1994, 231). In chapter 7 we will try to determine whether some of these conceptualizations had their origins in the heated rhetoric used by protest leaders to mobilize people.

3. *Political passivity (political apathy) and alienation from politics*
Uncertainty and cultural disorientation seem to have been correlated with another general malady of the transitory period, namely, political passivity. This phenomenon was clearly exemplified by the low trust in political parties and low electoral turnout during the first five years of postcommunism. Markowski, summarizing his detailed study of the nonvoting segment of the populace ("the silent majority"), wrote:

> From the whole [analysis] emerges a picture of political passivity as a phenomenon strongly related to the lack of faith in the new political class and the results of its actions. [This passivity] is based on and results from the lack of knowledge concerning the outside reality and is linked with the animosity toward the difference and the empowerment of minorities. (1992, 107)

Political passivity was frequently associated with an alienation from politics, succinctly summarized by Marody: "One of the major features of Poland's *habitus* has been a belief that politics is a sphere of life dominated by authorities whose decisions can be challenged but never influenced through participation" (1991, 112).

A survey conducted in January 1992 revealed that 46–58 percent of the respondents claimed that "during the past two years their ability to influence the affairs of the country, their locality, or work place has not changed" (Glinski 1993, 101). Only 14–20 percent believed that their ability had increased. A comparison with an October 1990 survey revealed an increase of 18 percent in the number of people who felt their influence over the country's affairs was actually waning.

4. *The lack of trust in the new political elite*
This alienation from politics was reflected by the low level of trust in political elites. Most Polish researchers agree that the political elite and most of the new political institutions (with the exception of the army and police), including political parties, were not perceived by a substantial portion of the Polish population as *trustworthy,* and their approval ratings were systematically declining throughout the 1989–93 period.[21] Kempny, having analyzed letters sent to new senators, noted that "the new power elite has been very often perceived in the same categories as the old regime" (1993, 99).

5. *Political indeterminacy*
Finally, several researchers observed what they called "political indeterminacy," whose major component was poorly developed and unstable electoral preferences (see Raciborski 1992, 162). In a series of CBOS studies, the re-

TABLE 8.   Index of Political Alienation

Country	Index of Alienation
Hungary	3.61
Poland	3.27
East Germany	3.01
Czechoslovakia	2.91

Source: Mason 1992.

spondents were asked to place themselves somewhere along the "left"—"right" political continuum.[22] The studies covered the period from July 1990 through May 1993 and revealed two striking trends. First, the number of people with right leanings and centrist political views declined considerably, whereas 16–20 percent of the respondents espoused consistently leftist viewpoints. Second, since the introduction of the "Hard to say" option in the July 1991 questionnaire, the majority of respondents (34–38 percent) repeatedly chose this response above all the others. This is a clear indicator of political indeterminacy (or incertitude), which seems to correlate with political passivity. Glinski observed, for example, that

> political identity of the society is completely undetermined. Poles are politically passive, because they do not have clearly articulated political views. They cannot therefore belong to political parties on a massive scale or support these parties in the elections. (1993, 100)

This general overview of the major studies on the political psychology of postcommunist Poland can be recapitulated in several points. From 1989 though 1993, many Poles felt *uncertainty, did not trust politics and politicians,* were experiencing *flux* and *indeterminacy.* The populace was largely *withdrawn from politics* and primarily *concerned with the economic situation.* Tellingly, this bleak picture was confirmed by other researchers. Mason discovered that Poles ranked high (second to Hungary) on the composite Index of Political Alienation (table 8).

Recapitulation and the Relevance for Our Study

In this chapter we offered a general overview of the postcommunist transformations in Poland from 1989 through 1993. For the remainder of the book, we will analyze the links between specific features of the Polish economic, political, or social post-1989 developments and the protest politics we studied in our research project. In other words, we will try to describe and explain certain elements of Polish postcommunist protest politics by placing them within the context of other political, economic, and social phenomena.

Specifically, we will examine the relationship among several features of protest and (1) changes in the economic situation; (2) people's grievances and perceptions of the socioeconomic reality; (3) the availability of material and symbolic resources; (4) historically shaped protest cultures; and (5) the institutional context of the polity within which such actions occur. This examination will be guided by several major questions, including:

> Did the increasing discontent with the political and economic changes, registered by the CBOS polls, lead to the increase in protest activity?
> Did the growing gap between the rich and the poor and the high level of political alienation lead to heightened protest activity?
> Or, rather, did increasing Polish approval of the postcommunist developments coexist with a lower and declining level of protest?
> Was the changing pattern of macroeconomic indicators, such as the GDP, reflected systematically in patterns of protest activity?

And finally, one of the most intriguing questions studies of social protest need to answer:

> Were people's grievances and perceptions of reality influencing protest leaders and their framing of events, or, rather, was it the other way around: the framing of issues by protest leaders influenced people's perceptions of reality?

Some answers to these questions will emerge from our analysis of aggregate protest data, presented in chapter 5. We believe, however, that more precise answers can be obtained through detailed analysis of protest rhetorics and symbolic frames of protest and through an in-depth case study of a major protest campaign. Such analyses are offered respectively in chapters 6 and 7.

Before we begin to address these questions, however, we have to specify our analytical model. Although there are several models and theories of protest politics and social movements, our choice of a suitable analytical framework was simple. Given the nature of our data (descriptions of events) and our goal (the role of protest in democratic consolidation or the institutionalization of the new polity), the choice of the "political process" approach was almost automatic. Theories belonging to this tradition place the institutional contexts of protest at the center of the researcher's attention. Additionally, protest frequency and characteristics are explained as results of people's more or less deliberate strategic choices within specific institutional settings. This approach, recently called the Synthetic Political Opportunity Theory (Lichbach 1996), has emerged as a dominant research program within the field of protest and movement studies. A version of this "integrated" approach to protest, utilizing structural, cultural, and rational variables and arguments (McAdam, Tarrow, and Tilly 1997), intermeshes almost seamlessly with our analytical model, designed to conceptualize the relationship between protest actions and various institutional arrangements of the wider political field. This model is presented in the next chapter, where we define the three realms of public life: the state, political society, and civil society. In the concluding chapter we offer several theses on how the relationships among these three institutional realms and protest politics shaped democratic consolidation in Poland.

CHAPTER 4

Three Realms of Politics and Regime Change

Poland's political developments strike at the heart of what Schmitter identified as "the most significant issue for contemporary political science: How can democracy be consolidated in the aftermath of the transition from authoritarian rule?" (1992, 157). The issue of consolidation of new democracies emerged as an explicit focus of systematic scholarly investigations in the early 1990s.[1] Until then, most research in the dynamically growing field of transitions to democracy had concentrated either on the structural preconditions and processes of the old regime's decomposition or on the intra-elite negotiations directly preceding the transfer of power and its immediate aftermath.

Two factors account for this dearth of studies on consolidation. First, until recently there have not been many consolidating democracies to study, and scholars' interests concentrated elsewhere. As Di Palma argued, "the most decisive role in establishing democracy belongs to the agreement phase, not to consolidation" (1990, 110–11). O'Donnell and Schmitter explain their group's similar position:

> The Wilson Center working group paid little attention to processes of consolidation and "advanced democratization" for the obvious reason that the cases and countries which preoccupied us were involved in the much more proximate and hazardous business of extricating themselves from various versions of authoritarian rule. (1986, 45)

Second, as Huntington suggested, the consolidation process is shaped by "contextual problems endemic to individual countries" (1991, 253) as well as "systemic problems stemming from workings of a democratic system." According to this view, a combination of historically contingent factors makes comparative analyses of consolidation difficult and cross-national generalizations uncertain.

During the last few years, however, the number of countries striving to consolidate their democracies increased sufficiently to warrant comparisons and generalizations. Before this is done, however, richer, more adequate conceptualizations should be developed and reliable descriptions and analyses of particular cases produced. In this chapter we propose a conceptual model that allows us to analyze democratic consolidation in broader terms than it is usually done.

In their pathbreaking work, Linz and Stepan offer a "narrow" definition of consolidation, specifying its three dimensions: behavioral, attitudinal, and constitutional. In a nutshell, democracy is consolidated when it is accepted as "the only game in town," that is, when no important social actor engages in actions to destroy it, contemplates its destruction in the future, or rejects its institutional order.[2] Linz and Stepan emphasize that there may exist many divergent types of democratic consolidation and that they may have in common only a very basic set of generalized procedures.[3] This thesis constitutes a starting point for our analysis. Each consolidating democracy may have a different set of principal actors, a different institutional makeup, and—in particular—a different style of institutionalizing political participation, including contentious collective action.

This book analyzes a particular type of consolidation represented by the Polish case: a postcommunist consolidation with a heightened level of contentious collective action. A careful analysis of this case should allow us to shed some new light on the way the major domains of the polity are institutionalized during the early stages of democratic consolidation. We intend to contribute to the debate on democratic (postcommunist) consolidation through a detailed examination of *contentious collective action*. While there are studies on the contributions made by the "popular sectors" or "civil society" to the fall of nondemocratic regimes,[4] people's activities during democratic consolidation have not been systematically analyzed.

To begin with, we propose to analyze the consolidation of democracy as a complex process occurring simultaneously on several levels (or within several institutional domains) of the sociopolitical organization of society. Linz and Stepan analyze consolidation in terms of five arenas (1996, 7–15). We propose a model containing three arenas: the state, political society, and civil society. This does not mean that we downplay the significance of the postcommunist economic transformations. Our analytical model simply reflects the way in which we want to examine the politics of democratic consolidation. We do not study how people engage in economic activities during the transition (the domain of economic society) and what the consequences of such activities are. We study how people act upon their economic and other preferences in the public sphere, how they organize themselves when they attempt to influence new governments' economic policies, and how they react to the results of these policies. The main domains (arenas) of such collective pursuits are political society and civil society. The interactions between individual and collective actors at and between the three arenas selected for our examination may foster the stabilization of the polity and consolidation of a democratic system or reinforce the political instability leading to the erosion of newly founded democratic institutions and liberties.

Additionally, we take an important cue from Shin, who argues that "consolidation and stability are not the same phenomenon" (1994, 144). In some cases, a budding democracy may appear politically stable, but a threat to overthrow its institutions remains a viable option for some significant actors. Valenzuela characterizes such a situation as a "vicious circle of perverse institutionalization" (1992, 68). In other cases, political stability may occur on a suboptimal level, that is, without the institutionalization of one or more elements of the fully consolidated democracy (specified below). Thus, we cannot conflate the absence of political instability with consolidation.

Democratic consolidation is a process that approaches its completion when the establishment of a political democracy is accompanied by *three additional conditions*. Following an emerging consensus, we subscribe to a minimalist, procedural definition of political democracy. Diamond, Linz, and Lipset offer one:

> Democracy denotes a system of government that meets three essential conditions: meaningful and extensive *competition* among individuals and organized groups (especially political parties) for all elective positions of government power, at regular intervals and excluding the use of force; a "highly inclusive" level of *political participation* in the selection of leaders and policies, at least through regular and fair elections, such that no major (adult) social group is excluded; and a level of *civil and political liberties*—freedom of expression, freedom of the press, freedom to form and join organizations—sufficient to ensure integrity of political competition and participation. (1990, 6–7)

The three additional conditions are:

1. the formation of a consensus concerning the boundaries of political community; that is, a situation whereby the "stateness problem" facing many newly democratized societies is resolved;[5]
2. the development of transparency and predictability at the institutional level;
3. the achievement of a sufficient level of what O'Donnell calls social and cultural democratization. (1992, 18)

Condition 2 is realized when the following elements are in place: (1) the basic democratic architecture, such as tri-division of powers, regular elections, rule of law, and guarantees of liberty, are assured by the constitution (see Elster 1993 and Lijphart 1992); (2) the state possesses a monopoly of means of coercion, control of the territory, stability, autonomy, and capacity to implement its policies;[6] and (3) the boundaries between the state and other institutional domains of the democratic polity (party system, civil society) are well defined. The domains are autonomous, but at the same time the linkages among them are well developed. Moreover, actors within these domains do not claim exclusive power to represent society as a whole.

Among the social and cultural conditions of consolidation, the following is most important: the basic institutional setup of the polity and political procedures must be considered legitimate by all significant social and political forces. As Diamond put it:

> It is by now a cardinal tenet of empirical democratic theory that stable democracy also requires a belief in the legitimacy of democracy. Ideally, this belief should be held at two levels: as a general principle, that democracy is the best form of government possible, and as an evaluation of the believers' own system, that in spite of its failures and shortcomings, their own democratic regime is better than any other that might be established for their country. (1993, 13)[7]

Political democracy is the necessary condition of consolidated democracy; without it, consolidation is meaningless. The three additional conditions are realizable and realized in various degrees, but their absence makes democracy weak and unstable. It is, however, not easy to specify a *threshold* beyond which a democracy can be declared consolidated.

We assume, moreover, that for each phase of democratization there is an optimal combination of developments in the main institutional domains of the polity. For example, the deconstruction of authoritarian or (post-)totalitarian regimes is facilitated by the simultaneous weakening of state power and mobilization (by necessity often poorly institutionalized) of civil society. Bermeo (1997) and Tarrow (1995b) demonstrate persuasively the existence of such a combination for Spain; it was also present in the first domino that fell through the Soviet bloc: in Poland. The actual transfer of power occurs most efficiently when civil society's mobilization does not escalate to violence and when a pact between elites and counterelites assures the inclusion of a broad range of political actors and sets the limits for political and economic change. Finally, the consolidation phase seems to be facilitated by a still different combination: the simultaneous strengthening of the state, political society, and civil society. We accept Stepan's conclusion that the relationship between institutional domains of society is not a zero-sum game: the power and capacity of the state and other collective actors may simultaneously increase or decrease (Stepan 1985).[8]

Our analysis concentrates on the second condition: the development of transparency and predictability at the institutional level. We will try to determine *how* the three institutional domains evolved after 1989, *whether* their power and capacity increased or decreased, and *what kinds* of linkages developed among them. Our answer will emerge from an overview of the changes occurring within the state and the party system, but primarily it will be based on a detailed analysis of protest politics. We consider the latter to be a solid indicator of civil society's condition, but we will also rely on evidence provided by other researchers, particularly those who study Polish NGOs.

The Three Realms of Politics

There are three realms within which political actions are generated, shaped, and structured. We understand politics broadly as various forms of collective action taking place within the established or emerging structures of authority, which are aimed at maintaining or changing the distribution of power and resources among individual or collective actors (groups, organizations, and institutions). Politics is also about the (re)construction of actors' identities.[9] For the sake of convenience we call these realms *the state, political society,* and *civil society.*[10] In each realm, politics are structured by different sets of institutions, social networks, identities, principles of authority, and specific modes of collective action. Each realm tends to have its specific public discourses, collective action frames, and modes of public participation.

   Although the boundaries between the three realms are constantly renegotiated and changed, their relative autonomy is a necessary condition of democracy (Gellner 1994). Moreover, the struggle over these boundaries is a critical element of consolidation. As Migdal noted, "The meeting grounds between states and other social forces have been ones in which conflict and complicity, opposition and coalition, corruption and co-optation have resolved the shape of countrywide social and political changes" (1994, 23). Similarly, Skocpol argues that "the meanings of public life and the collective forms through which groups become aware of political goals and work to attain them arise, not from society alone, but at the meeting points of states and societies" (1985, 27). During a rapid political change or regime transition, the boundaries between the three realms become porous and highly contested. Old and new individual and collective actors engage in intense political struggles, which often *transgress* from one realm to another, thereby redefining their boundaries.

The State

The state is the realm of authoritative and bureaucratic politics. It must be considered, following Stepan,

> as something more than the "government." It is a continuous administrative, legal, bureaucratic and coercive system that attempts not only to manage the state apparatus but to structure the relationship between civil and

public power and to structure many crucial relationships within civil and political society. (1988, 4)

The most distinct characteristics of the state are its control of coercive resources, its monopoly of rule making, and its capability to implement its decisions within a defined territory, despite public opposition or resistance. Imperative and bureaucratic-hierarchical decision making lies at the heart of state activities. Friedland and Alford describe the central logic of state action as "rationalization and the regulation of human activity by legal and bureaucratic hierarchies." This logic is "symbolically grounded, organizationally structured, politically defended and technically and materially constrained, and hence [has] specific historical limits" (1991, 248–49). Modern states monopolize a wide range of functions and tasks. They make and enforce laws, maintain order and security, provide and redistribute collective and distributional goods, and mediate social conflicts and interests. Their effectiveness in all these functions depends on their ability to raise and deploy financial resources (see Skocpol 1985, 17).

Bureaucratic hierarchies of the state assume diverse and historically developed organizational forms. The level of state centralization, the division of power between the state's hierarchies, and the presence or absence of federal arrangements define the state's strength and effectiveness. These factors also limit or expand a number of "access points" that actors outside the state have and, therefore, shape their potential to have an impact on state actions (cf. Kriesi 1995). In general, public participation in state actions is significantly limited. The institution of the popular initiative, which allows groups of citizens to put specific issues on the state agenda, and the institution of national referendum are not very common among contemporary states. Moreover, Kriesi emphasizes that "the procedures of compulsory and optional referenda give challengers an additional opportunity to intervene, but are of less importance because they allow intervention only after a decision has been taken by the political elite" (1995, 171). Similarly, conventional assumptions about the impact of elections and party politics on state activities are at least partially misleading. According to Alford and Friedland,

> the presumably most responsive sections of the state are not significantly influenced by variations in voting turnout and party competition. Unfortunately, electoral participation is not highly correlated with power as measured by public expenditures and other measures of state responsiveness. (1975, 432)

In fact, as Offe argues, the reverse process—that is, "the usurping of 'representative' function by the executive agencies of the state . . . for actors within civil society"—is increasingly more prevalent (Offe 1985, 8).

The main political actors within the state are organized networks of state officials. They are relatively insulated from the groups representing dominant socioeconomic interests (Skocpol 1985, 9). In fact, in some states the process of state-elite selection and promotion reinforces the autonomy of state actors and creates a stable elite with a particularly strong "esprit de corps" (cf. Evans 1992). In sum, despite the continuing ambiguity of the notion of state autonomy, the state—weak or strong—represents a distinct domain of society with its specific institutional logic, resources, capacities, and collective actors.[11]

Political Society

Political society is an intermediate realm within which the double process of translation and mediation takes place. It provides channels through which various societal interests and claims are aggregated and translated into generalized policy recommendations. According to Stepan, through political society "civil society can constitute itself politically to select and monitor democratic government" (1988, 4). For the state, however, political society is also an indispensable mediation instrument. Offe points out that "contemporary political parties often act as organs of communication for governments (when the party is in office) or for party elites aspiring to the office of government." He argues that while this two-way communication is a proper role of political society, the problem of welfare-state democracies is "the fusion of these channels of mediation through which actors within civil society act upon political authority, with those channels of communication through which, inversely, the state acts upon civil society" (1985, 7). Thus, through political society, state actions and policies are disaggregated, legitimized, and transmitted to localities, groups, and organizations within civil society.

Political society is the realm in which complex political alternatives and choices compete and are deliberated by political actors. A structured negotiation of competitive claims and actions is a fundamental modus operandi of political society in which coalitions of political actors are built and competition for political power takes place. As Stepan argues, political society "arranges itself for political contestation to gain control over public power and state apparatus" (1988, 4). In democratic polities it comprises universal suffrage, elections, competing political parties, and legislative bodies. According to Kitschelt,

> elections, parties and legislatures are generalized institutions of political choice; they are not specialized arenas for representing a specific set of citizens or deciding any particular subject matter. They are involved in an uncertain and in principle, unlimited set of citizens' demands for collective decisions. (1992b, 7)

Public participation in political society rests on the assumption of the equal and universal rights of all adults to choose their ruling elites through periodic elections. This type of participation is formalized and usually desocialized: in the act of voting a citizen is alone, and the secrecy of his/her choice is guaranteed. Additionally, the election process involves campaigning, another form of political participation that requires cooperation and social involvement.

In representative democracies, political society plays two seemingly contradictory roles. Kitschelt emphasizes that

> on the one hand, [it] opens the political process to an indeterminate and, in principle, all encompassing set of issues. . . . On the other hand, the resulting complexity of decision making and the corresponding risk of volatility in collective choices is reduced by closing the political process and restraining the alternatives that can be practically considered by a sophisticated array of institutional rules. (1992b, 8)

Civil Society

The concept of civil society, with its long and complex history, has enjoyed a remarkable renaissance during the 1990s. We suggest that the existing definitions of civil society fall into three basic types; the first two are descriptive and analytical, the third is normative. First, civil society can be construed as a specific *social space or sphere.* It is a space between family (household, domestic society) and the state. "It excludes both stifling communalism and centralized authoritarianism" (Gellner 1994, 12). Eley, quoting Habermas, offers the following formulation: "In a nutshell, the public sphere means 'a sphere between society and state, in which the public organizes itself as the bearer of public opinion'" (1992, 290). Second, civil society can be defined as a set or system of *specific social groups.* Schmitter elaborates this definition with great precision:

> "Civil society" is defined as a set or system of self-organized intermediary groups:
>
> (1) that are relatively independent of both public authorities *and* private units of production and reproduction, i.e., of firms and families;
> (2) that are capable of deliberating about and taking collective actions in defense/promotion of their interests/passions;
> (3) but do *not* seek to replace either state agents or private (re)producers or to accept responsibility for governing the polity as a whole;
> (4) but *do* agree to act within pre-established rules of "civil" or legal nature. (1995a, 4–5)

Finally, civil society can be defined as a "normative project," a discourse, a collective dream, that mobilizes people to action against the oppressive state.[12]

In our project we adopt both analytical definitions, understanding civil society as a space *and* as a set of specific groups inhabiting this space.[13] The space must be institutionally established, stabilized, and guaranteed usually, though not necessarily, by legal, particularly constitutional, regulations. The battle to create, enlarge, and protect such a space is carried out by organized groups constituting civil society in the second sense. It is, however, very important to remember that once such a space comes into existence, it can be populated not only by its creators and protectors but also by at least two other types of groups, enemies and free riders. Enemies use the institutional protection of civil society space to plot its destruction,[14] while free riders enjoy the protection but are not going to defend the space in case of danger.

We further assume that civil society is internally diversified and composed of various *sectors,* which are characterized by great fluidity. Their size and internal diversity may increase or diminish according to the independence they are accorded within the legal framework of the regime, certain characteristics of the society, and the dominant political practices of the elites. Thus the relative importance of these sectors, their various degrees of institutionalization, and their mutual relationships depend on the type of polity within which they operate.

In authoritarian and post-totalitarian systems, where there is no rule of law, civil society develops only within the confines of the arbitrary autonomy allowed either deliberately or inadvertently by the rulers. Totalitarian regimes allow little or no autonomy; authoritarian systems are more open and often tolerate some independent associations, whose operations are, however, unprotected by the law and are subject to arbitrary interference by the authorities. This situation can be called *uninstitutionalized autonomy:* civil society, as a set of groups, exists, but it does not exist as an institutionally protected space. Moreover, some organizations may be arbitrarily protected by the authorities, while others are ruthlessly persecuted. Under state socialism, the principle of uninstitutionalized autonomy allowed the existence of three types of organizations: (1) pseudo-autonomous (for example, official trade unions), (2) semi-autonomous (for example, the Roman Catholic Church in Poland), and (3) "illegally" autonomous (for example, dissident groups, black-market networks). In authoritarian systems, where the elite political actors reserve for themselves an almost complete monopoly over political activities, any independent action of civil society, particularly its third sector, becomes inadvertently political. On the other hand, mobilization for action within dissident groups is unthinkable without the support of familial, kinship, and friendship networks. For these two reasons, the borders that separate political society, civil society, and domestic society are very porous. In fact, civil society cannot exist without a base within domestic society: Gellnerian "cousins" are not civil society's greatest enemies, but rather its necessary benefactors.

In polities based on the rule of law, the situation is different. First, law allows for the constitution and protection of civil society as an autonomous public space. Thus the vitality of civil society organizations depends both on the comprehensiveness and durability of this autonomy and on their degree of separation from traditional, illiberal communities (primary groups).[15] It is a situation opposite to authoritarian systems, in which a civil society's strength depends on its interpenetration with traditional communities. Second, in lawful polities, the sectoral diversification of civil society is functional. All associations are *formally equal,* in the sense that they enjoy more or less equal expectations of institutional survival as long as their actions remain within an existing legal framework. Such an institutionally guaranteed freedom of association produces a multitude of organized collective actors and civil society sectors, each characterized by its particular institutional structure, functions, and political influence. The configuration, relative strength, and institutionalization pattern of these sectors differ from country to country, producing various types of civil society.

Civil societies differ from each other in terms of their organizational density, which varies significantly across regions and local communities. Moreover, different organizations of civil society may relate to each other in different ways. They may form complex horizontal networks, often based on close social ties as well as active and personal participation. They also compete for resources, members, and political access. It is thus not insignificant how big they are. In contemporary societies, large and centralized organizations tend to dominate associational life. Furthermore, sectoral organization of civil societies may be different. Without attempting to offer an exhaustive and precise classification, we suggest that contemporary civil societies are composed of at least seven sectors. They include (1) labor organizations, (2) traditional interest groups, (3) NGOs, (4) social movements, (5) youth organizations, (6) religious/ethnic associations, and (7) neighborhood and recreational associations. In Walzer's less formal enumeration, civil society "is the home ground of 'difference,' a realm of fragmentation made up of churches, ethnic groups, social movements, unions, professional associations, organizations for mutual aid and defence" (1993, 50).[16] Both the internal characteristics of these sectors (number and size of organizations, and the type of relations among them) and the relative importance of particular sectors account for variation of civil society forms. Finally, different civil societies can be dominated by liberal and democratic organizations or by civil society's enemies and free riders. Thus, the nature or character of civil society organizations accounts for the differences between existing civil societies.

There are many routine modes of public participation within the realm of civil society that include membership and/or participation in neighborhood and local organizations or projects, churches, or recreational associations. These can be described as *cooperative forms of public participation.* When civil society actors interact with the state, their actions often become competitive and contentious. There are two basic forms of contentious collective action: *resistance* and *protest.* These two forms of participation roughly correspond to Tilly's distinction between reactive and proactive collective action.[17] In short, whenever civil society interacts with the state in a contentious mode, the interests and identities of civil society actors (individuals and organizations) are defined, defended, and advanced through various forms of resistance or protest. Under oppressive regimes, resistance in its many forms plays the dominant role (Scott 1990). By contrast, in open political systems protest becomes a primary mode of civil society's contentious politics.

This brief overview was designed to convey a few simple points: there are many different civil societies, because they operate in various institutional spaces and are structured by different sets of organizations, social networks, identities, principles of authority, and specific modes of public participation.

The Relationships among the Three Realms

In different political systems, the center of political gravity can be found in civil society, political society, or the state. In authoritarian and statist regimes, the state is the most important arena of politics, and state actors have an almost exclusive capacity to structure political outcomes. Autonomy, political resources, and freedom of action in the other two realms are seriously restricted, if not abolished altogether. The state often attempts to substitute a network of corporatist arrangements for autonomous activities of civil and political society. In corporatist institutions, however, the variety of interests and claims that are allowed to be articulated and represented is limited. In some types of nondemocratic regimes, political and civil societies are almost completely destroyed or incapacitated. This is the case with communist and neopatrimonial regimes.[18] In contrast to neopatrimonial regimes, the destroyed organizations under communist regimes are replaced by a wide range of state-dependent, highly centralized, and fully controlled mass organizations that penetrate the entire sociopolitical order. This replacement of genuine civil society with its state-controlled substitute has important consequences for the consolidation of democracy in postcommunist regimes.

In contemporary liberal democracies, political society, with its party system, legislative assemblies, and elections, plays a dominant role. It selectively structures and channels claims advanced by the actors in civil society as well as controls the expansion of bureaucratic politics and the coercive capacity of the state. This point, however, must be qualified. Many students of modern democracies argue that the decline of political society and the expansion of state functions are undermining the stability and vitality of the democratic state (Linz 1992, 184–90). Offe, for example, points out that both the neoliberal critics of the welfare state and the representatives of new social movements share a common concern over the erosion of the nonstate underpinnings of the political system. They argue that "the conflicts and contradictions of advanced industrial society can no longer be meaningfully resolved through etatism, political regulation, and the inclusion of ever more issues on the agendas of bureaucratic authorities" (Offe 1987, 64–65). While such views offer important insights into contemporary democratic politics, the institutions of generalized political choice still retain their centrality in the public life of democratic societies. The importance and effectiveness of political society can be attributed to the fact that modern democratic polities emerged as a result of a long evolutionary process during which rich and transparent links between the three realms have been gradually established.

Situations in which civil society becomes the locus of political power are rare. They are usually the result of the collapse of national-level political institutions during revolutions, civil wars, or foreign invasions. Such cases are usually short-lived, and the unrestricted power of civil society is always drastically curtailed with the reestablishment of national-level state institutions and the recovery of the state's coercive capacity. The autonomous action of civil society is often romanticized by social theorists who believe in the virtues of cooperation and direct participation. The disintegration of the state and political society accompanied by the politicization of civil society, however, often produces aggressive mobilization and seems to delay the consolidation of the institutions of representative democracy (cf. Bermeo 1997; Schmitter 1995a; Valenzuela 1989, 450). The disintegration of the former Soviet Union and Yugoslavia provides some examples of the possible consequences of a shift of political power from the state to the amorphous and poorly institutionalized civil society (Beissinger and Hajda 1990, 316; Fish 1995b, 154–55, and 1995a).

During rapid democratization in former nondemocratic regimes, the locus of political power shifts among the three realms. The first phase of democratization, that is, the deconstruction of the old regime, entails the weakening of the state's coercive capacity and infrastructural power and the political mobilization of organizations and movements within civil society. When such a situation continues during the transfer of power and the establishment of incipient democracy, an anarchic transitory polity may result. Conflicts and disjunctions within and among the three realms emerge as each experiences autonomous and rapid changes. In some cases the very survival of a unified polity is at stake. Linz and Stepan noted that "in many countries the crisis of the nondemocratic regime is also intermixed with profound differences about what should actually constitute the 'state'. Some political activists simultaneously challenge the old nondemocratic regime and the existing territorial state itself" (1992, 123).

During the period of democratic consolidation, all three realms undergo important transformations; however, their character, scope, and speed depend on legacies left by the preceding nondemocratic system. The distribution of power among the realms and their institutional strength and coherence under nondemocratic rule have important consequences for the democratization process. As Hagopian emphasized in her analysis of Latin American experiences,

> to the extent that military regimes altered the societal bases for political association and participation, the relationship of political parties to their constituents, the networks of mediation through which states organize the consent of their societies, and in some cases even the institutional framework for political competition, their political legacies influence heavily the prospects for democratic consolidation and hence need to be brought into sharper focus. (1993, 466)

It seems, however, that constructing a viable and stable democratic polity entails "forgetting" authoritarian legacies and developing a "forward-looking" strategy that emphasizes the *simultaneous* rebuilding of civil and political societies as well as the redefinition of the state and its power. Thus, the successful crafting of democracy requires not only the elites' capacity to negotiate intra-elite pacts but also the ability of social groups to build the three public realms; to institutionalize—that is, make predictable and stable—links between them; and to reduce the level of mutual antagonism between collective actors in these realms.

In the remainder of this chapter, we will examine the transformations of the three institutional domains in Poland after 1989. We will take a closer look at Poland's postcommunist state, the newly emerged political society, and reconstituted civil society. Finally, we will analyze the relationships among the three main domains of the polity.

The Three Realms of Politics in Postcommunist Poland

The State

Despite some common misconceptions about the strength and capacity of communist party-estates, in the wake of the collapse of state socialism East European states were weak and ineffective (Stark and Bruszt 1998, 16). In Mann's terms, they had considerable "despotic power" and weak "infrastructural power," that is, the capacity to "penetrate civil society and to implement logistically political decisions throughout the realm" (1984, 188–89). They presided over the longest peaceful economic decline in the twentieth century and gradually lost their control and institutional grip on society. In 1989, the "despotic power" was gone with the inauguration of democracy and rule of law. The rebuilding of state institutions became one of the most critical tasks facing new political elites. The fall of state socialism opened up the opportunity for a redefinition of the state's power and functions. Yet, despite a flurry of reforms, changes, and debates, a comprehensive recalibration of the political system proved to be time-consuming. All countries have experienced difficulties in rebuilding and reforming their states. Institutional and legal reforms were slow in coming and have not been sufficiently deep to reshape the state apparatus in a fundamental way.

While political parties, elections, and vibrant civil societies are indispensable for modern democracy, the role of the state in shaping, fostering, and protecting democratic regimes cannot be minimized. According to Linz and Stepan, "modern democracy . . . needs the effective capacity to command, regulate, and extract. For this it needs a functioning state and a state bureaucracy" (1996, 11). Przeworski criticizes the dominant reform strategies in Eastern Europe for their lack of attention to the state. He argues that

> the principal mistake of neoliberal prescriptions is that they underestimate the role of state institutions in organizing both the public and private life of groups and individuals. If democracy is to be sustained, the state must guarantee territorial integrity and physical security, it must maintain the conditions necessary for an effective exercise of citizenship, it must mobilize public savings, coordinate resource allocation, and correct income distribution. And if state institutions are to be capable of performing these tasks, they must be reorganized, rather than simply reduced. (Przeworski et al. 1995, 12)

Paradoxically, during the 1989–93 period, a time in which many expected to see the huge, bureaucratic "communist Leviathan" cut down and limited, the Polish state actually grew in terms of employment and the number of central state agencies. At the same time, it became less efficient and frequently was unable to perform its functions and fulfill its citizens' expectations (Kurczewska, Staszynska, and Bojar 1993; Kochanowicz 1993; Taras 1993). It failed to prevent the steep rise of crime, massive tax evasion, and rapid expansion of the unofficial and black-market economy. The reforms of public spending and restructuring of the state-owned industrial sector have been delayed, while at the same time declining profitability of the state sector and underdeveloped tax systems led to the fiscal crisis of the state (Campbell 1995). Public opinion polls and media debates indicated that the Polish state had a serious performance deficit that produced a potentially destabilizing legitimization crisis. There are several reasons for this.

The first cause of weakness in the new Polish state was inherent in its institutional design. The set of compromises typical of negotiated transitions produced a semi-presidential system prone to deadlock and conflicts (Linz and Stepan 1996, 276–83; Michta 1993; Bernhard 1997). From the outset, the relationships between the government branches and their prerogatives were vaguely defined. Poland failed to enact a new constitution within the first five years of consolidation; thus, many fundamental systemic issues remained unresolved or were dealt with merely in a provisional fashion by the limited constitutional act introduced in 1992 (Sokolewicz 1992; Howard 1993; Rapaczynski 1993; Brzezinski 1997). As a result, Poland was plagued by an escalating political conflict between the presidency, government, and parliament over their prerogatives and responsibilities. At the same time, the country was plunged into legal purgatory: many old laws and legal regulations inherited from the communist regime were still in force and coexisted with new regulations introduced in response to emerging needs and pressures.

Despite fundamental changes in the domestic and international political and economic environments, the structure of the Polish government during the first five years of consolidation was almost exactly the same as the one inherited from the old regime. After 1989, two more ministries (Ministry of Ownership Transformation and Ministry of Communications) were added to the 19 that remained after the 1987 reform, and the overall number of central state agencies grew from 32 in 1988 to 43 in 1993 (Moldawa 1991, 44–48; GUS 1993, 77–83). At the same time, however, the state was insulated from old organized interests. It experienced a shift of "power within the state administration away from the branch ministries, which had served as the main venue for particularistic bargaining under communism, and toward agencies of macroeconomic regulation" (Bartlett 1996, 48). This shift away from the spending ministries and the breakdown of old networks and linkages between the state and organized social actors explain the capacity of the Polish government to introduce and sustain the radical economic reform.

The number of professional employees and overall employment in the central administration increased notably between 1989 and 1993. There were similar increases in local state administration. The growth of state employment can be attributed to the need to reorganize the old while building new spheres of state administration. Institutional infrastructure for capital, financial, and labor markets as well as a new revenue extraction system were necessary. The social security system had to be expanded and the police and legal apparatus thoroughly reformed. However, the new administrative structures did not effectively replace the old bureaucratic ones; often the reorganized institutions were bigger than their predecessors.[19] Surprisingly, employment in the Min-

TABLE 9.   Employment in Polish State Administration and Local Self-Government

	1987	1988	1989	1990	1991	1992	1993
Number of central state agencies	38	32	35	37	39	40	43
Total in central administration	45,463	42,525	42,934	46,062	60,794	68,728	88,561
Local state administration[a]	29,859	28,610	26,385	29,167	32,550	36,011	26,813
Local self-government	95,897	96,716	92,260	83,583	77,551	90,110	108,333
Total state employment[b]	171,219	167,851	161,579	158,812	170,895	194,849	223,707

Source: Rocznik Statystyczny, 1989, 1990, 1991, 1992, 1992, 1993, 1994 (Warsaw: GUS).

[a]For 1987–89, local state administration includes those employed in 49 provincial offices (*urzędy wojewodzkie*). For 1990 and later, it includes those employed in 49 provincial offices and in 254 newly created regional offices (*urzędy rejonowe*).

[b]Data do not include employees of the Ministry of Internal Affairs (employment increased from 145,014 in 1990 to 181,494 in 1993), Ministry of National Defense (employment and the size of the armed forces decreased from 363,400 in 1990 to 314,400 in 1993), and Ministry of Justice (employment increased from 60,600 in 1989 to 63,400 in 1993).

istry of Internal Affairs, responsible for internal security, increased from 145,014 in 1990 to 181,494 in 1992.

Second, in comparison with the pre-1989 period, the state's autonomy and relative capacity were seriously limited by the introduction of the rule of law and membership in supranational organizations. External controls over the state's administration were expanded and strengthened as a result of revived parliamentary, judicial,[20] and media oversight. Parliamentary politics and competitive elections imposed additional constraints on the executive's freedom of action and forced government agencies to respond to demands of various organizations and interest groups. Moreover, as a result of the reforms, the new state relinquished some of its power both "upward" to international agencies and organizations and "downward" to local self-governments. The Polish administrative reform introduced in March 1990 was the most extensive among East European countries at that time and granted local communities a number of administrative prerogatives and responsibilities they had not had earlier (Kubik 1994b; Wrobel 1994; Regulska 1998). The constraints imposed by international lending institutions (the World Bank, the International Monetary Fund, and the European Bank for Reconstruction and Development) were especially effective in reducing the state's capacity to freely implement policy changes that could increase the budget deficit and inflation. Similarly, multilateral organizations such as the Council of Europe or international nongovernmental organizations such as environmental groups had the capacity to influence policies of postcommunist governments and shape their legislation (Waller 1994, 29–31).

The third factor responsible for the state's declining strength was the lack of governmental stability, resulting from frequent cabinet changes and subsequent efforts to replace both the nomenklatura inherited from the old regime and the appointees of the prior postcommunist governments. During the 1989–93 period, Poland had six governments and eight prime ministers and experienced a substantial personnel turnover at the top executive positions. According to Wasilewski and Pohoski's study (1992), only 42.4 percent of the state administration officials in 1986 (deputy ministers, directors and deputy directors of ministry departments) were still employed in state administration in 1992.[21] By mid-1995, out of the 145 highest positions in the state administration, three were occupied by persons nominated during the communist period and only 28 by people nominated by the first four postcommunist governments. Old state functionaries who survived the post-1989 changes did not feel secure, while the newcomers brought into the administration by each new government had little professional and organizational experience. Moreover, government officials were often targeted in various political struggles; their ostensible privileges were criticized, and they were frequently accused of corruption and mismanagement, adding to their insecurity. Any attempts to create the institution of civil service, shielded from transient political configurations, failed.

The fourth source of the state's weakness was declining popular trust in its institutions, which in turn constrained government's capacity to introduce policy changes, especially those that involved cuts in state spending or old collective privileges and benefits. This decline was clearly reflected by public opinion polls conducted periodically since 1989. Figure 3 illustrates vividly the declining confidence in selected state institutions. After the initial surge of public trust following the 1989 elections and the formation of the Solidarity-led government, the polls registered a gradual drop in public confidence of over 50 points for most state institutions. "Traditional" state functions, such as maintaining public order, collecting taxes, controlling exports and imports, and policing the borders were not performed efficiently. This in turn was widely criticized in the media and during public political debates. For example, the number of criminal offenses increased rapidly (see table 10) in comparison to the pre-1989 period, exacerbating the general mood of insecurity engendered by the regime change and marketization (Sevelsberg 1995). While the overall number of criminal offenses more than doubled, the number of prisoners declined from 110,192 in 1985 to 50,165 in 1990 and 61,409 in 1993. Although the crime rate in Poland was significantly lower than in Switzerland, France, or Luxembourg, the widespread criticism of the state's performance in maintaining public order was registered by public opinion polls.

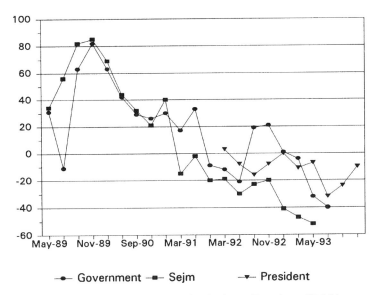

Fig. 3.   Net confidence in state institutions. (Data from CBOS.)

The Church and the Solidarity trade union, two pillars of anticommunist resistance in Poland, were not exempt from this growing distrust in public institutions. Rather unexpectedly, the two exceptions to this trend were the coercive organs of the state—the military and the police. Net confidence in the military increased from 39 percent in July 1989 to 71 percent in 1993. Net confidence in the police increased from −8 percent in July 1989 to 48 percent in 1993. The decline of public confidence in state institutions reflected not only the political turmoil that characterized the initial period of democratic consolidation but also the declining capacity of the Polish state to perform its functions, as well as its inability to satisfy citizens' high (maybe even unreal) expectations.

The state's obligations to its citizens became the subject of intense controversies. The Balcerowicz Plan imposed severe restrictions on the level of wage increases for public and state employees. Such policies of fiscal discipline were carried out against long-established popular expectations that the state should provide the resources for all the social, economic, and cultural needs of its citizens. In 1992, public opinion polls indicated that the majority of Poles expected that the state should assume full financial responsibility for maintaining schools, hospitals and health services, nursing homes and day-care centers, libraries, universities, theaters, and public transportation. Moreover, three-quarters of respondents believed that the state should pursue the policy of full

TABLE 10.   Selected Criminal Offenses in Poland, 1985–93

	1985	1990	1991	1992	1993
Murders	671	730	971	989	1,106
Violent robberies	8,511	16,217	16,110	17,717	21,034
Robberies	138,396	431,962	355,896	330,741	314,338

Source: GUS 1994.

employment, control prices, and expand social programs (CBOS 1992; Indraszkiewicz 1994). At the same time, only 6 percent were in favor of increased spending on the state administration (CBOS 1993). Paradoxically, after 1989 there was an increase in the percentage of the GDP allocated to social security and welfare programs, which led to higher social spending than in many richer countries.[22] Nonetheless, the state's social policies were strongly criticized in public debates and negatively assessed in public opinion polls. In 1992, 80 percent of Poles maintained that state social programs should be expanded and only 14.8 percent believed they should be limited (Indraszkiewicz 1994, 64–65). In 1993, the following percentages of Polish adults advocated more government spending on the following programs: 94 percent on health care, 84 percent on education, 83 percent on reducing unemployment, 81 percent on pensions and disability pensions, 70 percent on welfare programs, 67 percent on public housing. Clearly, the postcommunist state inherited not only a huge state sector in the economy but also an extremely broad social agenda legitimated by well-established protectionist expectations among the population: the majority of respondents in various public opinion polls asserted that the overall role of the state in the country should be expanded (Indraszkiewicz 1994, 104–7). The postcommunist state in Poland, despite the expansion of its social spending (as a percentage of GDP), could hardly fulfill such expectations.

Political Society

Paul Lewis summarized prevailing views on political parties in Eastern Europe the following way:

> political parties have not had a good press in post-communist eastern Europe. They have been seen as weak, fragmented, barely capable of sustaining effective government and poor at presenting themselves to the electorate, cliquish, divorced from the mass of society, increasingly unrepresentative of public interests and generally under-developed, divisive, self-seeking, antithetic to hopes of national recovery and harmful to state interests. (1994, 5)

Such views were expressed most often in papers and commentaries concerning Polish political developments, and a consensus seems to have emerged in the scholarly community that the process of party formation in Poland faced more obstacles than in any other East Central European country (Linz and Stepan 1996, 283; Bielasiak 1997, 40). We examined these claims through a systematic review of existing research and concluded that the weakness of the party system in Poland has been attributed to one or more of the following six factors: (1) excessive fragmentation within the party system and within the electorate; (2) unclear cleavages among the parties and political options; (3) the narrow social base of most parties; (4) low interest in politics, reflected in low electoral turnout; (5) a low level of political knowledge; and (6) weak linkages between parties and their electorates.

Many observers pointed out that from 1989 to 1993, the political spectrum was strongly fragmented, with larger political parties plagued by internal conflicts, divisions, and frequent splits (Zubek 1993). For example, at the beginning of 1993 Poland had 222 registered political parties.[23] Although the majority of these parties were not serious contenders for power, many did actually enter the political process.

It is useful to begin an analysis of political fragmentation with an examination of the electoral system, usually seen as a major factor contributing to the *parliamentary fragmentation.* In 1991, for the first fully democratic elections to the lower house of parliament, the Sejm, Polish legislators adopted a strictly proportional electoral law. One hundred eleven parties participated in the electoral contest. Among these parties, 69 registered their lists in only one electoral district, 42 were present in at least two districts, and 27 registered their national lists (Jasiewicz 1992, 497). As a result, the winner (the Democratic Union) received only 12.3 percent of the vote, and a fragmented Sejm was elected with 29 parties holding seats. Among these parties, 11 had enough seats to be "effective," that is, considered a possible partner in a potential ruling coalition.[24] As Linz and Stepan demonstrate, this was a much higher number of effective parties than in any democracy with a ten-year duration; consequently, formation of a stable governing majority proved to be very difficult (Linz and Stepan 1996, 275). On the other hand, the index of deviation from proportionality, calculated according to the formula provided by Taagapera and Shugart, was 12.8, a relatively high score compared to established democracies that use proportional representation, but much lower than after the 1993 elections (Jasiewicz 1996; Linz and Stepan 1996, 290–91).

The electoral reforms prior to the 1993 elections reduced the number of parties entering the electoral process and forced many to join in electoral coalitions. Still, there were 35 parties and coalitions represented in the national elections, with 15 registering national lists. Only seven parties and coalitions won seats in the lower chamber of parliament, but as a result of the existing electoral law, 35 percent of the votes went to parties that did not win any seats. The new parliament was less fragmented, but also less representative. The number of effective parties in the Sejm fell to 3.9, but the index of deviation from proportionality increased to 37.86, an unusually high score (Jasiewicz 1996).[25] This, and the fact that only 52.1 percent of the eligible voters cast their ballots, allowed the groups that did not make it to the parliament to question the representativeness of this institution.

A comparison of the two elections, as well as a comparative analysis of voting to the Sejm (lower house) and the Senate (upper house), demonstrates that the choice of electoral system contributed to the parliamentary fragmentation but was not its main cause. This fragmentation was primarily caused by the fragmentation of the political field, which—in turn—seems to have reflected the indeterminacy and divisions within the electorate.[26]

According to several authors, the second problem plaguing Polish political society, common to all postcommunist countries, was the absence of clear and stable political cleavages. Jowitt observed that "the cleavages in Eastern Europe are neither cross-cutting nor superimposed" but "diffused, poorly articulated, psychological as much as political, and for that reason remarkably intense" (1992, 216). In Poland, the two basic active cleavages (post-Solidarity versus ex-communist forces and reformists versus revolutionaries) cut across other divisions, engendered by various visions of the pace and content of economic reforms, the relationship between the state and the Roman Catholic Church, the definition of national interests, or the basic foundations of democratic politics.[27] These cleavages blurred other typical political divisions based on ideology (right-left), regional diversity (center-periphery), or class interests. In the 1989–93 period, the unclear cleavages were additionally complicated by frequent changes in positions and programs presented by specific parties. Many observers of the Polish political scene attributed the low electoral participation to the vague and confused positions advocated by major parties.

Not all analysts share such views. Kitschelt (1995) observed that the structuration of political cleavages was occurring and that the programmatic differences among various major political options were articulated with increasing clarity. Tworzecki (1996, 195) closed his study with a similar conclusion: not only were the voters presented with an increasingly clear and consistent set of political alternatives, but they also managed to develop well-defined political outlooks. Postcommunist politics in Poland was not as chaotic as it has often been portrayed to be.

The majority of parties, including those most influential in shaping the country's politics during the first years of consolidation, had weak social bases. Most of them had only a few hundred to a few thousand members;[28] the level of identification with political parties was also exceptionally low (see table 11).

TABLE 11.   Identification with and Trust in Political Parties,
1993–94 (by percentage change)

	Net Party Identification	Net Party Trust
Bulgaria	—	−62
Czech Republic	−8	−14
Hungary	−33	−54
Poland	−45	−64
Romania	—	−44
Slovakia	−24	−42

Source: Bielasiak 1997, 40, based on data from the New Democracies
Barometer III, November 26, 1993–April 14, 1994 surveys, conducted by
the Center for the Study of Public Policy, University of Strathclyde, under
the direction of Richard Rose.

In 1991, for example, only 1.1 percent of Poles admitted they belonged to a political party (Siemienska 1991). As a result, party activities came to be monopolized by a narrow, newly formed political class organized into a myriad of
small political parties. This class concentrated heavily on national-level politics, creating a political vacuum underneath. Thus, political activities on the local level were often divorced from national politics. As Kubik observed, "what
is truly revolutionary about the ongoing changes is the fact that national (central) level politics can be (and often is) irrelevant to local politics [and] the political groupings that dominate national politics . . . are often absent from the
local political scene" (1991, 16–17). In this context, the electoral successes of
political descendants of pre-1989 ruling parties testify to the role of effective
organizational structures, large membership, and an organizational presence in
local communities, as well as the ability to form alliances with a wide range of
organizations.

One of the most interesting puzzles of Polish postcommunist politics was
the low level of participation in consecutive elections. In the early 1990s, only
Bosnia and Hercegovina had a lower electoral turnout than Poland. Despite the
drama of regime change, the rise of political parties, highly charged political
and ideological conflicts, fundamental political and economic reforms, and frequent government changes and elections, many Polish voters withdrew from
the official political process. This gradual withdrawal from formal political participation predates the 1989 transition. During the last decade, electoral participation in Poland gradually declined. As Ekiert (1989) argued elsewhere, the
low voter turnout in elections that followed the imposition of martial law in
1981 can be attributed to active resistance that took the form of confrontational
nonparticipation in elections organized by the state. Approximately 25–30 percent of the electorate responded to appeals to boycott the elections issued by

TABLE 12. Electoral Turnout in Poland, 1984–93 (in percentages)

Elections	1984 Local	1985 National	1988 Local	1989 National	1990 Local	1990 Presidential	1991 National	1993 National
Round 1	74.9	78.9	55.0	62.7	42.3	60.6	43.0	52.1
Round 2				25.0		52.4		

Source: Gieorgica 1991; GUS 1991 and 1994.

Note: In the 1994 local elections, participation dropped to 33.8%, but in the politically charged presidential election of 1995 it increased to 64.7% in the first round and 68.23% in the second round. The electoral turnout during the 1997 parliamentary elections was 47.93%.

clandestine Solidarity organizations. The opening of the political system and the introduction of a genuine democratic mechanism in 1989 did not, however, reverse the decline in electoral participation. Even the 1989 founding elections did not produce high electoral turnout.[29] Table 12 illustrates the decline of electoral participation. Shortly before the 1993 parliamentary elections, in the poll conducted by Pentor, 91 percent of the respondents declared their lack of interest in the electoral campaign. Moreover, despite a multitude of political parties, the poll conducted by Demoskop in 1994 revealed that 67 percent of Poles believed that none of the existing parties represented their interests. This lack of interest in the formal political process went hand in hand with the rising pessimism and frustration reflected in the public opinion polls, reviewed in the previous chapter.

Also, the population's knowledge of and interest in politics were very low. A surprisingly high number of people were unaware that the former Polish prime minister, Hanna Suchocka, was a member of the Democratic Union. The majority of Poles were unable to match the names of well-known politicians with the parties they belonged to. Such results are surprising given the importance of national-level politics in shaping transitional policies; it is an indication that political knowledge that would foster participation at the level of political society was very weak.

Our systematic review of the major works on the Polish party system demonstrated that, although there existed significant regional and social differences in levels of formal political involvement and participation, the overall condition of Polish political society was not good. The Polish political scientist Wlodzimierz Wesolowski (1995) summarized his work on the party system in four points, which confirm our findings. According to him, from 1989 to 1993, political parties did not

- offer well-articulated and clear models of public life (ideologies);
- develop concrete yet comprehensive governmental programs;
- provide linkage mechanisms between people's interests and aspirations and party platforms and governmental decisions;
- mobilize people and organize them for more effective participation in public life.

As we have already pointed out, not all analysts conclude that the Polish political party system was excessively fragmented, political options poorly articulated and structured, and the public largely uninformed and disinterested. All of them emphasize, however, one basic weakness of this system: *the lack of strong linkages between the people and political parties.* Thus, we conclude this review with a thesis that has significant implications for our own study of protest politics: despite a gradual stabilization and consolidation of the country's political elites (Wasilewski 1994 and 1995) and a growing clarity of political cleavages (Kitschelt 1992b and 1995; Marody 1995), political parties had very weak social bases. In other words, many people did not consider political parties as organizations articulating their visions, protecting their interests, and representing their needs. The gap between the newly formed system of political parties and Poland's electorate in 1993 was almost as wide as it had been in 1989.

Civil Society

Democratization theory acknowledges that the "revival," "resurrection," or "reinventing" of civil society is an important part of transition to democracy and an essential precondition for democratic consolidation. Despite concerns expressed by many students of postcommunist political transitions (Bernhard 1996), civil society has become the rapidly developing realm of the polity. In the former communist countries, this aspect of democratization should be described as the process *combining the resurrection with the reconfiguration of civil society,* since many organizations inherited from the old regime became dominant players in the new public scene. Additionally, even if there is significant organizational continuity within all sectors of civil society, the pattern of reconfiguration and reinstitutionalization of various sectors differs from country to country. This in turn shapes the role and character of civil society organizations and the types of collective actors who become most active during the political transition and the consolidation of new democratic regimes in the region.

One of the understudied legacies of state socialism is the dense network of organizations and movements created during the consolidation of communist regimes in order to *colonize* public space and extend the party-state's penetration into all segments of society. These state-run organizations *simulated* the functions of organizations existing in democratic societies and performed vital political, ideological, and social tasks within the institutional design of the party-state. Especially in the earlier period of communist rule, they were nothing more than communist "fronts" with mandatory membership. As a result, the organizational density of state-socialist regimes was higher than in democratic countries: more people belonged to various formal organizations and movements (trade unions, youth and professional associations, etc.) than under any other type of political regime. Moreover, these organizations and movements provided their members with an entire range of benefits and services—the same as would be supplied by the marketplace, family, or local civic organizations under most other regimes.

The dependent status of these organizations, initially created as the de facto state agencies and instruments of control, changed over time. Beginning in 1950s, some of them were able to wrest a degree of autonomy from the party-state bureaucracy, accumulate considerable resources, and secure ever-expanding benefits for their members. They also acquired various degrees of influence and power, which allowed them to represent corporate interests and to shape or even occasionally defy party-state policies. During political crises, some of these organizations achieved full autonomy and were consequently purged or even dissolved and banned by the communist authorities. They were, however, always replaced or restored under tighter supervision of the party-state authorities. Usually, these new organizations were granted enough autonomy to achieve a modicum of credibility.

During the final years of communist rule, some of these organizations (at least in certain countries) achieved considerable autonomy, and thus the process of internal pluralization and general liberalization was initiated. The collapse of state-socialist regimes in 1989 left these organizations free and entirely responsible to fend for themselves. Some were significantly compromised by years of political servility and ideological rigidity, while others enjoyed limited credibility due to their long-standing tradition of promoting specific groups' interests. Thus, there were those that disappeared almost instantaneously (e.g., the Society for Polish-Soviet Friendship) whereas others swiftly adapted to the new situation. In fact, those that did adapt had distinct advantages over the newly emerging organizations and movements: they controlled sometimes sizable resources accumulated over the years, had legally defined functions, monopolized certain services, and had cadres of bureaucrats, organizers, and activists. As a result, they were important building blocks of the newly emerging organization of society. Hence, important sectors of civil society in postcommunist countries were characterized by organizational continuity. Old organizations changed their leaders, preserved their assets, and adapted quite successfully to a new democratic environment. Although they often lost a substantial number of members and had to downsize their organizational structures and personnel, they nevertheless were often more effective than new organizations that had to start from scratch.

In post-1989 Poland, thousands of new organizations and movements sprung up locally and nationally. By the end of 1994 there were 29,580 registered associations and 12,216 regional affiliates of these organizations. Moreover, there were 4,465 national-level foundations and 775 local foundations. Altogether, civil society in Poland comprised 47,036 organizations, while before 1989 there were only several hundred large, centralized organizations. A comprehensive database called Jawor (1993) tracking the development of associations in Poland listed 4,515 organizations in 1993. A year later, Jawor listed 7,000 associations and 4,500 foundations and estimated that 2 million Poles were active in these organizations. They had some 53,000 full-time employees, and 64 percent of their budget came from private and foreign sources

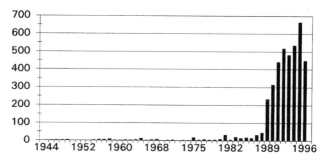

Fig. 4.   Number of civil society organizations by founding year. (Data from Krasnodebska et al. 1996.)

while 26 percent came from the state budget. Their activities were concentrated mostly in large urban centers (68 percent).[30] New organizations were rapidly emerging in all sectors of civil society, especially where existing organizations were unsuccessful in adapting to the new conditions or where new spaces and issue-arenas opened after the collapse of the party-state. The dynamic of the numerical growth of civil society organizations is illustrated by figure 4. It includes only those organizations tracked by Jawor. It should be noted that although the peak in the number of new organizations founded came in 1991, the number of organizations has increased gradually since 1980 and accelerated after 1987.

In general, three types of organizations comprise post-1989 civil society: (1) reformed organizations inherited from the communist period; (2) spin-off organizations, that is, those that broke away from their communist-era parent organizations; and (3) newly formed organizations.

The organizational continuity of civil society in Poland was most noticeable in the sector of professional associations. In 1985, 14 organizations represented the Polish artistic community with a combined membership of 16,900. In 1992, the same 14 organizations remained unscathed with an increased membership of 19,300. Similarly, the Main Statistical Office listed 105 nationwide scientific and professional associations that survived the regime transition intact. Although overall membership in these associations declined by some 50 percent (approximately 1 million members in 1987 and 404,000 in 1993), the membership losses were confined to a few organizations that had artificially inflated their membership numbers in the past.[31] Only organizations representing different professional groups of engineers had significant membership losses (on average 50 percent), due in part to the dramatic transformation of Polish state industry. At the same time, a large number of new professional associations appeared, such as those organized under the auspices of the Church. Their membership was usually small, however, and they lacked the resources of the older, established associations.

A sector where organizational continuity was relatively weak was the youth organizations. There was an "exodus" of membership from the four monopolistic, official youth organizations in 1989.[32] In 1990, the CBOS survey showed that 79 percent of high school graduates had no contacts with any political or social organization. At the same time, dozens of new youth associations and movements appeared after 1989. They have been, however, plagued by a lack of resources and interest from the state authorities, local communities, or other well-established organizations. As a result, they failed to attract a larger membership, and many of these organizations did not last. In 1992, there were some 80 youth organizations in Poland (Lipka 1992, 200–213). This number did not include the myriad of ephemeral countercultural groups and movements as well as less formalized groups, which formed across the country and distributed their own newsletters (so-called *fanziny*). The youth's rich informal activities contrasted sharply with their rejection of official organizations and their lack of trust in political elites and institutions. Among the social categories that did not participate in elections, the youth were the largest.

The NGO sector, supported by a variety of international organizations and foundations, expanded rapidly. New organizations raised many issues suppressed under the old regime; they included environmental problems, women's rights, and alternative lifestyles, as well as specific social problems. The number of registered foundations increased from 200 in 1989 to over 5,000 in 1994. The problems faced by NGOs are best illustrated by the environmental movement. In 1995, Poland had several hundred environmental organizations (700 by one count). There were several old, well-established organizations, such as the Polish Ecological Club or League for Nature Conservation, and hundreds of small new organizations, many with only a few members. The movement was plagued by political divisions and competition for resources; it was, however, becoming more professional, and attempts were made to unite various organizations around specific causes and tasks (Glinski 1994 and 1996).

The women's movement was also internally divided and competitive. It comprised 30 separate organizations. The dynamic growth of the NGO sector is perhaps best illustrated by the organizations focused on the problems of people with disabilities. By the end of 1992, there were 866 organizations representing the disabled—90 percent more than in 1980. They faced problems endemic to all sectors of civil society: fragmentation, competition for resources and members, and political divisions. As elsewhere, "old" organizations fared better than new ones (Czajkowski, Federowicz, and Iwanowska 1994).

Continuity and rapid development also characterized religious and ethnic minority organizations. In 1993, there were 58 churches and some 150 registered religious denominations with hundreds of organizations and charities.

Among religious organizations, the Catholic Church has traditionally been a powerful social and political actor. Its position was solidified by a new law that granted the Church legal status and a number of other rights, approved on May 17, 1989. In 1993, the Church had 9,266 parishes, 15,081 churches, and 25,187 priests. Almost 35 million Poles were baptized Roman Catholics.[33] Catholic organizations had over 800,000 members. The Council of Catholic Movements united the 52 largest organizations. In addition, there were four other national federations of Catholic organizations. All professional groups and business organizations had their own old or newly founded Catholic organizations (Mac 1995).

The Church controlled nearly 1,000 newspapers published by various parishes, one national daily, 10 weeklies, 11 biweeklies, and 78 monthly publications. It also ran several dozen radio stations and was working to establish its own television station. Despite major controversies and fierce political battles, the Church was successful in pushing through several major pieces of legislation, such as a ban on abortion and the introduction of religious instruction into all public schools. Beginning in 1990, however, the Church's popularity suffered a major decline.

The number of associations representing ethnic minorities increased rapidly. In 1993, there were 54 minority organizations with at least 50 members each. The majority of these organizations (33) represented Poland's German minority and had a combined total of 361,000 members. All other minority organizations had some 30,000 members combined. German minority organizations effectively established their own political presence: they ran their own candidates in parliamentary elections and in the 1993 elections won 3 seats in the parliament and one in the Senate. As Poland did not have any significant ethnic problems, these organizations focused primarily on cultural issues.

According to Valenzuela (1989, 447), labor movements always occupy a special place among the forces of civil society. He argues that "the labor movement has a greater capacity for extensive and effective mobilization at critical moments than any other social group." This special role and capacity of the labor movement comes from the fact that (1) "it has an organized network through its more or less permanently established unions"; (2) "the labor movement can disrupt the economy directly through work stoppages"; and (3) "Labor's demands can not be lightly ignored." The legacies of the 1980–81 political crisis brought labor organizations and especially Solidarity into the forefront of regime transition in Poland. It was the only state-socialist regime in the region where the labor organization became a main partner in negotiating the country's exit from communism. Moreover, in contrast to other postcommunist societies, Poland entered the democratic transition with decentralized, relatively autonomous, and pragmatic labor organizations. In December

1988, there were 138 national labor federations coordinated by the All-Poland Alliance of Trade Unions (OPZZ) with some 6.8 million members; by the end of 1989, their number increased to 144.[34] Thus it comes as no surprise that the development of the trade union sector after 1989 well exemplifies a pattern of continuity with the communist past. The new postcommunist labor sector emerged as a result of organizational competition and several splits of old and new organizations (Kloc 1992 and 1994; Marciniak 1992; Gortat 1994).

In 1989, as a result of the roundtable agreements, Solidarity was re-legalized in its trade union form. The ex-communist OPZZ and Solidarity became two major competitors within a highly pluralistic, competitive, but politically divided trade union sector. Solidarity had 1.7 million members, while the OPZZ boasted a membership of around 4 million. The OPZZ lost some 2 million members after 1989, and several unions left the organization, including the powerful Federation of Miners' Trade Unions with some 350,000 members. Yet it was a member of the postcommunist coalition, and its activists ran in the parliamentary elections on the ticket of the SLD (Alliance of the Democratic Left). It was, however, a decentralized organization with both largely independent industrial/professional unions and regional structures.

Solidarity never regained its 1980 strength and position. Not only was its membership a fraction of what it had been in 1980–81, but also its salaried staff were largely new. In the National Commission, only 30 percent of the members were union activists in 1980–81, and those mostly at the factory level. Solidarity was organized in 38 regions with 16 national industry secretariats and nearly 100 industry branch secretariats. There were a number of smaller and usually more radical federations, such as Solidarity '80, with approximately half a million members. The smaller, newly funded unions were critical of both Solidarity and the OPZZ for their cooperation with the government and became prominent in organizing protest actions in Polish industry.

Even though the Polish labor sector was dominated by two powerful federations, it was also fragmented. In 1993, there were 1,500 trade unions and some 200 nationwide federations. The Polish trade union law adopted in June 1991 set the framework for preserving a fragmented and decentralized union structure.[35] It was not unusual for the employees of one factory or firm to be represented by more than 10 different union organizations. For example, the Polish State Railroads (PKP) employed 260,000 people who were represented by 16 trade unions. The biggest union (Federation of Trade Unions of PKP Employees) had 91,500 members, while Solidarity had only 60,000. PKP by law paid the salaries of nearly 1,000 union activists. Trade unions fought against all attempts to reduce employment (PKP has the highest number of employees among European railroads) and defended all special benefits and social programs inherited by the firm from the past (housing complexes, day-care centers, health services, sport clubs, vacation centers, etc.). Another example of high fragmentation is provided by the mining sector. Polish miners were represented by 19 unions.

Fragmentation leads to competition. In turn, the competition between unions for new members, resources, and influence often entails higher militancy and an escalation of protest actions because, as Tarrow (1989, 20) points out, organizations in competition for the same constituency "try to outbid their competitors for support with more radical tactics." In a similar vein, Valenzuela (1989, 454, 457) argues that "a mobilization followed by restraint sequence would be more probable if union organizations and collective bargaining were highly centralized" and concludes that

> if the union organizations are decentralized and/or the union leadership highly divided for political and ideological reasons, the likelihood of a sharp rise in labor conflictuality which does not readily decline in order to secure the transition is very high. (1989, 457)

Thus, the militancy of the Polish unions owed as much to their historical-political importance as to the general pattern of labor movement institutionalization (fragmentation) and the failure of the Polish government to enforce an effective bargaining system based on the tripartite principle (Hausner 1994).

In short, the trade union movement

1. was highly fragmented and decentralized, by comparison with other East European states;
2. was highly competitive and politically divided on both the national and local levels;
3. had a mixed organizational form, with interlocking regional and industrial structures.

This overview illustrates the speed and intensity of the recovery of Polish civil society from 1989 to 1993, after four decades of communist rule. Across all sectors of civil society there emerged significant organizational continuity with the past as well as serious fragmentation, political divisions, and intense struggle for resources and members. Moreover, civil society's organizations and actors played an increasingly visible and vocal role in the country's politics, often confronting both the parliament and the government. The most striking feature of this new civil society was *its lack of systematic linkages with the party system.* As table 13 demonstrates, relationships of civil society organizations with political parties were *much worse* than their relationships with any other institutional sector.

In short, during the examined period, the reconfiguration of civil society

TABLE 13. Relationships between Polish Civil Society Organizations and Other
Actors of the Public Scene (in percentages)

	Willingness to Establish Contact	No Contact	Sporadic Contact	Mutual Assistance	Cooperation
Government	21	30	23	9	15
Voivodeship	18	13	29	17	22
Local government	12	5	21	27	35
Political parties	4	41	12	3	5
Church	6	14	26	15	34
Business	34	6	13	38	9
Local communities	14	9	16	28	31

Source: Krasnodebska et al. 1996.

Note: Representatives of NGOs were asked to assess their relationships with various other actors of the public scene.

was well under way, but the new institutionalization pattern foretold a highly contentious and fragmented domain, *strongly separated* from the emerging party system and confronting the state's policies by a variety of protest actions. As a result, many organizations of civil society were themselves politicized, although they faced serious identity dilemmas related to their unclear role in the country's politics (Sewerynski 1994; Waller 1994, 25–26). If fragmentation, competition, and political exclusion, accompanied by divisions, lead to an increase of protest activities, we should expect that the most militant and protest-prone sectors of civil society will include the labor movement, youth organizations, and social/political movements. This contention is supported by the data on protest activities presented in the next chapter.

CHAPTER 5

Protest Politics in Postcommunist Poland

During the 1989–93 period, collective protest in Poland was intense. Hardly a month passed without a serious protest campaign rocking the country. Waves of strikes swept through entire sectors of the economy. Huge marches and demonstrations were staged in Warsaw. Members of various professional groups, political parties, and movements frequently congregated in front of public buildings, expressing their disagreement with government policies.

Mass demonstrations began in earnest in 1991. In February 1991, some 20,000 people organized by the OPZZ labor federation marched through the streets of Warsaw in protest against the government's economic policies. In March, several thousand agricultural workers employed on state farms protested against agricultural policies. In May, the Solidarity union organized an antigovernment demonstration attended by some 5,000 people. In August, more than 1,000 pensioners assembled in front of a government building demanding higher pensions. In October, 10,000 teachers demanded higher salaries and more government spending on education. Demonstrations continued without abating in 1992. In February, 2,000 defense industry workers assembled in Warsaw and demanded more government contracts and rescue programs for their enterprises. In March, 2,000 nurses demonstrated, demanding more government spending on health care. In April, in the biggest demonstration since 1989, some 70,000 Solidarity members marched in Warsaw in protest against government economic policies. In August, some 6,000 people, led by striking Solidarity workers from the bankrupt Ursus tractor factory, displayed their frustration with government policies.

In 1993 the number of demonstrations escalated. In January, approximately 7,000 people demonstrated against the president and burned his effigy in front of his residence. In March, over 10,000 public sector employees marched through the streets of Warsaw demanding higher wages and increased state spending on education and health. In May, 4,000 farmers dumped stacks of hay in front of the government building, protesting the government's agricultural policies and demanding price controls, protective tariffs, and credit guarantees. In June, several thousand demonstrators clashed with police on the streets of Warsaw and ended the protest by burning the image of a red pig in front of the government building. These are only a few examples of the mass demonstrations organized by labor unions and political parties that ricocheted through Warsaw beginning in the early 1990s. They became a familiar political ritual, repeated almost weekly. These spectacular public demonstrations were, however, only the tip of the iceberg of protest activities taking place across Poland.

Protest actions ranged from single, isolated strikes and local demonstrations organized by small groups of activists to nationwide protest campaigns that would last for weeks and involve hundreds of public institutions and enterprises as well as thousands of workers and public sector employees. Small protests usually centered around a variety of local issues. They were spawned by grievances concerning housing, transportation, and various decisions and permits issued by local governments. They also included community actions directed against "porno shops" that appeared in many neighborhoods, or against unwanted construction projects. Sometimes they called for the removal of local officials. Large protests usually addressed larger economic and political issues and centered on government economic policies. During these protest campaigns, entire regions of the country and branches of industry and the public sector were the scene of escalating protest actions. Regional and national general strikes were declared many times. The most populous, urbanized, and industrialized areas of the country, such as the Katowice, Lodz, Walbrzych, Warsaw, and Gdansk regions, experienced the highest number of coordinated regional protest campaigns.

Every group of society was involved in the protests that engulfed the whole country. The most active participants were the workers of state-owned enterprises, public sector employees, peasants, and youth. Repeated protest campaigns, comprising strikes, demonstrations, and hunger strikes, swept through the troubled coal-mining industry, which was facing restructuring, mine closings, and cuts in state subsidies. In November 1990, the protest campaign of Silesian miners, organized by Solidarity, lasted for over three weeks. During the summer of 1992, their protest campaign of strikes and demonstrations lasted over a month. In December 1992, in another three-week-long campaign, 62 Polish coal mines with 300,000 workers were on strike, and coal deliveries to electricity- and heat-generating plants were blocked. The defense industry, facing rapid downsizing with domestic and foreign contracts drying up, experienced repeated protest campaigns involving dozens of enterprises. Polish State Railroads (PKP), the largest railroad in Europe in terms of employment, was the scene of repeated protests that paralyzed the country's transportation system beginning in May 1990. The several trade unions representing PKP employees tried to outbid one another by constantly demanding pay increases, resisting restructuring attempts, and opposing personnel and benefits cuts. Other huge state-owned industrial enterprises, including steel mills, the Gdansk shipyard, and the tractor manufacturer Ursus, became sites of lingering protests and union militancy, as workers resisted restructuring and layoffs. Their unions pressed the government for subsidies, credit guarantees, contracts, tax exemptions, and protective tariffs in order to save these insolvent flagships of socialist industrialization.

Repeated waves of protest swept the agricultural sector. Independent farmers and employees of state-owned farms organized by several militant organizations were among the first groups to challenge the new economic policies and resist government efforts to introduce market discipline. They demanded special protection against foreign competition, price supports, and credit guarantees. Scattered farmers' protests began already in 1989 and in 1990 escalated to form coordinated protest campaigns with demonstrations, strikes, road blockades, occupation of government buildings (including the Ministry of Agriculture), and hunger strikes, as well as physical assaults on government and bank officials attempting to foreclose insolvent farms and agricultural enterprises.

Large-scale protests erupted repeatedly in the public nonindustrial sector, whose employees were increasingly dissatisfied with governmental policies. Labor unions representing some half a million teachers, especially the postcommunist ZNP (Polish Teachers' Union), were the most active in organizing street demonstrations and sponsoring strike actions that affected entire regions of the country. The Main Statistical Office registered 5,316 strikes at schools in 1992 and 7,134 in 1993.[1] Health workers were the second major group involved in repeated protests, although the number of strikes they were involved in was not high (100 in 1993). The demands put forth by teachers and other public employees were similar: higher wages and more government spending on education, health, and culture.

The Solidarity union and its largely independent regional and sectoral branches were the most active protest organizers. They sponsored several countrywide protest campaigns during this period. The biggest took place in the spring of 1993, when hundreds of thousands of union members went on strike and Solidarity deputies in the parliament won a vote of no confidence, unseating the government. But Solidarity was not the only organization that sponsored major protest actions. Other labor federations, such as the ex-communist OPZZ, radical Solidarity '80, the Federation of Miners' Trade Unions, and farmers' unions, organized many countrywide and regionwide protests. Social and political movements and various interest groups staged their own protest actions as well, but they usually did not have the scope and significance of labor-organized campaigns.

The protests varied in intensity, duration, and methods. They included strike alerts, one-hour-long warning strikes, symbolic solidarity strikes (displaying flags, signs, and banners), publication of statements criticizing government policies and demanding policy changes, and rallies and demonstrations, as well as protracted and desperate strike campaigns that lasted for months. The use of blockades was widespread. Seaports were blocked by hundreds of fishing boats, border crossings by truck drivers, and roads by farmers. Many public buildings, including the government ministries of agriculture, education, and industry, were occupied for longer or shorter periods of time. Disruptive protests involving confrontational strategies that infringed on public order (such as strikes, demonstrations, blockades of public places, or occupation of buildings) outnumbered nondisruptive protests (that is, open letters, statements, legal and symbolic actions, or rallies in traditional gathering places such as auditoriums or sports arenas). Gradually, protest actions became more complex, with protestors intensifying their pressure through combining various strategies.

Farmers' organizations used the most disruptive strategies. The Union of Individual Farmers Solidarity and a militant farmer organization, Samoobrona, confronted local and national authorities with massive road blockades. In July 1990, Farmers' Solidarity organized road blockades across the country to protest government policies. Protestors used 29,000 vehicles to erect 979 road blockades. In March 1991, 500 road blockades were built. In June 1992, farmers barricaded national roads in 13 regions, demanding price supports, lower fuel costs, and forgiveness of debts owed by the farmers. Members of Samoobrona frequently occupied public buildings, including the three-week-long occupation of the Ministry of Agriculture in April 1992. The organization mobilized activists who prevented foreclosure of bankrupt farms and enterprises and intimidated and assaulted both bank employees and local officials. Its April 1993 demonstration in Warsaw ended in a skirmish with the police inside the parliament courtyard. Such disruptive and confrontational means were combined with other protest strategies.

As the previous examples demonstrate, the repertoire of protest was diverse. It consisted of both violent and nonviolent street demonstrations organized by various labor federations, social movements, and other organizations. Trade unions sponsored a variety of strikes and strike alerts. Dozens of dramatic hunger strikes were staged by workers and farmers in order to back demands with strong moral pressure. Hunger strikes took place not only in industrial enterprises and farms but also in front of government buildings. During many strikes, enterprises were taken over by protesting workers, management offices were occupied, and board members and managers were often assaulted or prevented from entering the premises. In some cases striking workers sold the firm's equipment in order to raise funds for relief payments to strikers and their families.

Various kinds of symbols were used during protest actions. National and black flags and banners covered buildings of striking firms. Protestors burned effigies of politicians, carried black coffins, and erected gallows in front of government buildings. Farmers dumped tons of butter inside the Ministry of Agriculture and other government buildings. Politicians attempting to address the crowds were verbally assaulted and hit with eggs, fruit, and balloons filled with paint. Symbolic displays were often used as substitutes for more disruptive protests and strikes. They were used, for example, by the police, teachers, and health workers who did not want to shut down schools or hospitals. Also, private enterprises used symbolic displays as a sign of solidarity with striking state enterprises. Avalanches of proclamations, statements, petitions, appeals, and protest letters were published and sent to the country's political leaders and various institutions during each wave of protest.

The national authorities were the primary targets of protest. Despite the government's efforts to distance itself from industrial conflicts, protestors consistently ignored other interlocutors and called for negotiations with and responses from the government and its officials. This was even the case with enterprises owned by foreign capital. There were some protest actions directed against local authorities and management; ethnic, professional, and political groups or movements were targeted rarely.

Economic demands were most frequent. They included calls for wage increases, payments of overdue wages and other compensations, tax benefits and exemptions (especially the repeal of the tax on excessive wage growth imposed on state-owned enterprises in order to control inflation, the so-called *popiwek*), protective tariffs to shelter domestic production, credit guarantees, protection of collective benefits and state subsidies, and reduction of price increases caused by price deregulation. Other frequently voiced demands concerned the recall, replacement, and punishment of managers, board members, and local and national politicians who were blamed for decisions harmful to enterprises, localities, and professional groups. There were, however, very few radical, antisystemic demands. Calls for abandoning market-oriented reforms or attacks on democracy were virtually nonexistent.

In short, after 1989 Poland's incipient democracy faced massive challenges from below. Collective protest became entrenched in the political landscape and a routine strategy for advancing various political and economic claims.

Protest in Poland: Overview

Our research indicates that during the first five years of democratic consolidation, Poland had a higher number of protest events than the other East Central European countries we studied (Ekiert and Kubik 1998). Table 14 bears this out.

Protest magnitude is determined by the number of protest events, but not exclusively. Other characteristics are also important. For example, protest events in Poland lasted significantly longer in comparison to other countries, due in part to the higher number of strikes. Protests in Poland were also char-

TABLE 14.   Number of Protest Events in Four Central European Countries, 1989–93

	1989	1990	1991	1992	1993	Total
Poland	314	306	292	314	250	1,476
Slovakia	—	50	82	116	47	295
Hungary	122	126	191	112	148	699
East Germany	222	188	291	268	283	1,252

acterized by the predominance of disruptive protest strategies, and they were much larger in terms of territorial scope and number of participants. Table 15 presents the picture of protest activities when duration is taken into account. In this table, protest events we recorded were translated into protest days.[2] Were we able to construct a more comprehensive index of magnitude, including territorial scope and the number of participants, the difference between Poland and other countries would be even more pronounced, but constructing such an index presents considerable difficulties. As mentioned in the introductory chapter, data collection from press sources is plagued by a great amount of missing information. This is especially the case with reporting the number of participants. In many studies this problem was resolved by replacing missing values with estimates. In our case, estimating missing values of some variables is unreliable, given the large percentages of missing data. We constructed an index of protest magnitude for Poland and other countries; we are convinced, however, that it should not replace a careful analysis of each facet of the protest event.

Despite the high incidence of protest, the number of protest events we recorded in Poland was not unusually high in comparison with established democracies. Given the drama of regime transition, disruptive economic transformations, and expanding opportunities for collective action, one could expect a much higher level of popular mobilization. Similar or even higher numbers of protest events were recorded for West European countries during periods of heightened political mobilization in the 1960s and 1980s.[3] The relative social

TABLE 15.   Number of Protest Days in Four Central European Countries, 1989–93

	1989	1990	1991	1992	1993	Total
Poland	2,033	1,684	3,253	3,529	4,382	14,881
Slovakia	—	302	532	851	521	2,419
Hungary	893	210	363	254	854	2,878
East Germany	391	544	535	2,733	1,146	6,076

quiescence is even more pronounced in other postcommunist countries. The incidence of protest was lower in Hungary and Slovakia, and protest events in these countries were more localized, smaller, largely nondisruptive, and short in duration. In the former East Germany, the unification triggered an evident increase in the number of protest events. This variation in levels of protest suggests that protestors in Poland and the former East Germany after reunification had at their disposal more resources to challenge the elite policies than did their counterparts in Slovakia or Hungary.

Our research confirms the thesis on the cyclical nature of protest formulated in other studies of social movements and contentious politics.[4] Our data show that in Poland, following the transfer of power and dissolution of the communist regime in 1989, there was a gradual increase in all relevant dimensions of protest events (e.g., duration, scope, number of participants, number of protest strategies per event, etc.). This observation allows us to argue that the magnitude of protest was growing during this period and that 1993 was a peak year in the protest cycle. Although our own data do not go beyond 1993, judging from the official strike statistics and media coverage, the number of protest actions in Poland declined significantly in 1994 and 1995. For example, the number of strikes registered by the Main Statistical Office declined from 7,443 in 1993 to 429 in 1994, and the number of strikers decreased from 382,222 to 211,442 (GUS 1995, 130).

Protest in Poland: Public Attitudes

As we argued in chapter 4, the high level of contentious politics in Poland was paralleled by the dynamic growth of civil society. Organizations of civil society, politicized yet fragmented and isolated from political parties, were bound to use protest as a major form of public participation. This potential was easily realized in practice, given the encouraging social climate that evolved in the 1980s. Following the experiences of the Solidarity movement and collective struggles after the imposition of martial law, most forms of protest were perceived by a growing number of people as appropriate ways of expressing collective grievances. Protest approval was on the rise, especially after 1989, when the fear of political repression abated and political rights and freedoms were guaranteed. By 1992, strikes, demonstrations, and boycotts of state decisions received the highest approval since the mid-1980s (Table 16). The high level of acceptance of disruptive protests, especially strikes, goes back to the legacies of the Solidarity movement, which elevated a strike to the most noble form of resistance against the unjust authorities and made it part of a routinized repertoire of political action. This fact supports Tilly's argument about the repertoires of collective action. He argues that "a population's repertoire of collective action generally includes only a handful of alternatives. It generally changes

TABLE 16. Net Approval of Specific Forms of Protest in Poland, 1981–92

Forms of Protest	1981	1984	1988	1989	1990	1992
Petitions, letters	39	61	60	50	68	84
Posting posters	−8	1	15	−4	38	41
Strikes	−2	7	−12	−15	22	47
Street demonstrations	−50	−3	−24	−35	7	39
Boycott of state decisions	−26	−14	1	−16	4	22
Occupying public buildings	−52	−72	−67	−71	−63	−55
Actively resisting police	−50	−41	−48	−39	−45	−47

Source: CBOS, "Opinia publiczna o roznych formach protestow spolecznych i skierowanych przeciw nim represjom" (Warsaw, February 1992); Adamski 1989, 192–93; Jasiewicz 1993a, 131.

Note: Net approval is the difference between the percentage of respondents who answer that citizens should have the right to use a specific form of action and the percentage of those who state the opposite.

slowly, seems obvious and natural to the people involved" (1978, 156). The repertoire of collective action available to a population is modified by several factors, including the efficiency of a particular method of advancing a group's goals, the populace's acceptance of repressive methods of control by the authorities, a group's familiarity with a particular method and its "heavy bias toward means it has previously used" (1978, 154), and cultural acceptance of some forms of collective action by the population. Judging from a set of comparative data, Poland of the early 1990s had a higher level of protest action approval than West European countries in the 1970s and 1980s.[5]

Another dimension of the Polish public's attitudes toward protest was the "repression potential," defined as "the tendency to grant authorities increasingly severe instruments of control to contain correspondingly severe challenges by protesters, strikers, or other unorthodox activists" (Barnes, Kaase, et al. 1979, 87). It was tested by the authors of *Political Action* and used by Polish sociologists in their research on political attitudes. The results of Polish surveys are presented in table 17. These results indicate the gradual yet consistently declining social approval of the authorized use of force. By 1992, the "repression potential" of the Polish authorities was rather low: roughly one-third of the Polish populace approved of the use of force against demonstrators and strikers. This very limited acceptance of repression was a clear legacy of the four decades of repressive rule: the new Polish state had even less public consent to intervene against disruptive political action than did the old communist state. Such a situation has important consequences for the postcommunist governments, for it restricts their range of legitimate, that is, popularly accepted, responses to protest actions.

According to the authors of *Political Action,* "three components of politi-

TABLE 17.   Net Approval of State Actions against Different Forms of Protest
in Poland, 1981–92

Types of Action	1981	1984	1988	1989	1990	1992
Police action against street demonstrations	−65	−51	−58	−74	−51	−70
Harsh penalties for resisting the police	−57	−47	−53	−66	−55	−65
Ban on protests and demonstrations	−35	−31	−29	−43	−50	−70
Using the military to break up strikes	−77	−67	−73	−84	−83	−91

Source: CBOS, "Opinia publiczna o roznych formach protestow spolecznych i skierowanych przeciw nim represjom" (Warsaw, February 1992); Adamski 1989, 192–93; Jasiewicz 1993a, 131.

Note: Net approval of a given repressive measure is the difference between the percentage of respondents who support the state's right to employ this measure and the percentage of those who do not.

cal action—protest potential, conventional participation, and repression potential—form the basic 'parameters of license' for protest" (Barnes et al. 1979, 60). It is, however, obvious that public opinion surveys do not provide sufficient knowledge about actual protest actions. As Tarrow observes, "Unless we trace the forms of activity people use, how these reflect their demands, and their interaction with opponents and elites, we cannot understand either the magnitude or the dynamics of change in politics and society" (1989, 7–8). The data presented in this chapter come from a systematic record of actual protest events that took place in Poland between 1989 and 1993. We will argue that during this period, collective protest emerged as one of the most important forms of participation in public life and became institutionalized as a routine means of advancing grievances and pressing for policy changes.

Protest in Poland: Main Features

The roundtable negotiations and the peaceful surrender of political power by the communist regime gave the impression that Poland's transition was an intra-elite affair. This is not the case: as we showed in the second chapter, beginning in the spring of 1988 Poland experienced a high level of protest and pressure from below. It did not take the form of mass public demonstrations, so conspicuous in East Germany and Czechoslovakia; the predominant strategies were strikes, strike alerts, and protest threats.

Furthermore, it is sometimes argued that the far-reaching post-1989 reforms were carried out with the nearly full support of all society. This support ebbed rapidly only after the monetary and budgetary discipline imposed in 1990 began to take its toll in growing social costs and dislocations. In addition, it is argued that the Solidarity trade union extended a protective umbrella over the first two postcommunist governments and began actively opposing the government's policies through sponsoring protest actions only in 1992. Earlier strikes and demonstrations were seen as organized by the ex-communist OPZZ labor federation or as spontaneously emerging actions. The data we collected and the statistical data available in Poland put such views in doubt.

The most striking finding that emerges from our study is that during the period from 1989 to 1993, *the number of protest actions in Poland remained relatively constant.* At the same time, *the magnitude of protest increased.* Moreover, the protest activities we observed seem to have constituted a wave that culminated during the early summer of 1993, greatly influenced the country's political situation, and then abated. Our database, which includes all protest actions reported by the six main Polish newspapers and weeklies, yields the picture presented in table 18.

Due to the specific definition of the term *protest event* that we chose, the number of protest events recorded in our database differs from figures found in other sources. For the purpose of our project, we assume that a protest event may include the activities of several separate groups or organizations. The activities of different groups are considered to be a part of the same protest event if (1) they relate to the same grievances and (2) take place at the same time or without any considerable delays. Thus strikes in several different enterprises or demonstrations in several cities were counted as a single protest event if demands and timing were similar. Although there is no comparable data set for the entire period, our count of protest events is lower than the number of protest actions registered by the labor ministry in 1991 and 1992. The Ministry of Labor compiled its count based on press information, its own data, and data from other state agencies. It registered 428 protests in 1992 and 401 protests in 1993 (see Swirska 1994).

TABLE 18.   Number of Protest Events in Poland by Category

	1989	1990	1991	1992	1993	Total
Single protest	246	261	235	256	203	1,201
events	78.3%	85.3%	80.5%	81.5%	81.2%	81.4%
Series of protest	41	27	17	17	6	108
events	13.1%	8.8%	5.8%	5.4%	2.4%	7.3%
Protest campaigns	27	18	40	41	41	167
	8.6%	5.9%	13.7%	13.1%	16.4%	11.3%
Total number						
of events	314	306	292	314	250	1,476

TABLE 19.   Strikes in Poland

	1990	1991	1992	1993
Number of strikes	250	305	6,351	7,443
Percentage of workers who participated in a strike	29.7%	41.4%	43.4%	55.2%

Source: GUS 1991–1995.

We were able to locate independent confirmation of our crucial finding that the magnitude (or intensity) of protest was increasing in the *Polish Statistical Yearbook* (GUS 1993, 1994, 1995), which reported data on the number of people who participated in industrial strikes, as shown in table 19.

While the number of protest events was relatively constant during the five-year period, a closer look at their more specific features reveals the growing intensity of protest. We singled out for consideration four such features: (1) the organizational complexity of the protest event, (2) the scope of the protest event, (3) the number of participants, and (4) the event's duration.

As table 18 illustrates, the number of large-scale, coordinated protest campaigns increased considerably. We assumed that if protest actions were officially (i.e., outwardly or publicly) directed or coordinated by one decision-making center, they constituted a protest campaign. In 1990, there were 18 campaigns, but from 1991 to 1993 their number climbed to 40 or more per year. They included nationwide protest actions, coordinated regional protests, and sectoral protest campaigns that were especially frequent in coal mines, the defense industry, transportation, the nonindustrial public sector (education, health), and agriculture.

The first social group to oppose government policies through countrywide protest campaigns were the farmers and agricultural workers. In 1990 farmers' unions organized regional protests and road blockades. At the same time, transportation workers staged a countrywide protest. Farmers continued in 1991 with road blockades, strikes, and demonstrations. In the spring of 1991, employees of approximately 1,000 collective farms (one-third of the country's state-owned farms) went on a strike that lasted almost a month. Their actions were coordinated by the National Strike Committee. Earlier in the year, trade unions had begun organizing large-scale protest campaigns. In January of 1991, the OPZZ launched a national protest campaign against the *popiwek* (tax on excessive wage growth). This tax was used by the government to limit wage increases and thus to control inflation. Between February 12 and 15, almost 2,000 state-owned enterprises participated in protests, mainly by displaying flags and banners demanding the abolition of the tax. At the same time, 2,000 miners demonstrated in Warsaw, and the following day more than 10,000 union members from all over Poland marched through the streets of the capital. For the next several weeks, street demonstrations were organized in many cities across the country. The national protest campaign ended with another big demonstration in Warsaw on April 12, but the tax remained in place nonetheless.

Massive protest campaigns were most common in 1992 and 1993. During the summer of 1992, a huge wave of protest actions rocked the country as several unions organized one strike after another. This wave involved coal mines; steel mills; automobile, tractor, and aircraft manufacturers; transportation workers; and a huge copper mining and smelting conglomerate, whose some 30,000 employees were on strike for a month. In August the National Committee was formed by six union federations. It presented the government with a list of 21 demands covering a range of political and economic issues.

The coal miners' unions, who organized their first major protest campaign in November 1990, continued with a number of protest actions in 1991 and struck again in 1992. This latter strike began in December and involved close to 70 mines and 300,000 workers. The miners were soon joined by the railroad workers. Deliveries of coal to industrial and commercial users were halted. Negotiations with the government secured a promise of a renovation program for the mining industry and brought the campaign to an end after 21 days. Strikes and other protests were only conditionally suspended, however, to give the government time to implement the promised policy changes. The miners' strikes were a prelude to a massive protest campaign that began in the spring of 1993; it involved mostly the nonindustrial public sector employees who were organized by several union federations. We will describe this campaign in more detail in chapter 6.

Organizing a large campaign requires considerable material, organizational, and human resources; therefore the increase in the number of large-scale campaigns is a strong indicator of the increased *institutionalization of protest* during the later part of the period studied. Protest campaigns not only became more complex and massive; they grew more confrontational and disruptive. Significantly, the increased salience of protest politics in the country's public life was confirmed by the increased number of protest actions whose scope was not local, but regional or national. Protest actions were unevenly spread throughout the country, and they did not always occur in the most depressed regions. Locations with the strongest organizational infrastructure and traditions of protest registered the highest number of contentious actions, many of which were very large in scope. Among the country's 49 regions, the most protest prone included the most populous and industrialized: the Warsaw region, Silesia, the Gdansk region, Krakow, Szczecin, and Lodz. These regions were strongholds of Solidarity in 1980–81 and centers of opposition against the post–martial law regime.

TABLE 20.   Number of Protest Events in Poland (by scope)

	1989	1990	1991	1992	1993	Total
Local	248	243	196	225	169	1,081
	79.0%	79.4%	67.1%	71.6%	67.6%	73.2%
Regional	22	21	27	40	34	144
	7.0%	6.8%	9.3%	12.7%	12.6%	9.8%
National	44	42	69	49	46	250
	14.0%	13.7%	23.6%	15.5%	18.4%	16.9%
Data unavailable	0	1	0	0	1	2
		0.3%			0.4%	0.1%
Total number of events	314	306	292	314	250	1,476

As stated before, there are considerable gaps in our data on the number of participants in protest actions, but general trends are sufficiently clear. Judging by the growing number of protests with large numbers of participants (above 2,000), the amount of people who engaged in contentious collective actions was increasing.[6] This was evident in 1992, when the Polish Copper conglomerate, employing nearly 40,000 workers, remained on strike for four weeks and when 64 coal mines employing nearly 300,000 workers went on a three-week strike. According to the Main Statistical Office, during 1992, 752,472 people participated in strikes and 2,360,392 workdays were lost. In the spring of 1993, several hundred thousand people participated in strikes, demonstrations, and rallies, coordinated as a nationwide protest campaign by Solidarity and other organizations.

TABLE 21.   Number of Protest Events (by number of participants)

	1989	1990	1991	1992	1993	Total
0–200	18	51	61	58	56	244
	5.7%	16.7%	20.9%	18.5%	22.4%	16.5%
201–2,000	15	28	37	41	39	160
	4.9%	9.1%	12.7%	13.1%	15.6%	10.8%
More than 2,000	9	11	20	36	28	104
	2.9%	3.6%	6.9%	11.5%	11.2%	7.0%
Not applicable	50	42	52	53	61	258
	15.9%	13.7%	17.8%	16.9%	24.4%	17.5%
Data unavailable	221	174	122	126	65	708
	70.4%	56.9%	41.8%	40.1%	26.0%	48.0%
Total number of events	314	306	292	314	250	1,476

TABLE 22.   Number of Protest Events (by duration of protest)

	1989	1990	1991	1992	1993	Total
One day or less	71	118	94	131	77	491
	22.6%	38.5%	32.2%	41.7%	30.8%	33.3%
2–7 days	36	21	31	18	28	134
	11.5%	6.9%	10.6%	5.7%	11.2%	9.1%
8 days –1 month	37	27	39	40	38	181
	11.8%	8.8%	13.0%	12.7%	15.2%	12.3%
More than	14	21	33	35	35	138
1 month	4.5%	6.9%	11.3%	11.1%	14.0%	9.4%
Not applicable	45	31	33	42	53	204
	14.3%	10.1%	11.3%	13.4%	21.2%	13.8%
Data unavailable	111	87	63	48	19	328
	35.4%	28.4%	21.6%	15.3%	7.6%	22.2%
Total number						
of events	314	306	292	314	250	1,476

Finally, other available numbers that can be interpreted as indicators of protest magnitude were growing as well. The Main Statistical Office recorded that the number of workers on strike doubled between 1990 and 1991 (from 115,687 to 221,547) and the number of workdays lost due to strikes tripled (from 159,016 to 517,647). Both the number of workers on strike and the number of lost workdays increased by close to 40 percent in 1992 (752,472 workers and 2,360,392 lost workdays) and then declined in 1993. Our data also suggest that between 1989 and 1993, there was a significant increase in the number of both participants and protest actions lasting over one month (from 14 in 1989 to 35 in 1993). The number of protest events lasting longer than two months went up from 6 in 1989 to 17 in 1992 and 14 in 1993.

This growing magnitude of protest in Poland can be captured by a composite index. Inspired by the method of calculating protest magnitude proposed by Tilly, who multiplies the size, duration, and frequency of collective protest (1978, 95–97), we constructed a similar index of protest magnitude. The yearly increases in the index's values demonstrate that during the first five years of the postcommunist consolidation, the *magnitude* of collective protest in Poland *increased* (table 23).

TABLE 23.   Index of Protest Magnitude

	1989	1990	1991	1992	1993
Index of magnitude	12.6	10.7	18.8	17.6	25.5
All valid cases	268	276	259	267	202

In short, our data reveal two phenomena: first, protest activities in Poland were widespread during the entire period under study; second, the magnitude of protest as measured by the number of participants, duration of protests, and their regional scope increased gradually throughout the period. The peak of the protest cycle following the collapse of the communist regime came in the spring of 1993.

Protest Participants: Social Categories

It is one of the tenets of political sociology that in complex, modern societies, most (if not all) types of political activities, including protest, tend to be systematically related to the actors' location in the social structure. Therefore, studies of protest often begin with an examination of *social cleavages* and their dynamic relationship with *political cleavages* (Kriesi and Duyvendak 1995). In the case of any postcommunist country, this idea must be applied with special care: social structures of state-socialist countries differed from the capitalist class structures usually analyzed by political sociologists. In Poland before 1989, the cleavage between the communist state and society became very pronounced and strongly influenced politics (Kubik 1994a, 230–38); yet this new social cleavage did not replace other cleavages, but rather complemented them. The question then arises: which of the pre-1989 social cleavages was reflected in the political cleavages and influenced the political actions of Poles after 1989? Can we, for example, find evidence that the "us versus them" cleavage survived the 1989 breakthrough and that the subsequent post-Solidarity governments were challenged by the representatives of the old classes—either the "Solidarity class" or the "state class"? Or, rather, did the fall of communism spell the demise of this cleavage? And did the post-1989 struggles therefore reflect more conventional social cleavages, such as those identified by Rokkan (1970): urban-rural, workers-owners, center-periphery, or religious divisions?

As the data collected in table 24 demonstrate, the protestors were mainly drawn from two groups or classes: industrial workers and public (state) sector employees.[7] Most of the protesting workers were employed by large state-owned industrial enterprises particularly privileged under the old regime. Miners, defense industry workers, steelworkers, heavy machinery builders, etc., had enjoyed better wages and benefits than workers employed in other sectors of the economy. Now they were losing their privileged positions and were ready to express their discontent. Among public sector employees, teachers and health sector workers were the most contentious; their sectors suffered the deepest budget reductions.

The most frequent opponent or target of protest for both groups (see table 29) was the state and its various agencies. Thus, we identified the most active cleavage of Polish protest politics between 1989 and 1993: *the state versus its*

TABLE 24.   Socio-Vocational Categories of Participants
(more than one per protest event)

	1989	1990	1991	1992	1993	Total
Workers	116	35	123	142	100	516
	36.9%	11.5%	32.2%	45.2%	35.0%	35.0%
Farmers/peasants	15	34	31	27	34	141
	4.8%	11.1%	10.6%	8.6%	13.6%	9.6%
Service sector	44	14	23	31	9	121
	14.0%	4.6%	7.9%	9.9%	3.6%	8.2%
Public state sector	78	70	70	79	53	350
	24.9%	22.8%	24.0%	25.2%	24.8%	23.7%
Youth/students	35	44	24	34	17	154
	11.1%	14.4%	8.2%	10.8%	6.8%	10.5%
Other	34	42	44	47	51	218
	10.8%	13.7%	15.1%	15.0%	20.4%	14.7%
Data unavailable	20	80	22	36	42	200
	6.4%	26.1%	7.5%	11.5%	16.8%	13.6%
Total number of events	314	306	292	314	250	1,476

own employees. This is an intriguing finding, since the structure of employment changed considerably during the analyzed period: the number of people employed by private firms increased significantly (from 47 percent in 1989 to 63 percent in 1995), and the private sector output as a share of GDP grew from 28 percent in 1990 to nearly 55 percent in 1995. Moreover, the output of industry and construction as a share of GDP declined from 52.3 percent in 1989 to 39.3 percent in 1995, while the share of services increased from 34.8 percent to 53.1 percent.[8] Thus, the sectoral composition of the Polish economy changed radically as well. Yet the number of protests involving employees of such enterprises was almost negligible. This may be attributed to three factors. First, trade unions have been conspicuously absent in the private sector. The public sector and state-owned large industrial enterprises have been their principal organizational strongholds. This situation is illustrated by the size of various sectors within the main trade union federations. For example, the Solidarity union's biggest sections include the Secretariat of Pensioners with 130,000 members, Health Service Employees with 120,000 members, and Coal Miners with 92,000 members. Second, market conditions favored new private and privatized enterprises, and they fared much better financially than did the state-owned firms. They were exempted from the tax on excess wage growth, and their wages were usually higher. Moreover, private firms were able to generate profits and did not face the necessity of mass layoffs. As a result, trade unions had a hard time organizing and mobilizing workers in this prospering sector of the economy. Finally, the private sector was composed of mostly small and mid-size firms. Existing research on strike activities indicates that there is a linear relationship between the firm's size and workers' militancy. The workers' level of participation in protest actions and union membership increase with the firm's size. Consequently, strikes in larger firms are more frequent and disruptive, and they are often accompanied by other forms of protest (Franzosi 1995, 86–89).

Structurally, the principal cleavage of protest politics after 1989 was very similar to the one driving anticommunist politics; in both cases it was "the state" versus "the people dependent on it." Protestors' identities and demands, however, differed considerably. If during the period before 1989 protestors constituted a powerful cultural-political class that expressed itself in the massive Solidarity movement and were primarily interested in the rejection and *delegitimation* of the state-socialist regime, during the early postcommunist era their identity was far less uniform and generalized. They were primarily concerned with contesting specific government policies or economic decisions and were trying to air various economic grievances.

The most protest-prone groups included various sections of the working class, nonindustrial public sector employees, and young people. This finding indicates that one of the "classical" cleavages of modern politics, between employees and employers (predominantly the state in our case), was *salient and noninstitutionalized* in Polish postcommunist politics.[9] Most protest actions were engendered by "group-based cleavages." "Issue-based cleavages," typical of Western new social movements, generated relatively few protests. Concerns with the environment, gender discrimination, human rights, and personal autonomy or lifestyles, which Offe characterizes as a "new paradigm" of Western politics, were overshadowed by "old" political issues of economic growth and distribution (see, for example, Offe 1987 and Larana, Johnston, and Gusfield 1994). Thus Polish protest politics was still "traditional" in Rokkan's sense: it was driven mostly by the economic grievances and distributional issues of well-defined social groups, and it was not fluid, "with participants joining and disengaging as the political context and their personal circumstances change" (Dalton, Kuechler, and Burkin 1990, 12).[10] It was therefore more similar to the class-based French pattern than the German, Dutch, or Swiss new protest industries, revealingly analyzed by Kriesi and his collaborators (1995).

Protest Participants: Organizations

As McCarthy reminds us, "scholars of social movements have come to a quite broad consensus about the importance of *mobilizing structures* [original emphasis] for understanding the trajectory of particular social movements and broader social movement cycles" (1996, 141). Limited by our methodology, which did not allow us to study the process of mobilization directly, we settled for a more modest task: the collection of data on organizations that were involved in protest actions, either as organizers or participants.

We also expected that a lot of protest actions would be organized by newly formed organizations, somewhat weakly institutionalized and spontaneous; furthermore, we hypothesized that we would find many organizations formed *as a result* of collective protest actions. None of these hypotheses was confirmed. New organizations did not emerge as a result of protest actions. They were formed as a result of divisions within existing organizations. For example, some militant trade unions were spin-offs from Solidarity and OPZZ. In the second half of the analyzed period they were more militant, and it is possible that their membership increased as a result of successful protests.

In principle, protests were organized by the "old," well-established organizations with considerable resources at their disposal (see table 25). Our data reveal also that protest actions were organized *predominantly by organizations belonging to civil society,* such as labor unions, peasant organizations, and social and political movements. The number of protests for which our coders were not able to determine organizers was low (11.3 percent). One of the most interesting findings of our study was the *very low* involvement of political parties

TABLE 25. Organizations Sponsoring or Leading Protest (more than one per protest event)

	1989	1990	1991	1992	1993	Total
None	25	27	48	28	39	167
	8.0%	8.8%	16.4%	8.9%	15.6%	11.3%
Political parties	22	29	6	20	12	89
	7.0%	9.5%	2.0%	6.4%	4.8%	6.0%
Labor unions	95	84	162	205	163	709
	30.3%	27.4%	55.5%	65.2%	65.2%	48.0%
Peasant/farmer	6	16	12	24	22	80
organizations	1.9%	5.3%	4.1%	7.6%	8.8%	5.4%
Interest groups	16	24	21	17	13	91
	5.1%	7.9%	7.1%	5.5%	5.2%	6.2%
Social/political	56	65	38	37	32	228
movements	17.8%	21.3%	12.9%	11.8%	12.8%	15.5%
Other	6	25	12	10	27	80
	1.9%	8.2%	4.1%	3.2%	10.8%	5.4%
Data unavailable	158	88	48	47	14	355
	50.3%	28.8%	16.4%	15.0%	5.6%	24.1%
Total number of events	314	306	292	314	250	1,476

in protest activities. Only 6.0 percent of protest events were sponsored by political parties. It was *much* lower than in our other three cases. Political parties (co-)sponsored or (co-)led 35.5 percent of protest actions in Hungary; 29.6 percent in Slovakia; and 23.3 percent in the former East Germany. This is a surprising finding: given the extreme fragmentation of the party system in Poland, one could expect small parties to encourage unconventional political participation. The low number of protest actions organized by political parties can be explained by the fact that despite fragmentation, ideological polarization was not significant (far right and far left antisystemic parties were absent or weak) and political cleavages remained unclear and unstable. Moreover, throughout most of the analyzed period, many smaller parties were represented in the parliament, due to the excessive proportionality of the electoral system; thus they had access to the formal legislative process. This situation changed following the reform of the electoral law, resulting in the much less fragmented parliament elected in 1993. Thus, there may yet be more involvement by extraparliamentary parties in protest politics.

During the period from 1989 to 1993, of all civil society organizations, trade unions were the main driving force behind collective protest. Among trade union federations, Solidarity was the most active protest organizer, despite its official support for the first democratic governments. During the 1991–93 period we noted, however, a significant increase in protests organized by other trade unions, mostly splinter groups from Solidarity. This can be explained by the competition among the growing number of union organizations that emerged in Poland during that period. As noted by other scholars, protest is a valuable resource for organizations lacking a strong financial and membership base (Lipsky 1968). For small, new unions, protest was the most readily available strategy of increasing their social and political visibility and attracting members and resources. This institutional explanation works very well when we compare Poland with Hungary, Slovakia, and the former East Germany. There were more strikes in Poland than in any of these other states. Assuming that strikes are the main "weapon" of labor unions and knowing that during the analyzed period Poland had the most pluralistic and competitive union sector in Eastern Europe, we conclude that the high number of strikes in Poland is, at least partially, explained by the inter-union competition. Table 26 illustrates union involvement in organizing protests.

Finally, we found additional support for our central argument that during the period analyzed, both the magnitude and the significance of protest were intensifying. Reviewing the data we collected on the number of organizers involved in each protest action, we discovered the following pattern: in 1990, 12.7 percent of protest events were sponsored by two or more organizations; in 1991, this number went up to 14.7 percent; in 1992 it was 17.8 percent; and in 1993 it was even higher: 19.6 percent. We submit that this growing *interorganiza-*

TABLE 26.   Labor Unions as Protest Organizers (more than one per protest event)

	1989	1990	1991	1992	1993	Total
Solidarity trade union	49	52	90	93	95	379
	51.6%	61.9%	55.6%	45.3%	58.3%	53.5%
OPZZ (ex-communist	1	7	10	33	18	69
federation)	1.1%	8.3%	6.2%	16.1%	12.2%	9.7%
Other labor unions	15	12	30	46	36	139
	15.8%	14.3%	18.6%	31.2%	22.1%	19.6%
Solidarity '80	30	13	32	33	14	122
	31.6%	15.5%	19.8%	16.1%	8.6%	17.2%
Number of events sponsored by unions	95	84	162	205	163	709

tional coordination of protest activities indicates the increasing routinization of protest, that is, its increasing significance as a mode of interaction between the state and its citizenry or among various actors of the public sphere.

Repertoire of Contention

In his groundbreaking book, Tilly remarked that "at any point of time, the repertoire of collective action available to a population is surprisingly limited. Surprisingly, given the innumerable ways in which people could, in principle, deploy their resources in pursuit of common ends" (1978, 151). He defines repertoire of contention as "a limited set of routines that are learned, shared, and acted out through a relatively deliberate process of choice" (1995a, 26). Collective protest in Poland fits this characterization well. The general repertoire of contention was limited and closely mirrored standard strategies used by protesting groups in contemporary politics. It was also relatively stable. Our database did not record any important shifts in protest strategies; dominant forms of protest were consistent throughout the entire period under study.

Postcommunist collective protest in Poland was *decidedly nonviolent*—a startling contrast to Latin America, where the so-called IMF riots exacted a heavy toll in casualties (150 to 190 dead) and property damage.[11] We defined violence broadly to include attacks on property, the use of force against officials, assassinations and accidental deaths resulting from protest activities, street confrontations, and riots. Only in 115 protest events (7.8 percent of all protests) was some form of violent behavior registered. Among all protest strategies, those using violence constituted only 4.9 percent. During the entire period there was only one fatality resulting from a protest action. Violence occurred most often when young people participated in protest actions: out of 154

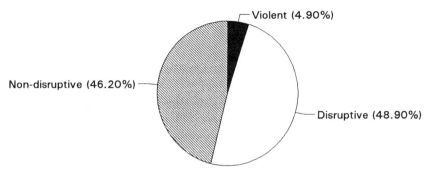

Fig. 5.   Violent, disruptive, and nondisruptive protest strategies, total
1989–93

events involving members of this category, 36 (23.4 percent) included some
form of violent incident. By contrast, out of the 479 protest actions workers
were involved in, only 13 (2.7 percent) were violent. As far as organizations are
concerned, violence most often accompanied protests sponsored by social and
political movements (16.2 percent of events involving such groups); when political parties were involved, protest turned violent in 11.5 percent of the cases;
only 3.5 percent of protest actions in which trade unions took part were violent!
Thus, not only was the level of violence low, but violence occurred mostly in
protest actions organized by small and loosely organized social movements
of young people. Major, well-established protest organizers, especially trade
unions, refrained from using violence. This regularity is an important sign of
democratic consolidation.

The most popular strategy of protest in Poland was *striking*. This included
a variety of strike forms (such as sit-down, revolving, slowdown, wildcat, symbolic, etc.), warning strikes, and strike alerts, and was often supported by rallies, mass meetings, demonstrations, and picket lines. Strikes did not dominate
the repertoire of protest only in 1990. Demonstrations, marches, and rallies
were the second most dominant form. Protest letters and statements followed.
The next most common forms of protest were more disruptive actions, such as
the occupation of public buildings and blockades of roads and public places.

The prevalence of strikes among protest actions reflects both the legacies
of the Solidarity movement, with its tradition of successful strikes, and the dominant role of the trade union sector in newly reconstituted civil society. It
also indicates the presence of significant organizational resources because, as
Franzosi points out, "strikes, more than sudden outbreaks of workers' protest,
require a complex organization" (1995, 105). The Polish repertoire of protest
has proven to be significantly different from the repertoires employed by Hungarians, Slovaks, and Germans from the former GDR. Protestors from the first

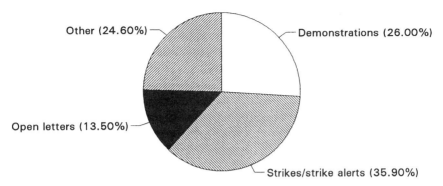

Fig. 6. Protest strategies, total 1989–93

two nations most often used street demonstrations and nondisruptive strategies of issuing open letters or statements and collecting signatures in order to oppose specific events or policies; German protestors most often employed marches and demonstrations and had a much higher proclivity to use violence than their counterparts in the other three countries of our sample. Violent strategies constituted the following percentages of all protest strategies: in Hungary, 1.7 percent; in Slovakia, 2.0 percent; and in the former GDR, 13.1 percent. Table 27 summarizes our findings on the repertoire of protest in Poland.

TABLE 27.   Protest Strategies (more than one per protest event)

	1989	1990	1991	1992	1993	Total
Demonstration/rally/	83	154	119	156	97	609
march/blockade	20.6%	37.7%	22.7%	28.7%	21.0%	26.0%
Strike	159	43	92	75	63	432
	39.5%	10.5%	17.5%	13.8%	13.7%	18.5%
Strike alert/threat of	50	53	106	100	99	408
protest action	12.4%	13.0%	20.2%	18.4%	21.5%	17.4%
Open letters/	39	37	77	79	84	316
statements	9.7%	9.1%	14.7%	14.5%	18.2%	13.5%
Occupation of public	10	44	21	33	25	133
buildings	2.5%	10.8%	4.0%	6.1%	5.4%	5.7%
Violent assault on	21	26	20	26	22	115
persons or	5.2%	6.4%	3.8%	4.8%	4.8%	4.9%
property						
Other	41	51	90	75	71	328
	10.2%	12.5%	17.1%	13.8%	15.4%	14.0%
Number of						
strategies	403	408	525	544	461	2,341

It is also worth noting that the tactical versatility (Tarrow's term) of Polish protestors improved: in 1990, three or more protest strategies were employed in only 7.4 percent of all events. In 1991, this figure rose to 19.2 percent of protest events; in 1992, 17.9 percent; and in 1993, 20.4 percent. This increased versatility involved more careful planning and coordination of protest actions; it testifies to the increased sophistication of the protest organizers and thus the higher institutionalization of protest as a mode of interaction with the authorities. This conclusion is supported by another finding: the number of protests involving two or more organizations rose as well—from 12.7 percent of all events in 1990 to 19.6 percent in 1993. The regularity we observed contradicts Tarrow's findings in Italy. He observed that "as the presence of known organizations was declining, people were learning to use more and more varied forms of collective action. Thus, as institutionalization increased, tactical versatility declined" (1989, 80). We would sum up our findings the opposite way: as institutionalization increased, so did tactical versatility.

Protest Demands

In the summer of 1992, Poland experienced a huge wave of protest actions that began as localized strikes and escalated into a nationwide protest campaign. Six union federations, including the militant Solidarity '80 and Samoobrona, formed a national coordinating committee. On August 10, the committee issued a list of 21 demands and threatened a nationwide general strike if the government did not respond and begin negotiations. The symbolic meaning of this action was unmistakable. The list of 21 demands issued by the striking workers in Gdansk in 1980 paved the way to Solidarity's revolution. As in 1980, the government was the exclusive target of protest, and demands combined both economic and political issues. They included a call for subordinating the government's economic policy to "national objectives," liquidation of unemployment, a demand for a change of the privatization law and restriction on the entry of foreign capital, protection of the domestic market against foreign competition, elimination of taxes paid by enterprises, and the cancellation of enterprise debts. Although the rhetoric of the 21 demands was political, they were asking for concrete economic changes. As our own study revealed, economic concerns were most often voiced by the protestors during the entire period.

The numbers presented in figures 7 and 8 illustrate a major finding of our study: during the 1989–93 period, protestors' demands had a predominantly economic character. Poles protested *mostly* to improve their standard of living. As a detailed examination of demands shows, calls for wage increases and expansion/preservation of other material benefits were by far the most frequently reported category. The second biggest category was demands for state subsidies and protection of state-owned enterprises. Surprisingly, we registered very

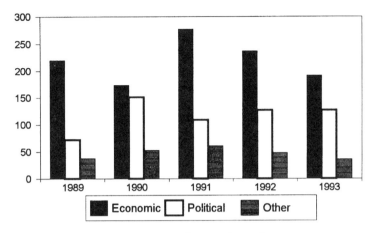

Fig. 7.   Types of protest demands

few demands against privatization policies (23, that is, 1.2 percent of all demands voiced). There were more demands (27) for accelerating or expediting
privatization. This finding undermines Kramer's (1995) conclusion that labor
unrest slowed down the pace of privatization. Our data show that the fiercest
opposition to the privatization efforts of post-1989 governments came from the
parliament, not from the striking and demonstrating workers.

Only a few contentious collective actions used radically polarizing symbolism and stated as one of their objectives the revolutionary overthrow of the
sociopolitical order instituted after 1989. As our database demonstrates, a demand to "modify/reform existing state or public institutions" was voiced in

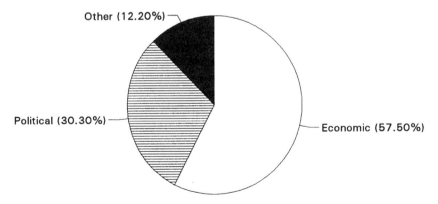

Fig. 8.   Types of demands, total 1989–93

only 0.6 percent of protests in 1989, 4.6 percent in 1990, 4.1 percent in 1991, 1.3 percent in 1992, and 2.0 percent in 1993. A more radical demand to "abolish/replace the post-1989 political order" was practically never voiced. *The tenor of the postcommunist protest in Poland was decisively reformist.* Protestors did not intend to challenge the legitimacy of the political system or the general direction of the economic reforms; instead, they wanted to correct specific state policies or express dissatisfaction with their outcomes. This critically important finding is supported by an extensive study of Polish workers:

> Workers' support for the market reform has a rather solid character and was formed already in the 1980s. . . . [This support] is of course conditional. . . . The key question that needs to be answered is—Which capitalism? Workers' postulates and demands are related to such problems as: (a) active employment policy, curtailing of unemployment, (b) limiting of the excessive income differential . . . , and (c) effective labor unions and employee participation (participation in decision making). (Gilejko 1995, 151; see also Gardawski and Zukowski 1994)

As we have already mentioned, protestors' demands reflected traditional politics and group-based cleavages. We registered very few demands typical of new social movements and issue-based cleavages. For example, in our database we recorded only 48 demands concerning ecological issues (2.5 percent of all demands), 28 concerning the abortion issue (1.5 percent of all demands), and 17 concerning the AIDS epidemic (0.9 percent of all demands). We also found a small number of nationalistic demands (14—0.7 percent of all demands) and a correspondingly small number of antinationalistic, pro-tolerance demands (15—0.8 percent of all demands). Moreover, international issues, including relations with the former USSR, were not high on protestors' agendas. We registered only 72 demands regarding international issues (3.7 percent of all demands).

The curve representing the intensity of political demands has a U shape: the number of protest events for which we registered such demands decreased temporarily in 1991, during the prime ministership of Krzysztof Bielecki. This may indicate that among the first four postcommunist prime ministers, he was the most acceptable to the protestors. The growing number of political demands from 1991 to 1993 seems to indicate *the increasing politicization* of protest during this period. In order to substantiate this thesis, we examined the pattern of data collected in response to the question "On whose behalf were the demands made?" Table 28 reports selected results.

Whereas the protesters' identities were predominantly and consistently "particularistic," the data presented in table 28 indicate an increasing usage of the more general identities, such as "nation," "social category" (for example,

TABLE 28.   Entities on Whose Behalf Demands Were Made
(more than one per protest event)

	1989	1990	1991	1992	1993	Total
Protesting group	143	99	216	127	174	759
	45.5%	32.4%	74.0%	40.4%	69.9%	51.4%
Territorial units	12	26	20	20	19	97
	3.8%	8.5%	6.8%	6.4%	7.6%	6.6%
Vocational and social	56	101	103	104	74	438
groups	17.9%	33.0%	35.3%	33.1%	29.6%	29.7%
Nation	3	4	3	11	6	27
	1.0%	1.3%	1.0%	3.5%	2.4%	1.8%
Society	24	31	28	49	37	169
	7.6%	10.1%	9.6%	15.6%	14.8%	11.4%
Other	1	9	2	21	7	40
	0.3%	2.9%	0.7%	6.7%	2.8%	2.7%
Data unavailable	92	68	45	83	11	299
	29.3%	22.2%	15.4%	26.4%	4.4%	20.3%
Number of protest						
events	314	306	292	314	250	1,476

"working class"), or "society." This trend may be interpreted as a sign of the growing politicization of collective protest. This *politicization through a generalization of identity* was mainly "civic" in character; the predominant general identity to which the protestors subscribed was "society." Such identities as "nation," indicating subscription to some form of nationalism, or "social category," meaning some form of class consciousness, were used far less frequently.

Judging by the number of political demands, workers' and farmers' protest actions were the least politicized (only 29 percent of events in which workers participated contained such demands). By contrast, protest actions organized or attended by young people were the most politicized. They put forth the highest number of political demands and the lowest number of economic demands. Youth protests were usually organized by various social and political movements. For protest events involving workers (479), we registered economic demands in 71 percent of all cases. When peasants/farmers were involved, economic demands were put forth in 73 percent of all events. By contrast, in protests attended or organized by "the youth" (154), economic demands were voiced in only 12 percent of all cases. As expected, protest actions involving political parties were the most politicized. We found political demands in 61 percent of the events involving political parties and only in 37 percent of events attended by labor unions. Economic demands were voiced most often during protests organized or attended by peasant organizations (76 percent of the cases) and labor unions (66 percent of the cases).

Targets of Protest

Our analysis would be incomplete without examining the targets of protest actions. We defined targets of protest as the person, institution, or organization whom the protestors want to respond or react to their demands or grievances. The state and its agencies were by far the most common target. As figure 9 shows, central and local state institutions as well as the parliament constitute 77.5 percent of all protest action targets during the analyzed period. A more detailed look (table 29) shows that among all state agencies, the central institutions of the state (the government, parliament, and the president) were targeted by the protestors more often than any other organizations or institutions. Moreover, the frequency with which the state institutions were targeted (particularly the government and various ministries) *increased considerably* during the examined period. Surprisingly, in 1989, when the transfer of state power took place and more-politicized protest could have been expected, management was a more favored target of protest than the state.

Table 29 illustrates an intriguing phenomenon: the *growing* number of protests targeted at all branches of the government, despite administrative decentralization and the rapid growth of the private sector in the economy. At the same time, the number of protests directed against management fluctuated without any appreciable growth or decline. Protests against domestic or foreign owners were infrequent. Given the predominance of economic demands, this finding indicates that protest actions responded to the continuing substantial involvement of the state in the economy. Protestors "lobbied" the state for subsidies, credit guarantees, tax exemptions, and protective tariffs. In addition, 70.1

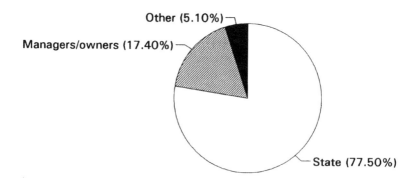

Other (5.10%)

Managers/owners (17.40%)

State (77.50%)

Fig. 9.   Targets of protest actions, total 1989–93

TABLE 29.   Targets of Protest Actions (more than one target per protest action)

	1989	1990	1991	1992	1993	Total
President	3	7	20	26	36	92
	1.1%	2.0%	5.0%	5.4%	8.1%	4.7%
Parliament	28	43	46	81	49	247
	10.7%	12.2%	11.4%	17.0%	11.0%	12.7%
Government/	91	142	207	258	217	915
ministries	34.9%	40.2%	51.4%	54.0%	48.9%	47.2%
Other state	7	26	7	15	19	74
agencies	2.7%	7.4%	1.7%	3.1%	4.3%	3.8%
Local government	17	50	42	27	41	177
	6.5%	14.2%	10.2%	5.6%	9.2%	9.1%
Management	95	54	69	45	59	322
	36.4%	15.3%	17.1%	9.4%	13.3%	16.6%
Domestic or foreign	1	0	0	9	5	15
owners	0.4%			1.9%	1.1%	0.8%
Other	19	31	12	17	18	97
	7.3%	8.8%	3.0%	3.6%	4.1%	5.0%
Number of						
targets	261	353	403	478	444	1,939

percent of demands were related to local or workplace issues, while only 29.1 percent concerned national and international issues for which a national government should be a proper target. The increasing targeting of state institutions may also signify that the "us-versus-them" conceptualization of politics, in which the "state" is seen as the main antagonist of the "society," was regaining its popularity after a short decline in 1989. The protestors seem to have been driven by an expectation shaped by the old regime—that the state is responsible for all aspects of economic and social life and, therefore, should solve all problems. Finally, we suggest that the increasing targeting of state institutions may be also interpreted as an aspect of the growing *politicization* of protest.

State Responses and Effectiveness of Protest

With the collapse of the communist regime, the cost of collective action for the actors within society declined markedly. Repressive policies toward all groups and organizations attempting to challenge the party-state policies, characteristic of state-socialist regimes, were quickly abandoned; legal guarantees of political rights, including the right of association, assembly, and strike, were enacted. As a result, a facilitating environment for collective action emerged. The gradual expansion of protest activities described in this chapter indicates that the newly reconstituted organizations of civil society took advantage of new liberties and benefited from the removal of fear of repression.

For the state, however, the democratization process increased the cost of coercive responses to protest and constrained its ability to prevent the disruption of public order. Oddly, public approval for the use of force against protestors was higher under the old communist regime than under the postcommunist regime. This limitation on the legitimate use of force was reflected in the state's responses to protest during the analyzed period. Following della Porta's typology of state responses to protest,[12] one can argue that the postcommunist state in Poland was remarkably tolerant, selective in its use of force, reactive rather than preventive, soft in using coercion, and respectful of legal and democratic procedures. Such features of state responses, according to della Porta, tend to be favorable for protest and encourage mass and peaceful protest activities (1996, 90). Our findings confirm her hypothesis: Polish protest was intensifying, yet at the same time its strategies were nonviolent and its demands had a reformist character.

During the analyzed period, police interference in protest actions was remarkably infrequent. We registered police interventions without the use of force in only 59 protest events (4 percent of all protests) and interventions with the use of force in 83 protest events (5.6 percent of protests). The use of police force was selective; only drastic attempts to disrupt public order, such as occupation of public buildings, road blockades, or unruly demonstrations, were counteracted by the police. The use of force was also limited to a handful of more militant organizations. Protests organized by the militant farmers' union Samoobrona often led to confrontation with the police and legal sanctions. In 1993, there were some 20 cases of criminal proceedings against individual members of this union, and the organization was under investigation by the prosecutor's office for violation of the law on a number of occasions. It is clear that Samoobrona used the most radical protest strategies, frequently involving violent assaults on public officials. The media complained about police inaction in the face of Samoobrona's blatant disregard for the law. Also, protest events organized by radical political movements and youth were more likely to invite police action than protests organized by trade union or other mainstream organizations.

Police interventions, when they took place, were remarkably restrained. We registered a very small number of people injured as a result of police action and an equally small number of protestors who were arrested or detained. The only fatality and serious injuries related to the use of police force were registered in September 1989 when police were called in to end violent riots in a number of prisons. Overall, complaints about police brutality or violation of legal procedures were largely absent. Administrative sanctions were employed in only a few cases, although our data collection method was not well suited for tracing long-term outcomes of protest events.[13] The postcommunist state was very reluctant to use force against protestors in part because it would resemble too closely the discredited communist tactics and in part because social sensitivities and democratic control over the police forces constrained more forceful actions and potential abuses of power.

An analysis of state responses to protest cannot be restricted to scrutiny of the police handling of protest events. State actions also included negotiations with protestors; mediation efforts when the state was not the target of protest; official pronouncements supporting or criticizing protestors' behavior or demands; and, more importantly, various policy changes to satisfy demands voiced by protestors. This includes the refusal to negotiate, avoidance of becoming one of the sides in the conflict, or rejection of demands. It seems that consecutive Polish governments were able to maintain an unyielding stance in dealing with strikes and other protests. The wave of strikes during the summer of 1992 was one of the most important moments in shaping the ways in which the government dealt with large-scale protests. After the unsuccessful conclusion of the 55-day strike at the FSM automobile plant in Tychy, Deputy Prime Minister Henryk Goryszewski remarked that "for the first time a strike has ended in something other than a victory for the strikers; this time the public and the democratic state won out" (Vinton 1992, 10). The largely unsuccessful end of the protest wave served as an important lesson for both sides. According to Vinton,

> while the strikers did not suffer the full economic and legal consequences of their action, the government managed to make several points. First, it would not be coerced into becoming a "side" in wage negotiations at the enterprise level; second, it would not revise macroeconomic policy to suit discontented segments of the work force; and, third, and most important, it would not allow strikes to provide better prospects for economic gains than legally negotiated settlements. (1992, 12)

Although one of the goals of our research was to investigate the impact of protest on government policies, it was not an easy task, because the *direct effects* of protest actions are notoriously difficult to measure.[14] Moreover, press accounts do not provide sufficient information on the outcomes of protest, which are often considerably delayed in time. Government policy changes are the result of multiple factors and pressures. It is difficult to assess whether protest actions, intergovernmental or parliamentary struggles, or foreign policy concerns were most responsible for various policy choices or reversals. Additionally, the time lag between protest actions and policy changes is often long.

Yet, despite these methodological limitations and the meager amount of information we collected on the effects of protest actions, we were able to observe some interesting facts.

First, we noted an interesting case of "social schizophrenia": an increase in negotiations and mediations did not result in a decrease of protests. Instead, protests were becoming institutionalized. Increasingly, they were the way society chose to advance its demands and claims. Institutionalized procedures of conflict solving provided by the law were weak and frequently disregarded. Moreover, in contrast to other postcommunist countries, the introduction of a tripartite mechanism was considerably delayed. Many aspects of the relationship between trade unions, employers, and the government as well as the status of state enterprises were clarified only through the package of 14 laws known as the "pact on state enterprises" introduced by the Suchocka government at the end of 1992. After lengthy consultations with trade unions, a tripartite commission (including representatives of the government, employers, and trade unions) was created as a national forum for collective bargaining in February 1994.

Second, although the direct impact of protest actions was hard to determine, it is clear that protests contributed to many policy changes and reversals of specific decisions of local and national authorities. Strikers often won wage concessions and received wages for the period they were on strike, despite the fact that the law explicitly prohibited such payments. Board members and managers were forced to resign. Guarantees from the government to restructure debts, purchase products, and finance firm restructuring were secured. The unions set out to modify policy implementation, and they achieved many of their goals. The main contours of economic policy introduced in 1990 were neither challenged nor drastically changed. In this respect Poland is not an exception. Summarizing the experiences of the Third World countries that attempted major economic adjustment programs, Nelson argues that

> Labor alone rarely can stall or drastically modify adjustment programs, although it may win limited concessions. Even in countries where unions are large and well-organized, governments have often faced down their opposition. But where union opposition combines with much broader protest, most commonly from the urban popular sector but sometimes also from business, programs have indeed been drastically modified or abandoned. (1990, 350)

In Poland, the linkage between actors within civil society and other actors in public life was very weak. Thus it seems that the opponents of economic policies, represented mainly by trade unions, would not have been able to build a broad coalition to block or reverse the pro-market reforms even if this had become their goal.

We can summarize the impact of protest action on government policies on three levels. First, protest did not have any substantial impact on macroeconomic policies, although some elements of the reform package were relaxed. For example, the punitive tax on excessive wage growth in state enterprises (*popiwek*), the main tool of the anti-inflation policy, was gradually relaxed (from 500 percent in 1991 to 300 percent in 1993, with a growing number of exemptions) and allowed to expire in March 1994. In August 1994, it was replaced by a new set of regulations. Second, contrary to some suggestions, the impact of protest on privatization policies was limited. Privatization was blocked in the parliament by a coalition of political forces hostile to the policy for a variety of reasons, but it was not a theme brought forth in many protest actions. Finally, protest was quite effective in blocking the restructuring of large state-owned enterprises. This was most evident in the coal-mining sector, where repeated protest campaigns prevented mine closings and mass layoffs as well as leading to an increase of state subsidies.

While assessing protest effectiveness proved to be difficult, during the 1989–93 period there was one event of tremendous political significance in which protest actions were effective. In the spring of 1993, the Solidarity trade union began a coordinated protest campaign designed to force the government, led by post-Solidarity parties, to relax its economic policies. This campaign was successful beyond all expectations: the Suchocka government was voted out of office. But success came only when a *massive protest campaign was combined with a vote of no confidence in the parliament,* initiated by Solidarity's parliamentary caucus. Solidarity's 1993 success suggests a specific combination of factors: to succeed, a well-coordinated protest must be supported by political action carried out through institutional channels. In brief, (the organizations of) civil society must act together with (the organizations of) political society if they want to maximize their chances of influencing state politics and policymaking. This finding supports a generalization that the effectiveness of protest actions increases when they are combined with more institutionalized types of pressure on states or governments (see, for example, Huberts 1989, 420–21). We will analyze this event in great detail in the next chapter.

CHAPTER 6

The Fall of the Suchocka Government: Interaction of Popular Protest and Conventional Politics

Traffic jams are nothing unusual in Warsaw; they are an accepted part of daily routine. Nonetheless, no one was prepared for what hit the streets on May 21, 1993. Tens of thousands of vehicles descended on the city, closing every available road; frustrated motorists took hours to move inches, while massive throngs of pedestrians swarmed in all directions. What was noticeably absent were city buses and streetcars. The Warsaw Metropolitan Transportation Enterprise (MZK) was on strike. The 1,300 buses and 600 streetcars that usually serve approximately 4 million passengers a day were nowhere to be found. City officials were only able to round up a mere thirty-some buses and 200 to 300 cars. If anyone had a car, they drove it. The number of vehicles on the streets more than tripled. The number of traffic police on duty also tripled—from the normal 50 to 160—but to no avail; nothing worked to dissolve this traffic nightmare.

The strike of the Warsaw Metropolitan Transportation Enterprise was part of a larger protest action organized by the Mazowsze regional chapter of the Solidarity union, one of the biggest and most influential in the country. A general strike of all enterprises and public institutions in the region began on May 20. It was the culmination of a wave of protests that had engulfed the country since March. Solidarity and other trade unions sponsored strikes and demonstrations in various regions and sectors of the economy. Most prominent, however, were protests in the nonindustrial public sector. Protestors everywhere demanded higher wages, state subsidies, and the relaxation of the state's fiscal policies.

By the end of the month, it was evident that May 1993 would go down as one of the most eventful and disruptive months of the postcommunist republic. On the twenty-eighth, the Suchocka cabinet crumbled following a vote of no confidence. President Walesa dissolved parliament on May 29 and called for new elections. This was the end of the first phase of Poland's transition led by a coalition of forces descended from the old Solidarity union and anticommunist opposition.

Were the protests and the government's collapse connected, and if so, how? What were the causes of the Suchocka cabinet's undoing? It is an important question, for the government's downfall resulted in new parliamentary elections and the unexpected victory of the ex-communist Alliance of the Democratic Left (SLD). Popular explanations of the Suchocka cabinet's fall emphasize the growing fragmentation of the post-Solidarity elite, engendered by growing divisions over the pace, direction, and extent of economic and political reforms. A part of this elite, the leadership of the Solidarity union in 1993, are often seen as the sole engineers of the government's fall. Some analysts point to the governing coalition's glaring political ineptitude; it was unable to discipline its troops at the critical moment, losing the vote of no confidence by only one vote. Almost all accounts dismiss the public (non-elite actors) as having a negligible impact on the chain of events.

We believe this is all wrong. The government's demise and the dissolution of parliament resulted from one of the most massive protest campaigns to hit Poland since the fall of state socialism. In fact, the sequence of events that engulfed the country in the spring of 1993 epitomizes the political style of the early years of democratic consolidation in Poland; it was a political style through which the trade union sector of civil society, by frequent protest actions, was *systematically* attempting to influence the decision-making process of the main organs of the state.

In July 1992 Hanna Suchocka formed the fourth Solidarity cabinet since June 1989. Her government's time in office was never free of protest. A long list of protests beginning in July 1992 includes (1) strike actions in the major state-owned enterprises whose employees felt threatened by economic reforms, (2) massive sectoral protests, and (3) extensive regional protest campaigns, usually involving the public sector employees.[1] The first category is best represented by (1) a strike in WSK PZL Mielec (a major manufacturer of military and civilian aircraft), employing some 4,000 workers. The protest was co-organized by all unions active in the enterprise and lasted, with interruptions, from mid-July until late fall of 1992; (2) the July–August strike in the Polish Copper SA Company (one of the biggest Polish exporters, employing approximately 30,000 people);[2] (3) the July–September strike in the car factory of Tychy (the manufacturer of the Polish Fiat, employing approximately 7,000 people); and (4) the August–September strike in Ursus, the Warsaw tractor manufacturer, where 5,000 to 6,000 people participated in a march and rally.

Among the sectoral protests, the strike wave that swept through the mining industry was the most massive. It began in July, gained strength in August–September, and peaked in December, when a general strike erupted in the Silesian mines. On December 23, all the mines shut down. Approximately 300,000 workers were idle in 65 out of the region's 70 mines. There were also massive protest campaigns in such sectors as the defense industry and transportation.

Huge protest campaigns paralyzed Silesia, one of the industrial centers of the country, where the Silesian Regional Directorate of the Polish State Railroads (PKP) went on partial strike, leading to the cancellation of 141 out of 801 scheduled trains. In February 1993, a general strike in the Lodz region, organized by Solidarity, immobilized economic activities in this region; in May 1993, a general strike produced a similar result in the Dolny Slask (Lower Silesia) region.

Some of these protests produced immediate results in the form of governmental concessions, including one-time payments, wage increases, and promises of revisions in restructuring policies. All of them received extensive media coverage, enhancing a growing sense of approaching crisis and political instability throughout the country. Nonetheless, two massive protest campaigns stand out due to their size and dramatic impact on the situation in the country: the prolonged protest action of the public sector employees and the general strike in the Mazowsze region of Solidarity. The transportation strike depicted at the beginning of this chapter was a culmination of the latter protest.

Spring of the People: The 1993 Protest Campaign in the Nonindustrial Public Sector

The beginnings of the statewide protest wave in the nonindustrial public sector,[3] employing about 1.1 million people,[4] can be traced back to March 1993. Various protest actions were organized by the sectoral or regional commissions of Solidarity and other unions. During the culmination of the protest wave in April–May 1993, protests were coordinated by the National Strike Committee, working closely with the National Commission of Solidarity (KK). On some occasions protests were co-organized by competing unions. Although the main union federations did not cooperate at the national level, their local chapters often did.

On March 12, approximately 10,000 representatives of all Solidarity regions participated in a march and rally in Warsaw. On April 13, the leadership of the teachers' Solidarity issued a statement announcing the beginning of preparations for a massive, continuous protest action that would begin a week before the final examinations in secondary schools (the so-called *matura*).[5] The strike was to be continued until the government accepted the union's postulates, including (1) dropping the 5 percent budget cut on education spending, which might lead to layoffs in the public sector; (2) making good on the delayed wage valorization for 1991; and (3) a wage increase of 600,000 zlotys (the government offered 390,000). Also during April, the Health Service Section of Solidarity began its own preparations for massive protest campaigns.

On May 5, 1993, the nationwide strike of teachers and other employees of the nonindustrial public sector, organized by Solidarity, began. At 6:00 a.m. the governmental hospital in Warsaw began sending its outpatients out to other hospitals. Most hospitals throughout the country were taking only emergencies.

Between 15 percent (according to the Ministry of Education) and 60–90 percent (in the National Strike Committee's estimate) of schools were closed. According to the Ministry of Education, 12 percent of elementary schools, 29 percent of college preparatory high schools, and 26 percent of vocational schools went on strike during the second day of the protest.

On May 10, as the protest wave engulfed the entire country, Ewa Tomaszewska, the head of the National Strike Committee of Solidarity, told journalists that the strike might continue for quite some time: "We do not trust the government with which we cannot have constructive conversations without strike pressure."[6] Negotiations with Deputy Prime Minister Pawel Laczkowski began and ended on May 10, when he told the Solidarity negotiators there was no possibility of meeting their wage demands.

The striking high school teachers posed a particular problem—the traditional high school examinations (*matura*) were scheduled for May 11. These exams are demanding and instrumental in determining a student's future; failure to pass bars the door to college. Moreover, they are a traditional rite of passage to the ranks of the intelligentsia and adulthood. It was unclear how many schools were going to cancel the *matura*s; it was up to local Solidarity chapters to make final decisions. On May 11, between 10 percent (according to the Ministry of Education) and 50 percent (according to Solidarity) of high schools did not hold them.

On May 12, the National Commission of Solidarity (KK) announced that if its demands were not met, it would oblige its parliamentary club to introduce a motion for a vote of no confidence on May 19. Additionally, the KK began preparation for the nationwide general strike. On May 13 the entire union was put on strike alert. On the same day, Maciej Jankowski, the chairman of the Mazowsze chapter of Solidarity (including Warsaw), announced a forthcoming regional strike on May 20.

On May 17 Prime Minister Suchocka went on national television to explain to the nation her policies and the reasons why her cabinet was unable to meet the protestors' wage demands (there was no "real money" to do so, she said). Marian Krzaklewski, the Solidarity chairman, commented immediately that after Suchocka's 11-minute TV presentation, the sides "were no closer to any solution."

On May 19 the National Commission officially rejected the governmental proposals and voted to introduce "immediately" before the Sejm a motion for a vote of no confidence (76 votes for, 3 against, 1 abstention). The next day the National Strike Committee of the Nonindustrial Public Sector decided to suspend its strike on May 24 and wait for the results of the no-confidence vote. And so on May 24 the massive protest campaign that had begun in earnest on May 5 was officially suspended.

It should be noted that during this protest campaign, Krzaklewski met several times with President Walesa, who declared his support for the protestors but expressed fear that the vote of no confidence contemplated by the union might lead to a serious political crisis. "Yes, and what next?" asked Walesa pointedly. What came next was beyond everyone's expectations. The vote of no confidence passed by one vote; the president dissolved the parliament and called for new elections. By the end of the year, the ex-communist Alliance of the Democratic Left (SLD) and its ally, the Polish Peasant Party (PSL), dominated the parliament and formed a government. The first era of postcommunist transformations, with Solidarity at the helm, was over.

Protestors' Demands and Goals

The protestors' goals were presented to the public in a barrage of official and unofficial statements and were widely reported in the media. The demands of the striking employees of the nonindustrial public sector were summarized in 10 points:

1. Maintaining the expenditures for health care, education, science, and culture at the previous year's level.
2. Abandoning the 5 percent employment reduction in the nonindustrial public sector.
3. Introduction of a more efficient taxation policy.
4. Valorization of wages in the nonindustrial public sector to the level of inflation, that is, an increase in the monthly wage by 600,000 zlotys.
5. Implementation of a ruling by the Constitutional Tribunal to valorize (raise) the wages for 1991.
6. Restoration of travel subsidies for employees of the budget sector.
7. Introduction of a new system of social security, with proper consideration given to the Solidarity proposal.
8. Valorization of the wage levels not bound by the tax on extra-normative wages.
9. Implementation of the existing legislative act on the financial restructuration of enterprises and banks.
10. Initiation of work on the budget amendment, in order to increase expenditures for social assistance.

These demands are specific, to the point, and moderate. They are focused on specific economic issues and speak mostly to concerns of the public sector employees. The broadest concerns deal with such elements of state policy as taxation, wages, banking reform, and social security reform. Significantly, the most critical political issues, such as the system's legitimacy or the appropriateness of the reform strategy, are absent from the list.

Quite clearly, however, the material demands were not limited to higher wages. Many statements reflected the protestors' concern that the severely underfunded educational system was on the verge of a virtual shutdown:[7]

> This is a strike in defense of the whole educational system, whose condition has been worsening daily. And this can lead to a civilizational collapse. There is no money in schools to purchase globes, maps, books for libraries, balls for physical education classes, and sometimes even for chalk.

At the same time, many striking teachers were painfully aware that by disrupting the education cycle, they were breaching some basic rules of their professional ethics: "This is not only about money, but about the entire educational system and its functioning. What we are doing now poses for us a true moral dilemma." The protest was, however, seen as necessary, for, as it was often emphasized, "This struggle is not only about salaries, about taking care of the basic economic needs, but about the future of the country." Moreover, in the perception of many strikers and certainly in the eyes of the Solidarity leadership, all other means of influencing the government's policies had been exhausted. Strikes were a method of last resort, and the fact that they had to be used further undermined the cabinet's credibility: "We do not trust the government, which proved by its attitude in many earlier negotiations that constructive exchanges are not possible without the pressure of strikes."

The main rhetorical style of this protest wave was, however, pragmatic; antisystemic or aggressive antigovernmental pronouncements were rare. The protestors set out to "correct" the government policies, even if it involved changing the cabinet. They chose the method of a general strike because all other means of communication with the ruling elites failed: "With the 4–5 percent growth of the gross domestic product, the expenditure of the budget sector is reduced by 10–11 percent. There is an error in the budget, and that error lies at the base of this conflict." Interestingly, Suchocka was often spared criticism, which was usually targeted at her cabinet ("Madam Prime Minister is a charming woman and it is hard to dismiss her, but the government is to be dismissed.") The cabinet and sometimes also the president were accused of incompetence:

> We have such a lack of order [nierzad] that the government [rzad] should be recalled. The general strike will force the president to take a more prostate attitude, because so far he has played for different sides and we are burdened with the costs. The president and the parliament must form a government not of ideologues, but of professionals.

As was the case with the critiques of economic policies, the tenor of the political criticism was moderate and concrete. Certain concrete politicians were asked to resign because of their performance or their erroneous policies, while calls for a wholesale systemic change were few and far between.

The Mazowsze General Strike

The protest wave that engulfed the "budget sector" constituted a powerful challenge to the Suchocka government's ability to govern. The death blow, however, was delivered by the Mazowsze chapter of Solidarity.

On May 14, newspapers printed a statement made by Maciej Jankowski, the chairman of the Mazowsze regional chapter of the Solidarity union. He announced the region was beginning preparations for the general strike called for May 20. Their central demand was a change of cabinet. As he put it:

> Madam Suchocka makes a "sympathetic" impression. It is hard to dismiss such a woman. But her government—yes. In its present composition it will not do anything constructive. It is preoccupied with the maintaining of its own existence, not with the reforms.[8]

This indolent government should be replaced with a "cabinet of experts," demanded Jankowski.

The pressure on the government increased when it became known that on May 14, the Solidarity parliamentary club and the National Commission of Solidarity were taking steps toward a vote of no confidence against the Suchocka government. The ensuing debate revealed deep divisions in the Solidarity leadership. A few influential deputies, including Jan Rulewski and Bogdan Borusewicz, threatened to change their party affiliation. There was also a lot of uncertainty as to the objective of such a move: some deputies wanted merely to "scare" the government and force it to consider issues the union deemed important.[9] Suchocka invited the union leadership for a special meeting on May 18, but the presidium of the National Commission of Solidarity immediately replied that this offer was not enough—they wanted to meet with the cabinet immediately.

Also on the fourteenth, Jankowski met with the parliamentarians from the KPN (the nationalistic Confederation for an Independent Poland) and the PSL (Polish Peasant Party) to convince them of the necessity of voting against the government. He told journalists that a strike was "95 percent certain," since the government was unwilling to accept the union's postulates.

After several weeks of preparations and warnings, on May 20, the Mazowsze region of Solidarity began the general strike.[10] The protest action took various forms, from hour-long stoppages to daylong strikes and rallies. According to Solidarity's own assessment, *one-third* of all enterprises in the region joined the protest action. Out of 2,300 enterprise chapters of Solidarity, only five refused to participate in the strike. Some enterprises could not join the strike because they were not scheduled to work that day. The most conspicuous absence in the strike was the Ursus tractor factory, the most militant Solidarity stronghold, which announced that it would join the strike only on the following day.

The demands, announced to the press a day earlier, included:

1. Freezing of price hikes for heating, gas and oil, and rents until the end of the year. Delaying the introduction of the VAT (value-added tax) until the next year.
2. Introduction of a uniform tax code for all enterprises, regardless of the type of ownership. Tax preferences should encourage investment, particularly when it creates new jobs.
3. Articulation of a policy regarding public utilities.
4. Increasing state expenditure for education, health care, and social welfare. Allocation of new resources for combating economic crimes and banditism, by introducing changes to the 1993 budget.
5. Extension of unemployment benefits in regions particularly threatened by structural unemployment.
6. An end to the labor law violations by private and state employers, particularly the infractions of the Labor Code and the agreements between the Union (Solidarity) and the government.

This set of demands differs from the demands articulated by the striking employees of the nonindustrial public sector; they clearly reflect the specific fears of the industrial workers and their insecurity engendered by enterprise restructuring.

On May 21, the Mazowsze protest action intensified; according to Solidarity, 85–90 percent of the region's enterprises joined in.[11] Its most spectacular component was the strike of the Warsaw Metropolitan Transportation Enterprise (MZK), described at the beginning of this chapter. By day's end, the Executive Committee of Mazowsze Solidarity decided to suspend the general strike in anticipation of another series of negotiations with the government and the National Commission decision on the nationwide general strike.

The political impact of the Mazowsze strike was much more extensive than its somewhat limited scope (particularly on May 20) would indicate. First, it was designed as a warning. As Jankowski put it, "the Mazowsze region action is a prelude to the nationwide action." Second, the nation's most important public space—its capital—was paralyzed by the strike. Third, it was the culmination of the earlier, massive, budget sector protest campaign that became the catalyst for the motion for a vote of no confidence in the Sejm, the lower house of parliament.

This motion was brought before the deputies by Alojzy Pietrzyk representing Solidarity on May 20. It was supported by 50 deputies from the opposition parties. The vote was held on Friday, May 28. Out of the 445 deputies present, 223 voted in favor of the motion. The government lost parliamentary confidence by one vote. This political drama was not without ironic overtones. One of the deputies of the governmental coalition was late for the vote by seven minutes; had he been there and voted with his party, the vote of no confidence would not have passed. Even more astounding is that some deputies did not understand the consequences of their actions. One of them confessed later on:

> A large group of deputies, members of the Lower House (Sejm), did not know the law sufficiently and did not foresee all the consequences of such a decision [to support the no-confidence vote]. I would venture to say that we did not have enough imagination to realize what was going to happen, within the limits of the Small Constitution and the Regulations of the Sejm, after the vote of no confidence. It is true that ignorance of the law hurts.[12]

On the following day, President Walesa refused to accept the government's resignation, dissolved the parliament, and called for new elections. This move was strongly supported by the populace.[13] The first phase of Polish postcommunist transformations—the Solidarity era—was over.

Contexts of the 1993 Protest Wave: Governmental Politics, the Economic Situation, Fluctuations of Public Opinion, and the Magnitude of Protest

As the protest wave kept swelling, the Suchocka government was busy working on several projects while trying to deal with its chief weakness: the disunity of the governing coalition. Among the governmental projects, two had high priority: the reorganization of the state administration (preparation for the second stage of the self-government reform) and the regulation of the government-labor relation through a tripartite commission (neocorporatist arrangement).

The governing coalition's disunity was increasingly apparent. For example, on March 18 the Sejm rejected the Program of Universal Privatization. This was due in part to the 12 coalition deputies who voted against their own program, while 23 others were absent. In late April, the Agrarian Alliance left the coalition over disagreements concerning agricultural policy. The increasing tension between the government and the Solidarity union, which through its deputies belonged to the coalition supporting the government, was most destabilizing.

For the Suchocka cabinet, designing and implementing the second stage of local administration reforms was a priority. What was at stake was the further power devolution from the central administration to local and regional levels. The first reform of 1990 empowered local communes; the second stage of reform was designed to create the second tier of self-government: counties (*powiaty*). The reform's blueprint was already before the parliament for deliberation and a vote when the government collapsed.

What is particularly striking in the drama of the Suchocka government is the fact that her cabinet was not insensitive to labor issues. Already by the end of July, Labor Minister Jacek Kuron presented to the parliament a draft of the "Pact on State Enterprises."[14] The six major legislative proposals constituting the pact were discussed in the Sejm on May 13, amidst the growing protest crisis. They were designed to regulate (1) the massive privatization program, (2) the rules of financing and (3) profit sharing in state enterprises, as well as such labor-related problems as (4) unemployment benefits, (5) social obligations of enterprises, and (6) workplace safety regulations.[15] The pact was comprehensive and dealt with several problems raised by the protestors. Its passage was, however, delayed by the intensifying protest wave, and it was never enacted before the government's fall. It was later approved, in February 1994, under the new government of ex-communists.

The political drama of spring 1993, in which protest politics took center stage, unfolded against the background of a robust economic recovery.[16] First, the GDP, which had already increased by 2.6 percent in 1992, grew by 3.8 percent in 1993. This growth was led by the recovery of industrial and construction output and fueled by increased consumption.[17] Second, although the unemployment rate for 1993 was 15.7 percent (compared with 13.6 percent in 1992), its growth rate during 1993, compared with the three previous years, was curtailed.

What is particularly important for our analysis is the fact that unemployment—often invoked as a major determinant of public opinion (Przeworski 1993)—began growing *only after* the political drama of May–June was over. In January 1993 unemployment stood at 14.2 percent; by May it increased merely by 0.1 percent to 14.3 percent! It reached the level of 15.7 percent only in December. In fact, as the Polish press reported, in April, compared with March, unemployment went down slightly (by 6,234 persons); it decreased even more between April and May (from 14.4 to 14.3 percent) (Vanous 1994, 22). It needs to be emphasized, then, that during the first five months of 1993, there appeared clear signs that the relentless and seemingly endless trend of increasing unemployment was halted. This observation has a theoretical significance.

Przeworski developed an argument that "among economic factors, the decline of public confidence in democratic institutions (and in the church) and the increase of confidence in the army (and recently in the police) are due almost

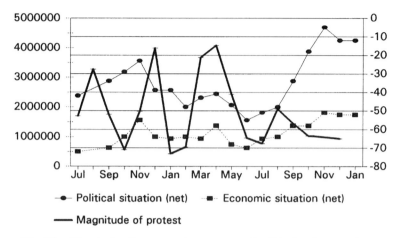

Fig. 10.   Magnitude of protest and assessment of political and economic situation, by month, July 1992–January 1994. (Data from CBOS and authors' own data.)

exclusively to mounting unemployment" (1993, 174). He also noted that "cross-sectional evidence shows that those who feel threatened by unemployment are much more likely to oppose reforms" (1993, 165). Given the data on unemployment presented above, our analysis of protest demands, and the data on protest magnitude (figure 10), Przeworski's argument does not hold for the protest wave that overwhelmed the budget sector in early 1993 and contributed to the government's fall. First, the "objective" threat of unemployment subsided in early 1993. Second, as a review of protest demands reveals, unemployment *was not* a major issue in this wave of strikes and demonstrations. Among the goals and demands of the nonindustrial public sector protest, unemployment was not mentioned at all. Third, the Warsaw region, where protests were most intense, had the lowest unemployment rate in the country. Fourth, if the magnitude of protest is taken as an indicator of people's opposition to reforms (in some general sense), then during those critical months a positive correlation between the rate of unemployment (or the rate of its increase) and opposition to reforms *did not exist.* Between October 1992 and January 1993, as unemployment was slowly but surely rising, people's assessment of both the political and economic situation of the country declined (in correlation with, or perhaps under the impact of, the swelling tide of protest actions). Between January and June 1993, as unemployment stabilized and even slightly declined, people's assessment of the political situation first stabilized, then declined. Between June and November, as unemployment increased from 14.3 to 15.5 percent, people's assessment of the country's situation (both political and economic) improved so dramatically that in November it reached the highest level in two and a half years!

If unemployment was not the primary factor determining people's attitudes toward the reforms during these eventful months, then what was? Zagorski claims that "it seems that economic and general sentiments are influenced predominantly by political rather than economic events" (1994, 372). He points out that the temporary improvement in people's evaluations in April 1993 might have been caused by such events as the adoption of a new electoral law and international celebrations of the Ghetto Uprising anniversary in Warsaw that "crowned a great improvement in Polish-Jewish relations" (1994, 372). We emphasize another factor: the magnitude and the rhetorical intensity of protest. To substantiate this claim, we will now turn to a more systematic, quantitative analysis of our data and the trends in public opinion.

As is clearly illustrated by figure 10, the magnitude of protest peaked in April. But people's assessment of the country's political and economic situation reached its lowest point since May 1992 in June. It is not easy to identify all the factors influencing public opinion and to evaluate their relative impact. Our data suggest, however, that it was not a plunge in people's independent assessment of the country's situation that led to an increase in protest activity. It was, rather, the other way around: people's assessment declined *as a result of the unprecedented intensification of protest.* The evening news was filled with reports of a large protest campaign, threats of a general strike, incessant criticism of the cabinet, and eventually the Solidarity-led vote of no confidence. People could easily conclude that "the situation of the country was bad," regardless of what the economic indicators were showing. A critical discourse developed by oppositional politicians (including union leaders) and disseminated through massive protest campaigns does not simply mediate between "objective" economic trends and public perceptions of the political and economic situation; it can directly shape these perceptions.

The spring 1993 protest wave defies predictions derived from the relative deprivation theory. In essence, this theory holds that discontent (or deprivation) begets protest. We have already suggested that in spring 1993 the relationship seems to have been reversed: protest (in one sector) begot discontent (in the population at large). Let us, however, examine other elements of the situation. As we have already mentioned, the analysis of demands indicates that protests in the budget sector were not driven by people's concern with unemployment. The protests were primarily over wages and declining state expenditure for health care and education. It became known, for example, that the total expenditure for education constituted 12.8 percent of the state budget in 1990, 11.6 percent in 1991, 10.1 percent in 1992, and 8.9 percent in 1993.[18] Furthermore, the growing discontent of the "budget" employees was justified by the relative decline of their wages compared with other sectors of the economy. In 1993 real

TABLE 30.   Wages in the Nonindustrial
Public Sector as a Percentage of Wages
in the Industrial Public Sector

1990	107.0
1991	94.0
1992	93.8
1993	88.9
1994	82.0

Source: Nowa Europa, February 7, 1995, 3.

wages in the Polish economy increased for the first time in five years (by 3.6 percent according to the Polish Statistical Office; by 1.2 percent according to Vanous 1994). But in the nonindustrial public sector, real wages *declined* by 3 percent.[19] In fact, an analysis of the ratio between wages in the nonindustrial public sector and wages in the industrial public sector demonstrates that the gap between them was systematically growing (see table 30). If we focus on the 1990–93 period, the relative deprivation theory would predict what we found in our data: the increasing magnitude of protest in the budget sector. The wages in this sector in 1993, *relative* to the wages of the industrial sector, were at their lowest since 1989. But if we include 1994 in the analysis, the theory fails: during this year, the wage gap between these two groups increased over the previous year, yet the magnitude of protest among the nonindustrial public sector employees was nowhere near its 1993 level. Ted Gurr, the main exponent of the relative deprivation theory, argues that the magnitude of protest is not simply a reflection of the level of deprivation but is, rather, co-determined by a number of factors. Among these factors, the institutional context of protest politics seems to be most critical; we will return to this issue in the final chapter. Suffice it to observe here that the lower level of protest in the budget sector in 1994 seems to have been related to the country's new political situation. From November 1993 the new social democratic (at least nominally) government was enjoying its "honeymoon" period; people were waiting to see whether its policies would reflect its pre-election promises.

The Politics of the Spring 1993 Protest:
Contentious Reformism

As we observed in chapter 5, the magnitude of protest reached its maximum since the fall of state socialism during Suchocka's term in office. The rhetoric of protest was predominantly "reformist" and nonpolitical, that is, focused on concrete economic issues. On the other hand, as we show in chapter 7, during the same period radical polarizing frames, epitomizing the "revolutionary" option in Polish politics, were used more often than during the early years of post-communist transformations. There exists, however, strong evidence indicating that these two trends, the intensification of protest and the radicalization of protest rhetoric, were at least partially unrelated.

A perfect exemplification of this bifurcation is a political fault line that opened in Solidarity during the May protests. While the Mazowsze region, led by its chairman Maciej Jankowski, went on strike on May 20–21, the militant Network Alliance and the Ursus organization, led by Zygmunt Wrzodak, organized a separate protest on May 18. On that day about 2,000 to 5,000 people, led by the Network activists, marched from the Sejm building to the government headquarters and on to the Belweder, the presidential palace. They carried with them several gallows, prepared, as they announced, for the president, the prime minister, and other officials. The demonstrators were yelling short, rhyming slogans, including "Rokita—bandit," "We will find a two-by-four for the fat Lech," "Krzaklewski is a pathetic chap," and "Put the Judeo-government on trial." The written slogans illustrated the political opinions of the protestors. "Go back to the Styrofoam" was a clear rejection of the legacy of the "first Solidarity." During the Lenin Shipyard strikes in 1980, some workers occupying the yard slept on Styrofoam sheets. The "buddies from the Styrofoam" was a rhetorical figure used to convey the camaraderie of the first great strikes that shook the communist system. Slowly, however, a new interpretation appeared: this time the invocation of "Styrofoam" meant a corrupt network of old buddies. This was the meaning intended in the May 18 march. Another slogan, "Down with the Wachowcy government," reflected the protestors' criticism of Walesa's chief of staff, Mieczyslaw Wachowski, often accused of having an unconstitutionally strong influence on the president. Relentless gossip that Walesa was somehow tainted by some form of collaboration with the communist government found an expression in another slogan: "We want a president, not an agent." On the leaflet announcing the rally, Walesa and his advisers were crossed out and an inscription announced: "Enough!" The political sympathies of the group were also clearly expressed. They displayed a placard: "Long live the Christian government of Jan Olszewski." Finally, this protest had strong nationalistic and antisemitic undertones. Several aggressively antisemitic individuals, including a young man who displayed a placard "Kill Walesa, kill Jews," were apprehended and escorted away from the demonstration.

The key Solidarity personalities involved in the 1993 "Spring of the People" included Marian Krzaklewski, the Solidarity chairman; Maciej Jankowski, the Mazowsze region chairman; and Zygmunt Wrzodak, the Ursus Solidarity chairman. It is clear that while Jankowski positioned himself as the leader of the growing wave of discontent, the pressure mounted on Krzaklewski. Thus many observers rightly pointed out that the differences between the two leaders amounted to the beginning of an intense power struggle for the union leadership before an upcoming (June) Solidarity congress. But such analyses miss the critical point that their political positions have been almost identical. A much more significant difference emerged between Krzaklewski and Jankowski on the one side and Wrzodak on the other. The first two wanted to put pressure on the government to force significant reorientation of the official state policies, but the replacement of the cabinet was not a goal in itself; both expressed respect for Suchocka; both kept the protest campaign sharply focused on labor-related issues; and, finally, both distanced themselves from the explicit "polarizing" politicization of the strikes and demonstrations, the "polarization" so characteristic of the May 18 march, organized by the Network and led by Wrzodak. Given these facts, any interpretation that casts the entire 1993 wave of protest as a populist "overreaction" to the governmental policies is erroneous.[20]

A comparison of the symbolism and rhetoric used during the May 18 demonstration with the goals and demands of both the budget sector strike and the Mazowsze general strike reveals a significant split. That fissure opened between the more moderate "pragmatist-unionist" line, represented by the leadership of the Mazowsze region and its chairman Maciej Jankowski, and the increasingly revolutionary, nationalistic option, organized through the Network Alliance and having its most visible spokesman in Zygmunt Wrzodak. The split was not merely symbolic; its political significance went well beyond the May protests. The chairman of Solidarity, Krzaklewski, and the Executive Committee of the union's National Commission condemned the May 18 demonstration and declared that the use of the Solidarity name and insignia by its organizers was illegal. The union did not endorse the "revolutionary," antisystemic stance of the Network Alliance; it framed its protest in "reformist" terms.

Such pragmatic usage of protest indicates that it was perceived as a political strategy designed to *influence* the government's reform policies, not to destabilize the new democracy or reverse economic transformations. It was a method of dialogue between "the people" and "the authorities." In fact, the government was seen as a target of protest actions even by the striking workers in private enterprises. A strike in the Luchini (formerly Warsaw) Steelworks may serve as an example. This protest was organized as part of the general strike of the Mazowsze region. The representatives of the Italian concern were understandably upset that their employees were striking although the company had already met its contractual obligations. They learned to their amazement that the protest was not directed against them but against the Polish government.[21]

The choice of protest strategy was dictated by the realization that other methods of political struggle were ineffective.[22] The existing surveys of public opinion indicate that this choice resonated with the opinions of a substantial portion of the population. For example, the CBOS asked the following question in several surveys: "Which of the following statements is closer to your opinion? (1) In the present situation only striking can lead to desired results;

and (2) In the present situation striking is basically useless." In September 1992, 21 percent of the respondents chose (1) and 59 percent chose (2). But in March 1993, option (1) was shared by 35 percent of the respondents and option (2) by 51 percent.[23]

Another study, conducted on a representative sample of the employees of larger enterprises, revealed that between November 1992 and April–May 1993, the approval of strikes as a legitimate political method increased considerably. For example, a dramatic reversal occurred in the pattern of answers to such questions as "Given the present situation, do you agree that striking indicates a lack of responsibility for the country?" While in November 1992 47 percent of the respondents agreed with this statement and 36 percent disagreed, in April–May 38 percent agreed and 45 percent disagreed.[24]

At the same time, yet another study demonstrated that the Suchocka government received *the highest ranking* of all postcommunist cabinets. Such was the opinion of 43 percent of respondents in a Pentor study. According to the same study, in July 1993, 38 percent of the respondents favored the continuation of the Suchocka cabinet's policies, while 35 percent opted for their rejection. A whopping 80 percent of respondents supported Walesa's decision to dissolve the parliament and call new elections.[25]

The picture that emerges from these and other public opinion polls and our own data indicates that during the first six months of 1993, a specific political situation developed in Poland. It may be characterized in five points:

1. The legitimacy of democracy was increasing (although radical, antisystemic rhetoric intensified, it was present in fewer than one-third of protests).
2. The Suchocka government enjoyed considerable support.
3. The party system was regarded as inefficient and unresponsive (see chapter 4).
4. The dissolution of the parliament was widely supported, for—as the Pentor study demonstrated—most people believed that was the only available method of resolving the political stalemate. Given the composition of the existing lower house of parliament, the parliament elected in 1991 was seen as unable to produce a stable and effective government.
5. Protest was seen as a legitimate method of interacting with the authorities.

This analysis brings us to one of the most important findings of our study. The volatility of the Polish political scene during the first several years of postcommunist transformations was not caused by people's dissatisfaction with the results of economic reforms alone; its causes were often located in the *specific institutional pattern* of the new polity. If we take the fall of the Suchocka government as an example, we notice that her cabinet was deposed not because of a deteriorating economic situation or a particularly acute fear of unemployment or a sudden drop in popularity among the population at large. Suchocka's government was forced to resign as a result of a concerted action by a powerful union, whose leadership and rank-and-file members decided that in order to resolve specific problems (low wages and deteriorating finances) of specific sectors (education and health care services), they had to use drastic measures of intense protest pressure in the workplace and in the streets as well as a motion on the vote of no confidence introduced by their parliamentary representation. These methods were chosen with some reluctance, after several months of failed (from the union's point of view) negotiations; they were chosen because such conventional channels of interaction with the government as political parties or the parliament were deemed *ineffective,* while neocorporatist institutions (a tripartite commission) were not yet created.[26]

The analyses presented here and in chapter 4 indicate that throughout the whole period (1989–93), protest was used as a method of influencing the government's policies or modifying governing coalitions, rather than undermining democracy. Kloc and Rychlowski reached a similar conclusion:

> The employee supporting a strike is convinced that this method will allow him/her to realize their intended goals. For its supporters, the strike is not an act of despair in a hopeless situation; it is, rather, an effective tool for forcing the realization of demands. (1994, 21)

Given these findings, the dominant political style that developed in Poland between 1989 and 1993 should be called *contentious reformism.* Bresser Pereira, Maravall, and Przeworski (1993, 208) offered a useful typology of policy styles in reforming polities.[27] They isolated four dominant types:

1. decretism, whereby a strong executive rules by decrees and imposes "from above" tough reform measures on society;
2. mandatism, whereby an executive, supported by a majority in the legislature, imposes reform measures on society without consulting with opposing parliamentary or extraparliamentary forces;
3. parliamentarism, whereby a strong majoritarian or coalition government consults and negotiates its policies with a wide range of parliamentary forces in order to obtain a strong consensus and support;
4. corporatism (concertation), whereby a government consults on its policies with a wide range of parliamentary and nonparliamentary organizations (unions, employers' associations).

The reformist style adopted by the Polish elites during the initial months of the postcommunist period can be best described as mandatism with an admixture of parliamentarism. However, as Przeworski rightly emphasizes, Polish reforms cannot be adequately categorized by considering merely the main tenor of economic policy-making. The first several years of Polish reforms were characterized by a considerable institutional feebleness (Bresser Pereira, Maravall, and Przeworski 1993, 209) and a multiplicity of political cleavages. Economic reforms were designed, adjusted, and implemented in a political context whose main features were institutional indeterminacy and political volatility. At the same time, such organizations of civil society as trade unions were bypassing the ineffectual (certainly in their perception) organizations of political society (parties and the parliament) to engage the state directly. The method of this engagement, employed with increasing magnitude, was protest. The most spectacular success this method brought about was the fall of the Suchocka government, and its most unexpected consequence was the return to power by the ex-communist forces.

Thus, while Bresser Pereira, Maravall, and Przeworski's conceptualization adequately captures the political style of the several *initial* battles over policy formation and implementation, the overall political style of the reform period's first stage (January 1, 1989–September 9, 1993) should be construed as *contentious reformism*.[28] During the early years of democratic consolidation, Poland developed neither effective parliamentarism nor neocorporatism. In parliamentarism, the inclusion of societal interests in the policy-formation process takes place through party competition inside and outside the legislative forum. To be effective, however, parties need to have a strong popular mandate and be perceived as effective representatives of social interests. In neocorporatism, institutionalization of inclusion is usually achieved through a tripartite arrangement. In postcommunist Poland, parliamentarism was weak due to the low effectiveness of political parties; neocorporatism remained uninstitutionalized until 1994. Due to such institutional developments, the Polish political system began showing many features of mandatism. It is not our task here to determine whether this political style was deliberately chosen by the Polish elites; we are merely observing that its elements became pronounced in the newly emerging institutional system.

In democratic contexts, decretism and mandatism are unstable, since sooner or later they are challenged by the excluded struggling for inclusion. If the conventional, "Western" styles of inclusion such as parliamentarism or neocorporatism do not develop, mobilized people may bypass the democratic institutions altogether by engaging in antisystemic, populist protest.[29] In Poland none of these options was realized; history and the existing institutional constraints suggested an original solution to the problem of exclusion. This solution—*contentious reformism*—emerged soon after the fall of state socialism and became the dominant style of Polish politics during the first phase of democratic consolidation.

CHAPTER 7

Cultural Frames and Discourses of Protest

At least three dimensions of postcommunist transformations, though important, are understudied. They include (1) the revival of local and regional politics, (2) cultural dilemmas associated with dramatic social, economic, and political changes, and (3) collective action and social protest. The material we collected through our research project enables us to analyze the latter two together; therefore, in this chapter we will explore the link between culture and collective action in post-1989 Polish social and political life.

We are not alone in suggesting that the cultural dimension of the recent regime transitions/transformations deserves more scholarly attention than it has hitherto received. Despite the fact that most endeavors have concentrated on the economic and political aspects of the ongoing political change, it is the remodeling of culture, and particularly *political culture,* that is often perceived as the key to successful consolidation of new regimes. Claus Offe claims, for example, that "the unique and unprecedented nature of the East European process of transformation" results to a large degree from the fact that "at the most fundamental level a 'decision' must be made as to who 'we' are, i.e., a decision on identity, citizenship, and the territorial as well as social and cultural boundaries of the nation-state" (1991, 869). Similarly, Michael Kennedy argues "that the cultural landscape matters in the construction of communism's successor, and that the formation of ideologies and identities is more complicated than most discourses of transition or revolution allow" (1994a, 1). The cultural dimension of the ongoing transformations is explicitly chosen as a fundamental yet neglected research topic by several Polish authors (Jawlowska and Kempny 1994; Tarkowska 1991).

This dimension can be conceptualized and analyzed in two basic ways: (1) as a syndrome of attitudes predominant in the postcommunist states, recorded mainly through surveys and public opinion polls;[1] or (2) as a field of sociopolitical discourses developed by individual and collective actors, which can be studied through various techniques of content analysis of imagery, rhetoric, and public behavior (e.g., rituals and ceremonies). We will employ both conceptualizations and rely on results of sociological surveys to reconstruct the popular political culture, reconceptualized, however, as political habitus. The elite political culture will be approached as a field of discourses to be deciphered through content analysis of public statements by leading politicians.

There is at least one good reason to postulate the necessity of incorporating cultural analysis into the studies of East European, particularly Polish, postcommunist transformations: in Poland, cultural revolution preceded the political revolution, and they have been intricately interwoven (Kubik 1994a, 1994c). Moreover, neglect of the cultural dimension of the postcommunist transformations in a region where culture has always been strongly and intricately intertwined with economics and politics would be a serious analytical oversight (Bibo 1991; Szporluk 1990).

As we argued in the introduction, the Polish anticommunist "refolution" (*reform* and *revolution*) was a cultural-political phenomenon of massive—by comparison with other East European countries—proportions. During the 1970s and early 1980s, a substantial number of people engaged in the formulation, development, and defense of a counterhegemonic vision, which served to delegitimize the state-socialist system and, simultaneously, allowed these people to constitute themselves as an "oppositional" cultural class. We interpret Solidarity not as a trade union or a movement, but as a cultural class *in statu nascendi,* never fully "consolidated," subjected to the tremendous internal centrifugal tensions that operated together with the centripetal forces of symbolic unification. By 1991, the centrifugal political (both programmatic and personal) tensions destroyed Solidarity (as a specific "cultural" class), but throughout the 1980s a substantial portion of the Polish populace "belonged" to it—either actively, by engaging in various clandestine activities, or passively, by giving it their "moral support." The cultural frame that held this class together was built as a polar vision of "us/the people/Solidarity" versus "them/authorities/communists."

The events that helped the "opposition" to construct this hegemonic polar cleavage included two papal visits to Poland, the murder of Father Jerzy Popieluszko and the immediate emergence of his cult, and countless street demonstrations and clashes with the police, as well as large industrial strikes in 1988. Not everybody, of course, participated in this ongoing political and symbolic confrontation with the regime, and not everybody accepted the polar vision of the conflict. In fact, the actual numbers of those who supported Solidarity kept declining throughout the 1980s and rebounded only after Solidarity's spectacular electoral victory in 1989 (Jasiewicz 1993a, 129–30). Yet the perception of the hegemonic conflict between "us" and "them" continued to be the most characteristic feature of Polish popular political culture.[2]

To summarize, during the waning years (1976–89) of state socialism in Poland, the extreme, polar conceptualization of the public space ("us" versus "them") was a crucial weapon in the society's struggle against the regime.[3] This bipolar conceptualization, or (di)vision, was not shared by everybody, yet it served as a mobilizing frame for the *most active* individuals and groups. An intriguing question emerges: what happened to this polarizing vision or, at least, to a predilection to visualize the world in bipolar terms after the fall of state socialism in 1989? Has its political significance as a mobilizing frame diminished? Has it evolved, changing content while retaining the basic polar structure? During the initial stages of our project, we hypothesized that since the Polish "refolution" was symbolically most elaborate, the postcommunist consolidation in Poland should be besieged by "oversymbolized" politics, that is, politics excessively preoccupied with questions of the political actors' identity. Furthermore, we suspected that this oversymbolization should be routinely expressed in bipolar terms.

Popular Political Culture, Elite Political Culture, and Collective Action Frames

For Tarrow, the relationship between culture ("ideational materials") and action, and in particular "the construction of meaning in social movements," is best conceptualized when the culture—a "catch-all" concept—is broken down into three "concepts of successively declining generality and increasing purposiveness—social mentalities, political cultures, and collective action frames" (1992b, 176). We will work with another, similar triad, including popular political culture, elite political culture, and collective action frames.

We define political culture, following Gamson, as "the meaning systems that are culturally available for talking, writing, and thinking about political objects: the myths and metaphors, the language and idea elements, the frames, ideologies, values, and condensing symbols" (1988, 220).

Popular political culture includes the politically relevant "meaning systems" utilized and constructed by the "followers," the "average" people. Since in any modern, complex society there are many separate social groups, networks, milieus, strata, and classes, and many of them have their own meaning systems, it is crucial to conceptualize the situation as a multitude of popular political cultures. What they have in common is the fact that they are all cultivated by "amateurs," that is, people who rarely "professionally" produce frames, ideologies, values, etc., but rather take them for granted as pre-given systems of categories that organize their thoughts and direct their actions. Elite political culture is the system of meanings produced by the political elite.[4] It may be quite diversified, so again it may be advisable to think about several elite political cultures. What they share is a high level of elaboration and articulation in comparison with popular political cultures; moreover, they are usually deliberately (re)produced by Bourdieu's "professionals."[5]

In this chapter we do not attempt to reconstruct various popular political cultures of postcommunist Poland; we will merely attempt to outline some of the most general features that many of these cultures seem to share. Most of these features will be extracted from the writings of Polish sociologists, who did not study systems of meanings (semiotic phenomena) per se, but rather syndromes of attitudes and people's actions (psychosocial phenomena). The nature of the bulk of the evidence—sociological generalizations based on attitudinal surveys—calls for a specific reconstruction and conception of culture. We cannot reconstruct political culture (as a meaning system) directly, but instead we can summarize certain features of people's actual political and politically relevant reactions and actions, in most cases revealed through attitudinal surveys. Since these actions and reactions are intricately interwoven with people's "everyday" conceptualizations of their situation, we will use Bourdieu's habitus to conceptualize this complex syndrome of acting and thinking.[6] A brief characterization of this *political habitus,* presented in chapter 3, must suffice in place of an analysis of the popular political culture construed as a *semiotic* phenomenon.

Elite political culture will be reconstructed through the analysis of political rhetoric and symbolic displays by leading politicians. The same method will be used to reconstruct collective action frames: we will analyze dominant demands, types of action, slogans, visual symbols, songs, and rhetoric employed by the protestors. We take the concept of "frame" from Snow and Benford, who in turn borrow it from Goffman (1974, 21). It denotes "'schemata of interpretation' that enable individuals 'to locate, perceive, identify, and label' occurrences within their life space and the world at large. By rendering events or occurrences meaningful, frames function to organize experience and guide action, whether individual or collective" (Snow and Benford 1988, 214). The concept "frame of meaning" closely corresponds to the concepts of "schema" developed by Ortner (1989) and "root paradigm," prominently featured in Victor Turner's writings (1978, 248–49). Ortner emphasizes the tremendous flexibility and variability of the relationship between actors and cultural schemas. As she puts it: "Some actors are manipulating it (the schema); some are 'driven' by it; some are moved merely by the logic of the moment; and some use the schema to interpret the behavior of others. At one level the variations matter." But in a conclusion she claims that "at another level they [the variations] add up to many modes of 'enacting' the schemas, the notion of enactment here being a shorthand for the varying ways in which people hold, and are held by, their culture" (1989, 129).

Our analysis will be based on an assumption that the creators of collective action frames in postcommunist Poland, in their attempts to mobilize people, had to take into consideration *two* types of cultural capital: the "mundane" capital of the popular political habitus and the more "elaborate" capital of the elite political culture(s). In order to assess the mobilizing efficacy of frames employed by protest organizers, we will compare the main features of the popular political habitus with *both* the central characteristics of the elite political culture and the dominant collective action frames. Finally, it should be emphasized that the influence of elite political culture on the people's perceptions of reality is not just hypothesized; it has been corroborated by empirical studies. Swida-Ziemba writes:

> Another specific phenomenon that was not found under communist rule is that contents appearing in the discourse (statements of politicians, journalists, and publicists) are not rejected nowadays as before but internalized by their recipients. (1994, 230)

Additionally, Swida-Ziemba determined that this internalization is selective: people tend to accept mostly *negative visions of the post-1989 reality.*

Polish Popular Political Culture (as Portrayed by Polish Sociologists)

A composite portrait of the Polish postcommunist habitus emerges from a review of several major studies completed by Polish sociologists. We presented this portrait in chapter 3. Here we will merely list its major features. The Polish "political habitus," encompassing a range of "dispositions" influencing people's perceptions, evaluations, and actions they undertake within the public arena, was dominated by

1. cultural chaos;
2. uncertainty and insecurity;
3. political passivity (political apathy) and alienation from politics;
4. lack of trust in the new political elite;
5. political indeterminacy.

Additionally, the public tended to perceive the political field as fragmented and divided across several cleavages. The 1989 "refolution" brought down the communist regime and elevated to power a new elite—initially drawn almost completely from the Solidarity movement. However, the popular perception of the new elite was not bipolar ("communists" versus "Solidarity"), but rather fragmented. In table 31, we present the results of two studies revealing this fragmentation.

This complex perception of political cleavages in the country was confirmed by several sociological studies. They demonstrated that after 1989, the predominantly bipolar vision of the sociopolitical reality, so characteristic of the 1970s and 1980s (if not most of the communist period), was losing its hegemonic power over people's political imagination: *di*vision was replaced by *mul-tivision.* Table 32 summarizes Jasiewicz's report on the distribution of answers

TABLE 31.   Visions of the Post-1989 Political Elite (in percentages)

	"Poles 1990"	CBOS 1992
The communist dictatorship has been replaced by democracy.	19.9	9
The communist dictatorship has been replaced by a new dictatorship under the Solidarity banner.	12.5	16
The new authorities have replaced communists, but the end result is still uncertain.	32.1	27
The clergy, the (Roman Catholic) Church, rule behind the backs of the new authorities.	Option not included	18
The same people who used to rule under communism continue to rule behind the backs of the new authorities.	19.0	15
No opinion	15.8	15

Source: Jasiewicz 1993a, 125.

Note: The data for the "Poles 1990" study was collected in October 1990. Kolarska-Bobinska (1992) presents the results of the October 1992 CBOS study.

when respondents were asked which groups or institutions were the parties to conflict in post-1989 Poland.

This trend toward increased fragmentation of the popular vision of the elite was, however, quickly reversed. Already in 1992, a CBOS study discovered a *renewed* salience of the bipolar "authorities versus society" vision. Answering the question "Who are the participants in social conflicts in Poland?" 33 percent of the respondents chose the "conflict above our heads, within the political elite" option, while 23 percent felt that the sides in this conflict are "the authorities and society" (Kolarska-Bobinska 1992, 11). Whereas in 1990 the latter

TABLE 32.   Answers to the "Who Are the Parties to the Conflict?"

Authorities, government, etc., and nation, society, etc.	4.2%
Towns and country	9.8%
Authorities (old or new) and Solidarity	2.9%
PZPR, communists, party members, and others	2.6%
The rich and the poor	4.5%
Old authorities and new authorities	3.5%
Different parties with one another	6.0%
Conflict with the government, among the authorities	2.8%
Conflict within Solidarity	3.5%
Walesa and Mazowiecki	3.5%

Source: Jasiewicz 1993a, 137.

option was selected by 4 percent of the respondents, in 1992 it was chosen by almost *one-quarter* of the surveyed sample.

To recapitulate, the dominant features of the Polish habitus (representing here popular political culture) in the 1989–93 period were uncertainty, lack of trust in politics, flux, indeterminacy, and fragmentation. The populace was largely withdrawn from politics, primarily concerned with the economic situation (see chapter 3), and quite involved in civic initiatives (see chapter 4). There existed, however, pockets of vulnerability to extreme rhetoric, which mobilized some groups to political protests expressing total dissatisfaction with the post-1989 changes.

Dualism of the Polish Elite Political Culture

During periods of rapid social change, culture becomes fragmented and *decentered,* yet at the same time the link between culture (discourses, symbols, rhetoric, etc.) and politics intensifies (Jawlowska 1994). There seem to be two basic mechanisms that propel this process. First, as Swidler observes:

> Culture has independent causal influence in unsettled cultural periods because it makes possible new strategies of action—constructing entities that can act (selves, families, corporations), shaping the styles and skills with which they act, and modelling forms of authority and cooperation. (1986, 280)

Second, many people during such unstable periods tend to retreat to their private or "parochial" worlds. It is well established that "the pattern of retreat into parochial institutions . . . is a characteristic response for many people when faced with a larger society that is culturally unfamiliar" (Wilson 1991, 213). If escapism is the frequent reaction to unfamiliarity resulting from instability and rapid change, then the public space is left to elites and political entrepreneurs (Bourdieu's professionals). As a result, they have a unique opportunity to "model the forms of authority and cooperation" in political space without the challenge they would have had to encounter had the situation been more stable and had civil and political societies been more active.[7] In brief, during the period following the downfall of the "ancien régime," social control over political entrepreneurs is relaxed, and consequently they face a unique opportunity to engage in defining the shape of the new, emerging political and social order. Under such circumstances, protest is not simply a symbolic tool to *challenge* or *support* a specific hegemonic frame legitimating the incumbent regime's power; it becomes a part of the struggle to *establish* a new hegemonic framework for all present and future political conflicts.[8]

This is exactly what has been happening in Poland since 1989. Polish elites have engaged in a bitter struggle to find suitable and acceptable cultural capitals and construct out of them a viable hegemony, that is, a durable cultural frame that would be able to produce enough consensus around their programs of postcommunist consolidation. In postcommunist Poland there existed many building blocks (types of political capital, discourses) that could be used in the creation of such hegemony. They included, for example, "nationalism," "Catholicism," "socialism," and "liberalism." Quite often they were combined in bizarre—from the Western point of view—ways. For example, most actors supported the creation of a market economy, but some of them simultaneously espoused welfarist-statist views. Thus, their rhetoric and programmatic statements tend to fluctuate, seemingly due to their assessment of the changing balance of forces in the social and political fields. The picture that emerges from the analyses provided by several Polish political sociologists indicates a fragmented and awkwardly complicated (by Western standards) political field. Moreover, it is a field with several intersecting cleavages. Yet, as we claim in chapter 3, during the "early" consolidation phase (1989–92), Polish elite political culture was polarized.[9] A bipolar cleavage emerged "above" or "beyond" the multiplicity of other cleavages and can be best construed as an opposition between *the logic of the rule of law,* espoused by the reformists, and *the revolutionary logic,* developed by the revolutionaries. Differences between both styles of politics, discussed in chapter 3, are summarized in table 33.

The cleavage between revolutionaries and reformists cut across other cleavages. It did not manifest itself clearly on the left side of the political spectrum, where both the "post-Solidarity left" (Labor Union) and the "ex-communist left" (Alliance of the Democratic Left) tend to be by and large reformist.

TABLE 33.   Revolutionaries versus Reformists

	"Revolutionary" Option	"Reformist" Option
Diagnosed relation of the post-1989 political order to state socialism	Continuity (at least partial)	Discontinuity (considerable)
Postulated regulation of transition	Revolutionary logic	Rule of law
Postulated logic of transition	Clean-cut (*ruptura*)	Gradual (*reforma*)
Postulated basic principle of regime	Substantivist (rule of majority)	Formalist (rule of law)
Principal cause of economic problems	Post-1989 policies	Pre-1989 policies
Principal political objective	Completion of state socialism's deconstruction	Acceleration of the new order's consolidation
Attitude toward tighter incorporation within "Europe"	Reserved, sometimes hostile	Supportive, often enthusiastic

The right side of the spectrum was, however, more clearly divided. There was the so-called progovernmental right (they supported the Mazowiecki, Bielecki, and Suchocka governments), Aleksander Hall and his Polish Convention being the most clear exponent of this "reformist" option. The revolutionary right (the "center-right," the "independence right," or the "antigovernmental right") was represented by, among others, the Movement for the Republic, led by Jan Olszewski, Antoni Macierewicz, and Jan Parys; and the Center Alliance, led by Jaroslaw Kaczynski.

As this split within the right camp indicates, the revolutionaries/reformist cleavage belongs to these symbolic and rhetorical fault lines that divide people very deeply, for they locate them in separate political-symbolic realms. Aleksander Hall observed: "To say that [the ruling] coalition belongs to the left, is simply to say something patently false. And here lies the basic difference between us: in *naming and understanding reality*" (emphasis added).[10] It is, however, important to remember that many revolutionaries (e.g., Olszewski or Kaczynski) did not transgress the rules of the democratic political game *in practice;* their revolutionary inclinations were, however, clear in their rhetorics.

Frames of the Elite Political Culture

Public discourse developed by Polish political elites during the 1989–93 period provides many examples of the dualistic (bipolar) conceptualization of the country's political field and political culture. For example, the reformists often saw themselves as *enlightened Europeans* and their opponents as *hateful revanchists*. Revolutionaries in turn defined themselves as *true anticommunists* who faced *the alliance of the Reds and Pinks*. In extreme conceptualizations, the revolutionaries' enemies were portrayed as *alien manipulators,* including "foreign capitalists," "Masons," and "Jews." Master frames of the elite political culture contain several elaborate versions of these basic distinctions. What follows is a collection of statements illustrating this phenomenon.

A. Reformists Conceptualizing Revolutionaries

Reformist frame 1: Revolutionaries are extreme. Jan Litynski (an influential politician of the Democratic Union), when asked whether accusing Walesa of secretly collaborating with the communist security forces was a political game or a folly, answered:

> Game comes in later; initially you have revolutionary vigilance, as in the case of Nechayev, Dzerzhinsky, or leftist and rightist terrorists: the rejection of what exists or existed in the name of the total elimination of evil. This must lead to folly, to the disavowal of values in whose name one is acting. (*Gazeta Wyborcza,* July 22, 1992)

Reformist frame 2: Revolutionaries are populist, for they prevent or delay the consolidation of the "normal" parliamentary system. For example, Aleksander Hall described the main dilemma of Polish politics in the following fashion:

> I believe, that the time has come to consolidate the forces of all [political] groups which want to stabilize parliamentary democracy in Poland. And this calls for a cooperation of people representing christian-democratic, conservative, and moderately social-democratic (in the western sense of the word) views. In my interpretation the program of the party or coalition that is being formed around Jan Olszewski, is based on a conviction that the system we now have in Poland must be replaced through early elections . . . [which they] want to win by rousing people's anger directed against elites.[11]

Reformist frame 3: Revolutionaries are unsophisticated. This frame was rarely used in the official public discourse, yet it emerged in many private conversations we had with various reformists during the 1989–93 period. It has been reported, for example, that a prominent politician of the "reformist" Democratic Union referred to the "revolutionary" politicians as "stinking men with wet palms."

Reformist frame 4: Revolutionaries are evil (demonizing). Antoni Macierewicz was often accused of having "evil eyes."[12]

B. Revolutionaries Conceptualizing Reformists

Revolutionary frame 1: Reformists are crypto-communists, for they collaborate with or at least protect the interests of the former communists. Macierewicz observed: "Today's Poland needs the unification of the right. In order to shatter *the vicious circle of the post-roundtable drama* [emphasis added], which is being played in front of our eyes." "We need to liberate Poland from the rule of the left, which is based on lies, enslaves our nation, and attempts to subdue it to the power from the East" (*Polityka,* May 12, 1992).

Revolutionary frame 2: The break between the Polish People's Republic and the post-1989 system has not yet occurred or has not been decisive enough. Another quote from Macierewicz illustrates the usage of this frame: "First of all, the communist system still continues. . . . It is a personal, economic, political, but also legal continuity, since the Stalinist constitution still holds. Only the labels have changed. In Russia the system's continuity is even more pronounced than in Poland" (*Ilustrowany Kurier Polski,* September 18–20, 1992).

Revolutionary frame 3: Solidarity politicians who participated in the roundtable negotiations and later formed the ROAD (Civic Movement—Democratic Action) and the Democratic Union are associated with "the Reds"—

the former communists from the PZPR. This association is so close that they merit the name "Pinks." The "Pinks" frame was very influential in the elite political culture of the early 1990s; we will discuss it in detail in the next section.

Revolutionary frame 4: Reformist economic policies ruined the Polish economy. Macierewicz observed:

> We are talking—first of all—not about instigating a wave of demands for entitlements. This wave of social discontent exists. It is a drama that such parties that call themselves "the right"—like yours—do not want to notice this wave, or perhaps they believe that they can ignore it. But this wave results from the mistakes that are being committed [now].

The "Pinks" Master Frame: A Case Study

For a politician to align himself or herself with "socialist" or "social democratic" discourse in postcommunist Poland proved to be a much more treacherous undertaking than to take on the mantle of the "liberal" or "Christian democrat." In a country emerging from forty-some years of "actually existing socialism," almost everything that could be even loosely associated with "the left" was turned into an unpredictable political weapon. However, a politician identifying herself or himself as an exponent of such an ideology/program could count on increasing (as the 1993 election demonstrated) sympathy from those who found it difficult to abandon the ideals of egalitarianism and the practical comforts of the welfare-state safety net or those who would like to see the reversal of history and the return of "actually existing socialism." Yet this was a hazardous step. Politicians had to remember that by declaring publicly their "socialist" identity, they would subject themselves to fervent "negative" framing by the influential parties of the "center" and the "right." This framing strategy boiled down to a simple two-step precept: (1) keep hammering into people's minds that there is only one "left"—the same one they know so well from their experience with "actually existing socialism"; and (2) label your political enemy as a member of this "left." The conclusion, explicitly stated or merely suggested, was obvious: if a party, person, movement, etc., was identified or identified itself as "left," it had to be classified as a successor of "actually existing socialism" (totalitarian communism), which had left the country in ruins.

An elaborate version of this strategy was applied by the Center Alliance (PC) and other parties of the right in their competition with the ROAD, and later with the UD (Democratic Union), for primacy over the Polish political scene (the PC, the ROAD, and the UD evolved out of the Solidarity movement). In what follows, we will reconstruct the logic of this strategy, which constituted the backbone of one of the most influential political discourses in Poland in 1990–91.

Thesis 1. The new political order that emerged after the collapse of communism is fragile and constantly endangered by a counteroffensive from the postcommunist forces. In a PC programmatic pamphlet, *Why Acceleration?* Jaroslaw Kaczynski wrote:

> A serious danger is associated with such a course of transformations in our country, which allows the groups that in essence are in a minority and whose orientation is antidemocratic (postcommunist) to retain very significant positions in social life and exercise control over essential elements of the economic, political, and informative infrastructure. (1990, 4)

Moreover, PC activists often argued that "the forces of the old regime are on the offensive";[13] thus something must be done to terminate a harmful continuity between the new Polish Republic and the communist Polish People's Republic. Kaczynski demanded: "The Polish state must be new, it cannot continue the traditions of the Polish People's Republic" (1990).

Thesis 2. The "left" segment of the political spectrum includes not only the postcommunist Social Democracy of the Polish Republic and post-Solidarity left parties (PPS [Polish Socialist Party], Solidarity of Work, Democratic-Social Movement), but also some significant parts, if not the whole, of the Democratic Union, particularly such leaders and supporters of this party as Kuron, Michnik, and Mazowiecki. Kaczynski expounded this thesis frequently:

> We do not consider our political opponents to be communists; nevertheless, they belong to the left—their attitude toward the Polish communist past is different from the attitude of the non-left people, it is based on the concept of a "thick line," it is an attitude that rejects the uprooting of this past. (1990)[14]

Thesis 3. Mazowiecki, Michnik, Kuron, and the Democratic Union (formerly ROAD), as well as their allies—that is, "the post-Solidarity left"—strive to achieve a monopoly of power in the country[15] and, perhaps inadvertently, create such political conditions that allow the former communists to preserve, if not expand, their economic and political influence. In various political writings of the Center Alliance publicists, the reasoning contained in this thesis was often taken one step further. A modified version of thesis 3 would usually take the following form:

Thesis 3'. There exists an "objective" convergence of interests between the postcommunist and the post-Solidarity "left." This thought was fully developed in a Center Alliance pamphlet, *The Essence of the Controversy: The Center versus ROAD:*

> Since the completion of the roundtable negotiations, the opposition group, which achieved power through these negotiations, quite naturally devel-

oped an interest in the maintenance of the division of power designed at the roundtable. What has been created, then, is an objectively paradoxical alliance of the former functionaries and the groups who were earlier brutally persecuted by them. Both formations can lose their influence when the far-reaching systemic reforms are instituted in this country. The Solidarity left could retain its influence through the preservation of unity of the citizens' movement that it headed, at least until the free elections, which it would win decisively, earning four more years to strengthen its influence. In such a situation, the old apparatus would take positions next to the citizens' movement, assuming Solidarity's mantle as their own and supporting Solidarity's leadership, but at the same time blocking structural changes. The forces of the center and the right, striving for the possibly fastest possible transformation, became the common enemy [of this alliance]. (Drozdek 1990, 18)

Finally, in the pronouncements of the more radical politicians of the Center Alliance or the "right" parties, the line of reasoning represented by theses 3 and 3' would culminate in its politically most explosive form, thesis 3".

Thesis 3". There exists an actual political alliance between "the postcommunist left" and "the post-Solidarity left." This idea was expressed in various forms. Adam Gwizdz, an influential Center Alliance activist in the Bielsko region, declared in an interview: "According to public sentiment, not only are the present authorities incompetent, but also, together with the postcommunists, *they oppress the nation*" (emphasis added; *Kronika Beskidzka,* April 25, 1991). The Supreme Council of the ZChN (the Christian National Union, a vocal representative of the "right") issued a statement declaring that the Democratic Union "has been, for some time now, linked through an actual political alliance" with the communists. Moreover, this "alliance of the postcommunist and Solidarity left" is driven by the desire to "reinforce in Poland a system originating in communism" (*Gazeta Wyborcza,* March 19, 1991). Stefan Niesiolowski, a leader of the ZChN, claimed: "We do not invent the alliance of the 'pinks' with the 'reds.' The leaders of the 'pinks' talked about this alliance already in the fall of 1989" (*Gazeta Wyborcza,* May 6, 1991).

Jacek Kuron, a vice-chairman of the Democratic Union, and Adam Michnik, the editor of *Gazeta Wyborcza,* commonly perceived as a close ally of this party, vehemently denied that there existed an "actual alliance" between them and the postcommunists. They also rejected the "left" label attributed to them by the Center Alliance. Kuron declared:

I would like to belong to the "left" very much. But at this moment Polish society faces the problem of building what I would call a capitalism with a human face. I cannot build capitalism proclaiming that I am "the left," because that would be a deception. We believe that an ideological party, a "worldview" party, is not a precept for a party in the current situation of our country at all. Moreover, I will honestly confess that a party based on a "worldview" is a very bad thing. (TV program *Klincz,* March 14, 1991)

Michnik was even more poignant in his denial. In a TV "duel" with Kaczynski, he said:

let's stop labeling each other. Please do not call me "the secular left," or any "left," and I promise I will not call you a "Muslim right." (November 21, 1990)

Despite such straightforward denials, the Center Alliance continued to depict its political opponents as "the people of the left," with all the ensuing consequences we outlined above. It constructed and disseminated a discourse in which their political opponents (1) were defined as "the people of the left" or as "the post-Solidarity left" and (2) were equated with or presented as a close ally of "the postcommunist left." Significantly, in this discourse "communism" and "socialism" were never clearly defined, but meshed imperceptibly with each other. Thus, a bipolar master frame was created, which served not to legitimize one's political power but to delegitimize a political opponent.

Although it is difficult to assess its popularity and influence, we concluded that the "Reds-Pinks versus others" bipolar frame was the most pervasive and elaborate of all frames we were able to detect within the elite political culture during the 1989–91 period. Through further, less systematic observations we came to the conclusion that later (1992–93), the usage of this frame *among the political elite* declined. Wasilewski's work on the Polish political elite confirmed this insight: by 1993 this elite was less polarized than earlier and more fragmented along several cleavage lines. Moreover, amid this fragmentation, new, more systematic *political* divisions were slowly emerging. As Wasilewski put it: "The new structure reflects political and ideological differences in a more distinct and coherent way than the old bipolar structure" (1995, 129).

Frame Resonance, or On the Conditions
of Successful Protest Mobilization

Having identified the main frames of the elite political culture, we set out to determine (1) whether these or similar frames were employed by organizers and participants of collective actions, and (2) how strongly these protest frames resonated with basic everyday frames, organizing the post-1989 Polish habitus.

The basic concept used in these investigations is resonance. Resonance occurs when an "obvious" or at least "convincing" linkage between a protest frame proposed by the mobilizers and a commonsense frame guiding the mobilized in their everyday life (*Lebenswelt,* habitus) is formed.[16] The mobilizers include party and union leaders or various activists ("professionals"). The mobilized are the people to be involved in collective action.

Our research protocol contained three items designed to record both the slogans displayed or recited by protestors and the comments they offered to journalists. Unfortunately, the press accounts did not always have this kind of information. In 1989, out of 314 recorded protest events, accounts of only 32 (10 percent) provided information concerning the *political rhetoric* of slogans and participator comments. Information for the following three years is, however, more comprehensive. For 1990, out of 306 event descriptions, 67 (22 percent) contained relevant information; for 1991, 100 out of 292 case descriptions (34 percent) contained information pertaining to rhetoric. For 1992 the ratio is 117 out of 314 (37 percent); for 1993, 83 out of 250 (33 percent).

Slogans and participator comments from 399 protest events were grouped into five basic types of frames.[17] While constructing this typology, our primary consideration was to determine how often the polarizing frames developed within the elite political culture were employed by the protestors; in other words, we wanted to determine the strength of the alignment between the most radical frames of the elite political culture and the framing (conceptualization, symbolization) of protest. The five types, 10 subtypes, their examples, and relevant comments follow.

1. *Anticommunist and anti-Soviet frames.* These frames were particularly suitable to challenge the legitimacy of the pre-1989 political order and those of its institutions that continued to exist afterward. They should therefore be used frequently in 1989 and 1990, when the institutions of communism were gradually phased out, and afterward their usage should decline. Examples of such frames include "Down with communism," "Down with the commune," "Soviets go home," "Down with the Soviets," and "Communists, consider your own Nuremberg."

2. *Polarizing frames (nationalistic and antisemitic).* They were employed *systematically* only by four types of organizations: (*a*) radical nationalists such as Tejkowski's Polska Wspolnota Narodowa—Polskie Stronnictwo Narodowe (Polish National Union—Polish National Party) or the Narodowy Front Polski (Polish National Front); (*b*) moderate nationalists such as the KPN; (*c*) radical trade unions such as Chrzescijanski Zwiazek Zawodowy "Solidarnosc" imienia J. Popieluszko (the J. Popieluszko Christian Trade Union "Solidarity") or Federacja Zwiazkow Zawodowych Gornikow (Federation of Miners' Trade Unions), led by Rajmond Moric; and (*d*) radical populist organizations such as Samoobrona (Self-Defense). We identified three subtypes of polarizing frames:

2.1. Polarizing frames rejecting the post-1989 political order as illegitimate. Employment of such frames could mean only one thing: a total (even if only "symbolic") rejection of the post-1989 political order. We were particularly interested in finding out whether protestors were inclined to employ the "Pinks" master frame and/or its derivatives. The dominant frames of this group were "the commune" (*komuna*)—in reference to the Solidarity governments and institutions; "crypto-commune"; or "Judeo-commune" (*Zydokomuna*). We decided, however, to classify the latter with other antisemitic frames. Many frames in this category were used in slogans beginning with "Down with . . . ," as in "Down with the commune," "Down with the Judeo-commune." They served to delegitimize the post-1989 political order by defining it as a continuation of communism. Other examples of frames belonging to this group include "Communists to Cuba," "Magdalenka = Targowica,"[18] "Crypto-commune, stay away from our property" or "Enough of the crypto-commune's rule," "Solidarity is betraying the interests of the working people and selling out to the nomenclature," and "Okapizm + Walesism = Komunism."[19]

2.2. Nationalistic polarizing frames (purity frames). They seem to have served to delegitimize the post-1989 political order by defining it as ethnically/nationally *impure* and calling for its purification. The most frequent examples: "Poland for Poles," "Long live Great Poland," "We won't allow Polish soil to be taken away."

2.3. Antisemitic polarizing frames. They served to reject the post-1989 political and social order by defining it as controlled by or associated with the Jews. There appear to have been two basic subtypes of such frames: (1) frames associating Jews with communism, as in "Down with the Judeo-commune" (Precz z Zydokomuna); and (2) clear-cut antisemitic slogans, including "A good Jew is a dead Jew." Any issue, it seems, could be incorporated into an antisemitic frame, which then served to turn a political opponent into an "alien," as in "Walesa, the Jew." For example, social policies of the Mazowiecki government, personified by the Labor Minister Jacek Kuron, were attacked in the slogan that read "Shame! We do not want soups. Let Kuron himself eat them!"[20] But on another occasion the following quasi-syllogism was displayed: "'Jews to the oven,' 'Kuron to the oven,' 'Make soup out of Kuron.'"

3. *Reformist political frames.* Slogans employing these frames did not call for the rejection or abolition of the regime; neither did they seek to delegitimize it by indicating its national impurity or "Jewish connections," etc. They simply expressed criticism of some policies or politicians. For example, on March 7, 1990, a demonstration organized by Citizens' Committees displayed a placard that pronounced, "The government is not enough—[local] self-government is needed." On May 1, 1992, during a rally co-organized by Social Democracy of the Polish Republic, a journalist noted the following slogans: "Enough corruption!" "Stelmachowski to a parish office," "Lech Walesa must go—no replacement."

4. *Frames criticizing specific economic policies.* "Economic" slogans and

self-comments expressed a wide range of the populace's concerns. They were often moderate, as exemplified by the following quotation: "The aim of the strike is not to force pay raises but to defend the enterprise against bankruptcy." Other examples: "We protest against the drastic salary reductions in light industry"; "Amnesia can be cured. Kaszpirowki—heal our ministers."[21]

Slogans expressing criticism of governmental economic policies were sometimes personalized. Then their most frequent target was Leszek Balcerowicz, deputy prime minister and finance minister in both the Mazowiecki and Bielecki governments. For example, on May 24, 1990, demonstrators displayed: "The Balcerowicz program—to be corrected." On one occasion the slogan "Replace Balcerowicz" was accompanied by another one pronouncing "We apologize for the [road] blockade" and a comment: "We do not want to block Poland, but we want to unblock thinking about agriculture."

5. *Frames concerning specific issues (ecological, feminist, AIDS-related, local problems).* According to our analysis, this type had three subtypes. They included:

5.1. Ecological slogans. Examples: "Life in Zabrze = death sentence," "The Czorsztyn dam = the death of nature," "Nuclear energy—stop."

5.2. Slogans and statements expressing feminists' issues as well as pro-choice or pro-life concerns. The slogan "Spring is yours—ass is ours" was yet another take on the theme "Something is yours, something else is ours," initiated with "The winter is yours, the spring is ours," often heard after the imposition of martial law on December 13, 1981. It was also used by Michnik in the summer of 1989 in his famous proposal "Your president, our prime minister."

5.3. Slogans related to AIDS. Examples: "We do not want Kotanski and his protégées,"[22] "Fags—get out."

5.4. Slogans or statements expressing concrete, specific (often local) concerns and demands. Examples: "The Holocaust will never happen again," "The PZPR buildings for the University," "The press, radio, and television lie," "Remove the sex shop," "Poles demand the recognition of Lithuania's independence."

The frequency distribution of the five types of frames is presented in figure 11. We have to assume that due to the methodology of data gathering, our database is incomplete and its representativeness is hard to determine; thus the following conclusions must be taken with a grain of salt and should be read only as an attempt to identify general trends. These trends are, however, clear.

First, throughout the whole period, the protest rhetoric was predominantly focused on concrete, often economic, issues. Frames related to economic and various specific problems were used in 60–70 percent of protests, regardless of which government was in power.

Second, radical polarizing frames, explicitly indicating the symbolic rejection of the post-1989 political and social order, were used infrequently dur-

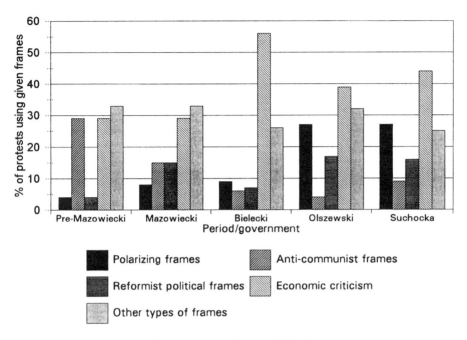

Fig. 11. Protest frames, 1989–93

ing Mazowiecki's and Bielecki's terms in office. However, the use of such frames was intensifying systematically. In the pre-Mazowiecki period of 1989, they constituted 4 percent of all slogans and self-comments; during the Mazowiecki reign, 8 percent; in 1991, under Bielecki, 9 percent. Their usage increased dramatically under Olszewski (27 percent) and under Suchocka (27 percent).

More specifically, both antisemitic and nationalistic protest rhetoric *intensified* in 1992. Our researchers did not detect such rhetoric prior to April 5, 1989 (the conclusion of the roundtable negotiations) at all; during Mazowiecki's term in office, antisemitic and nationalistic frames constituted 2 percent of all recorded frames; during Bielecki's tenure (mostly 1991), 1 percent; but during the premierships of Olszewski and Suchocka (1992–93), their usage went up to 18 and 16 percent respectively.

Third, anticommunist and anti-Soviet rhetoric, so prominent in the 1989–90 protests, was gradually disappearing during the subsequent years. It must be noted, however, that its basic frame "Down with the commune" was transferred from one set of circumstances to another: first it was used against the communists, then, with increasing frequency, against the post-1989 regimes. "Down with the commune" and "Down with the Judeo-commune" were the two most popular polarizing frames used to delegitimize the post-1989 political regimes.

Resonance of Protest Frames with the Dominant Frames of the Political Habitus

In order to estimate the success of protest leaders' framing efforts, we will attempt to assess the degree of resonance between protest frames and the popular political habitus, particularly people's fluctuating perceptions of the country's political and economic situation.

The precise motivations of most protest organizers not to choose radical polarizing frames during the 1989–91 period are unknown. Behaving rationally, protest organizers and leaders might have not chosen them realizing that such frames would not resonate well with the popular political culture. There are three possible reasons for such a conclusion: (1) moderation resulting from the recognition of belonging to the common tradition of Solidarity; (2) a desire to reflect and express people's main concerns: for the bulk of the population, economic problems were at the top of their worries; and (3) a preference to produce frames congruent with people's own understanding of political reality: public perception of the political field was unfocused and fragmented, and thus the crisp, bipolar frames could be seen as "out of touch."

The first reason for not choosing polarizing frames could have been deliberate restraint resulting from recognition of the fact that both the subsequent governments and most of the leading protest organizers shared common roots: Solidarity. If so, one expects that as the myth of Solidarity was fading away, the post-Solidarity governments should be labeled as "postcommunist" (the main function of the "Pinks" frame) with increasing frequency. Such a trend is indeed confirmed by our data.

The second reason for not using polarizing political frames could be found in people's preoccupation with economic issues. According to Pentor (a public opinion research firm), in late June 1992, 80 percent of Poles believed that the state authorities should concentrate first of all on the economic problems of the country. Most of the respondents believed that society was increasingly alienated from the disputes and quarrels within the political elite (*Wprost,* June 28, 1992). Another piece of evidence indicating the preeminence of economic concerns in people's minds is a finding that political passivity (defined as nonparticipation in elections) was most strongly connected with the negative assessment of the Balcerowicz Plan; it was an "economic motive" that kept people away from the voting booths. Judging from demands and slogans collected in our study, it was the same motive that pushed most of the participants to engage in protest actions.

It seems, therefore, that protest organizers "read correctly" those economic indicators that directly affected people's lives, that is, falling real wages and rising unemployment. If we look at the general trends in the existing data sets, we must conclude that these two negative economic developments were reflected in the rising *magnitude* of collective protest and the decisive predominance of economic demands over the political ones throughout the whole period (see chapter 5).

A closer look, however, reveals that the pattern of economic decline and renewal (reflected in such economic indicators as changes in unemployment and real wages) *was not automatically reflected* by the fluctuating pattern discernible in the use of protest frames. Neither did the fluctuating intensity of the critical "economic" rhetoric follow more optimistic indicators, such as yearly changes of GDP, which displayed signs of improvement already in 1991. Real wages fell most dramatically between 1989 and 1990, yet the amount of "economic criticism" expressed through protest rhetoric actually *decreased* during the same period. Between 1990 and 1991 real wages *stagnated,* whereas the "economic protest rhetoric" *intensified* considerably. The GDP fell most drastically in 1990 and continued falling in 1991, but in 1992 Poland was the only postcommunist state in Eastern Europe that registered a growth of GDP (2.6 percent), and in 1993 it experienced the fastest rate of economic growth in Europe (3.8 percent). Yet the economically focused protest rhetoric was the loudest not in 1990—the year of the most shocking decline in *all* economic indicators—but in 1991. What is even more striking is the fact that the good performance of GDP in 1992 and 1993 (the Olszewski and Suchocka governments), accompanied by the drastically decelerated growth of unemployment, was

1. accompanied by a muting of economic criticism (compared with 1991); but also by
2. a steadily increasing magnitude of protest overall; and
3. *a sharp increase* in political criticism, particularly the use of radical polarizing political frames (figure 11).[23]

The conclusion is inevitable: from 1989 to 1993, the changes in protest rhetorics did not simply follow the fluctuations in the economic situation ("objective" or "perceived"); they were, rather, dictated by protest leaders' political calculations and their specific understandings of the sociopolitical reality.

Thus, the third reason for the relatively infrequent use of polarizing frames during the 1989–91 period may be the leaders' close reading of the predominant popular conceptualization of the political field. During that time, popular political culture seems to have been poorly crystallized and fragmented—that is, people perceived the sociopolitical reality as a somewhat hazy entity divided by multiple, often overlapping cleavages. Jasiewicz observed that already in

1990 Poles were conceptualizing the sociopolitical reality with the help of several different "visions":

> The variety of those visions was reflected in the pluralization of the political scene and in the number of candidates. It was a situation *qualitatively different* [emphasis added] from that of the 1980s, which was a rigid and polarized structure of conflict, in which demands and proposals had only one direction, toward the single center of power. (1993a, 139)

During the 1992–93 period (the Olszewski and Suchocka cabinets), protest became more radical. The magnitude of protest increased compared with the reigns of the earlier postcommunist governments. Moreover, this increased magnitude of protest was paralleled by the more frequent use of radical polarizing frames by some protest organizers. On the other hand, Kolarska-Bobinska observed that the "we–society versus them–the authorities" vision of the political field became much more popular in 1992–94 than it was in 1990:

> The "us" (society) versus "them" government division perceived in the 1980s disappeared entirely in the [early] 1990s, giving way to conflicts in the various structures of state authority, as well as within the various groups within Solidarity. Two years later *in 1992, the "us"–"them" dichotomy came back to life in full vigor.* [emphasis added; in 1992, 23 percent of these who perceived conflict mentioned such a division; in 1994, 21 percent] (1994, 154)

A comparison of our results with Kolarska's conclusions reveals, therefore, an intriguing correlation: during the 1992–93 period, the "us versus them" bipolar vision *reemerged* both within the political habitus and in protest framing. Unfortunately, we are unable to determine which caused which. Was it radical protest rhetoric that helped people to sharpen their vision of reality, or was it people's increased radicalism that forced the leaders of radical organizations to employ more radical frames in order to "stay in tune" with the populace? We do not know, since our data set is not reliable enough to venture beyond generalizations concerning the most general trends. Yet the radicalized perception of reality is firmly confirmed, and what is puzzling is the fact that it occurred while the economic situation of the country (at least as measured by the main macroeconomic indicators) was sharply improving and Polish sociologists registered clear signs of depolarization within the elite political culture. Our hunch, based mostly on the detailed analysis we presented in chapter 6, is that the radicalized rhetoric of some groups and the parallel intensification of protest caused or at least contributed to the worsening of people's assessment of the political and economic situation of the country during the 1992–93 period.

Summary of Conclusions

The analyses of protest rhetoric and symbolism presented in this chapter support our conclusions based on the examination of other features of protest, presented in chapter 5. During the 1989–92 period, most Poles engaged in protest (strikes and demonstrations) to put forth demands related to their everyday (mostly "economic") concerns; only some of them turned to militant populism,[24] finding in its polarizing master frames a guide for their actions. For the majority of protestors, it seems, collective protest was a mode of civic action based on an acceptance of the existing order and merely aimed at the correction of governmental—mostly economic—policies. "It's Economy, stupid" could have been the principal motto of most protest organizers during the first five years of the postcommunist transition. The most popular political program that emerges from the analysis of protest frames seems to have been the one that combined decisive economic demands with moderate political claims ("do not topple the whole system, but change some ministers").[25]

Second, during the Mazowiecki and Bielecki terms in office (fall 1989–winter 1991), the eclectic set of collective action frames identified through our research resembled structurally and semantically the *multi*polar mosaic of the political habitus (representing here the popular political culture) rather than the *bi*polar universe of the elite political culture, divided between revolutionaries and reformists. Radical polarizing frames, akin to the bipolar conceptualizations of the political field, were mostly used by a few radical fringe groups.

Third, the usage of radical polarizing frames intensified during the Olszewski and Suchocka governments (1992–93). Interestingly, during the same period the significance of the bipolar division within the political elite declined (Wasilewski 1995), but the perception of the bipolar "us versus them" division of sociopolitical reality among the populace increased (Kolarska-Bobinska 1994, 154). Therefore, we conclude that by and large, protest organizers were more in tune with the popular visions of the political field than many/most members of the political elite. This finding dovetails with our generalization that in postcommunist Poland, protest politics was more developed than in other Central European countries (Ekiert and Kubik 1998) and with a well-established fact that trust in political elites and political parties among the Poles was very low.

Fourth, the patterns we detected within the protest rhetorics, in particular its *growing radicalization through polarization,* were not simply following the changing patterns of the economic situation, as reflected by major macroeconomic indicators such as the rate of growth of GDP, the unemployment rate, changes in real wages, etc. As the economic situation was getting better, protest was becoming more intense and, in some sectors, more radical. We conclude that protest politics was not driven by socioeconomic mechanisms, but rather by the *political calculations* and *understandings of reality* of protest leaders and organizers.

Fifth, until the fall of the Olszewski government (June 1992), the way protest rhetorics changed reflected or followed the changes in popular evaluations of the post-1989 transformations: as these evaluations declined, protest was becoming increasingly more politicized and its rhetorics more radical. During Suchocka's term in office (July 11, 1992–October 24, 1993),[26] the following trends emerged:

1. approval of the political regime and economic system increased (figure 2);
2. the economy showed signs of decisive recovery;
3. people's evaluations of the country's political and economic situation briefly improved (until November 1992) and then began declining again, dropping more radically just before the vote of no confidence in the parliament (May 1993; see figure 1);
4. the bipolar vision of the political field regained some of its earlier attractiveness (in 1992 it was accepted by one-quarter of the populace);
5. during 1992 and the first half of 1993, the magnitude of protest increased and the usage of polarizing protest frames intensified.

Although we cannot establish precise causal order among these trends (the available data is not "hard" enough for statistical analysis), one conclusion seems to be reasonably well founded: the downward trend in people's assessment of their country's political and economic situation coincided with the intensification of protest and the radicalization of protest symbolism and rhetorics. At the same time, there was a noticeable improvement in the major economic indicators. We surmise that the popular political culture (political habitus) was influenced by the protest organizers' framing more than by the changes in the economic situation.[27] This conclusion is particularly well supported by our analysis of the Suchocka government's fall, presented in chapter 6.

CHAPTER 8

Conclusions: Collective Protest
and Democratic Consolidation

Many observers of Eastern Europe assumed that the collapse of state socialism and rapid transition to a market economy and democracy would involve
high social costs and dislocations, at least in the short run. And, in fact, during the first years of postcommunism, the transitional recession resulted in a
dramatic decline of GDP and industrial production and spawned high unemployment. Under such circumstances, it was argued, maintaining social peace
was going to prove a great challenge for all postcommunist states (Bruszt
1992). People subjected to dramatic political and economic transformations
were believed to have little tolerance for the social costs of reforms. It was expected they might rebel against the reforming elites, despite the enthusiasm
engendered by the fall of the repressive regimes and the inauguration of democratic politics. Dahrendorf warned about "the possibility of a profound disenchantment on the part of a majority with the promises of democracy" (1990,
112). Some predicted massive protest actions that would force politicians to
reconsider their goals and strategies or even to call a halt to political and economic transformations.

It was not easy, however, to assess whether this scenario was being realized because the existing empirical studies on popular responses to the transformations either were fragmentary and unsystematic or relied on public opinion polls, which provided no data on people's actual behavior. We embarked
therefore on an empirical comparative study of protest politics among the postcommunist states of Central Europe. Our research project focused on four countries, and this analysis of Poland's initial years of transformations is the first
book-length outcome of our project. Poland warranted a separate book all its
own. It was Poland, after all, that was renowned for its rebellious civil society,
which generated more protest than in any other communist state. We wanted to
know whether Poles continued to protest after the fall of communism, and if so,
how. Moreover, Polish economic reforms were the most radical among the postcommunist states, and the initial social costs of these reforms were higher than
elsewhere. At the same time, recovery from the economic recession was swift,
and from 1992 Poland had robust economic growth, paralleled by a rise in real

wages and the standard of living. Thus Poland's experiences are an ideal reference point for the study of other postcommunist transitions.

In this book we have analyzed the first five years of postcommunist transformations in Poland from a specific empirical and analytical perspective. This perspective is determined by our main research question: what role does protest play in the early stages of democratic consolidation? In order to answer this question, we gathered data on all forms of collective protest that occurred during such a period in Poland. The protest event analysis we employed produced a database with information on 1,476 protest events. This is currently the most complete and detailed set of information on protest activities compiled on any Central European country. This database makes possible a systematic investigation of popular mobilization patterns and the relationship between the state and society in a new democracy. It also enables us to answer a number of specific questions on the various dimensions of protest politics: Which social groups were challenging the new government's policies through unconventional political actions? Which organizations were the most active protest organizers? What cleavages were most visible in protest politics? What were the demands put forward during protest actions? Who or what were the targets of protests? What kinds of rhetoric and symbols were used by protestors? Was protest effective in shaping the policies of the new democratic state?

We also set out to contribute to the theory of democratic consolidation. The elite bias of current literature and the selective focus of existing analyses of East European transitions left a void that we wanted to fill. We wanted to know much more about the patterns of activities undertaken by civil society's organizations and their impact on the process of democratic consolidation. In order to accomplish this task, we conceptualized consolidation as a complex process transpiring concurrently within the three realms of politics: the state, political society, and civil society. Next we reconstructed the major developments occurring within each of these realms and the relationships among them. Empirical material came mostly from Poland, but the framework we developed is applicable to other cases of democratic consolidation.

In this chapter we summarize both our major empirical findings and the key elements of our theoretical argument. Our conclusions are structured in the following way. First, we summarize the main characteristics of protest. Second, we propose explanations for the patterns our analyses revealed. In order to understand and explain the role of protest in the democratic consolidation in Poland, we analyzed the relationships among protest and (1) the main trends of the post-1989 political and economic developments, (2) the configuration of the three main institutional domains of the new polity (the state, political society, civil society), and (3) changes in people's attitudes, particularly the evaluations of the economic and political situation. Third, we consider the relationship between contentious politics and the consolidation of democracy.

Main Features of Protest in Poland, 1989–93

In this section we present the most important findings of our analyses. Emphasis is placed on the main characteristics of protest, reconstructed through our empirical study.

1. During the regime transition and the initial period of democratic consolidation, collective protest was widespread and used by various groups and organizations to express a variety of economic and political demands. Our comparative research shows that in Poland, protest was more frequent and became a more salient element of political transformations than in other Central European countries. Also, protest activities displayed a specific trajectory. The patterns we observe in all relevant variables (duration, number of participants, tactical versatility, etc.) indicate a growing magnitude of protest from 1989 to 1993. After 1993 this rising tide of protest began to abate. While we have no data of our own beyond 1993, the information collected by the Main Statistical Office show a marked decline in the number of strikes. We explain the greater occurrence of protest in Poland and its rising magnitude over the 1989–93 period by referring to the historical legacies of protest and peculiar patterns of institutionalization within the political realms.

2. Although protest actions were organized by a variety of social groups and spread to all parts of the country, some groups were more prone to protest. Our findings show that protests were not organized by marginal groups; rather, it was the members of "mainstream" social categories such as industrial workers (almost exclusively from state-owned enterprises) and public sector employees who were most likely to engage in protest activities. We suggested this pattern of protest activities reveals the most active cleavage of the postcommunist social order: the state versus its own employees. Other frequent protest participants included the youth, students, and peasants, both those who owned their farms and collective-farm employees. Most of the protest participants in all the years under study came from these four main social categories. The numbers of protests involving a given group did not change significantly from year to year. This may explain the consistently high level of certain protest strategies and demands; each social group seems to have developed its "favorite" repertoire of protest.

3. Our database does not provide much evidence for our initial hypothesis that through protest actions people would forge new identities and set up new organizations. The decisive majority of protest actions were organized by existing organizations, which mobilized people in the name of existing identities. The only exception was youth protests, which spawned a large network of new "countercultural" organizations.

4. Protest organizers came most often from civil society. Labor unions were the most active, followed by social and political movements. Among the labor unions, the trade union Solidarity was the most frequent organizer of protest actions. Political parties protested infrequently. Thus, relying on our own data and other available sources of information, we conclude that Polish civil society *was not demobilized* after the downfall of the old regime. If this is so, then either Karl and Schmitter are wrong in claiming that demobilization "of various mass publics" during democratic consolidation is "the almost universal fact" (1995, 976), or Poland constitutes an exception to such a regularity. More importantly, the whole discussion on the weakening or strengthening of civil society during the transition process may be the result of a definitional confusion: civil society under communism and civil society in democracy are two different entities. The role or meaning of civil society in the political process *changed*. Whereas under state socialism civil society (i.e., various illegal and semilegal associations) was simply coterminous with political society (oppositional parties, political movements), during democratic consolidation the public domain underwent a rapid bifurcation. Two *separate* (at least in Poland) domains emerged: a *vibrant and growing* domain of civic associations and organizations, and a more *torpid and elitist* domain of political parties and "political" interest groups.

5. The repertoire of protest was stable and predominantly nonviolent. Violent strategies were used very rarely. Striking was the dominant form of protest (including strikes and strike alerts), followed by demonstrations and rallies, and nondisruptive protests (open letters, statements, symbolic displays, etc.). The prevalence of strikes among protest actions reflected both the legacies of the Solidarity movement and the dominant role of the trade union sector in the newly reconstituted civil society. A growing tactical versatility of protest indicated the presence of significant organizational resources and a learning process among protest organizers.

6. Demands voiced during protest actions were predominantly economic and reformist. Radical demands, such as the abolition of the entire post-1989 order, were infrequent. Only a small minority of protestors turned to the highly polarized symbolism of militant populism; instead, most of them engaged in strikes and demonstrations to put forward their demands related to everyday (mostly "economic") concerns. For them, it seems, collective protest was a mode of *civic* action based on an acceptance of the existing order and intended to *correct* governmental—mostly economic—policies. We call this phenomenon *contentious reformism*. Thus our initial expectation of finding a considerable number of oversymbolized, militant, and highly politicized protests was not confirmed.

7. The most popular targets of protest actions were top state institutions such as the government, parliament, and presidency. During the period under study, they were targeted with increased frequency. There was no increase in protest actions directed at management. Domestic and foreign owners were targeted very rarely. This pattern suggests that the political cleavage inherited from the communist period (us versus them, the state versus society) still played a dominant role in shaping contentious politics. The multidimensional, cross-cutting cleavages with many challengers and targets—characteristic of open, democratic societies—were not emerging. Quite the contrary; in 1992–93, a polarized vision of politics, with the state as society's main adversary, regained some of its earlier popularity, which had declined briefly at the outset of consolidation.

8. Protestors' identities were predominantly particularistic, although the invocation of more general identities (such as "nation" and "society") increased. Collective protest did not acquire an "oversymbolized" form, but rather a more pragmatic one; demands remained primarily economic throughout the whole period. Nor did the increased magnitude of protest manifest itself through the intensification of protest-sponsorship by political parties. It occurred, first of all, through the *generalization* of protestors' identities and through the growing "seriousness" of the addressees (or targets) of their actions. In brief, as the years went by, the protestors acted more often on behalf of "the whole of society" and targeted the country's highest authorities with increasing frequency.

9. The state's responses to protest were measured, and the whole field of protest politics was remarkably nonviolent. The postcommunist state was very reluctant to use police force against protestors even when serious disruption of public order took place. We showed that the postcommunist state in Poland was remarkably tolerant, selective in use of force, reactive rather than preventive, soft in using coercion, and respectful of legal and democratic procedures.

10. The effectiveness of protest is difficult to measure; policymakers may take protestors' demands seriously but treat them as only one of many elements influencing their decisions. Moreover, such decisions may come months after actual protest actions occurred. Despite such obstacles, we believe our data allow us to form three conclusions concerning the effectiveness of protest.

First, inasmuch as protest actions aimed to reverse or considerably slow down the implementation of the major provisions of the Balcerowicz Plan, they failed. There were no major reversals in the macroeconomic policies of Polish governments during the analyzed period, despite the fact that the consecutive coalition governments represented different political options and policy agendas.

Second, some protestors achieved considerable successes in *modifying* certain elements of governmental economic policies. They won such policy concessions as the relaxation of the punitive tax on excessive wage growth (*popiwek*), the introduction of protective tariffs, and slowing down the pace of enterprise restructuring.[1] After analyzing a subsection of our database, Maryjane Osa concluded that "constantly high levels of protest kept pressure on the government to take workers' interests into account when planning continued economic reform" (1998, 38). In particular, she found that protest pressure kept unemployment well below the level it could have reached, given the depth of the early transformational recession.[2] Finally, it should be noted that protestors often secured promises of increased governmental involvement in solving regional and sectoral problems.

Third, strikes were most successful in winning limited concessions, such as wage increases, reinstatement of collective benefits, or the removal of unpopular managers.

Protest Politics in Poland in a Comparative Context

We are now ready to place our findings on protest in Poland within a wider theoretical framework and attempt some generalizations based on the empirical material collected also in the former East Germany, Hungary, and Slovakia. As we indicated in chapter 3, our primary interest in the institutionalization of a new democratic polity led us to accept the basic tenets of the political process approach to protest politics. Within this approach, protest is construed as a reasoned tactic or strategy of interacting with the authorities when other tactics or strategies fail or are perceived as less effective. It is, however, clear that much thinking about postcommunist transformations is at least implicitly grounded in another model of protest politics: a model derived from a relative deprivation theory.[3]

The reasoning inspired by the deprivation model goes as follows: (1) Rapid, "neoliberal" economic reforms produce higher social costs and more dissatisfaction among the populace than slower, more gradual reforms. (2) High social costs of reforms anger the public, whose members utilize the newly acquired freedoms and newly established democratic procedures to obstruct or decelerate economic transformations and attempt to depose the reforming elites. (3) In particular, the heightened level of dissatisfaction with the reforms and the elites that designed and implemented them is likely to result in increased protest magnitude. (4) As the "Olsonian" logic suggests, in this climate of dissatisfaction and a heightened readiness for protest, the "losers" should be much easier to mobilize than the beneficiaries of the reforms; the latter are scattered throughout the society, while the former are concentrated in such easily mobilizable sectors as large enterprises of heavy industry.[4] (5) Finally, protest may/

should bring about the downfall of the reforming, neoliberal elites. In fact, as various analyses of Latin American cases amply demonstrate, the public reaction to neoliberal reforms, particularly in the "losing" sectors, is likely to take a form of mass protest, which may turn violent and exact a heavy toll in casualties.[5]

Let us turn to empirical evidence to verify this theoretical sketch. We determined that although the Poles approved of the newly established, democratic political system and the postcommunist economic system in gradually increasing numbers, their evaluations of the economic and political situation initially kept declining and then stabilized at a relatively low level. We also know that the gap between the rich and the poor was wider than during the last years of state socialism. Moreover, blue-collar workers began losing the privileged position they enjoyed under the old regime. During the same period, the level of protest was high and its magnitude was rising. This confirms the basic tenets of the relative deprivation theory: the worsening economic situation of an important segment of the population bred dissatisfaction and led to increased protest activity by its members.

Yet a closer examination of the economic data that should corroborate or refute the propositions of the relative deprivation theory produces ambiguous results. It is sufficient to consider two important data sets. As table 30 in chapter 6 illustrates, the gap between wages in the industrial sector and wages in the nonindustrial public sector was systematically growing. In the first half of 1993, a tremendous protest wave shook the country. It was organized by the unions representing the public sector employees, mostly teachers and health care workers. The relative deprivation theory predicts such a result, but only for the 1989–93 period. By 1993, wages in the nonindustrial public sector, relative to wages of the industrial sector, were at their lowest since 1989. In 1994, however, while the wage gap between these two groups opened even wider than in the previous year, the magnitude of protest within the nonindustrial public sector rapidly declined. Additionally, as we demonstrated in chapter 6, protest was not driven by some generic sense of deprivation or a need to manifest rejection of the post-1989 changes. Rather, protest actions were organized to communicate to the authorities very specific concerns of labor unions and their constituents. Moreover, we suggested that the dissatisfaction with the progress of the reforms or some of their effects was not the main force behind protest actions. Instead, the growing magnitude of protest seems to have influenced negatively people's assessment of the country's political and economic situation. Hence, the causal relationship between attitudes and actions implied by the relative deprivation theory is questionable.

Another opportunity to test the relative deprivation theory is provided by a data set on the rate of decline of real wages within different groups of the population, presented in table 34. Peasant and peasant-worker families suffered a

TABLE 34.   Change in Families' Real Incomes (1989 = 100)

	Workers	Peasants	Workers/peasants	Pensioners and retirees
1989	100	100	100	100
1990	66	75	71	72
1991	66	62	60	90
1992	61	57	52	73
1993	67	64	59	87
1994	77	72	70	101

Source: The Institute for Statistical and Economic Research of the Polish Academy of Sciences and the Main Statistical Office, reported in *Tygodnik Solidarnosc,* July 2, 1993.

steeper decline in their incomes than did the families of nonagricultural workers. It was, however, precisely the employees of the nonagricultural sectors who were the most active protestors throughout the whole period.

The analyses presented above do not constitute rigorous tests of the predictions derived from the relative deprivation theory. Nonetheless, it is obvious that the basic regularities suggested by this theory are not unequivocally corroborated by the existing data sets on social and economic changes after 1989 and our own data on protest activities. We conclude, together with many other critics of the relative deprivation theory, that protest politics is governed by complex mechanisms, which are only partially dependent on the sense of relative deprivation among the social groups from which the protestors come. In particular, this theory cannot provide any answer to the question of why certain institutional channels for airing grievances and exerting pressure on the authorities are chosen over others. In order to answer such a question we will turn to (neo)institutional theories, which dovetail almost seamlessly with the political process model of protest politics.

In order to make the institutional analysis more effective, it is necessary to consider protest as a multidimensional phenomenon and consider how various features of protest are shaped by specific institutional constraints and opportunities of a given polity. In the following analysis, we will focus on the magnitude of protest and protest repertoires. As table 15 illustrates, the magnitude of protest in Poland was higher than in the three other countries we studied. Other characteristics of protest also show considerable variance among the four countries (see table 35). For example, the Polish protest repertoire was dominated by strikes and strike threats.

The higher incidence of these protest forms in Poland than in Hungary, Slovakia, and the former East Germany can be explained by invoking three analytically distinct institutional mechanisms.

TABLE 35. Protest Magnitude and Repertoires in the Former East Germany,
Hungary, Poland, and Slovakia, 1989–93

	East Germany	Hungary	Poland	Slovakia
Population, ages 15–64 (in millions)	11	7	25	4
Protest events	1,254	699	1,476	295
Protest days	5,349	2,574	14,881	2,206
Protests/year	251	140	295	74
Protest days/year	1,070	515	2,976	441
Protest days/million population (15–64)	97.3	73.6	119.0	110.3
Strikes	107	61	432	24
Demonstrations	607	244	544	87
Ratio of demonstrations/ strikes	5.70	4.00	1.26	3.63
Strikes/year/million population (15–64)	1.95	1.74	3.50	1.50
Demonstrations/year/ million population (15–64)	11.04	6.97	4.35	5.45

1. Cultural-historical. We expect more strikes in a country that has a long and extensive (in comparison with other East European states) history of institutionalizing such forms of protest.
2. Rational-instrumental. We expect people to engage in protest as a rational, calculated response to their lack of access to policy-making through other channels. For example, labor unions are more likely to organize frequent protest actions if the country does not have a tripartite collective bargaining institution and thus there is no neocorporatist inclusion of labor into the governmental decision-making processes. We also expect more protest in a country where people do not trust the existing political parties, which undermines their effectiveness as mechanisms of interest aggregation and representation.
3. Sociological-institutional. We expect more strikes if there are many unions competing for the same "audience." Under such circumstances, unions increase their "protest" visibility in order to outbid each other in wooing potential supporters. As a result, a specific (protest-intensive) institutionalization of the interorganizational competition develops.

In the East European field, the well-known dilemma of more variables than cases makes impossible a rigorous test to pinpoint the best explanation. In fact, a comparison of Poland, Hungary, Slovakia, and the former East Germany provides evidence supporting all three explanations.

First, let us consider a hypothesis that the repertoire of contention is shaped by history (unique cultural trajectories). Among the East European states, Poland has by far the strongest tradition of political conflicts disguised as industrial conflicts with strikes as a dominant form of protest. Hungary, by contrast, has a well-established tradition of street demonstrations and struggles (1956 in particular), which played a significant role during the power transfer period (1988–90) (Hofer 1993). The unions and other protest organizers in the former East Germany should be influenced by the dominant action repertoire brought over by West German unions and other SMOs (social movement organizations), which organize most of the protest actions there. As Koopmans and Kriesi (1995, 44–50) report, demonstrative strategy dominated the German action repertoire. Given these facts, the Polish ratio of street demonstrations to strikes should be considerably lower than in Hungary or Germany. The empirical data reported in table 35 strongly confirm this hypothesis.

Hungarian protestors chose street demonstrations four times more often than strikes; German protestors demonstrated six times more often than they went on strike. Poles, by contrast, were almost equally prone to strike and to demonstrate. This is an *expected result* given the relatively long, established tradition of using strikes as a weapon in political conflicts and struggles in Poland. In Slovakia, the most frequently used protest strategy was letter writing. Again, it is not an unexpected result in a state that is a successor to Czechoslovakia, where letter writing was the main form of political participation during the Prague Spring (1968) and where the anticommunist opposition (Charter 77) used open letters as its main tool of pressuring the authorities.

Two other explanations are also confirmed by a comparison of institutional arrangements in the four countries. If Hungary, Slovakia and the former East Germany instituted top-level neocorporatist arrangements while Poland did not, one should expect more strikes in the latter country. As Schmitter (1981), Wallace and Jenkins (1995, 134), and Nollert (1995, 147) noted, the institutionalization of neocorporatist bargaining diminishes the likelihood of protest. Countries with a strong social democratic party (Hungary and Poland after 1993) and a centralized labor sector (Hungary, the former East Germany, and Slovakia) are expected to have fewer industrial conflicts and strikes than would a more pluralistic country with several unions that do not have "direct," neocorporatist access to the political process (Poland).

These expected regularities are indeed confirmed by our data. One of the most prominent features of Hungarian, Slovak, and East German transitory politics was the early institution of top-level neocorporatist arrangements. In Hungary, the Council for Interest Reconciliation was established already in 1988,

Slovakia's Council of Economic and Social Agreement was formed in 1990, and in Germany neocorporatist institutions expanded to the new Länder in 1990, during the early stages of unification (Hethy 1994; Thirkell, Scase, and Vickerstaff 1995; Wiesenthal 1995). And as expected, Poland, where a tripartite mechanism was not established until 1994, had by far the highest incidence and magnitude of strikes, organized predominantly by trade unions.

There exists one more rational-instrumental mechanism helping to explain why Poles protested in such high numbers and with such intensity. From the evidence presented in chapter 4, it is clear that many of them were uncomfortable with routine parliamentary democracy and dissatisfied with party politics (see table 11) and turned to *contentious collective action* as a substitute for or alternative to such conventional forms of political participation as voting or supporting political parties. Growing dissatisfaction with political parties as channels of interest articulation and representation is documented both in our study and in other works. It is also reflected in the "Klon" data, which reveals that for the decisive majority of NGO activists there was a *dramatic chasm* between civil and political societies and that systematic relationships between them were extremely weak (see table 13). The postcommunist party system in Poland might have become more consolidated and structured, but its ability to articulate and represent people's interests—in light of our research—*remained problematic.*

A theory emphasizing sociological-institutional mechanisms is also confirmed by the evidence we marshaled. The Polish trade union sector was more diversified and decentralized than in other countries; therefore—exactly as sociological institutionalists would argue—Poland had more interorganizational competition and thus more protest actions.[6]

Since the empirical evidence we gathered corroborates the regularities suggested by three different institutional theories, it turns out that the high magnitude of protest in Poland from 1989 to 1993 and the dominance of protest repertoire by strikes and strike threats were causally overdetermined. This means that the specific pattern of Polish democratic consolidation our analysis revealed—the pattern we call institutionalized contentiousness (or contentious reformism)—was not accidental but rather resulted from a unique combination of a specific cultural and institutional legacies and specific postcommunist institutional arrangements.

This pattern, characterized by gradually intensifying contentious collective action, occurring mostly within civil society, has been largely overlooked in the existing analyses of post-1989 Polish politics. As a consequence, the critical early stages (1989–93) of Polish democratic consolidation have been misinterpreted. In the final section we will recapitulate our definition of consolidation, determine how Polish consolidation measures up against the definitional criteria, and discuss the wider applicability of our analytical model.

Protest, Democratic Consolidation,
and the Three Domains of the Polity

In chapter 4 we introduced our definition of democratic consolidation. We proposed that it should be understood as a process that approaches its completion when the establishment of a *political democracy* is accompanied by *three additional conditions*. These three conditions include (1) the formation of a consensus concerning the boundaries of a political community; (2) the development of transparency and predictability at the institutional level; and (3) the achievement of a *sufficient level* of social and cultural democratization, particularly the emergence of the legitimacy of the new order. The second condition is realized when (2.1) the basic democratic institutions, supported by a constitution, are in place; (2.2) the state possesses the stability, autonomy, and capacity to implement its policies; and (2.3) the boundaries between the state and other institutional domains of the democratic polity (party system, civil society) are well defined and the linkages among them are well developed.

One of the goals of this book was to determine to what degree the second condition was fulfilled during the early consolidation period (1989–93). In particular, we set out to determine *how* the three institutional domains evolved after 1989, *whether* their power and capacity increased or decreased, and *what kinds* of linkages developed among them.

It needs to be emphasized at the outset that conditions 1 and 3 of democratic consolidation were met by Poland from the beginning of the postcommunist period. In contrast to several other countries of the region, Poland's boundaries were never disputed by any major political force within the country nor by the governments of the neighboring states. Moreover, Poland's small ethnic minorities were effectively incorporated into democratic politics. Also, the legitimacy of the democratic order was not contested by any significant force and gradually increased: approval of the new political regime grew from 52 percent in November 1991 to 69 percent in December 1993. Similarly, Poles increasingly approved the new economic system (from 31 to 50 percent over the same period; see Rose and Haerpfer 1996a, 25, 47; see also Kolarska-Bobinska 1992, 11).

The problems of Polish consolidation were related to the imperfect fulfillment of the criteria listed under condition 2 of our definition. First, throughout the entire early consolidation period (until the second parliamentary elections in 1993), Poland did not have a full-fledged democratic constitution. An ill-defined division of powers among the legislative, executive, and judicial branches of government alone contributed to political instability. Second, the Polish postcommunist state had considerable autonomy but was often less efficient than the communist party-state and burdened by high welfare expectations. Third, political society was fragmented and estranged from the electorates, though arguably increasingly more consolidated (structured). Fourth, civil society was rapidly expanding, and various new and old organizations played an important role in the country's politics. The activities of civil society actors, as we documented, were increasingly *contentious;* protests became a salient feature of the newly democratized polity. At the same time, protest strategies were largely nonviolent, demands put forward by protest organizers usually moderate, and their rhetoric only infrequently antisystemic and inflammatory.

The findings of our research should be carefully interpreted. Our analysis focused on a highly volatile and unsettled period of early postcommunist transformations. Moreover, our project covered a relatively short period of time. Nonetheless, we are convinced that the formative experiences of the new regime are critically important, for they leave long-lasting political legacies. In this context the *nature of Polish contentiousness* needs to be examined, and we need to assess its role in the democratic consolidation. As we demonstrated, protest had a profound impact on the institutionalization of the new regime, on the political practices developed by major collective actors, and on a specific trajectory of Poland's postcommunist transformations.

People's civic activities often took the form of *contentious collective action* rather than *interorganizational negotiation and mediation:* instead of engaging in well-institutionalized interorganizational games (negotiations, lobbying, etc.), organizations such as trade unions were very quick to organize or sponsor strikes and demonstrations. In a sense, then, civil society (at least its significant segment) was specifically institutionalized, that is, the rules of routine conflict resolution were not established and/or legitimized. This kind of institutionalization was not the result of organizations' passivity, but rather of their tendency to employ contentious forms of participation in public life, as a form of communication with the authorities.[7] Contentious actions were carried out by well-established organizations of the civil society that challenged specific policies of postcommunist governments. Yet these often intense protests did not lead to major policy reversals, though they prompted policy adjustments and modifications. In brief, protest activities became a routine mode of interaction between the state and civil society; hence, the emerging set of norms and rules should be referred to as *institutionalized contentiousness.*

What transpired in Poland was, therefore, a different kind of consolidation of democracy than the one Bresser Pereira, Maravall, and Przeworski seem to have had in mind. They observe that "if reforms are to proceed under democratic conditions, distributional conflicts must be institutionalized: All groups must channel their demands through the democratic institutions and abjure other tactics" (1993, 4). But what if protest becomes a part of the bargaining process and a frequent mode of political participation? Is democratic consolidation threatened by such an increased magnitude of contentious collective action?

Such a situation developed in Poland. For most observers, that country passed the point of no return early during the consolidation process—an authoritarian reversal became highly unlikely. Yet it was Poland that experienced a high magnitude of strikes and massive street demonstrations, which on one occasion led to a government's fall and early elections. By contrast, Slovakia, the country with a low level of strike activity and the least disruptive (most benign) repertoire of protest, has been commonly perceived during the same period as the least consolidated democracy in Central Europe.

In order to determine whether the heightened level of contentiousness in Poland constituted a threat to democratic consolidation, we need to determine to what degree protest activities were institutionalized, that is, whether they were routinely accepted as a legitimate mode of interaction between the state and citizens. The existing literature on institutionalization suggests that a social practice is institutionalized when one of the following two criteria is present:

1. It is widely regarded as "normal" or "taken for granted," or recognized as legitimate by the wider community and legally permitted.
2. It is routinized, that is, repeated almost always when a problem or issue it is designed to deal with emerges and conformity is enforced by sanction and/or rewards.[8]

In postcommunist Poland, protest became an increasingly routinized and institutionalized form of participation in politics. Although classical modernization theory made the link between institutionalization and order or stability one of its most fundamental assumptions, institutionalization of a social practice (or interaction pattern) has to be dissociated from the notion of order. It is clear that different levels of conflict, contention, and disruption may be taken for granted, legitimized, and/or routinized in a given political system (cf. Wolfsfeld 1988 on Israel; Wilson 1994 on France). Therefore, political stability can coexist with heightened levels of contentious political participation. In postcommunist Poland, a high level of contentious collective action was institutionalized as a significant element of the newly formed democratic polity. This fact confirms Eckstein and Gurr's observation that

> the risk of chronic low-level conflict is one of the prices democrats should expect to pay for freedom from regimentation by the state—or by authorities in other social units, whether industrial establishments, trade unions, schools, universities, or families. (1975, 452)

We conclude, therefore, that if protest does not involve violence and if protestors do not promulgate antidemocratic programs, unconventional but institutionalized political participation ("chronic low-level conflict") is a sign of democratic vitality or successful democratic consolidation. It is not a threat to democratization, but rather its significant component.

What, however, does the relatively high level of protest in Poland tell us about the type of linkages that developed among the various institutional domains of the new polity? Our study confirms a generalization that during a regime transition, when the *boundaries* between the institutional realms of the polity are unclear and contested, organizations of civil society penetrate political arenas with greater vigor than in more stable polities. There were many examples of political actors crossing the boundaries between the realms, but without any procedures regulating such "trespassing." Polish trade unions ran candidates in elections and aspired to an independent parliamentary representation. In fact, it was the Solidarity parliamentarians who orchestrated the no-confidence vote against Suchocka's government and forced the new elections in 1993. Also, some political parties acted as oppositional movements by, for example, organizing demonstrations against the government in which they were the official partner.

Thus, Poland turned out to be an excellent example of the disjointed and chaotic development of the institutional realms of the polity during a period of transition. All three domains had their own transformational dynamics, and the formation of institutional structures *within* each of them was far more advanced than the formation of the formal institutional linkages *among* them. It should be noted, however, that informal linkages between some powerful interest groups and the state developed, and, as some observers claim, such groups were able to influence state policies more effectively than political parties (see Rychard 1995, 11; and Staniszkis 1995). On the other hand, each of the three domains had a relatively high level of *autonomy* vis-à-vis the other two, which prevented any of them from monopolizing political power. But the formal and transparent linkages between civil society organizations and the party system (political society) were extremely weak. Rychard formulates a similar thesis: "numerous studies and observations of everyday life indicate that the society is outside politics. It does not mean that the society is passive; it means, rather, that it does not use political instruments to articulate its interests" (1995, 10). In contrast to state socialism, postcommunist Poland during early consolidation did not have a formal institutional mechanism that would link and coordinate various institutional orders: an equivalent of the system of nomenklatura was not developed. Corporatist institutions that could provide such an alternative developed slowly and were ineffective during the analyzed period. The dialogue between the state and its citizens often took the form of contentious collective action and governmental responses to it. As a result of this specific institutionalization of the links between civil society, political society, and the state, the effectiveness of the whole polity suffered.

The peculiarity of Polish consolidation can be summarized in the following formula: the legitimacy and stability of the political regime and the absence of disruptive shifts in state economic policies *coexisted* with governmental instability, short electoral cycles, a relatively high level of protest activities, and a weak system of linkages among the institutional domains of the polity. Paradoxically, the very same pattern may have contributed to the coherence and continuity of the radical economic reforms. As long as opposition to the reforms was expressed through protest actions and protestors called for modifications of the reform strategy, not its termination, the authorities often responded to criticisms and modified their plans accordingly. Radical calls for the termination of the Balcerowicz strategy were infrequent, and when they occurred, the government ignored them. When such calls reached a level of political articulation, they came usually from several smaller parties and were voiced in an uncoordinated and thus impotent fashion. In general, our findings support Geddes's conclusions that

> labor has not been able to translate its opposition to adjustment policies into credible threats to punish the initiators of adjustment. Labor has not lacked the capacity to mount opposition; there have been numerous strikes and demonstrations. But this opposition has not routinely led to threats of regime breakdown, the defeat of the incumbents at the polls, or the wholesale abandonment of market-oriented policies. (1994a, 111)

As we assumed at the outset of this project, a specific angle provided by our study on protest politics allowed us to gain fresh and original insights into democratic consolidation in Poland. We determined that the high level and specific features of protest in Poland typify two important, though contradictory, features of the Polish postcommunist situation. On the one hand, the high magnitude of protest reflected institutional chaos, particularly the lack of well-defined and routinely accepted channels of interest articulation and mediation. Protest actions were not an expression of growing disenchantment with democracy and economic reforms: protest continued to intensify while the legitimacy of the whole system was systematically increasing and people's assessment of their situation leveled off. Such a high magnitude of protest demonstrated instead disappointment with the *inaccessibility of the state* and the *ineffectiveness of political parties*. On the other hand, the high institutionalization of protest activities meant that they became a routine mode of political participation and, rather than undermining democratic consolidation, they enhanced it. A threat to consolidation comes from spontaneous, poorly institutionalized outbursts of collective rage, often accompanied by violence (see Walton 1991; Walton and Ragin 1990; and Walton and Seddon 1994). Protest actions of such kind were marginal in Poland.

Through this set of general conclusions concerning Poland, we arrive at more general lessons generated by our study. The comparison of Polish post-1989 developments with other countries undergoing democratic consolidations demonstrates that there is no single pattern to this process. Rather, there exist several different types of consolidation. They may differ from each other on every dimension specified in our definition. What our study demonstrated is that in addition to obvious differences resulting from the higher or lower legitimacy of the new regime or from the degree to which the "problem of stateness" remains unresolved, institutional differences are equally important. We began our work with the assumption that democratic consolidation is facilitated by a simultaneous strengthening of the state, political society, and civil society. We quickly realized that there are many combinations of features exhibited by these three domains. For example, Poland between 1989 and 1993 was characterized by a semireformed, autonomous, and often inefficient state, a party system that was fragmented and poorly embedded in society, and strong though contentious civil society. It is, however, difficult to say whether such a combination of features facilitated early Polish democratic consolidation. It is not easy to distinguish between optimal and suboptimal levels of consolidation. A specific type is optimal for a set of traditions and institutions of a given country and the specific set of problems it faces, particularly during the early stages of consolidation.

Various patterns of institutionalization will also characterize the linkages among the basic domains of the polity. The most obvious example is the relationship between organized labor (a crucial sector of civil society) and the state. The countries with corporatist institutions will experience different patterns of state-society interaction than countries without it, a regularity strongly suggested by our study. Also, the strength of the linkage between civil society and political society will vary. In Poland, the remarkably weak linkage between civil society and political society was exemplified by the very low level of trust grassroots activists had in political parties. This, in turn, weakened the institutional system's ability to aggregate people's interests and its capacity to facilitate institutionally mediated resolution of conflicts.

Finally, protest will be tolerated in various polities in various degrees. As our analyses revealed, Poland had a high degree of tolerance for and acceptance of protest activities (or unconventional political participation). This high legitimacy or institutionalization of protest has consequences for the future development of Polish democracy: Poles are more likely to resort to contentious collective action as a means of political participation than other Central Europeans. But it is also a legacy of many decades of protest politics in Poland.

This brings us to the final point. As many astute observers of East and Central Europe have noted, democratic consolidation in this part of the world is heavily influenced by the legacies of ancien régimes. Patterns of institutionalization of (1) the basic domains of the polity, (2) linkages among them, and, in particular, (3) various levels of tolerance for protest reflect more or less distinct developments. It is not just the result of recent institutional configurations that trade unions remain a very influential political force in Poland, that they rely on strikes as a trusted political weapon, and that Solidarity has proven, over and over again, to be the most powerful "kingmaker" in Poland. It toppled the communist regime in 1989, it brought down its "own" government in 1993, and it was the nemesis of the ex-communist government in 1997. All this is a result of the specific political trajectory Polish people traveled almost since the inception of the communist regime in 1944.

While it is difficult to generalize about democratic consolidations and offer "the general laws of consolidation," it is possible to identify the main building blocks of this process through *analytical generalization*. This strategy leads to a precise identification of the crucial elements of the basic model of democratic consolidation. We identified several elements of such a model through a careful analysis of the Polish case, reconstructed the "Polish pattern," and began investigating three other patterns on the basis of the Hungarian, Slovak, and German data. So far our conclusions are unequivocal: in each case there has developed a different pattern or combination of the several basic elements, indicating the existence of at least four different democratic consolidations in Central Europe. They are not shaped merely by a single, uniform "Leninist legacy,"[9] but rather each of them constitutes a specific constellation of "past legacies and current circumstances" (Crawford and Lijphart 1995, 194; see also Bunce 1999). Among the basic elements of such constellations, analyzed by various authors, are specific patterns of opposition to state socialism, trajectories of "de-totalization," modes of the communist regime breakdown, mechanisms of the power transfer, and choices of reform strategies at the outset of the process. Crawford and Lijphart discuss the role of new institutions, hegemonic norms, and international imperatives. Our study of protest politics led us to the conclusion that in addition to these factors, it is imperative to analyze the patterns of institutionalization both within the major domains of the polity (the state, political society, and civil society) and among them.

APPENDIX A

Data Collection Protocol

I. Basic Data

001. Identification Number (IN):
     Date of first publication: Year   Month   Day   Number
002. Sources: 01. *Gazeta Wyborcza*   02. *Rzeczpospolita*
                  03. *Tygodnik Solidarnosc*   04. *Zycie Gospodarcze*
                  05. *Polityka*   06. *Wiesci*
                  07. Other. Specify:

Coding History:
Completing questionnaire:
Researcher's full name   Completion date   Acceptance date
Coordinator's signature
Coding:
Coder's full name   Coding date   Acceptance date
Receiver's signature

003. Brief description of protest (1. main actor(s); 2. type of protest;
     3. location [workplace/town/voivodeship])
004. Date protest began: Year   Month   Day
005. 01. Exact
     02. Approximate
     03. Day missing
006. Date protest ended: Year   Month   Day
007. 01. Exact
     02. Approximate
     03. Day missing
008. Duration of protest:
     01. 8 hours or less   04. 8 days–1 month
     02. One day   05. More than a month
     03. 2–7 days   06. Other (letters, statements)
     99. Data unavailable
009. Scope:
     01. Local
     02. Voivodeship
     03. Regional
     04. National
     99. Data unavailable

010. Demands are related to:
- 01. Local level
- 02. Voivodeship
- 03. Region
- 04. Nation
- 05. Workplace
- 06. Branch of industry
- 07. International/foreign affairs
- 99. Data unavailable

011. Type of protest event:
- 01. Single, separate protest
- 02. Series of protests
- 03. Protest campaign
- 99. Data unavailable

012. Related protests: 013. How many:
- 01. None
- 02. One or more

014. Brief description of related protests:
Type of protest action: Identification Number:
                               (use numbers from question 024)

015. Type of institution or enterprise where protest took place:
Production enterprise:
- 01. Category not specified
- 02. State-owned
- 03. Individual partnership with national treasury
- 04. State-owned, in the process of liquidation
- 05. Cooperative
- 06. Cooperative in the process of restructuring
- 07. Communal
- 08. Communal in the process of privatization
- 09. Private or privatized without foreign investment
- 10. Private or privatized from foreign investment

Service enterprise:
- 11. Category not specified
- 12. State-owned
- 13. Individual partnership with national treasury
- 14. State-owned, in the process of liquidation
- 15. Cooperative
- 16. Cooperative in the process of restructuring
- 17. Communal
- 18. Communal in the process of privatization
- 19. Private or privatized without foreign investment
- 20. Private or privatized with foreign investment

State or local self-government agency:
- 21. State
- 22. Local government
- 23. Other. Specify:
- 24. No specific institutional location (i.e., demonstration, rally, road blockade, letters, statements)
- 99. Data unavailable

II. Protest Participants

016. Number of participants:
      01. 0–20
      02. 21–200
      03. 201–500
      04. 501–1,000
      05. 1,001–2,000
      06. 2,001–10,000
      07. over 10,000
      99. Data unavailable

017. Social-vocational category of participants:
      01. Workers (with no additional specification)
      02. Miners and other employees of mining industries
      03. Workers in heavy industry/construction (without mining)
      04. Workers in light industry
      05. Farmers/peasants (with no additional specification)/employees of agricultural services
      06. Individual farmers/peasants
      07. Farmers in cooperative farms
      08. Farmers in state-owned farms
      09. Employees of service industries/trade/crafts
      10. Employees of the state-run public sector (with no additional specification)
      11. Health services/welfare institutions
      12. Education/science
      13. Culture/arts
      14. Transport/railways/airlines/shipping
      15. Mass media (radio/TV/press)
      16. State and local government/administration employees/judicial institutions
      17. Police/armed forces/firefighters
      18. Employers/owners/landlords
      19. Unemployed/homeless
      20. Retirees/pensioners/disabled
      21. Women
      22. Youth/students
      23. Ethnic minorities
      24. Religious minorities
      25. Neighborhood, local, or regional organizations
      26. Other. Specify:
      99. Data unavailable

018. How many categories:

019. Organizations leading or sponsoring protest: 020. How many:
      01. None
      02. Political parties. Specify: 021. How many:
      03. Political representatives of social organizations.
      Specify: 022. How many:
      Organizations of civil society: 023. How many:
      04. Labor unions: Solidarity

05. Labor unions: OPZZ
06. Labor unions: Solidarity '80
07. Other labor unions: Specify:
08. Siec
09. Samoobrona
10. NSZZ RI
11. Other peasant/farmer organizations.   Specify:
12. Professional organizations/interest groups.   Specify:
13. Youth organizations.   Specify:
14. Ethnic minority organizations.   Specify:
15. Alternative-culture movements (e.g., Skinheads).   Specify:
16. Social movements (e.g., ecological, peace, feminist, Monar).
    Specify:
17. Radical political movements/extraparliamentary opposition.
    Specify:
18. Regional or local organizations.   Specify:
19. Roman Catholic Church
20. Other churches:
21. Other organizations:
22. Strike committees, employees' councils
99. Data unavailable

III. Strategies and Methods of Protest

024. Protest:
Violent:
01. Attack on property (sabotage, theft, destruction) and terrorist action resulting in property damage
02. Use of force against management (battery, preventing management from carrying out duties)
03. Homicide, death resulting from terrorist actions, riots, etc.
04. Confrontation of two or more groups
05. Altercations, street riots, mutiny (resulting in beatings and property damage)
06. Revolt, civil war, armed confrontations, partisan/guerrilla activity
Nonviolent Disruption of the Public Order:
07. Strike
08. Occupation of public buildings
09. Demonstration, march, rally
10. Blockade of road or public place (e.g., square), picket
11. Takeover of enterprise
12. Refusal to acknowledge or carry out a legal decision
13. Forfeit of debt (taxes, loans, rent, etc.)
With No Disruption of the Public Order:
14. Rallies, meetings in traditional gathering places (auditoriums, sports arenas)
15. Strike alert and threat to undertake protest action
16. Open letters, statements, and appeals to authorities or community

17. Legal action
18. Symbolic manifestation (e.g., wearing armbands, insignia, displaying flags)
19. Boycotts of individuals, organizations, products
20. Hunger strikes
21. Other. Specify:
99. Data unavailable

025. Did the methods of protest change during the event's progression?
    01. No change
    02. Original methods were retained, although new methods were also introduced. Specify:
    03. Original methods were rejected and replaced by new ones. Specify:
    99. Data unavailable

026. Were the protest actions legal (meaning, were they undertaken and carried out in accordance with existing laws)?
    01. No
    02. Yes
    03. Began illegally, later recognized as legal by official authorities
    04. Began legally, later outlawed
    99. Data unavailable

Detailed Description of Strategy and Protest Method (quote):

IV. Scope of the Protest

027. Demands and grievances: 028. How many:
      Economic demands: 029. How many:
    01. Material compensation (e.g., wage raise, bonuses, financial disbursement, strike pay). Specify:
    02. Change in specific political-economic policies or the removal of individuals responsible for policy and economic decisions. Specify:
    03. General, abstract demands
    Political demands: 030. How many:
    04. Increased influence in decision making or greater participation in the political process. Specify:
    05. Change in specific policies or removal of certain members of political bodies. Specify:
    06. Dissatisfaction with current policies (expressed in general terms). Specify:
    07. Recognition of the protestors' identity (subjectivity). Specify:
    08. Demands related to the abortion debate. Specify:
    09. Demands related to the AIDS epidemic. Specify:
    10. Other demands. Specify:

031. Did additional demands arise during the protest activity?
    01. No
    02. Yes
    99. Data unavailable

032. If additional demands did arise, specify (categorize using the numeration from question 027):
033. How many:
034. Were any of the initial demands abandoned?
    01. No
    02. Yes
    99. Data unavailable
035. If so, which ones? (categorize using the numeration from question 027):
036. How many:
037. Was the protest action an expression of solidarity with protests organized by other persons, groups, or organizations?
    01. No
    02. Yes
    03. Partially a solidarity action, partially original
    99. Data unavailable
038. Mottoes and slogans used during the protest (quote):
039. Songs:
    01. National anthem
    02. Religious songs
    03. Patriotic songs
    04. Revolutionary songs (not including the International)
    05. The International
    06. Other. Specify:
    99. Data unavailable
040. Slogans appearing on flags, posters, and/or pamphlets (quote):
041. Symbolic objects used in protest:
    01. Flags. Specify:
    02. Crucifixes
    03. Religious objects (excluding crucifixes)
    04. National emblem
    05. Symbols and emblems of organization. Specify:
    06. Other. Specify:
    99. Data unavailable
042. Self-commentary by the participants of the protest (quote):
043. In whose name were the demands made?
    01. Protesting groups
    02. Vocational category. Specify:
    03. Territorial units (e.g., "the residents of Radom"). Specify:
    04. Social groups (e.g., ethnic, religious). Specify:
    05. Social category (e.g., "senior citizens"). Specify:
    06. The nation
    07. Society
    08. Other. Specify:
    99. Data unavailable

V. The Direct Object and the Ultimate Target of the Protest Event

044. Direct object of the protest action: 045. How many:
     National institutions: 046. How many:
     01. President
     02. Parliament
     03. Government
     04. Commissioner (ombudsman) on civil rights
     05. Armed forces
     06. Ministers and/or ministries. Specify:
     07. Members of parliament/senators. Specify:
     08. Police
     09. Voivode and voivodeship government
     10. Other:
     11. Local government (mayor, bailiff, municipal council, etc.)
     12. Political parties. Specify: 047. How many:
     13. Political representatives of social organizations.
         Specify: 048. How many:
     Organizations of civil society: 049. How many:
     14. Labor unions: Solidarity
     15. Labor unions: OPZZ
     16. Labor unions: Solidarity '80
     17. Other labor unions: Specify:
     18. Siec
     19. Samoobrona
     20. NSZZ RI
     21. Other peasant/farmer organizations. Specify:
     22. Professional organizations. Specify:
     23. Youth organizations. Specify:
     24. Ethnic minority organizations. Specify:
     25. Alternative-culture movements (e.g., Skinheads). Specify:
     26. Social movements (e.g., ecological, peace, feminist, Monar).
         Specify:
     27. Radical political movements. Specify:
     28. Regional or local organizations. Specify:
     29. Roman Catholic Church
     30. Other churches:
     31. Other:
     32. Management, boards of directors
     33. Domestic owners
     34. Foreign owners
     35. International institutions, foreign governments, trade offices
         (e.g., the World Bank, embassies). Specify:
     99. Data unavailable

050. Ultimate target or the protest action:
     National institutions:
     01. President
     02. Parliament
     03. Government
     04. Commissioner (ombudsman) on civil rights
     05. Armed forces
     06. Minister and/or Ministry of Ownership Transformations
     07. Minister and/or Ministry of Industry
     08. Other ministers and/or ministries. Specify:
     09. Members of parliament/senators. Specify:
     10. Police
     11. Voivode or voivodeship government
     12. Other:
     13. Local government (mayor, bailiff, municipal council, etc.)
     14. Political parties. Specify: 051. How many:
     15. Political representatives of social organizations.
         Specify: 052. How many:
     Organizations of civil society: 053. How many:
     16. Labor unions: Solidarity
     17. Labor unions: OPZZ
     18. Labor unions: Solidarity '80
     19. Other labor unions: Specify:
     20. Siec
     21. Samoobrona
     22. NSZZ RI
     23. Other peasant/farmer organizations. Specify:
     24. Professional organizations. Specify:
     25. Youth organizations. Specify:
     26. Ethnic minority organizations. Specify:
     27. Alternative-culture movements (e.g., Skinheads). Specify:
     28. Social movements (e.g., ecological, peace, feminist, Monar).
         Specify:
     29. Radical political movements. Specify:
     30. Regional or local organizations. Specify:
     31. Roman Catholic Church
     32. Other churches:
     33. Other:
     34. Management, boards of directors
     35. Domestic owners
     36. Foreign owners
     37. International, foreign institutions (e.g., the World Bank).
         Specify:
     99. Data unavailable

VI. Reactions to Protest Event

055. Did the authorities (e.g., police) intervene? If so, how?
    01. No intervention
    02. Intervention without the use of force
    03. Intervention with the use of force
    99. Data unavailable
056. If yes, who intervened?
    01. Police
    02. Armed forces
    03. Special forces
    04. Other. Specify:
    99. Data unavailable
057. Did the use of force result in casualties or property damage?
    01. No
    02. Human casualties (death)   058. How many:
    03. Wounded/injured   059. How many:
    04. Arrested and detained   060. How many:
    05. Convicted   061. How many:
    06. Material losses   062. Amount (in zlotys):
    99. Data unavailable
063. Were administrative sanctions brought against the protestors (e.g., dismissal from work, fines, banning of organization, etc.)?
    01. Yes. Specify:
    02. No
    99. Data unavailable
064. Were negotiations undertaken with the protestors?
    01. No
    02. Yes
    99. Data unavailable
065. Who negotiated:
066. Was mediation attempted?
    01. No
    02. Yes
    99. Data unavailable
067. Who mediated:
068. If yes, was the mediation:
    01. Rejected by the protestors
    02. Rejected by the target of the protest
    03. Accepted though did not lead to conflict resolution
    04. Accepted and led to conflict resolution
    99. Data unavailable
069. Was a counter-protest carried out by another group or organization?
    01. No

      02. Yes. Specify:

      99. Data unavailable

070. Were the demands of the protestors met?

      01. No

      02. Yes, entirely

      03. Yes, partially. Specify (use numeration from question 027):

      99. Data unavailable

071. Was there any political reaction (statements, speeches, etc.)?

      01. No

      National institutions: 072. How many:

      02. President

      03. Parliament

      04. Government

      05. Commissioner (ombudsman) on civil rights

      06. Armed forces

      07. Ministers and/or ministries. Specify:

      08. Members of parliament/senators. Specify:

      09. Police

      10. Voivode and/or voivodeship administration

      11. Local government (mayor, bailiff, municipal council, etc.)

      12. Other:

      13. Political parties. Specify: 073. How many:

      14. Political representatives of social organizations.

          Specify: 074. How many:

      Organization of civil society: 075. How many:

      15. Labor unions: Solidarity

      16. Labor unions: OPZZ

      17. Labor unions: Solidarity '80

      18. Walesa before he became president

      19. Other labor unions: Specify:

      20. Siec

      21. Samoobrona

      22. NSZZ RI

      23. Other agricultural organizations. Specify:

      24. Professional organizations. Specify:

      25. Youth organizations. Specify:

      26. Ethnic minority organizations. Specify:

      27. Alternative-culture movements (e.g., Skinheads). Specify:

      28. Social-action movements (e.g., ecological, feminist, Monar).
          Specify:

      29. Radical political movements. Specify:

      30. Regional organizations. Specify:

      31. Catholic Church

      32. Other churches:

      33. Other. Specify:

      34. Management, boards of directors

      35. Domestic owners
      36. Foreign owners
      37. International, foreign institutions (e.g., the World Bank, embassies)
      99. Data unavailable
076. What kind of political responses resulted, if any?
      01. Supportive. Who (using numeration from 071):
      02. Neutral. Who (using numeration from 071):
      03. Condemning. Who (using numeration from 071):
      04. Difficult to evaluate (source only indicated that there was a reaction). Who (using numeration from 071):
077. Did the demands and/or grievances of protestors result in any long-term policy changes?
      01. No change
      02. Policy modified
      03. Policy changed
      99. Data unavailable
078. If a policy change or modification took place, describe it briefly:

Chronology of Major Events, 1989–1993

Compiled by Jacek Stefanski
Translated, edited, and revised by Martha and Jan Kubik
(Several entries for 1992 were translated from Roszkowski 1994)

1989

2/6   The roundtable negotiations began. The communist delegation was headed by Minister of the Interior General Czeslaw Kiszczak; the Solidarity delegation, by Lech Walesa. The meeting opened with Kiszczak's speech, in which he listed an agreement on "nonconfrontational" parliamentary elections as one of the chief aims of the negotiations. In accordance with an earlier decision, special committees (subtables) were created to discuss specific issues: economic and social policy, party pluralism, political reform, and others.

3/29   During an informal meeting in the Villa Magdalenka, Kiszczak and Walesa decided that an Agreement Commission should be created that would supervise the implementation of the roundtable accords.

4/5   The final session of the roundtable. The leaders of both delegations signed the agreement. In retrospect, the most important documents were those concerning parliamentary elections. At first, opposition circles saw the agreements as concessions to the communist regime in return for granting Solidarity official recognition. Later, these agreements became the gateway to the transformation of the Polish political system.

4/7   The Sejm legislated major changes in the constitution. Two new government institutions were created: the office of the president, and the Senate. The Solidarity National Commission (KKW "S") asked the Citizens' Committee advising the Solidarity chairman to supervise the parliamentary elections under the name of the Solidarity Citizens' Committee (KO "S"). Regional offices of the trade union were urged to set up local Solidarity Citizens' Committees.

4/13   The State Council of the Polish People's Republic (PRL) set the election dates for June 4 (first round) and June 18 (second round) and established the State Electoral Commission (PKW).

4/17   The District Court in Warsaw registered NSZZ (Independent Self-governing Trade Union) Solidarity. Three days later, NSZZ "S" of Individual Farmers was legalized.

5/8	The first issue of the opposition newspaper *Gazeta Wyborcza* was published. Adam Michnik was the editor in chief.
6/4	The first round of elections to the Sejm and the Senate. Sixty-two percent of registered voters participated. Solidarity candidates triumphed, gaining 160 out of 161 lower house seats and 92 of 100 upper house seats they were allowed to contest. In the second round of elections, Solidarity won the remaining independent seat in the Sejm and seven more seats in the Senate. Only five candidates running for the 299 seats reserved for the communist coalition received the required 50 percent of votes.
6/17	Solidarity's governing body (KKW "S") decided to dissolve local Citizens' Committees, saying their task was already accomplished. This decision was later revoked as being too hasty.
6/23	The Citizens' Parliamentary Club (OKP) was created at a meeting of Solidarity deputies and senators. Bronislaw Geremek was elected its chairman.
6/30	The Thirteenth Plenary Meeting of the Central Committee of the PZPR. General Wojciech Jaruzelski, uncertain of his support, announced he would not run for president. He proposed General Kiszczak should take his place.
7/3	*Gazeta Wyborcza* published Michnik's article entitled "Your President, Our Prime Minister," proposing a division of power between the communists and Solidarity.
7/4	During the inaugural session of the parliament, M. Kozakiewicz and A. Stelmachowski were elected, respectively, Speaker of the Sejm and Speaker of the Senate. Prime Minister Mieczyslaw Rakowski announced his cabinet's resignation.
7/18	After participating in a meeting of the Polish United Workers' Party (PZPR) Parliamentary Club, Jaruzelski announced he would run for president.
7/19	The National Assembly (joint houses of the Sejm and the Senate) elected General Wojciech Jaruzelski president with 270 votes. The required minimum was 269.
7/25	President Jaruzelski suggested to Lech Walesa the creation of a "great coalition" with Solidarity's participation. Walesa asked that the opposition be allowed to form a new government.
7/29	The second part of the Thirteenth Plenary Meeting of the Central Committee of the PZPR. Jaruzelski resigned as First Secretary of the Central Committee. Mieczyslaw F. Rakowski was elected in his place.
7/31	In a conversation with the Citizens' Parliamentary Club (OKP) chairman, Bronislaw Geremek, General Kiszczak announced his intention to run for the office of prime minister. The OKP was not happy with Kiszczak's decision and maintained its readiness to create a new government.
8/1	The Sejm accepted the resignation of Rakowski's cabinet. Heated discussions over Kiszczak's candidacy were held in the Sejm lobbies.
8/2	As a result of a motion put forward by President Jaruzelski, the Sejm appointed General Kiszczak prime minister.
8/7	Lech Walesa proposed that the SD (Democratic Party), the ZSL (United Peasant Party), and the OKP form a new government coalition.
8/17	Solidarity chairman Lech Walesa, ZSL chairman Roman Malinowski, and

SD chairman Jerzy Jozwiak issued a communiqué regarding the creation of a new government coalition. President Jaruzelski received the three politicians in Belweder (the presidential palace). On the same day, the president received a letter from Prime Minister Kiszczak asking to be relieved of his position.

8/19   Acting on Walesa's suggestion, the president recommended Tadeusz Mazowiecki as the candidate for prime minister to the Sejm.

8/24   The Sejm dismissed Kiszczak and appointed Mazowiecki in his place. The new prime minister said in his inaugural speech: "I want to form a government capable of acting for the good of the society, the nation, and the country. This will be the government of a coalition for a fundamental reform of the state. . . . It is necessary to reintroduce in Poland the mechanism of a normal political life. The rule of struggle, which sooner or later leads to the elimination of opponents, has to be replaced by the rule of partnership. Otherwise we shall not pass from a totalitarian system to a democratic one. The long-run strategic aim of the government's activities will be the reinstatement of well-known and proven economic institutions in Poland. By this I understand the return to a market economy. . . . It is necessary to introduce the rule of law, to grant each citizen rights conformable to international treaties, agreements, and conventions. . . . The government that I will create will not be responsible for the legacy that it inherits. This legacy, however, influences the environment in which we have to act. We are drawing a thick line underneath the past. We shall be responsible only for what we will do to extricate Poland from the current state of depression."

9/12   The Sejm accepted the new government proposed by Mazowiecki. The new cabinet consisted of 24 ministers, representing four parliamentary clubs. The OKP took 12 seats and gave the Ministry of Finance to Leszek Balcerowicz, who became also deputy prime minister. The ZSL and SD received four and three ministries, respectively. Four ministries were assigned to the PZPR, including the Ministry of Internal Affairs, which was given to the other deputy prime minister—General Kiszczak. The only independent cabinet member was Krzysztof Skubiszewski, the foreign minister.

10/26   A meeting of the Warsaw Pact countries' Committee of Ministers of Foreign Affairs was organized. The closing statement recognized the right of every state to self-determination without external interference as the basis for security and peace in Europe.

10/28   Three hundred delegates, representing more than 10 national-Catholic movements, formed the Christian National Union (ZChN). Wieslaw Chrzanowski was elected chairman of the organization. The representatives of the ZChN in the Sejm decided to form their own lobby within the OKP.

11/9   Visit of West German Chancellor Helmut Kohl to Poland. The next day the chancellor returned unexpectedly to Germany for 24 hours, prompted by the events that culminated in the destruction of the Berlin Wall.

11/28   Minister of Foreign Affairs Skubiszewski said that Poland's attitude toward the unification of Germany will depend on whether the new German state will accept the commitments of East Germany, resulting from the Zgor-zelec Accord of 1950, and West Germany, defined in the December 1970 accords. Both treaties concerned the recognition of the Polish border on the rivers Odra and Nysa (Oder and Neisse). He added that the unification of Germany was a European issue and should happen with the consent of the whole of Europe.

12/6   The government asked the parliamentary clubs for an expedient decision on the package of 16 economic legislative acts that would create a legal ba-sis for the planned reforms.

12/9–10   A Conference of the Civic Movement was organized on the topic "The Ethos of 'Solidarity.'" Several hundred delegates participated in the con-ference, including the leading representatives of "Solidarity circles," such as Walesa, Mazowiecki, and Geremek. Jaroslaw Kaczynski criticized the proposal to formalize the civic movement. He feared that this might lead to the creation of a strong party, which would take over the role of a political monopolist from the communist party (the PZPR).

12/13   Ministers of foreign affairs of the 24 developed Western countries met in Brussels and confirmed the creation of the so-called stabilization fund for Poland.

12/27–29   The Sejm passed the package of legislative acts regarding economic reforms, later known as the Balcerowicz Plan.

12/29   The Sejm ratified a constitutional amendment that changed the name of the state from the Polish People's Republic (PRL) to the Republic of Poland (RP). The articles granting the PZPR the leading role in the country, defin-ing international alliances, and formalizing the socialist economy were repealed.

1990

1/17   During a meeting of the KKW "S" Walesa said: "I will support the gov-ernment until the next congress of Solidarity, although I do not agree with its ideas. But at the congress I will say, 'The government! sail alone.' And if its ideas are proven wrong, I will do everything to let new people and new ideas in."

1/27–30   The Eleventh Congress of the Polish United Workers' Party (PZPR). In the evening of the first day, the debate was suspended and the founding con-gress of a new party began, with the participation of the same delegates. The new party was called Social Democracy of the Republic of Poland (SdRP). Aleksander Kwasniewski became the chairman of the party's Na-tional Council.

2/10   Representatives of 500 shop-floor organizations of Solidarity opposed to Lech Walesa formed a new union, Solidarity '80. Marian Jurczyk was elected chairman.

2/13   Ministers of foreign affairs of the Warsaw Pact and the NATO countries agreed on a schedule of future negotiations concerning German unification. Representatives of the FRG (Federal Republic of Germany), the GDR

(German Democratic Republic), and the four world powers—the United States, the USSR, the United Kingdom, and France (the "2 + 4" formula)—were to participate in the negotiations. On the following day Prime Minister Mazowiecki announced that Poland would try to change the formula of the negotiations regarding the unification of Germany, to include a representative of the Republic of Poland.

3/14   Poland was invited to participate in the negotiations concerning the Polish-German border during the 2 + 4 conference.

3/31   Walesa and Mazowiecki participated in a meeting of the National Citizens' Committee. Solidarity's chairman and the prime minister expressed different views on the future of political changes in Poland. Walesa criticized the government for its inefficiency and sluggish reforms. The committee's chairman, Zdzislaw Najder, declared that the "roundtable formula" had outlived its usefulness, and fully democratic parliamentary elections were a necessity.

4/7   In an interview for *Zycie Warszawy* (Warsaw Life), Jaroslaw Kaczynski said, "I believe that a change in the president's office is unavoidable, and Walesa is really the only candidate for this office . . . Walesa's presidency is not an aim per se, it is the result of an exhaustion of possibilities of the current political system."

4/11   The Sejm repealed the censorship law and dissolved the Main Office for the Control of the Press, Publications, and Public Performances.

4/12   The Soviet Union publicly acknowledged its responsibility for the Katyn massacre.

4/19–24 During the Second Congress of the NSZZ Solidarity, Walesa was reelected as the union's chairman by a large majority. Delegates supported early parliamentary and presidential elections in the spring of 1991.

5/10   In an interview for the *Washington Post,* Walesa predicted a "permanent political war" that would cause a governmental shake-up. He accused Mazowiecki's cabinet of "blurring of political differences in Poland." He added that during the previous year, the prime minister had convinced him that Poland needed peace, and that political debates had to be quieted. Walesa added: "I placed too much faith in Polish intellectuals and I used their advice too often. They misled me. Now I will go against them and that is why I am suggesting the idea of a permanent political war."

5/12   A new party, the Center Alliance (PC), was formed by various political parties and clubs, regional Citizens' Committees, and several individuals. A. Anusz, A. Arendarski, J. K. Bielecki, J. Eysymontt, A. Glapinski, P. Hniedziewicz, J. Kaczynski, A. Kern, J. Lewandowski, T. Liszcz, J. Maziarski, J. Olszewski, and S. Siwek were among the founding signatories of the PC charter.

The PC announced its program, which stated: "Either there will be an acceleration of changes in the political system, leading to full democracy, full sovereignty, and a radical transformation of property rights in the economy, or the current political configuration will persist, preserving the communist heritage." It further stated that the roundtable accords were no longer valid and that parliamentary and presidential elections should take place no later than the spring of 1991. The new president should coauthor the reforms; the candidacy of Lech Walesa would guarantee the realization of such a reform program.

5/27   Local elections were held. The turnout was 42.13 percent.

6/1   Walesa dismissed Adam Michnik as editor in chief of *Gazeta Wyborcza* and took away the paper's right to use Solidarity's insignia. Michnik retained his position since *Gazeta Wyborcza* was privately owned. In so doing, Walesa initiated a conflict that ultimately destroyed the unity of the Solidarity camp.

6/10   Following Jerzy Turowicz's initiative, the informal movement Alliance for Democracy was formed in Krakow. Concerned with conflicts within the Solidarity camp and the radical tenor of the PC's program, they decided to form a more moderate political movement. Most of the Alliance's participants later became the leaders of the Democratic Union (UD).

6/21   The parliaments of both German states passed identical resolutions confirming the Polish-German border on the Odra (Oder) and Nysa (Neisse) Rivers.

6/27   The Democratic Right Forum (FPD) was formed. Aleksander Hall and Tadeusz Syryjczyk were among its founders.

6/29–30   The first congress of the Liberal-Democratic Congress (KLD). The party's manifesto declared liberty, private property, and tolerance as the foundation of social order. Freedom of religion and the separation of church and state were also included in the party's program. Janusz Lewandowski and Donald Tusk became, respectively, the chairman and deputy chairman of the Congress.

6/30   Representatives of several Citizens' Committees came to Warsaw for a conference chaired by Walesa. They expressed their support for him and decided not to build any central structures, but to hold from time to time national conferences. On the following day, representatives of Citizens' Committees met again, this time in response to an invitation issued on June 17 by the supporters of Prime Minister Mazowiecki. Some delegates participated in both conferences, others arrived only for this one. There was a great deal of confusion as to who represented whom, and who possessed voting rights. A discussion concerning the future of the movement was inconclusive.

7/6   Mazowiecki reconstructed a part of his cabinet. The Sejm dismissed Kiszczak as minister of internal affairs and General Siwicki as minister of defense. Both had been members of the communist party.

7/7   Mazowiecki and Walesa met in a convent near Warsaw. There was no rapprochement; their ideological differences prevailed.

7/16   A group of Solidarity activists, including Z. Bujak, W. Frasyniuk, M. Edelman, Z. Kuratowska, B. Labuda, J. M. Rokita, J. Turowicz, and H. Wujec, formed the Civic Movement—Democratic Action (ROAD). The organization's manifesto stated that parliamentary democracy, civil liberty, and an independent court of justice should be the foundations of a sovereign Poland. The role of the state should be limited, and many of its functions should be transferred to local self-governments. The planned economy should be replaced by a social market economy. The ROAD also advocated early direct presidential elections.

7/17   Poland's and West Germany's foreign affairs ministers agreed to sign two bilateral treaties during the third round of the 2 + 4 conference in Paris. The first treaty, concerning the border on the Oder and Neisse Rivers, was to be signed immediately after the German unification and added to the final documents of the conference. The drafting of the second treaty, concerning good-neighbor relations and friendship between the two countries, was postponed until a later date.

7/27   About 100 members of the parliament signed a petition addressed to President Jaruzelski asking him to resign.

8/31   Mazowiecki and Walesa met in the residence of Bishop Goclowski of Gdansk in the hope of ending their standoff. Walesa offered the prime minister another term in office in exchange for Mazowiecki's promise not to run for president. Mazowiecki suggested that neither of them run but that they together propose another candidate. No compromise was reached.

9/17   Walesa announced his candidacy for the office of president.

10/3   The National Commission of NSZZ Solidarity officially announced their support for Walesa's candidacy.

10/4   Mazowiecki announced his candidacy for the office of president.

10/25   Six candidates collected the 100,000 signatures required to run for the office of president. The last to register was Stanislaw Tyminski, an unknown Polish entrepreneur from Canada, considered to be a marginal candidate.

11/8   Miczyslaw Gil became the new leader of the OKP, following Geremek's resignation. Solidarity's increasing fragmentation was evident in the seven factions that emerged within its parliamentary club. They included ROAD—52 deputies and senators, 49 independent members of parliament; PC—39 members; Christian Democrats—39 members; the combined clubs of NSZZ RI Solidarity and the PSL "S"—28 members; FPD—6 members; ZChN—also 6 members. The remaining members of parliament who had belonged to the originally 260-person OKP either did not declare their support for any of the above groups or had left the club.

11/25   The first round of presidential elections. No candidate reached the required 50 percent threshold. The turnout was 60.63 percent of registered voters. Of these, 39.96 percent voted for Walesa. Tyminski unexpectedly came in second with 23.1 percent of the votes. Mazowiecki was third with 18.08 percent. The ex-communist candidate, Wlodzimierz Cimoszewicz, received 9.2 percent; Roman Bartoszcze of the PSL, 7.15 percent; and Leszek Moczulski of the KPN, 2.5 percent. There would be a runoff between Walesa and Tyminski on December 9, 1990.

11/27   Mazowiecki handed in his cabinet's resignation. The president asked the prime minister to continue as head of the government until the presidential elections were over and a new prime minister appointed.

12/2	Members of Mazowiecki's electoral committees, the ROAD, the FPD, and the Alliance for Democracy formed the Democratic Union (UD). Mazowiecki became the Union's leader. The new party asked its supporters to vote for Walesa in the second round of elections.
	Walesa authorized Jan Olszewski to begin preparations for a new government.
12/9	Walesa won decisively the second round of the presidential elections with 74.25 percent of the vote.
12/14	Following a motion introduced by Prime Minister Mazowiecki, the Sejm dismissed the old government and asked the prime minister to continue in his office until the appointment of a new prime minister.
12/18	Olszewski announced, "As a result of significant differences between the President-elect and myself in our views on the composition of the government, I abandoned the mission entrusted to me."
12/22	President Walesa appointed Jaroslaw Kaczynski, the Center Alliance's leader, his chief of staff.
12/29	Jan Krzysztof Bielecki, one of the KLD leaders, was designated by the president as the new prime minister.

1991

1/4	Bielecki was approved by the Sejm.
	The Democratic Union's parliamentary club left the OKP. Several days later, Geremek was elected the new club's chairman.
1/6	In a letter to the Citizens' Committee, President Walesa called for a final, gala meeting of the committee. He stated that the committee's activities "have become part of the glorious pages of History." The members of the committee decided that the organization should continue to exist but under the name of the National Civic Committee (KKO).
1/8	The PC's political council called for new parliamentary elections to be held as soon as possible.
1/12	The Sejm approved the new cabinet proposed by Bielecki. Four members of the previous cabinet remained in their offices, including Deputy Prime Minister and Finance Minister Leszek Balcerowicz and Minister of Foreign Affairs Krzysztof Skubiszewski. The majority of new ministers came from the Liberal-Democratic Congress (KLD) and the Center Alliance (PC).
2/12	President Walesa received a letter from President Mikhail Gorbachev of the Soviet Union, who proposed to dissolve the military structures of the Warsaw Pact by April 1, 1991.
2/15	In Vysehrad, Prime Minister Jozsef Antall of Hungary, President Vaclav Havel of Czechoslovakia, and President Lech Walesa of Poland signed a declaration of cooperation between their three countries.
2/23–24	During the Third National Congress of NSZZ Solidarity, Marian Krzaklewski became Walesa's successor as chairman. The congress decided to

	field its own candidates in the upcoming parliamentary elections. Their number was not to surpass 60–70 names.
2/25	The Warsaw Pact Political Advisory Committee, which met in Budapest, accepted a protocol concerning the repeal of the Warsaw Pact military agreements and the dissolution of the pact's organs and structures as of April 1, 1991.
3/9	The Sejm decided to dissolve itself by the fall of 1991.
3/13	Stanislaw Tyminski's Party "X" was registered.
3/23	The First Congress of the Center Alliance labeled the party "Christian democratic." Jaroslaw Kaczynski was elected chairman. The delegates advocated that the parliamentary elections take place on May 26, 1991. It was also decided that the new parliament should produce a law on the decommunization of the state.
3/25	Members of the nine-person "Labor Solidarity" faction left the OKP.
4/20	Zbigniew Bujak and his supporters left the ROAD and formed the Social-Democratic Movement (RDS).
4/21	Poland signed an agreement with the Paris Club that reduced the Polish debt (about $3 billion) by half. Implementation of the plan was conditional on the Polish government's compliance with an accord between Poland and the IMF.
5/10	The Sejm passed several laws on the parliamentary elections. The Senate was to be elected according to a majoritarian system (first-past-the-post); the Sejm according to a combination of two rules: 115 deputies were to be chosen by majority in single-seat districts, while the remaining 345 deputies would be elected from party lists in proportion to the number of votes won by their parties.
5/11–12	The Unification Congress of the Democratic Union (UD) was held. Members of the ROAD and the Democratic Right Forum (FPD) decided to retain their autonomy and formed separate factions within the party. The ROAD created the Social-Liberal Faction (FSL); the Forum, the Democratic Right Faction (FPD). Mazowiecki was elected chairman of the UD; Wladyslaw Frasyniuk (FSL), Aleksander Hall (FPD), and Jacek Kuron became his deputies. The main aims of the Democratic Union were stated in its declaration of principles: representative democracy, the rule of law, a social market economy, Poland's participation in a unified Europe.
5/19	The Liberal-Democratic Congress changed its leadership. Donald Tusk replaced Janusz Lewandowski. It was decided that the KLD's parliamentarians should leave the OKP and form their own club.
6/6	In a letter to the Sejm Speaker, President Walesa proposed changes to the recently passed electoral law. In his judgment, the law was complicated and politically irrational. After an exchange of letters with the Sejm, the president formally vetoed the new electoral law.
6/13	The Sejm failed to override the presidential veto (a two-thirds majority was needed to succeed). Walesa's amendments were accepted, and the Sejm passed the amended version: a Hare version of the proportional represen-

tation (PR) system. Three hundred ninety-one deputies were to be chosen from party lists in 37 multimember districts; the remaining 69 were to be chosen from national lists. For the Senate elections, a plurality system with a single ballot was adopted.

6/17 Prime Minister Bielecki and Chancellor Kohl signed the "Treaty on Good-Neighbor Relations and Friendly Cooperation between Poland and Germany."

6/21 The president's spokesman announced that Walesa was still unhappy with the format of the electoral law and was debating whether to dissolve the parliament. The PC and the ZChN supported the president's position. At the same time, the ZChN accused the UD of "a conscious intention to delay the reconstruction of a democratic and independent Polish state."

6/26 President Walesa vetoed the amended electoral law. Two days later, his veto was overturned by the Sejm.

6/29 An emergency congress of the Polish Peasant Party (PSL) dismissed Roman Bartoszcze from the post of party chairman. Waldemar Pawlak became his successor. One of the reasons for Bartoszcze's dismissal was his appeal to decommunize the party and to expel the leading members of the former ZSL.

7/1 The Warsaw Pact was dissolved at a meeting of its Political Advisory Committee.

President Walesa signed the electoral law. The election date was set for October 27, 1991.

7/11 The National Committee of NSZZ Solidarity reversed its previous position and decided not to limit the number of its candidates in the elections.

8/7 Representatives of the Christian National Union (ZChN) and the Christian Civic Movement jointly formed the Catholic Electoral Action (WAK) coalition.

8/8 The Center Alliance, most Citizens' Committees, and several smaller parties formed the Center Civic Agreement (POC) electoral committee.

8/19 The Moscow Putsch. President Walesa met Prime Minister Bielecki and consulted many leading politicians. In the evening President George Bush telephoned Walesa. The conversation concerned the situation in the USSR and Poland's security.

8/21 The defeat of the Moscow Putsch. Walesa talked to Boris Yeltsin.

8/26 The Polish government recognized the sovereign states of Lithuania, Latvia, and Estonia.

8/29 Wieslawa Ziolkowska of the Labor Deputy Club (earlier a member of the Polish Social-Democratic Union) put forward a motion to dismiss the government, blaming it for the country's deepening economic crisis. On the following day in the Sejm, Prime Minster Bielecki offered his cabinet's resignation, stating that "the possibilities for effective cooperation between the government and the parliament under the present conditions have been exhausted."

8/31	The Sejm refused to accept Bielecki's resignation. Two hundred eleven deputies opposed Ziolkowska's motion, while only 114 voted in favor and 26 abstained.
9/3	Thirty electoral committees registered lists in every region of the country; numerous parties registered lists in five or fewer regions.
9/16	Jaroslaw Kaczynski, the PC's leader, categorically denied that the Alliance was at any time the "party of the president," rejected the possibility of forming a government jointly with the KLD and the UD after the elections, and strongly criticized Balcerowicz's economic policies.
9/23	President Walesa met with the Electoral Committee of the POC. Kaczynski later commented: "This shows the president's political support for our coalition."
9/26	The Sejm amended the budget, increasing the deficit to about 3 percent of GDP and above 10 percent of the planned budget expenditures, a deviation from the IMF financial directions. The IMF suspended its credits to Poland.
10/5	A summit of the Vysehrad Triangle in Krakow, with the participation of President Havel, President Walesa, and Prime Minister Antall. The three leaders expressed their desire to enter into close cooperation with the NATO. Poland signed bilateral declarations concerning friendly relations, solidarity, and cooperation with Czechoslovakia and Hungary.
10/17	Polish bishops issued an appeal asking people to vote for parties that "stand clearly for human life from the moment of conception, respect family rights, show their care for Poland and their respect for Poland's traditions stemming from Christian roots."
10/27	Parliamentary elections. The voter turnout was low: 43.2 percent. In the Sejm election, the UD won 12.3 percent of the votes (62 seats), the post-communist SLD—11.99 percent (60 seats), the WAK—8.7 percent (49 seats), the PSL—8.7 percent (48 seats), the KPN—7.5 percent (46 seats), the POC—8.7 percent (44 seats), the KLD—7.49 percent (37 seats), the PL (a peasant party)—5.47 percent (28 seats), and the NSZZ Solidarity—5.05 percent (27 seats). Nineteen other electoral committees won between one and 16 seats in the Sejm.
10/29	The president began a series of meetings with representatives of the main political parties. Kuron was his first interlocutor. The ZChN proposed forming a broad Christian coalition that "would take over the responsibility for the government." In addition to the WAK (ZChN's electoral committee), the coalition would be composed of the PC, PL, PChD (Christian Democracy of Poland), and ChD (Christian Democracy) deputies. An agreement with the PSL was also expected.
	Donald Tusk (KLD) met with Jaroslaw Kaczynski (PC). The KLD's chairman investigated the possibility of forming a coalition of the two parties and the UD.
11/4	The president met with representatives of the ZChN, KLD, and KPN. He proposed that the Center Alliance (PC) and these three parties form a gov-

	ernment. He recommended Jan Krzysztof Bielecki of the KLD for prime minister.
11/7	Walesa and the "Four" (ZChN, PC, KPN, and KLD) met again. The coalition wanted Jan Olszewski as the new prime minister. Walesa was opposed to this candidacy and asked the UD to come up with their own candidate for the post of prime minister. The next day he asked Bronislaw Geremek to form a cabinet. Geremek gave up this mission after several days.
11/14	The president met again with representatives of the "Four" and the PL. He still refused to appoint Olszewski prime minister. The political deadlock lasted for several days.
11/25	The inaugural session of the Sejm. The five parties (ZChN, PC, KPN, KLD, and PL) had a sufficient majority in the lower house to form a government. Wieslaw Chrzanowski (of the ZChN) was elected the Speaker of the Sejm. The coalition parties divided the seats in the Presidium of the Sejm among themselves.
11/26	Poland became an official member of the Council of Europe.
12/2	Poland became the first country to recognize the independence of Ukraine.
12/5	The Sejm accepted the resignation of Bielecki's cabinet. The Speaker of the Sejm, Chrzanowski, informed the deputies that President Walesa had designated Jan Olszewski as the new prime minister.
12/6	The Sejm appointed Olszewski prime minister. The new government leader announced: "I will try to form a government of clear intentions and clean hands."
12/10	The "Five" coalition tried unsuccessfully to work out a common position regarding economic issues. The Liberals (KLD) threatened to leave the coalition; they did so two days later.
12/14	Prime Minister Olszewski informed the "Four" of the tentative composition of his new cabinet. It was dominated by the members of the PC and ZChN. The KPN was given no ministerial portfolios. After the meeting, its leader, Leszek Moczulski, told the press: "I have no good news. The prime minister has decided that the KPN will remain outside the government."
12/16	Poland, Hungary, and Czechoslovakia signed an association agreement with the European Economic Community (EEC).
	President Walesa expressed his disapproval regarding the composition of the new government proposed by Olszewski. Further discussions were announced.
12/17	Olszewski announced his resignation, faced with the dissolution of the coalition and with the lack of presidential acceptance. In his letter to the Sejm Speaker, Olszewski wrote: "During our conversation yesterday, Mr. President said that he would not cooperate with a government whose composition and program I had proposed to him." Walesa stated that he accepted Olszewski as prime minister but wanted the coalition to include the PSL and the UD. On the following day the Sejm rejected Olszewski's resignation.

12/21	Prime Minister Olszewski delivered the government's exposé in the Sejm. He criticized the two previous Solidarity governments of Mazowiecki and Bielecki. He said: "I would like the swearing in of the government I proposed to mark the beginning of the end of communism."
12/23	The Sejm accepted Olszewski's government. Krzysztof Skubiszewski remained as minister of foreign affairs. Jan Parys was appointed minister of defense. Antoni Macierewicz was to head the Ministry of Internal Affairs.
12/27	The Polish government recognized the national sovereignty of Armenia, Azerbaijan, Belarus, the Russian Federation, Kazakhstan, Kyrgyzstan, Moldova, Tajikistan, Turkmenistan, and Uzbekistan.

1992

1/6	Prime Minister Olszewski met with the SLD Parliamentary Club. He discussed the problem of decommunization, which, according to him, would affect not more than several hundred persons—symbols of the old regime.
1/10	The Samoobrona (Self-Defense) Agricultural Trade Union, headed by Andrzej Lepper, was registered.
1/20	The minister of the interior, Macierewicz, stated that all high civil servants, public prosecutors, judges, and members of parliament who had been Security Service (SB) informers should resign from public offices.
2/9	Kaczynski called for an expansion of the government coalition by the UD and KLD. Olszewski, who shared Kaczynski's opinion, allegedly authorized him and his brother to begin negotiations regarding this matter with the UD.
2/13	Following the prime minister's authorization, Lech Kaczynski met with Mazowiecki. Shortly afterward, Jan Gugulski, the government spokesman, denied any knowledge as to who authorized the Kaczynski brothers to conduct negotiations with the UD on behalf of the coalition. This announcement sparked a long exchange of statements between the PC's leader and the prime minister regarding the question of the authorization.
2/22–23	The Third National Conference of the KLD criticized the economic policy of the Olszewski government and called for the formation of a pro-reform coalition with the UD and the PC.
2/27	The Sejm appointed Andrzej Olechowski minister of finance.
3/11	The prime minister met with Mazowiecki. The two politicians discussed the potential entry of the Democratic Union into the governing coalition. A compromise on economic issues was a precondition. The Union also requested the participation of the KLD in the negotiations.
3/15	The UD Council authorized Mazowiecki to negotiate the government's reconstruction. Key topics were the economic program, further reforms of public administration, and defense and foreign policy. Two days later Prime Minister Olszewski and Mazowiecki held another round of negotiations but did not reach a compromise. Olszewski did not consent to the participation of the KLD in an expanded coalition; his preference was to add several

	Democratic Union politicians to the government and avoid major governmental reconstruction.

3/21 Mazowiecki (Democratic Union), Donald Tusk (Liberal-Democratic Congress), and Bankowski (Polish Economic Program—PPG) formed a "Small Coalition," declaring their parties' desire for close cooperation.

3/26 Prime Minister Olszewski and Waldemar Pawlak agreed on the principles of the PSL's participation in the government coalition.

4/6 Defense Minister Jan Parys implicated the military in a political power play and plans to abolish democracy. A deep crisis between the government and the president ensued. The crisis ended when Parys was suspended.

4/22 Negotiations aimed at forming a great coalition failed. Prime Minister Olszewski did not accept the postulate of the "Small Coalition," which requested that each coalition party participate in the government in proportion to the number of seats it held in the parliament.

4/27 President Walesa told the press: "I do not exclude the possibility of suggesting to the prime minister that he resign." In the president's estimate, the effectiveness of the government was low. In the evening the president met with the prime minister, who sought Walesa's support.

5/2 At a meeting of the Warsaw Civic Agreement—a structure formed three weeks earlier by the supporters of Jan Parys—the suspended defense minister appealed for the establishment of National Defense Committees.

5/6 Prague: Lech Walesa participated in a summit of the Vysehrad Triangle together with the Czechoslovak president Vaclav Havel and the Hungarian prime minister Jozsef Antall. In a joint declaration, the three leaders announced their countries would form a free trade area and jointly apply for full membership in the EEC and in the NATO security structures.

5/8 In an address to the Sejm, President Walesa accused politicians of engaging in ceaseless disputes that disorganized the state. He demanded from the Sejm the right to appoint and dismiss cabinets.

5/18 Minister Parys handed in his resignation. His deputy, Romuald Szeremietiew, became acting defense minister.

5/19 Several ministers threatened to resign should Skubiszewski continue as head of the Ministry of Foreign Affairs. The conflict was caused by the minister's plans to sign a treaty with Russia. Skubiszewski's adversaries wanted to include in the document a preamble passing on to Russia the Soviet Union's responsibility for the effects of the Ribbentrop-Molotov Pact. They also criticized the pact concerning the withdrawal of Russian troops from Poland.

5/20 President Walesa announced that despite the opposition of several government members, the treaty would be signed. He strongly criticized Prime Minister Olszewski, blaming him for fomenting confusion and for the declining international prestige of the country.

5/21–22 President Walesa's visit to Moscow. Two hours before Yeltsin and Walesa were to sign the treaty, Prime Minister Olszewski questioned the validity of the pact by dispatching a coded message with his objections to the treaty to the Polish embassy in Moscow. The treaty was, however, signed. Walesa condemned the prime minister's actions, stating: "The government's lack of responsibility could have led to a complete failure of the negotiations."

5/26   In his letter to the Speaker of the Sejm, President Walesa withdrew his support from the government and advised the Speaker to begin preparations for appointing a new cabinet. The prime minister announced that the cabinet would continue to carry out its responsibilities. He said: "The president's letter does not include a motion to dismiss the government."

5/28   Another governmental crisis was caused by a motion by Deputy Korwin-Mikke obliging the minister of internal affairs to make public the information about the collaborators with the communist Security Bureau (UB) and the Security Service (SB).

5/29   The "Small Coalition" proposed a motion to dismiss Olszewski's government.

5/30   Prime Minister Olszewski began talks regarding the entry of the KPN into the coalition. The negotiations failed.

6/2   President Walesa met with Waldemar Pawlak, asking him to form a new government coalition.

6/3   The PSL (Pawlak's party) announced that it would vote in favor of the motion to dismiss the government.

6/4   Minister Macierewicz handed over to the state authorities and parliamentary clubs lists of names of deputies, senators, and high civil servants who, according to the Ministry of the Interior, had been agents of the UB, the SB, and other communist special services. The lists included dozens of persons, including many politicians who had belonged to anticommunist opposition groups. The "Portfolio Affair," as it was called, was a great scandal. The presence of many people on these lists was questioned. Macierewicz explained that this was only the information "found in the materials that were at the disposal of the Ministry of the Interior and not a list of agents." Several hours later, President Walesa stated that the lists were doctored, and he put forward a motion calling for immediate dismissal of the government. Shortly after midnight, the Sejm dismissed Olszewski's government.

6/6   As a result of a motion proposed by the president, the Sejm appointed Waldemar Pawlak prime minister.

6/7   Olszewski and several other members of parliament from the Christian Democratic Thought Forum (the Christian Democratic faction of the PC) formed the founding committee of a new parliamentary club, which assumed the name Movement for the Republic (RdR) on June 19, 1992.

6/10   The representatives of the ZChN, the PC, the PL, the Solidarity Parliamentary Club, and the FPD faction of the UD debated the possibility of a political alliance, opposing Prime Minister Pawlak.

6/11   The Fourth Congress of the NSZZ Solidarity was held. President Walesa, who participated in the discussions, was accused by some speakers of helping to overthrow Olszewski's government. However, a motion to withdraw the union's support for Walesa was defeated.

6/12   During the Second Congress of the Center Alliance (PC), Jaroslaw Kaczynski described Prime Minister Pawlak's efforts to form a government as an attempt to establish the rule of a new nomenclature and of the "old circle of agents." He blamed Walesa for this state of affairs, accusing him of "defending the postcommunist system." He advocated the creation of a "broad front of opposition against recommunization" inside and outside of the parliament.

6/30   The "Small Coalition" decided not to participate in the Pawlak government.

7/2   Pawlak asked the president to relieve him of the task of forming a new government. On the following day, the "Small Coalition" began negotiations with the "Five" (ZChN, PC, PL, SLCh, [Christian-Peasant Party] and PChD). The Democratic Union and its coalition partners proposed the candidacy of Hanna Suchocka for prime minister. Deputies of the Solidarity Parliamentary Club assumed the duties of mediators between the "Small Coalition" and the "Five."

7/4   The Sejm ratified the association agreement between Poland and the European Community (EC). Deputies of the ZChN and KPN voted against the agreement.

7/8   President Walesa accepted the candidacy of Hanna Suchocka as well as the proposed composition of her cabinet.

7/10   After dismissing Waldemar Pawlak, the Sejm appointed Hanna Suchocka prime minister. On the next day, the Sejm approved her cabinet.

7/31   A new parliamentary club was formed under the name of the Union of Labor (UP).

8/1   The "Little Constitution" was passed by the Sejm.

8/7   Representatives of OPZZ, Solidarity '80, the Mining Union Federation, and Samoobrona formed the National Trade Union Committee for Negotiations and Strikes. They threatened a nationwide general strike if the government did not immediately begin negotiations with the striking workers of the Lubin copper-smelting conglomerate, the mines, and the Tychy car factory.

8/10   Two other trade unions joined the National Committee for Negotiations and Strikes—the miners' union and the railway workers' union. A list of 21 postulates was drawn up.

8/19   Prime Minister Suchocka declared the government would not give in to the strikers.

8/20   The Strike Committee and the board of directors of the Lubin copper plant reached a wage agreement. The strike was suspended.

9/14   An agreement was signed in the Tychy car factory.

10/6   The government began negotiations with the trade union leaders regarding a legislative proposal, known as the Pact on State Enterprises. It was designed to regulate the restructuration and privatization processes.

10/14   A copy of the Soviet Politburo decision from March 5, 1940, authorizing the murder of Polish officers in Katyn was presented to Walesa by Yeltsin's special envoy. The decision was kept secret for 50 years, including the Gorbachev period.

11/6   The Sejm Internal Affairs Committee determined that no coup d'état was attempted by Olszewski on June 4.

11/17	Walesa signed the "Little Constitution," which increased the presidential powers.
11/23	The bishops issued an appeal against the referendum on abortion. It was read in all churches.
12/3	A proposal to hold a referendum on abortion was signed by half a million people.
12/6	The Conservative Party was formed. Aleksander Hall was elected chairman.
12/17	Sixty-three out of 70 mines were on strike.
12/22	The strike in Silesian mines was suspended.
12/29	The Sejm passed a new act regulating radio and television. It upheld the Senate's amendment obliging the media to respect "Christian values."

1993

1/4	The regional Strike Committee suspended the mine strike.
1/7	The Sejm passed a bill on "family planning, safeguarding the human fetus, and stating the conditions under which abortion may be permitted" (the abortion law). Simultaneously, it rejected a bill authorizing a referendum on the penalization of abortion.
1/23–24	The first Congress of the Union of Labor (UP). Ryszard Bugaj became its leader. The party announced its desire to create an economic program, an alternative to the existing programs of the liberals and the ex-communist coalition.
2/15	The ex-communist Teachers' Union (ZNP) threatened to organize a massive teachers' strike if the government did not accept the union's demands.
2/17	Beginning of negotiations between Solidarity and the government regarding salaries in the nonindustrial sector.
2/22	The government and the main labor unions signed a Pact on State Enterprises.
2/23	No salary agreement between the ZNP and the government. The nonindustrial public sector branch of Solidarity announced a strike alert.
3/8	The IMF confirmed its agreement with Poland. Valid for one year, this agreement enabled Poland to obtain a $650 million credit and to begin the second round of debt reduction negotiations with the Paris Club.
3/18	The Sejm unexpectedly rejected the mass privatization program (PPP). The vote demonstrated once again the lack of unity within the governing coalition. Twelve deputies of the coalition voted against the plan; 23 were absent.
3/20–21	The Second Congress of the SdRP (ex-communists). Aleksander Kwasniewski, elected party leader for a second term, said: "There was an attempt to throw us out with the trash, to isolate and ostracize us. Today we have the largest club in the Sejm and an ever-growing number of supporters."
3/30	The ZNP decided to hold a one-day teachers' strike on April 22. The nonindustrial budget sector branch of Solidarity announced its plan to organize a large protest campaign on May 4.

4/15	The Sejm passed a new electoral law that stipulated that 391 mandates were to be divided among the electoral committees receiving at least 5 percent of the vote. The threshold for coalitions was raised to 8 percent. The remaining 69 seats were to be proportionally distributed among those committees that would obtain more than 7 percent of the national vote.
4/22	A nationwide strike organized by the ZNP was supported by a large majority of teachers.
4/24–25	A congress of the Democratic Union elected Mazowiecki party chairman. It also expressed its support for the Suchocka government.
	At a congress of the Center Alliance, Jaroslaw Kaczynski declared "an unconditional war, but without transgressing democratic rules," against the SLD (ex-communist coalition), the Democratic Union, and the president. He invited several parties of the so-called post-Solidarity right to form a center-right coalition.
4/28	The parliamentary club of the Agrarian Alliance (PL) decided to leave the governing coalition.
4/30	The Sejm passed a bill on National Investment Funds.
5/4	A massive teachers' strike, organized by Solidarity, began.
5/7	Marian Krzaklewski, chairman of Solidarity, met with Prime Minister Suchocka and President Walesa. They decided to begin negotiations between the government and the union on May 10.
5/10	Negotiations between the government and Solidarity's Strike Committee failed on the first day.
5/12	Suchocka met with the leaders of parliamentary clubs. She said that the government would not meet the financial demands of the protestors. She promised that the budget expenditure in the nonindustrial public sector (education and health services) would increase the following year.
	The National Commission of Solidarity instructed its parliamentary representatives to introduce a motion for a no-confidence vote if the government failed to address the protestors' demands. The whole union was placed on strike alert.
5/17	Suchocka addressed the nation in a televised speech. She explained why the government could not give in to the protestors' financial demands.
5/19	The National Commission of Solidarity authorized its deputies to introduce a motion for a vote of no confidence against the government.
5/20	President Walesa announced his support for the government.
5/22	The Center Alliance's political council obligated its deputies to vote for the dismissal of the Suchocka cabinet.
	The SdRP's Chairman Kwasniewski announced his party's conditions under which they would support the government. The conditions included earlier parliamentary elections (spring 1994), access to mass media, changes in the state budget reflecting the strikers' postulates, and consultations with the opposition concerning the government's work schedule.

5/24   The National Strike Committee of the Nonindustrial Public Sector suspended the strike.

5/25   Suchocka announced her cabinet's readiness to undertake negotiations with any political group, but without any prior conditions.

Pawlak announced that the Polish Peasant Party (PSL) would support the motion for a vote of no confidence.

5/26   The Alliance of the Democratic Left (SLD) decided to vote in favor of the no-confidence motion.

5/27   The Solidarity Parliamentary Club introduced before the Sejm the motion for a vote of no confidence in the government. During the debate, Prime Minister Suchocka stated that her cabinet had not yet exhausted its potential and that it would be a paradox to dismiss the government just as the long-awaited economic revival had been achieved and rising unemployment halted. She said: "Backing the no-confidence vote with a threat of the general strike poses the question about the union's attitude not only toward the government, but also toward the parliament and the democratic procedures of the state."

5/28   The Suchocka government was dismissed. Two hundred twenty-three deputies voted in favor of the motion of no confidence. The required minimum was 222. After the vote, President Walesa refused to accept Suchocka's resignation.

5/29   Citing his constitutional prerogative, President Walesa dissolved the parliament.

6/2   Walesa set the date for new parliamentary elections—September 19, 1993.

6/5   Walesa announced his intention of forming a new party, the Nonparty Bloc for the Support of the Reforms (BBWR). It was intended as his political base.

6/12   The National Council of the Union of Labor (UP) rejected a possible electoral alliance with the ex-communist coalition SLD.

6/17   Suchocka met with the party leaders of the outgoing government coalition. Her proposal was to form one common electoral list or two mutually nonaggressive electoral blocs representing the post-Solidarity forces. One bloc would be led by the UD and KLD, the other by the ZChN. The idea was rejected.

In contrast to the 1992 elections, the episcopate did not endorse officially any specific party or coalition. It appealed to the populace to vote according to their Christian moral standards.

Jan Olszewski's RdR and Jaroslaw Kaczynski's PC formed the Polish Union electoral coalition.

6/24   Several days of negotiations between the UD and the KLD concerning their electoral alliance did not produce any results.

6/25–26   The Fifth Congress of NSZZ Solidarity decided not to form any electoral alliances. In particular, they rejected Walesa's offer to form a coalition with his BBWR.

Walesa announced that he and Solidarity had parted ways.

7/3   Olszewski's RdR left the Polish Union coalition it formed earlier with the Center Alliance. The partners could not decide who would lead the coalition.

7/6   Olszewski formed a new electoral bloc, Coalition for the Republic (RdR). A few small right-wing parties joined his RdR.

The Christian National Union (ZChN) and Gabriel Janowski's Agrarian Alliance (PL) failed to form a coalition.

7/13   The ZChN and three smaller Christian democratic and Christian agrarian parties constituting the Polish Convention formed the Catholic Electoral Committee "Fatherland" (KKW "Ojczyzna").

7/28   Poland and the Vatican signed a concordat in Warsaw. The president and the prime minister were present. It needed to be ratified by a new parliament.

8/3   The last unit of the Russian Army left Poland.

8/10   The last day of registration for the regional party lists in the Sejm elections. Four hundred sixty mandates would be contested by approximately 9,000 candidates. Fifteen parties and coalitions won the right to be represented in all regions: BBWR, KdR (Coalition for the Republic), KLD, KPN, KKW "Ojczyzna," Party "X," PC, PSL, PSL-PL, UD, UP, UPR (Union of Real Politics), Samoobrona, Solidarity, and SLD.

8/24   While visiting Poland, Boris Yeltsin expressed his "understanding" for Polish plans to join NATO.

9/7   President Walesa proclaimed that he would respect the voters' verdict in case of the ex-communist coalition's electoral victory and would approve the left's candidate for prime minister. Public opinion polls showed a large lead by the ex-communist Alliance of the Democratic Left (SLD) and the Polish Peasant Party (PSL). Among the very divided post-Solidarity forces, only the Democratic Union (UD) had double-digit support.

9/19   Parliamentary elections. Voter turnout was 52 percent. Of the 15 parties and coalitions that fielded candidates, only five passed the 5 percent threshold. The ex-communist SLD won 20.4 percent of the valid vote and 37.2 percent of the Sejm seats. The "peasants" (PSL) came in second with 15.4 percent of the vote and 28.7 percent of the seats. The UD placed third, winning 10.6 percent of the vote and 16.1 percent of the seats. Three other parties that won seats were the Union of Labor (UP), the Confederation for an Independent Poland (KPN), and Walesa's BBWR. Four seats went to representatives of the German minority. None of the parties of the so-called post-Solidarity right crossed the threshold. They represented together well over 20 percent of the valid vote.

9/20   Negotiations to form a government began. The UD excluded the possibility of forming a government in coalition with the ex-communist parties.

The presidents of France, Germany, and Poland met in Gdansk to discuss cooperation within the so-called Waimar triangle.

9/24   The SLD, the winner of the elections, assured the president that his constitutional prerogative to control the ministries of foreign affairs, internal affairs, and defense would be respected. The party also announced that it planned no major changes in the economic and foreign policies.

9/28   A breakthrough in the coalition negotiations between the SLD and PSL. Waldemar Pawlak emerged as a common candidate for prime minister.

9/30   Despite his earlier Warsaw declaration, President Yeltsin opposed the NATO expansion in a letter to Western governments. At the same time, he proposed that both NATO and Russia offer security guarantees to the Central European countries.

10/2   The post-Solidarity Union of Labor participated in coalition negotiations with the SLD and PSL.

The UD Council proposed a merger with the KLD.

The National Council of the ZChN issued an appeal to consolidate the post-Solidarity right.

10/12   The SLD, PSL, and UP signed a coalition agreement. Ryszard Bugaj, the UP's chairman, opposed his party's participation in the ruling coalition.

10/13   The UP left the coalition with the SLD and PSL.

10/14   Jozef Oleksy from the SLD was elected Speaker of the Sejm.

10/15   Andrzej Struzik from the PSL was elected Speaker of the Senate.

10/26   A new government was sworn in.

10/27   As one of his first decisions, Prime Minister Pawlak suspended a test program for the second stage of the state administration reforms.

11/8   In his inaugural speech, Prime Minister Pawlak announced the continuation in foreign policy, expedient ratification of the concordat, increased assistance for the poorest sections of the population, and protection of agriculture against foreign competition.

11/9   The Sejm passed a vote of confidence in Pawlak's cabinet. During the debate, Aleksander Kwasniewski, the SdRP chairman, said: "We apologize to all . . . who experienced injustice and villainy at the hands of the pre-1989 authorities and system."

11/10   The ZChN, PC, and PL signed a cooperation agreement. The next day, several other parties of the post-Solidarity right (PK [Conservative Party], PChD, SLCh, and UPR) signed a separate agreement. The former group was united by the idea of decommunization; the latter, by a liberal-conservative economic platform.

12/12   Congress of the Movement of the Second Republic (RdR). Romuald Szeremietiew was elected chairman over the previous leader, Jan Olszewski. The new leader announced his desire to join the ZChN-PC-PL coalition.

12/14   The mayors of 46 cities selected for the test program of the second stage of administrative reforms accused Prime Minister Pawlak of introducing policies reviving state centralism and limiting the role of local and regional self-government.

12/16 The Sejm passed a bill increasing considerably the income tax for the next year. The measure passed on the strength of the votes of the governing coalition's deputies.

12/29 Prime Minister Pawlak presented his government's economic program to the Sejm. It criticized the privatization policy of the previous governments and promised to slow down privatization.

Notes

Chapter 1

1. For a similar argument, see Elster, Offe, and Preuss 1998, 31.

2. See, for example, Crawford and Lijphart 1995; Huntington 1991; Linz and Stepan 1996, 55–83; Geddes 1995; Bova 1991, 126; Kitschelt 1992a; and Shin 1994.

3. See also Pridham 1990; Linz 1992; and Kitschelt 1992a.

4. For useful reviews of this literature, see Parrott 1997 and Dawisha 1997.

5. For the most recent examples of this growing interest in the role of civil society in democratization, see Bermeo 1997; Collier and Mahoney 1997; Fish 1995a, 1995b; Oxhorn 1995; Perez-Diaz 1993; Schmitter 1995a; Tarrow 1995b; and Valenzuela 1989.

6. See, for example, the impressive series Studies in Public Policy, produced by the Centre for the Study of Public Policy, University of Strathclyde, and coordinated by Richard Rose (Rose and Haerpfer 1996a and 1996b); McDonough, Barnes, and Lopez Pina 1986; and Zagorski 1994.

7. See also Johnston and Klandermans 1995; McAdam 1994; and Tarrow 1992a, 1992b.

8. See, for example, Czyzewski, Kowalski, and Piotrowski 1997; Kennedy 1994b; Verdery 1996; and Parrott 1997, 21–27. The role of cultural factors in democratization is poorly understood. In his review of Adam Przeworski's work, Kitschelt observes: "What Przeworski teaches us is that macro-historical comparison must be supplemented by a historical hermeneutics of political action, developed within 'cognitive political science.' Only within a framework of structural and cognitive analysis does it make sense to explore the extent to which game-theoretic rational-choice analysis illuminates the actual process and outcome of democratization" (1992a, 425).

9. Charles, Louise, and Richard Tilly, in their studies of collective action in France and Britain, convincingly demonstrate that over the last two centuries, organizations of civil society were the typical vehicles of protest (Tilly, Tilly, and Tilly 1975; Tilly 1979). This regularity is confirmed by all systematic studies of protest in contemporary societies.

10. For a discussion of differences between American and European approaches to the study of collective action, see Duyvendak and Koopmans 1995.

11. For overviews of methodological issues pertaining to protest event analysis, see Franzosi 1987; Olzak 1989; Rucht and Ohlemacher 1992; Tilly 1995b, 55–105; and Rucht, Koopmans, and Neidhardt 1998.

12. Validity refers to "measuring what we think we are measuring. The unemployment rate may be a good indicator of the state of the economy, but the two are not syn-

onymous" (King, Keohane, and Verba 1994, 25). In the context of newspaper-based event analysis, validity refers to the extent to which newspapers provide valid—that is, generalizable—information about events, such as strikes or street demonstrations (see Franzosi 1987, 6–10). Validity increases when the inferences from newspaper articles, notes, etc., are confirmed by inference from other data sets, based on other techniques (for a brief discussion of various types of validity and the distinction between validity as correspondence versus as generalizability, see Weber 1990, 18–21).

13. *The Media in Eastern Europe, RFE/RL Research Report,* 2, 19 (May 7, 1993), 22–23. See also Margueritte 1995.

14. An excellent, though rather forgotten, manual defines "prestige" papers in the following way: "The prestige paper has become an institution in all modern major powers. In each there is one paper, and usually only one, easily identified as being addressed to an elite audience and providing statements of public policy which are not available to readers of the ordinary papers. This paper is often, although not always, a great paper in the sense of having widespread news coverage" (Lasswell, Lerner, and de Sola Pool 1952, 42).

15. While coding the number of participants, coders were asked not to estimate this number on the basis of general description or on the basis of specific terms used by journalists. Although this is a fairly well established procedure, we felt that it extends the boundaries of arbitrariness too far.

Chapter 2

1. Hann argues that "the reputed strength of these states may be little more than a construction of Western analysts, who have demonized the states of Orient and of communist Eastern Europe in order to highlight by contrast the virtues of their own systems of government" (1995, 137). See also Stark and Bruszt 1998, 15–16.

2. For a critique of such approaches, see, for example, Hankiss 1989 and Stark and Nee 1989.

3. In fact, more recent research on state-socialist regimes suggests that "in institutional structures of state socialism noncompliance and apathy assumes a collective character and have a specific political significance" (Xueguang 1993, 66).

4. Some scholars attempted to introduce more nuanced distinctions between types of behavior defying oppressive regimes. See, for example, Kershaw 1983, 2–3; and Friszke 1991.

5. Pomian describes Poland as the only Soviet-bloc country where "authorities were afraid of the working class, not the other way around" (1985, 10).

6. Brumberg, for example, argues that "nowhere had the endemic communist failures to erect an economic system at once rational, productive, and at least moderately equitable been so disastrous as in Poland" (1983, x).

7. Bermeo (1992) emphasized the importance of political learning in regime transitions. See also Hall 1993 and Levy 1994.

8. These rehabilitations were restricted to former party members and leaders purged by Stalinists in internal fighting for power. Most of them, like Gomulka, Spychalski, and Kliszko in Poland or Kadar, Szakasits, and Marosan in Hungary, played a crucial role in subsequent political events. In Poland rehabilitation affected some 200 people, includ-

ing the leaders of the Polish prewar communist party killed by Stalin. Moreover, about 35,000 prisoners, mostly political, were released in the spring of 1956, and investigations of political offenses were terminated.

9. More detailed descriptions of the Poznan events and interpretations of the revolt can be found in Syrop 1957; Karpinski 1982; and Staniszkis 1984, 278–312. Official documents concerning the revolt were published in Zinner 1956. Also, during the Solidarity period in Poland, the conference of historians organized on the anniversary of the events examined carefully the whole episode (cf. Maciejewski and Trojanowiczowa 1990). The Polish regime responded to this work with its own interpretation of events (cf. Czubinski 1986). After 1989, several new analyses of the Poznan rebellion were published (cf. Bombicki 1992 and Nalepa 1992).

10. For detailed accounts of party meetings and intraparty conflicts and struggles, see Lewis 1958 and Karpinski 1982. It should be emphasized that, surprisingly, the Polish crisis of 1956 was not studied and examined in as comprehensive a way as other cases of crises were (Sakwa 1978). Only recently have Polish historians published systematic analyses of these events (cf. Rykowski and Wladyka 1989; Dymek 1989; Wladyka 1989; Machcewicz 1993; Wladyka 1994).

11. A detailed description and interpretation of the events can be found in Karpinski 1982, 105–38; Bielasiak 1988; and above all in Eisler 1991. See also Flis 1988 for an original interpretation. The official point of view of the Polish regime may be found in Hillebrandt 1986.

12. For more detailed analysis of December 1970 events in Poland, see Karpinski 1982, 157–66; Laba 1991, 15–82; Korybutowicz 1983; Glowacki 1990; and Eisler and Trepczynski 1991. Testimonies of participants in Szczecin events may be found in Szejnert and Zalewski 1986 and Instytut Literacki 1986. For an interpretation reflecting the point of view of the Polish communist party, see Rakowski 1981.

13. The actual number of casualties is still unknown and estimated at several hundreds (see Eisler 1990, 5–27).

14. During these events, regular military forces were employed in some 100 actions in all regions of the country, involving 61,000 soldiers, 1,700 tanks, 1,750 personnel carriers, and units of the air force and navy (see Kuklinski 1987, 14). In the Baltic coast cities, 27,000 soldiers, 550 tanks, and 750 personnel carriers took part in pacifying the workers' rebellion. See also Nalepa 1990; Fajfer 1993 and 1996; and Eisler and Trepczynski 1991, 19–20, 137–66.

15. In Szczecin in 1970, for example, workers demanded "regular and reliable information about the country's political and economic situation in the national mass media." In 1980 in Gdansk, they demanded "the enforcement of freedom of speech, print, and publication as guaranteed in the Polish constitution." In Szczecin in 1971, workers demanded the "immediate and legitimate elections of trade union authorities, workers' councils and . . . democratic elections in the party and youth organization on the factory level." In 1980 in Gdansk, workers demanded the "recognition of free trade unions independent from the party and employers as codified in the World Labor Organization's convention No. 87 ratified by the Polish government." See Marciniak 1989, 153–54; see also Laba 1991, 155–82.

16. For the debate on the origin of the Solidarity movement, see Bernhard 1991 and Kubik 1994c.

17. Street demonstrations also took place in Plock but were much less violent than in the other two places. For a detailed analysis of the June 1976 events, see Terry 1996; Bernhard 1987 and 1993, 46–75; Lipski 1985; and Karpinski 1982, 191–97. For a selection of documents, see Mizerski 1991.

18. For a detailed analysis of independent groups and initiatives, see Bernhard 1993; Raina 1981; Lipski 1985; Kawalec 1979; and Holzer 1984. See also Brumberg 1983; Myant 1982; and Lepak 1988.

19. For a comprehensive analysis of this period, emphasizing the significance of papal visits to Poland for the emergence of the Solidarity movement, see Kubik 1994a.

20. The period of Solidarity in Poland already has an extensive bibliography. Competent analyses of events can be found in Ash 1985; Touraine et al. 1983; Staniszkis 1984; Holzer 1984; Ost 1990; Laba 1991; Goodwyn 1991; and Kennedy 1991.

21. See also Krzeminski 1987 and Marciniak 1989.

22. See also Staniszkis 1981 and Kulpinska 1990.

23. The evolution of political attitudes is the best-documented aspect of Poland's developments between 1980 and 1989, thanks to systematic empirical research conducted by a team of leading Polish sociologists (Adamski et al. 1981, 1982, 1986, 1989, 1991) and summarized in English in Adamski 1993. The comprehensive list of publications based on these surveys can be found in Adamski et al. 1991, 186–88.

24. For an analysis of the cultural dimension of the political crisis in Poland, see Kubik 1994a and 1994c; Bakuniak and Nowak 1987; Modzelewski 1989; Kowalski 1990; Grudzinska-Gross 1987; and Uhlig 1989).

25. Institutional transformations and policies of the Polish regime are analyzed in Ekiert 1996; Kaminski 1991a; Karpinski 1990; and Zielonka 1987.

26. See also Smolenski and Gielzynski 1989 for detailed accounts of strikes in the Lenin Shipyard and the Nowa Huta steel mill. See also Blaszkiewicz, Rykowski and Werenstein- Zulawski 1994.

27. See Dokument nr 39, "Informacja o konfliktach spolecznych i akcjach protestacyjnych w zakladach pracy i srodowiskach zawodowych," in Perzkowski 1994, 303–4. See also Dokument nr 3, "Kalendarium akcji strajkowych w okresie 15–30 sierpnia 1988 r." (Perzkowski 1994, 15–31; and Pernal and Skorzynski 1990).

Chapter 3

1. The roundtable agreement and its effects have been extensively analyzed. See, for example, Osiatynski 1991; Linz and Stepan 1996, 264–49; Staniszkis 1991, 190–202; Castle 1996, 230–35; and Taras 1996, 133–38.

2. See Olson 1993; Lewis 1990; Heyns and Bialecki 1991; and Kaluza 1989.

3. *Polityka,* June 3, 1989, 5.

4. "In the first round of elections, each seat will be voted for on a separate election card, on which the candidates will be listed in alphabetical order, *without any additional descriptions* [emphasis added]; political symbols, the names of organizations, etc., can be, though, at the request of a candidate, placed on election lists, posters, etc." (*Tygodnik Mazowsze,* June 12, 1989).

5. Assessments of the size of various minority groups vary. According to *The Warsaw Voice* (September 15, 1991), in Poland there were about 350,000 Germans, 350,000

Ukrainians, 200–250,000 Byelorussians, 30,000 Slovaks and Czechs, 25,000 Lithuanians, 25,000 Gypsies, and 15,000 Jews. All the minorities total about 1 million, which is about 2.5 percent of Poland's population. According to minority associations, there are 250,000 Byelorussians, 250–300,000 Ukrainians, 700,000 Germans, 25–30,000 Slovaks, 15–20,000 Lithuanians, and about 10,000 Gypsies (Klosinska 1992, 54).

6. The dichotomy we are proposing here partially overlaps with several other dichotomous conceptualizations of post-1989 politics in the former Soviet bloc. Jowitt writes about "civics" and "ethnics" (1990, 195). Wnuk-Lipinski (1994) came up with a very similar conceptualization, defining "two responses to a radical social change" as fundamentalism and pragmatism. In a systematic study of Polish political parties, Tworzecki (1996, 53–54) identified two distinct political options: "traditionalists" and "modernizers." The latter tended to support Mazowiecki; the former would rather opt for Walesa, although a clear-cut match between these options and the two politicians did not exist. Ziolkowski (1993) develops a contrast between the "universalistic-market-achievement-modernization-individualistic-anti-egalitarian" and "particularistic-protective-claiming-traditional-communitarian-egalitarian" constellations. He writes about the two general orientations *within the populace at large,* whereas we concentrate on a cleavage within the elite political culture, yet it seems that our "reformists" may count on the support of Ziolkowski's "universalists." Our "revolutionaries" should find more following among Ziolkowski's "particularists."

7. Another observer characterized Polish politics in 1991 as permeated by "increasing fragmentation and alienation of new elites, exacerbated by the bad economic and social situation" (Roszkowski 1992, 61).

8. After the vote of no confidence on May 28, 1993, Suchocka stayed on as the head of a caretaker government until October.

9. Differences between decentralization, devolution, and other related processes are succinctly analyzed in Lake and Regulska 1990. For a discussion of problems associated with the self-government reform in Poland, see Regulska 1993 and 1998.

10. For example, in August prices went up by 40 percent, while wages increased by almost 90 percent. See Balcerowicz 1992, 36.

11. The following description is based on Balcerowicz 1992, 39–55; Sachs 1993, 45–46; Poznanski 1996, 172–77; and Slay 1994.

12. Monthly inflation rates: November 1989—22.4%; December 1989—18.3%; January 1990—77.3%; February 1990—15.8%; March 1990—4.5%. See Sachs 1993, 61.

13. Changes in industrial production: 1990—23.3%; 1991—11.9%; 1992—4.2%; 1993—5.6%; 1994—11.9%. See Slay 1995, 30. Poznanski argues that "this recession in production was basically limited to the state sector, while private businesses continued to expand" (1996, 180). See also *OECD Economic Surveys, Poland 1994.*

14. All data and analyses in this section come from Slay 1994.

15. Privatization was completed in 1,166 enterprises. Out of this number, 115 enterprises were sold, 813 were leased or franchised, and 238 were partially or completely privatized through liquidation (Halicki 1994, 54). See also Frydman, Rapaczynski, and Earle 1993; Lieberman, Nestor, and Desai 1997.

16. Rutkowski calculates that if real wages for 1987 are taken to be 100, then real wages for 1988 = 114.4; 1989 = 124.7; 1990 = 94.3; 1991 = 94; 1992 = 91.4; 1993 = 90.5 (1996, 5).

17. Real income (previous year = 100): 1986—102.4; 1987—101.2; 1988—113.6; 1989—106.0; 1990—85.3; 1991—105.9; 1992—103.5. See Ksiezopolski 1995, 172.

18. The World Bank analysts came to the same conclusion; in Poland the gap between rich and poor became wider than in Slovakia, Hungary, or the Czech Republic. See *From Plan to Market* 1996, 69; and Wyzan 1996, 24–27.

19. The answer "No one does" to the question "Do you or anyone in your family have a second job to earn some extra money?" was given by 83 percent of Bulgarians, 85 percent of Czechs, 83 percent of Slovaks, 82 percent of Hungarians, and only 74 percent of Poles (Rose and Haerpfer 1996b, 57).

20. See Linz and Stepan 1996, 283; and Bielasiak 1997.

21. See Wesolowski 1995, 9–10; Kolarska-Bobinska 1994, 102, 138–40; Bielasiak 1997; and Linz and Stepan 1996, 283. We will discuss this phenomenon in chapter 4.

22. CBOS, "Lewica—Prawica—Rzad: Komunikat z badan" (Warsaw, May 1993).

Chapter 4

1. See, for example, Huntington 1991 (in particular chapter 5, "How Long? Consolidation and Its Problems"); Schmitter 1995b; Mainwaring, O'Donnell, and Valenzuela 1992; Higley and Gunther 1992; Gunther, Diamandouros, and Puhle 1995; Haggard and Kaufman 1995 (in particular part 2, "The Political Economy of Adjustment in New Democracies"); Bresser Pereira, Maravall, and Przeworski 1993; and Shin 1994.

2. This brief characterization of Linz and Stepan's approach is based mostly on 1996, 5–7.

3. Schmitter also argues that "no single format or set of institutions embodies modern democracy" (1992, 162). See also Schmitter and Karl 1991 and Karl and Schmitter 1991.

4. For the most recent examples of this growing interest in the role of civil society in democratization, see Perez-Diaz 1993; Bermeo 1997; Schmitter 1995a; and Tarrow 1995b.

5. Linz and Stepan offer a seminal analysis of this problem (1992 and 1995, 16–38). Similarly, Schmitter believes that most "consolidologists" would agree that "It is preferable, if not indispensable, that national identity and territorial limits be established before introducing reforms in political (or economic) institutions" (1995b, 29).

6. We define autonomy, following Shafer, as "the extent to which the state is not merely an arena for conflict but is distinct from nonstate actors" (1994, 6). State capacity is defined, following Barkey and Parikh, "as the state's ability to implement strategies to achieve its economic, political, or social goals in society" (1991, 526). They argue that "the state may acquire capacity through institutions such as the bureaucracy, or through resources such as external ties to entrepreneurs and finance capital [but it is also] determined by the state's relations to society." See Shafer (1994, 7–8) for a useful distinction between absolute and relative capacity.

7. In a similar vein, Mainwaring observes that "Legitimacy is every bit as much the root of democratic stability as objective payoffs, and it is less dependent on economic payoffs than Przeworski or Lipset (1959) indicate" (1992, 306). Similarly, Schmitter argues that "the core of the consolidation dilemma lies in coming up with a set of institutions that politicians can agree upon and citizens are willing to support" (1992, 159).

8. Fish notes that in postcommunist Russia "the fragmentation and decay of old structures of power and authority may actually *inhibit* [original emphasis] the rapid emergence of a genuine civil society. A state that lacks effective economic and administrative functions, structures permitting the intermediation of interests, and capacity for the universalization of law, can actually impede the emergence of a 'modern' civil society" (1995b, 154).

9. For a useful discussion of difficulties in delineating boundaries of the political and politics, see Maier 1987. Politics of identity is well defined in Dirks, Eley, and Ortner 1994, 32.

10. These are three terms that have a long history and are the subject of intense debates. See, for example, Keane 1988; Cohen and Arato 1992; and Seligman 1992. In this project we follow Stepan, who argues that "it is conceptually and politically useful to distinguish three important arenas of the polity: civil society, political society, and the state. Obviously, in any given polity these three arenas expand and shrink at different rates, interpenetrate or even dominate each other, and constantly change" (1988, 3).

11. For examples of debates on state strength and weakness, see Mann 1984; Nordlinger 1987; and Migdal 1988 and 1994.

12. See, for example, Keane 1988, 25–29; Engelstein 1995; and Ogrodzinski 1991, 70–72.

13. Weigle and Butterfield utilize a similar conceptualization. They distinguish between civil society as a specific legal framework (institutional base) and as a specific "identity of the social actors and the goals toward which their activity is directed" (1992, 3).

14. Both communists and fascists used this strategy during their ascent to power. See, for example, Allen 1984.

15. In Gellner's words: "we must first of all distinguish it [civil society] from something which may in itself be attractive or repulsive, or perhaps both, but which is radically distinct from it: the segmentary community which avoids central tyranny by firmly turning the individual into an integral part of the social sub-unit" (1994, 8).

16. Verba, Nie, and Kim describe these organizations as "private organizations," rightly emphasizing that membership is not always strictly voluntary (1978, 100).

17. According to Tilly, reactive collective actions "consist of group efforts to reassert established claims when someone else challenges or violates them." Proactive collective action "asserts group claims which have not previously been exercised" (1978, 145–46). Tilly gives here an example of strikes for higher wages or better working conditions.

18. For the distinction between authoritarian, totalitarian, and neopatrimonial regimes, see Linz 1975 and Linz and Stepan 1996, 38–54. The concept of incapacitation is developed by Gross 1991, 232–40.

19. For example, the Office for the Protection of the State, founded in 1990, employed 6,073 functionaries, while the reorganized security police, abolished at the beginning of the same year, had 3,524 full-time functionaries, down from 24,000 in June 1989. See *Wprost,* July 11, 1993, 29–32.

20. Poland was the only country in the Soviet bloc that established a set of institutions for external administrative control before 1989. The Supreme Control Chamber (NIK), controlled by the parliament, was supplemented in the 1980s by the Administra-

tive Court, the Constitutional Court, the State Tribunal, and the Office of the Ombudsman.

21. See also "Wierzcholek piramidy," *Polityka* 1995, no. 34, pp. 12–13; no. 35, pp. 22–23.

22. According to Inglot (1995), Poland's economic transition did not lead to radical cuts in social spending. To the contrary, social expenditures dramatically increased in proportion to the GDP. He shows that in 1992 Poland spent 17.5 percent of its GDP on social payments in cash, which was almost double the amount spent in 1989. See also Kramer 1997.

23. By the end of 1995, the number of political parties increased to 297. The number of parties reflects a very liberal party registration procedure. In order to register a political party, 15 signatures had to be collected on a registration form and three people had to appear in the District Court in Warsaw, and the process was free of any charge.

24. The number of effective parties was calculated according to the Taagapera/Shugart formula (1989). After the 1991 election it was 10.7 (Jasiewicz 1996).

25. Linz and Stepan briefly review various measures of disproportionality and calculate the Lijphart Index for Poland. It was 35.1—much higher than in any other known democracy (1996, 290).

26. Jasiewicz compared the patterns of voting to the Sejm (two versions of the PR system) and to the Senate (two versions of the plurality system) and concluded that "electoral regulations matter, but cannot alone prevent political fragmentation and instability which are a reflection of a very complex process of economic, political, and social transformation" (1996, 20). See also Gebethner 1996.

27. For an overview of various conceptualizations of the Polish postcommunist field, see Ekiert 1992 and Jasiewicz 1993b. See also Bielasiak 1997; Grabowska and Szawiel 1993; Kitschelt 1992b and 1995; Szawiel 1993; and Wesolowski 1995.

28. For example, the Liberal Democratic Congress, one of the most influential parties—whose leader, Krzysztof Bielecki, served as prime minister—has approximately 3,000 members. The Christian National Union, the most important representative of Catholic views—which had several ministers in the last three governments and a deputy prime minister in Suchocka's government—has approximately 6,000 members. Seven hundred members were in Warsaw, and one in every 100 members holds a parliamentary seat. See Maciej Janicki, "Czysto i ubogo," *Polityka,* February 27, 1993; and *Polityka,* October 9, 1993.

29. This situation departs from experiences of other democratizing countries where, according to O'Donnell and Schmitter (1986, 62), "founding elections are . . . moments of great drama. Turnout is very high. Parties advocating cancellation, postponement, or abstention are swept aside by the civic enthusiasm that attends such moments." In fact, voter turnout in founding elections in Spain in 1977, for example, was 79.1 percent and decreased in 1979 elections to 68.3 percent (Caciagli 1984).

30. According to another source, by the end of 1992, there were more than 2,000 nationwide voluntary associations registered in the Warsaw District Court, a majority of which existed before 1989 (*Polska '93,* 148). This number did not include associations whose activities were limited to the regional or local level and were registered by provincial courts (Prawelska- Skrzypek 1996).

31. A comparison between 1987 and 1993 data on professional organizations com-

piled by the GUS (Główny Urzad Statystyczny, the Main Statistical Office) shows that the Federation of Regional Clubs Technology and Technical Improvement lost 118,000 members, the Polish Economics Association lost 37,000 members, the Association of Management and Organization lost 21,000, and the Polish Association of Nurses, with 60,000 members in 1987, disappeared from the list.

32. The Polish Scouting Union (ZHP), which had over 2 million members in 1987, had only 450,000 in 1993. Still, this was the biggest and most successful youth organization. After 1989, several new scouting organizations were founded, but with only about 21,000 members, they did not pose a serious challenge to the ZHP.

33. The Orthodox Church comprised 410 churches, 259 priests, and 570,000 members in 1993. Protestant churches had 1,110 congregations with 150,000 members (GUS 1994, 69–70).

34. This was approximately half the size of the trade union movement before martial law was imposed in December 1981. Solidarity as well as all other unions were dissolved, and during the 1980s the Polish regime gradually reestablished union organizations to regain control over workers (Kolankiewicz 1987; Mason 1987).

35. The law stipulates that as few as 10 employees may found a union and apply for its registration. In an enterprise where there are 150 or more union members, the enterprise has to finance one full-time union position.

Chapter 5

1. GUS 1994 and 1995.

2. The duration of each protest event was expressed in days (or 24-hour units). Then the total number of protest days for each year was calculated.

3. See, for example, Tarrow 1989; Kriesi et al. 1995; and Koopmans 1995.

4. See Tarrow 1995a and McAdam 1995.

5. For data reporting research on protest potential, see Barnes et al. 1979 and Hastings and Hastings 1984.

6. These numbers include only those protest events for which we have exact information regarding the number of participants.

7. The category "public sector employees" comprises the following subcategories of state employees: health services and welfare institutions, education and science, culture and arts, transport (including airlines and railways), state-owned media, state administration, local government and judiciary, police, armed forces, and fire brigades.

8. *OECD Economic Surveys, Poland 1997,* 57–61.

9. "The institutionalization of a cleavage does not imply that it no longer gives rise to political competition. It only implies that the competition is no longer taking place in unconventional terms" (Kriesi and Duyvendak 1995, 6).

10. On the relationship between social cleavages and (new) social movements, see also Kriesi and Duyvendak 1995.

11. See Bienen and Gersovitz 1996; Walton 1991; Walton and Ragin 1990; Walton and Seddon 1994; and Greskovits 1994.

12. She proposes to analyze responses of the state, and in particular the police, to protest in five dimensions: "(1) 'repressive' versus 'tolerant,' according to the range of prohibited behaviors; (2) 'selective' versus 'diffused,' according to the range of groups

subject to repression; (3) 'preventive' versus 'reactive,' according to the timing of police intervention; (4) 'hard' versus 'soft,' according to the degree of force involved; (5) 'dirty' versus 'lawful,' according to the degree to which respect for legal and democratic procedures is emphasized" (della Porta 1996, 66).

13. For example, in July 1993 the protest against the decision of the city government in Swinoujscie regarding the new location of the open air market ended in a rampage during which city officials were physically assaulted and battered. Criminal proceedings against participants in this action were concluded only in December 1995 with the sentencing of 28 people to suspended prison terms and fines.

14. The existing critical-methodological literature bemoans the difficulty of measuring the influence, success, or effectiveness of movements rather than protest actions. It is, however, relevant for our study, since movements' principal mode of operation is protest or "noninstitutionalized tactics." See Burnstein, Einwohner, and Hollander 1995; Klandermans 1989b; Huberts 1989; and Gundelach 1989.

Chapter 6

1. The following list was compiled on the basis of two articles in the two leading weeklies (*Polityka,* June 5, 1993, 12; and *Wprost,* March 20, 1994, 19) and our own database.

2. Most sources do not provide any information on numbers of participants in strikes and other protest actions listed here. Existing estimates are often contradictory. Whenever we can, we are providing the number of employees in affected enterprises, branches of industry, or sectors for 1994 (from Balicka and Balicki 1995).

3. The nonindustrial public sector ("budget sector" in Polish nomenclature) includes primarily the employees of the educational system, the state administration, and the health care system. The protest campaign discussed in this chapter mobilized employees of the educational system and the health care sector.

4. *Polityka,* May 15, 1993, 1.

5. *Gazeta Wyborcza,* April 13, 1993, 2.

6. *Rzeczpospolita,* May 10, 1993, 1.

7. All quotations in this section come from our database.

8. *Gazeta Wyborcza,* May 14, 1993, 1.

9. *Gazeta Wyborcza,* May 15–16, 1993, 1.

10. The following account is based mostly on *Rzeczpospolita,* May 21, 1993, 1–2; *Gazeta Wyborcza,* May 21, 1993, 1; *Wprost* (various issues); and *Polityka* (various issues).

11. *Rzeczpospolita,* May 22–23, 1993, 2.

12. *Polityka,* June 5, 1993.

13. In a poll, whose results were published on May 31, 51 percent of respondents supported the president's decision, 24 percent would rather see him appoint a new cabinet, and 25 percent had no opinion. See *Rzeczpospolita,* May 31, 1993, 1.

14. For an analysis of the pact, see Kramer 1995, 100–102.

15. *Rzeczpospolita,* May 14, 1993, 1–2.

16. This observation is shared by most analysts. See, for example, Kramer 1995, 102.

17. Vanous 1994, 1–2. See also Poznanski 1996, 179.

18. *Polityka,* May 15, 1993, 13.

19. This is a December 1992 to December 1993 comparison. It should be noted here that in August 1993 the Central Planning Office reported that in June 1993, compared with June 1992, real wages in the budget sector increased by 20 percent (*Polityka,* August 14, 1993, 3). As far as we can determine, this information did not play any role in shaping the thinking of the protesting employees of the budget sector.

20. For example, after the vote of no confidence, the influential daily *Rzeczpospolita* published a comment by its editor in chief, Dariusz Fikus. In his opinion, the government fell because Solidarity turned its back on it and chose "radicalism and populism." See *Rzeczpospolita,* May 29–30, 1993, 1.

21. *Polityka,* June 5, 1993, 12.

22. Ewa Tomaszewska, chairwoman of the National Strike Committee of the Nonindustrial Public Sector, *Rzeczpospolita,* May 10, 1993, 1.

23. CBOS, "Spoleczny stan 'gotowosci strajkowej': Komunikat z badan" (Warsaw: April 1993).

24. CBOS, "Pracownicy o strajkach" (Warsaw: May 1993). A representative sample of 988 employees of enterprises employing at least 500 persons. The "agree" answer combines "strongly agree" and "rather agree"; the "disagree" answer combines "rather disagree" and "strongly disagree."

25. Pentor study as reported in *Wprost,* July 25, 1993, 15–17.

26. This observation confirms generalizations offered by, inter alia, Schmitter (1981, 287) and Nollert (1995) that in polities that do not have neocorporatist arrangements for interest articulation, the magnitude of protest is going to be heightened.

27. See also Haggard and Kaufman 1994 and Przeworski 1992, 56.

28. The September 9, 1993, election brought to power the ex-communist coalition, thus ending the first Solidarity period of Polish postcommunist reforms.

29. An extensive discussion of inclusion through incorporation can be found in Collier and Collier 1991, 40–55.

Chapter 7

1. For a review, see Sztompka 1991 and 1992. For further examples, see Reisinger et al. 1994 or Vainshtein 1994.

2. Jasiewicz and Adamski summarized a longitudinal study of Polish attitudes in the following fashion: "Spontaneous answers show that in 1988 somewhat fewer respondents than in 1984 perceive the presence of conflict in Polish society, which is, however, perceived by almost half the respondents. The great majority of those who perceive conflict define it as between the authorities and society" (1993, 55). Uhlig (1989, 61) observed that "after December 13, 1981, the opposition's drive to make a distinction between 'our Poland' (the Solidarity Republic) and 'their Poland' (the Polish People's Republic) intensifies."

3. Staniszkis's (1989) theorizing on the construction of "social subjects" under state socialism is similar to our conception of the cultural-political class founded on such a polarizing discourse.

4. We follow the work of Putnam, who defines "'political elite' very loosely as those who in any society rank toward the top of the (presumably closely intercorrelated) dimensions of interest, involvement, and influence in politics" (1971, 651).

5. In distinguishing "amateurs" and "professionals," we follow Bourdieu (1991; see also Bourdieu and Wacquant 1992, 241–43). Both categories are socially constructed and thus always historically situated and challengeable. In particular, professionals' claims to dominance in a given field may or may not be recognized by the "amateurs." For example, in postcommunist Eastern Europe, politicians (as a certain group of professionals) have very low legitimacy and authority.

6. Bourdieu defines habitus as "the strategy-generating principle enabling agents to cope with unforeseen and ever-changing situations . . . a system of lasting and transposable dispositions which, integrating past experiences, functions at every moment as a matrix of perceptions, appreciations and actions and makes possible the achievement of infinitely diversified tasks" (1977, 95).

7. As Tarrow observed (following Wildavsky), it takes "entrepreneurs making deliberate culture *choices* to turn mentalities into collective action" (1992a, 55).

8. On the concept of symbolic struggle over the regime's legitimacy, see Gamson 1988, 219.

9. We owe to Krzysztof Jasiewicz the realization that this dichotomy was predominantly, if not exclusively, manifested in the elite political culture.

10. Hall in his discussion with Antoni Macierewicz on the situation of the Polish right. Hall, one of the leading politicians of the "Mazowiecki camp" and the Democratic Union, left this party to lead the "pro-reform right." Macierewicz, an influential politician of the "anti-Mazowiecki camp," was the minister of internal affairs in the Olszewski cabinet and one of the leaders of the "revolutionary" right. See RFE/RL Research Institute, *Polish Monitoring* 438 (October 2–4, 1992): 27–31.

11. Ibid.

12. Interestingly, according to Garrison and Arensberg, in the Mediterranean, where the phenomenon of the "evil eye" is particularly widespread, it is associated with clientelism (i.e., weak formal institutionalization). Certain forms of the "evil eye" phenomenon correlate with "a system of plural, stratified, societies organized in unstable states with redistributive economies" (Galt 1982, 666).

13. Kaczynski, the leader of the PC, during the first congress of his party (*Rzeczpospolita,* March 4, 1991).

14. In a TV show, "100 Questions to Jaroslaw Kaczynski," he developed this thought: "I do not treat the term 'left' as an epithet; the left has its place in Polish tradition, has its place on the present political scene . . . if I used the term 'commune' [a pejorative term used to describe the communist regime], that would be an epithet; when I am saying that he is a person of the left, it is simply a description, nothing more."

15. Kaczynski said during a TV debate with Michnik (November 21, 1990): "there was an effort made [in Poland after the roundtable agreement, i.e., after April 1989, we presume] to construct a certain new mono-party or a hegemonic party, which, in addition, would be based in its internal structures on the hegemony of a single group. . . . A very meritorious group . . . yet, nonetheless, a specific group, holding specific views, which I would call left-wing."

16. This definition is influenced by Snow and his collaborators as well as by Tarrow, who developed a cognate concept of frame alignment. See Snow and Benford 1988 and Tarrow 1992b.

17. The resulting typology produced mutually exclusive categories that covered al-

most completely all the reported cases; it therefore comes quite close to the ideal of proper classification. It must be remembered, however, that our database, derived from journalistic accounts, is incomplete, and all the conclusions must remain somewhat tentative.

18. Magdalenka is a location where unofficial talks took place during the roundtable negotiations of 1989. For some people, it came to symbolize the beginning of the alliance between some segments of the opposition ("the Pinks") and the communist authorities ("the Reds"). Targowica, a place where a pro-Russian confederacy was announced in 1792, functions in the Polish collective memory as the ultimate symbol of national treason.

19. "Okapizm" refers to the OKP, the Citizens' Parliamentary Club—representing Solidarity in the parliament, dominated by the people who later formed the Democratic Union. "Walesism" means an ideology, a type of thinking characteristic of Walesa and his supporters. Since the politicians related to both the OKP and Walesa in 1990 decisively dominated the political scene, the slogan equates the whole of Polish politics with communism.

20. Demonstration co-organized by the KPN and the PPS-RD (Polish Socialist Party-Democratic Revolution) on January 22, 1990. Kuron helped to set up a system of soup kitchens for the poor, which became popularized as "Kuron's soups."

21. Kaszpirowki was a Russian faith healer often working in Poland, where he was extremely popular.

22. Kotanski was the main organizer of help and social services for drug users and people infected with AIDS.

23. Between the end of 1990 and the end of 1991, unemployment almost doubled (it went from 6.3 percent to 11.6 percent). Between the end of 1991 and the end of 1992, it grew only by 14 percent (from 11.6 percent to 13.6 percent).

24. Following Conovan, populism is defined here in the most general sense: "All forms of populism without exception involve some kind of exaltation of and appeal to 'the people', and all are in one sense or another antielitist" (1981, 294).

25. Kolarska-Bobinska reports that "Almost half of all Poles evaluate the development of democracy in our country very negatively. Yet the lack of acceptance of parties and the rulers in a democratic system leads to the replacement of elites, not to the rejection of the whole system. Delegitimation of democracy may lead to its replacement by an authoritarian rule, but the latter system of governance is accepted by only 20–25 percent of Poles" (1992).

26. This includes the term in office of her caretaker government.

27. If so, Lippmann's (1956, 15) and Lipset's (1993) contentions that people's political behavior is shaped by their *perceptions* of economy (and polity) and is not simply determined by a configuration of "objective" economic (or political) factors would be confirmed.

Chapter 8

1. This conclusion has been confirmed by Jerzy Osiatynski, Minister of Finance and Privatization in 1992, who admitted that protests had a modifying impact on the government's decisions. See Osa 1998, 39.

2. In this part of her analysis Osa relies on Carnoy's work, who argues, against more conventional views, that the level of unemployment in postcommunist Eastern Europe was actually surprisingly low, given the depth of economic transformation and "a tremendous loss of output" (see Carnoy 1996).

3. We employ a modified version of the relative deprivation theory, proposed by McCarthy and Zald (1987, 17). In this version, the concept of "deprivation" replaces "relative deprivation," which considerably changes the nature of the argument. We will, however, follow this common practice, mostly because there is no comparative study of relative deprivation in the four East Central European states we know of, while we found several comparative studies dealing with various aspects (indicators) of political and economic "deprivation" or "intensity of grievances."

4. See, for example, Shafer 1994, 39–42; or Hellman 1998, 206–8. Hellman demonstrates that under partial reforms in postcommunist systems, the collective action dilemma produced by the dispersal of "winners" from economic reforms does not occur.

5. See Walton 1991; Walton and Ragin 1990; and Greskovits 1998.

6. In Hungary, for example, labor continued to be dominated by ex-communist federations, mostly the MSZOSZ (National Federation of Hungarian Trade Unions) (Greskovits 1995).

7. A focus group study of the striking miners conducted on December 28 and 29, 1992, concluded that "For the miners, the strike is a form of communicative behavior" ("Gornicy o sobie, strajku i wladzy," *Rzeczpospolita,* January 5, 1993).

8. For a fuller analysis of the institutionalization of protest during early democratic consolidation, see Kubik 1998.

9. For an examination of the concept of "Leninist legacy" within a comparative perspective, see Crawford and Lijphart 1995 and Geddes 1995.

Bibliography

Adamski, Wladyslaw W. 1989. "Afiliacje zwiazkowe, stosunek do protestow i wartosci obywatelskich jako przejaw konfliktu interesow." In *Polacy '88: Dynamika konfliktu i szanse reform,* Wladyslaw Adamski et al., 159–222. Warsaw: Uniwersytet Warszawski.

———, ed. 1993. *Societal Conflict and Systemic Change: The Case of Poland, 1980–1992.* Warsaw: IFiS Publishers.

Adamski, Wladyslaw W., et al. 1981. *Polacy '80: Wyniki badan ankietowych.* Warsaw: IFiS PAN.

———. 1982. *Polacy '81: Postrzeganie kryzysu i konfliktu.* Warsaw: IFiS PAN.

———. 1986. *Polacy '84: Dynamika spolecznego konfliktu i konsensusu.* Warsaw: Uniwersytet Warszawski.

———. 1989. *Polacy '88: Dynamika konfliktu i szanse reform.* Warsaw: Uniwersytet Warszawski.

———. 1991. *Polacy '90: Konflikty i zmiana.* Warsaw: IFiS and ISP PAN.

Alford, Robert R., and Roger Friedland. 1975. "Political Participation and Public Policy." *Annual Review of Sociology* 1:429–79.

Allen, William Sheridan. 1984. *The Nazi Seizure of Power.* Rev. ed. New York: Franklin Watts.

Anusz, Andrzej. 1991. *Niezalezne Zrzeszenie Studentow w latach 1980–1989.* Warsaw: Akces.

Armijo, Leslie E., Thomas J. Biersteker, and Abraham F. Lowenthal. 1994. "The Problems of Simultaneous Transitions." *Journal of Democracy* 5 (October): 161–75.

Ash, Timothy Garton. 1985. *The Polish Revolution: Solidarity.* New York: Vintage Books.

Aslund, Anders. 1985. *Private Enterprise in Eastern Europe.* London: Macmillan.

Bakuniak, Grzegorz, and Krzysztof Nowak. 1987. "The Creation of a Collective Identity in a Social Movement: The Case of 'Solidarnosc' in Poland," *Theory and Society* 16:401–29.

Balcerowicz, Leszek. 1992. *800 Dni: Szok kontrolowany.* Warsaw: BGW.

———. 1993. "Demokracja nie zastapi kapitalizmu." *Przeglad Polityczny,* special issue, 24–31.

———. 1994. "Understanding Postcommunist Transitions." *Journal of Democracy* 5 (October): 75–89.

———. 1995. *Socialism, Capitalism, and Democracy.* Oxford: Oxford University Press.

Balicka, Mariola, and Wladyslaw Balicki. 1995. "Najwieksze Polskie firmy 1994." *Polityka,* April 22, 1–4.

Barkey, Karen, and Sunita Parikh. 1991. "Comparative Perspectives on the State." *Annual Review of Sociology* 17:523–49.

Barnes, Samuel H., Max Kasse, and Klaus R. Allerbeck, et al. 1979. *Political Action: Mass Participation in Five Western Democracies.* Beverly Hills: Sage.

Bartlett, David. 1996. "Democracy, Institutional Change, and Stabilisation Policy in Hungary." *Europe-Asia Studies* 48 (1): 47–83.

Beissinger, Mark R. 1998. "Event Analysis in Transitional Societies: Protest Mobilization in the Former Soviet Union." In *Acts of Dissent: New Developments in the Study of Protest,* ed. Dieter Rucht, Ruud Koopmans, and Friedhelm Neidhardt, 284–316. Berlin: Sigma Press.

Beissinger Mark R., and Lubomyr Hajda. 1990. "Nationalism and Reform in Soviet Politics." In *The Nationalities Factor in Soviet Politics and Society,* ed. L. Hajda and M. Beissinger, 305–22. Boulder: Westview Press.

Bermeo, Nancy. 1992. "Democracy and the Lessons of Dictatorship." *Comparative Politics* 24 (3): 273–91.

———. 1997. "Myths of Moderation: Confrontation and Conflict during Democratic Transitions." *Comparative Politics* 29 (April): 305–22.

Bernhard, Michael. 1987. "The Strikes of June 1976 in Poland." *East European Politics and Societies* 1 (3): 363–92.

———. 1991. "Reinterpreting Solidarity." *Studies in Comparative Communism* 24 (3): 313–30.

———. 1993. *The Origin of Democratization in Poland.* New York: Columbia University Press.

———. 1996. "Civil Society after the First Transition: Dilemmas of Postcommunist Democratization in Poland and Beyond." *Communist and Post-Communist Studies* 29 (3): 309–30.

———. 1997. "Semipresidentialism, Charisma, and Democratic Institutions in Poland." In *Presidential Institutions and Democratic Politics,* ed. Kurt von Mettenheim, 177–203. Baltimore: Johns Hopkins University Press.

Bibo, Istvan. 1991. *Democracy, Revolution, Self-Determination: Selected Writings.* Ed. Andras Boros-Kazai. Highland Lakes: Atlantic Research and Publications.

Bielasiak, Jack. 1983. "The Party: Permanent Crisis." In *Poland: Genesis of a Revolution,* ed. Abraham Brumberg, 10–25. New York: Random House.

———. 1988. "Social Confrontation to Contrived Crisis: March 1968 in Poland." *East European Quarterly* 22 (1): 81–105.

———. 1997. "Substance and Process in the Development of Party Systems in East Central Europe." *Communist and Post-Communist Studies* 30 (1): 23–44.

Bienen, Henry S., and Mark Gersovitz. 1996. "Consumer Subsidy Cuts, Violence, and Political Stability." *Comparative Politics* 19 (October): 25–44.

Blasiak, Wojciech. 1989. "Centra i peryferie ruchow chlopskich w Polsce, 1980–1981." In *Studia nad ruchami spolecznymi,* vol. 2, ed. Piotr Marciniak and Wojciech Modzelewski, 201–27. Warsaw: Instytut Socjologi, Uniwersytet Warszawski.

Blaszkiewicz, Anna, Zbigniew Rykowski, and Jerzy Werenstein-Zulawski. 1994. "The Solidarnosc Spring?" *Communist and Post-Communist Studies* 27 (2): 125–34.

Bombicki, Maciej. 1992. *Poznan '56.* Poznan: Lawica.

Borkowski, Tadeusz, and Andrzej Bukowski, eds. 1993. *Komitety Obywatelskie: Powstanie—Rozwoj—Upadek?* Krakow: Universitas.

Bourdieu, Pierre. 1977. *Outline of a Theory of Practice.* Cambridge: Cambridge University Press.

———. 1991. "Political Representation: Elements for a Theory of the Political Field." In *Language and Symbolic Power,* 170–202. Cambridge: Harvard University Press.

Bourdieu, Pierre, and Loic J. D. Wacquant. 1992. *An Invitation to Reflexive Sociology.* Chicago: University of Chicago Press.

Bova, Russell. 1991. "Political Dynamics of the Post-communist Transition: A Comparative Perspective." *World Politics* 44 (October): 113–38.

Bozoki, Andras. 1988. "Critical Movements and Ideologies in Hungary." *Sudosteuropa* 37:377–87.

Bresser Pereira, Luiz Carlos, Jose Maria Maravall, and Adam Przeworski. 1993. *Economic Reforms in New Democracies.* Cambridge: Cambridge University Press.

Bright, Charles, and Susan Harding. 1984. "Processes of Statemaking and Popular Protest: An Introduction." In *Statemaking and Social Movements,* ed. Charles Bright and Susan Harding, 1–15. Ann Arbor: University of Michigan Press.

Brumberg, Abraham. 1983. Introduction to *Poland: Genesis of a Revolution,* ed. Abraham Brumberg, ix–xii. New York: Random House.

Brus, Wlodzimierz. 1978. "Trwale konsekwencje 'Polskiego Pazdziernika.'" In *1956 w dwadziescia lat pozniej z mysla o przyszlosci,* 53–62. London: Aneks.

Bruszt, Laszlo. 1992. "Transformative Politics: Social Costs and Social Peace in East Central Europe." *East European Politics and Societies* 6 (1): 55–72.

Brzezinski, Mark F. 1997. *Law vs. Power: The Struggle for Constitutionalism in Poland.* London: Macmillan.

Brzoza, Czeslaw. 1996. *3 Maja 1946 w Krakowie.* Krakow: Ksiegarnia Akademicka.

Bugajski, Janusz. 1987. *Czechoslovakia: Charter 77's Decade of Dissent.* New York: Praeger.

Bunce, Valerie. 1999. *Subversive Institutions: The Design and Destruction of Socialism and the State.* Cambridge: Cambridge University Press.

Burawoy, Michael. 1985. *The Politics of Production: Factory Regimes under Capitalism and Socialism.* London: Verso.

Burawoy, Michael, and Janos Lukacs. 1992. *The Radiant Past: Ideology and Reality in Hungary's Road to Capitalism.* Chicago: University of Chicago Press.

Burnstein, Paul, Rachel L. Einwohner, and Jocelyn A. Hollander. 1995. "The Success of Political Movements: A Bargaining Perspective." In *The Politics of Social Protest,* ed. J. Craig Jenkins and Bert Klandermans, 275–95. Minneapolis: University of Minnesota Press.

Burton, Michael, Richard Gunther, and John Higley. 1992. "Introduction: Elite Transformations and Democratic Regimes." In *Elites and Democratic Consolidation in Latin America and Southern Europe,* ed. John Higley and Richard Gunther, 1–36. Cambridge: Cambridge University Press.

Caciagli, Mario. 1984. "Spain: Parties and the Party System in the Transition." *West European Politics* 7:84–98.

Campbell, John L. 1995. "State Building and Post-Communist Budget Deficits." *American Behavioral Scientist* 38 (3): 760–87.

Carnoy, Martin. 1996. "Notes toward an Analysis of the Transition in Eastern Europe: The Case of Poland." Manuscript. Stanford: Stanford University.

Castle, Marjorie. 1996. "The Final Crisis of the People's Republic of Poland." In *Poland's Permanent Revolution: People vs. Elites, 1956–1990,* ed. Jane Leftwich Curry and Luba Fajfer, 211–41. Washington, D.C.: American University Press.

CBOS. 1989. "Zycie codzienne Polakow w 1989r." December. Warsaw.

CBOS. 1992. "Serwis Informacyjny." No. 4 and No. 10. Warsaw.

CBOS. 1993. "Podatki a budzet." August. Warsaw.

Chmiel, Beata, and Elzbieta Kaczynska, eds. 1988. *Postulaty 1970–71 i 1980.* Warsaw: Uniwersytet Warszawski.

Cohen, Jean, and Andrew Arato. 1992. *Civil Society and Political Theory.* Cambridge: MIT Press.

Colburn, Forrest, ed. 1989. *Everyday Forms of Peasant Resistance.* Armonk: M. E. Sharpe.

Collier, Ruth Berins, and David Collier. 1991. *Shaping the Political Arena.* Princeton: Princeton University Press.

Collier, Ruth Berins, and James Mahoney. 1997. "Adding Collective Actors to Collective Outcomes: Labor and Recent Democratization in South America and Southern Europe." *Comparative Politics* 29 (April): 285–303.

Conovan, Margaret. 1981. *Populism.* London: Junction Books.

Crawford, Beverly, and Arend Lijphart. 1995. "Explaining Political and Economic Change in Post-communist Eastern Europe." *Comparative Political Studies* 28 (July): 171–99.

Curry, Jane Leftwich. 1984. *The Black Book of Polish Censorship.* New York: Vintage.

———. 1990. *Poland's Journalists: Professionalism and Politics.* Cambridge: Cambridge University Press.

Czajkowski, Tomasz, Michal Federowicz, and Anna Iwanowska. 1994. "Srodowisko ludzi niepelnosprawnych w perspektywie spoleczenstwa obywatelskiego." In *Droga przez instytucje,* ed. Michal Federowicz, 181–213. Warsaw: IFiS PAN.

Czubinski, Antoni. 1986. *Czerwiec 1956 w Poznaniu.* Warsaw: KAW.

Czyzewski, Marek, Sergiusz Kowalski, and Andrzej Piotrowski, eds. 1997. *Rytualny chaos: Studium dyskursu publicznego.* Warsaw: Aureus.

Dahrendorf, Ralph. 1990. *Reflections on the Revolution in Europe.* New York: Random House.

Dalton, Russell J., Manfred Kuechler, and Wilhelm Burkin. 1990. "The Challenge of New Movements." In *Challenging the Political Order,* ed. R. J. Dalton and M. Kuechler, 3–20. New York: Oxford University Press.

Dawisha, Karen. 1997. "Democratization and Political Participation: Research Concepts and Methodologies." In *The Consolidation of Democracy in East-Central Europe,* ed. Karen Dawisha and Bruce Parrott, 40–65. Cambridge: Cambridge University Press.

della Porta, Donatella. 1996. "Social Movement and the State: Thoughts on the Policing of Protest." In *Comparative Perspectives on Social Movements,* ed. Doug McAdam, John D. McCarthy, and Mayer N. Zald, 62–92. Cambridge: Cambridge University Press.

Diamond, Larry. 1993. "Introduction: Political Culture and Democracy." In *Political Culture and Democracy in Developing Countries,* ed. Larry Diamond, 1–27. Boulder: Lynne Rienner.

Diamond, Larry, and Juan J. Linz. 1989. "Introduction: Politics, Society, and Democracy in Latin America." In *Democracy in Developing Countries: Latin America,* ed. Larry Diamond, Juan J. Linz, and Seymour Martin Lipset, 1–58. Boulder: Lynne Rienner.

Diamond, Larry, Juan J. Linz, and Seymour Martin Lipset. 1990. "Introduction: Comparing Experiences with Democracy." In *Politics of Developing Countries: Comparing Experiences with Democracy,* ed. Larry Diamond, Juan J. Linz, and Seymour Martin Lipset, 1–37. Boulder: Lynne Rienner.

Di Palma, Giuseppe. 1990. *To Craft Democracies: An Essay on Democratic Transitions.* Berkeley: University of California Press.

Dirks, Nicholas B., Nicholas Geoff Eley, and Sherry B. Ortner. 1994. Introduction to *Culture/Power/History,* ed. Nicholas B. Dirks, Nicholas Geoff Eley, and Sherry B. Ortner, 3–45. Princeton: Princeton University Press.

Dobieszewski, Adolf. 1992. "Polityka kolektywizacji wsi i represje wobec chlopow." In *Elity wladzy w Polsce a struktura spoleczna w latach 1944–1956,* ed. Przemyslaw Wojcik, 429–58. Warsaw: ISNS UW.

Drozdek, Jan. 1990. *Istota sporu.* N.p.

Duyvendak, Jan Willem, and Ruud Koopmans. 1995. Conclusion to *New Social Movements in Western Europe: A Comparative Analysis,* by Hanspeter Kriesi, Ruud Koopmans, Jan Willem Duyvendak, and Marco G. Giugni, 238–51. Minneapolis: University of Minnesota Press.

Dymek, Benon, ed. 1989. *Pazdziernik 1956: Szkice historyczne.* Warsaw.

Eckstein, Harry, and Ted Gurr. 1975. *Patterns of Authority: A Structural Basis for Political Inquiry.* New York: John Wiley.

Eckstein, Susan. 1989a. "Power and Popular Protest in Latin America." In *Power and Popular Protest: Latin American Social Movements,* ed. Susan Eckstein, 1–60. Berkeley: University of California Press.

Eckstein, Susan, ed. 1989b. *Power and Popular Protest: Latin American Social Movements.* Berkeley: University of California Press.

Eisler, Jerzy. 1990. "Przedslowie." In Edward Nalepa, *Wojsko Polskie w Grudniu 1970,* 5–27. Warsaw: Bellona.

———. 1991. *Marzec 1968.* Warsaw: PWN.

———. 1993. "Polskie radio wobec wydarzen w kraju w 1956 r." *Krytyka* 40:146–63.

Eisler, Jerzy, and Stanislaw Trepczynski. 1991. *Grudzien '70: Wewnatrz 'Bialego Domu.'* Warsaw: Colibri.

Ekiert, Grzegorz. 1989. "Recent Elections in Poland and Hungary: The Coming Crisis of Ritualized Politics." Center for Research on Politics and Social Organization Working Paper Series, no. 14, Department of Sociology, Harvard University.

———. 1991. "Democratization Processes in East Central Europe: A Theoretical Reconsideration." *British Journal of Political Science* 21:285–313.

———. 1992. "Peculiarities of Postcommunist Politics: The Case of Poland." *Studies in Comparative Communism* 25 (December): 341–61.

———. 1993. "Prospects and Dilemmas of the Transition to a Market Economy in East Central Europe." *Research on Democracy and Society* 1:51–82.

———. 1996. *The State against Society: Political Crises and Their Aftermath in East Central Europe.* Princeton: Princeton University Press.

Ekiert, Grzegorz, and Jan Kubik. 1998. "Contentious Politics in New Democracies: East Germany, Hungary, Poland, and Slovakia, 1989–93." *World Politics* 50 (July): 547–81.

Eley, Geoff. 1992. "Nations, Publics, and Political Cultures: Placing Habermas in the Nineteenth Century." In *Habermas and the Public Sphere,* ed. Craig Calhoun, 289–339. Cambridge: MIT Press.

Elster, Jon. 1993. "Constitution-Making in Eastern Europe: Rebuilding the Boat in the Open Sea." *Public Administration* 27:168–217.

Elster, Jon, Claus Offe, and Ulrich K. Preuss. 1998. *Institutional Design in Postcommunist Societies: Rebuilding the Ship at Sea.* Cambridge: Cambridge University Press.

Engelstein, Laura. 1995. "The Dream of Civil Society in Tsarist Russia: Law, State, and Religion." Paper presented at the conference "Civil Society before Democracy," Princeton University, October 6–7.

Evans, Peter. 1992. "The State as Problem and Solution: Predation, Embedded Autonomy, and Structural Change." In *The Politics of Economic Adjustment: International Constraints, Distributive Conflicts, and the State,* ed. Stephan Haggard and Robert R. Kaufman, 139–81. Princeton: Princeton University Press.

Fajfer, Luba. 1993. "The Polish Military and the Crisis of 1970." *Communist and Post-Communist Studies* 26 (2): 205–25.

———. 1996. "December 1970: A Prelude to Solidarity." In *Poland's Permanent Revolution: People vs. Elites, 1956–1990,* ed. Jane Jeftwich Curry and Luba Fajfer, 55–108. Washington, D.C.: American University Press.

"Farmers' 'Solidarity,' 1981–1987." 1988. *Polish Agriculture* 8:18–22.

Ferge, Zsusa. 1995. "The Evaluation of Freedom, Security, and Regime Change." Paper prepared for the Euroconference on Social Policy organized by ICCR-Vienna, Lisbon, November 8–11.

Fish, Steven M. 1995a. *Democracy from Scratch: Opposition and Regime in the New Russian Revolution.* Princeton: Princeton University Press.

———. 1995b. "The Emergence of Independent Associations and the Transformation of Russian Political Society." In *The Soviet System: From Crisis to Collapse,* rev. ed., ed. Alexander Dallin and Gail W. Lapidus, 147–59. Boulder: Westview Press.

Flis, Andrzej. 1988. "Crisis and Political Ritual in Post-war Poland." *Problems of Communism* 37 (May–August): 43–54.

Franzosi, Roberto. 1987. "The Press as a Source of Socio-Historical Data: Issues in the Methodology of Data Collection from Newspapers." *Historical Methods* 20:5–16.

———. 1995. *The Puzzle of Strikes.* Cambridge: Cambridge University Press.

Frentzel-Zagorska, Janina, and Krzysztof Zagorski. 1989. "East European Intellectuals on the Road of Dissent: The Old Prophecy of a New Class Re-examined." *Politics and Society* 17 (1): 89–113.

Friedland, Roger, and Robert R. Alford. 1991. "Bringing Society Back In: Symbols, Practices, and Institutional Contradictions." In *The New Institutionalism in Organizational Analysis,* ed. Walter W. Powell and Paul J. DiMaggio, 232–63. Chicago: University of Chicago Press.

Friszke, Andrzej. 1991. "Opozycja i opor spoleczny w Polsce (1945–1980)." In *Mate-*

rialy konwersatorium z 20 lutego 1991 r., ed. Andrzej Friszke and Andrzej Paczkowski, 3–18. Warsaw: ISP PAN.

From Plan to Market: World Development Report. 1996. Published for the World Bank. Oxford: Oxford University Press.

Frydman, Roman, Andrzej Rapaczynski, John S. Earle, et al. 1993. *The Privatization Process in Central Europe.* Budapest: CEU Press.

Gabor, Istvan. 1989. "Second Economy and Socialism: The Hungarian Experience." In The *Underground Economies: Tax Evasion and Information Distortion,* ed. Edgar Feige, 339–60. New York: Cambridge University Press.

Galt, Anthony. 1982. "The Evil Eye as Synthetic Image and Its Meaning on the Island of Pantelleria, Italy." *American Ethnologist* 9 (4): 664–81.

Gamson, William A. 1988. "Political Discourse and Collective Action." In *International Social Movement Research,* vol. 1, *From Structure to Action: Comparing Social Movement Research across Cultures,* ed. Bert Klandermans, Hanspeter Kriesi, and Sidney Tarrow, 219–44. Greenwich, Conn.: JAI Press.

Gardawski, J., and Tomasz Zukowski. 1994. *Robotnicy 1993: Wybory ekonomiczne i polityczne.* Warsaw.

Gebethner, Stanislaw. 1992a. "Sejm rozczlonkowany: Wytwor ordynacji wyborczej czy polaryzacji na polskiej scenie politycznej?" In *Wybory '91 a polska scena polityczna,* ed. Stanislaw Gebethner and Jacek Raciborski, 51–80. Warsaw: Polska w Europie.

———. 1992b. "Wprowadzenie." In *Wybory '91 a polska scena polityczna,* ed. Stanislaw Gebethner and Jacek Raciborski, 7–26. Warsaw: Polska w Europie.

———. 1996. "Proportional Representation versus Majoritarian Systems: Free Elections and Political Parties in Poland, 1989–1991." In *Institutional Design in New Democracies,* ed. Arend Lijphart and Carlos H. Waisman, 59–75. Boulder: Westview Press.

Gebethner, Stanislaw, and Krzysztof Jasiewicz, eds. 1993. *Dlaczego tak glosowano: Wybory prezydenckie '90.* Warsaw: ISP PAN.

Geddes, Barbara. 1994a. "Challenging the Conventional Wisdom." *Journal of Democracy* 5 (October): 109–18.

———. 1994b. *Politician's Dilemma: Building State Capacity in Latin America.* Berkeley: University of California Press.

———. 1995. "A Comparative Perspective on the Leninist Legacy in Eastern Europe." *Comparative Political Studies* 28 (July): 239–74.

Gellner, Ernest. 1994. *Conditions of Liberty: Civil Society and Its Rivals.* New York: Allen Lane.

Gieorgica, J. Pawel. 1991. *Polska lokalna we wladzy PZPR.* Warsaw: Uniwersytet Warszawski.

Gilejko, Leszek. 1995. *Robotnicy i spoleczenstwo: 1980–1981, 1989–90.* Warsaw: Szkola Glowna Handlowa.

Glinski, Piotr. 1993. "Aktywnosc aktorow spolecznych w transformacji." In *Spolecznstwo w transformacji: Ekspertyzy i studia,* ed. Andrzej Rychard and Michal Federowicz, 97–108. Warsaw: IFiS PAN.

———. 1994. "Environmentalism among Polish Youth." *Communist and Post-Communist Studies* 27 (2): 145–59.

———. 1996. *Polscy zieloni: Ruch spoleczny w okresie przemian.* Warsaw: IFiS PAN.

Glowacki, Andrzej. 1990. *Kryzys polityczny 1970 roku.* Warsaw: Instytut Wydawniczy Zwiazkow Zawodowych.

Gnatowska, Helena. 1985. "Strajki w Polsce w latach 1945–1947 w swietle dokumentow PPR." *Z Pola Walki* 3:103–12.

Goffman, Erving. 1974. *Frame Analysis.* New York: Harper Colophon.

Goldfarb, Jeffrey. 1989. *Beyond Glasnost: The Post-totalitarian Mind.* Chicago: University of Chicago Press.

Goodwyn, Lawrence. 1991. *Breaking the Barrier: The Rise of Solidarity in Poland.* New York: Oxford University Press.

Gorlach, Krzysztof. 1989. "On Repressive Tolerance: State and Peasant Farm in Poland." *Sociologia Ruralis* 29 (1): 23–33.

Gortat, Radzislawa. 1994. "The Feud within Solidarity's Offsprings." In *Parties, Trade Unions, and Society in East Central Europe,* ed. Michael Waller and Martin Myant, 116–24. Portland: Frank Cass.

Grabowska, Miroslawa, and Ireneusz Krzeminski, eds. 1991. *Bitwa o Belweder.* Warsaw: Wydawnictwo Mysl.

Grabowska, Miroslawa, and Tadeusz Szawiel. 1993. *Anatomia elit politycznych: Partie polityczne w postkomunistycznej Polsce, 1991–93.* Warsaw: Instytut Socjologii Ewa Lewicka- Banaszak and Piotr Marciniak.

Grabowski, Maciej H. 1994. "Polacy pracuja na czarno." *Przeglad Polityczny* 25:62–63.

Grabowski, Tomek. 1996. "The Party That Never Was: The Rise and Fall of Solidarity Citizens' Committees in Poland." *East European Politics and Societies* 10 (spring): 214–54.

Greskovits, Bela. 1994. "Is the East Becoming the South? Where Threats to Reforms May Come From." Paper presented at the 16th World Congress of the International Political Science Association, Berlin, August 21–25.

———. 1995. "Hungerstrikers, the Unions, the Government, and the Parties: A Case-Study of Hungarian Transformation: Conflict, the Social Pacts and Democratic Development." Occasional Papers in European Studies 6, Center for European Studies, University of Essex.

———. 1998. *The Political Economy of Protest and Patience: East European and Latin American Transformations Compared.* Budapest: Central European University Press.

Grochowski, Miroslaw. 1991. "Praktyki spoleczne wladz lokalnych." In *Miedzy nadzieja a rozczarowaniem: Samorzad terytorialny rok po wyborach,* ed. Bogdan Jalowiecki and Pawel Swianiewicz, 91–118. Warsaw: Uniwersytet Warszawski.

Gross, Jan. 1991. *Revolution from Abroad.* Princeton: Princeton University Press.

Grudzinska-Gross, Irena. 1987. "Culture as Opposition in Today's Poland." *Journal of International Affairs* 50 (2): 367–90.

Gundelach, Peter. 1989. "Effectiveness and the Structure of New Social Movements." *International Social Movement Research* 2:427–42.

Gunther, Richard, Nikiforos Diamandouros, and Hans Jurgen Puhle, eds. 1995. *The Politics of Democratic Consolidation: Southern Europe in Comparative Perspective.* Baltimore: Johns Hopkins University Press.

GUS. 1991. *Rocznik Statystyczny 1991.* Warsaw: GUS.
GUS. 1993. *Rocznik Statystyczny 1993.* Warsaw: GUS.
GUS. 1994. *Rocznik Statystyczny 1994.* Warsaw: GUS.
GUS. 1995. *Rocznik Statystyczny 1995.* Warsaw: GUS.
Haggard, Stephan, and Robert R. Kaufman. 1994. "The Challenges of Democratic Consolidation." *Journal of Democracy* 5 (4): 5–16.
———. 1995. *The Political Economy of Democratic Transitions.* Princeton: Princeton University Press.
Hagopian, Frances. 1993. "After Regime Change: Authoritarian Legacies, Political Representation, and Democratic Future of South America." *World Politics* 45 (April): 464–500.
Halamska, Maria. 1988. "Peasant Movements in Poland, 1980–1981." *Research in Social Movements, Conflicts, and Change* 10:147–60.
Halicki, Andrzej. 1994. "Prywatyzacyjna batalia." *Przeglad Polityczny* 25 (Fall): 54–55.
Hall, Peter A. 1993. "Policy Paradigms, Social Learning, and the State: The Case of Economic Policymaking in Britain." *Comparative Politics* 25 (April): 275–96.
Hall, Peter A., and Rosemary C. R. Taylor. 1996. "Political Science and the Three New Institutionalisms." *Political Studies* 44 (3): 952–73.
Hankiss, Elemer. 1989. "Demobilization, Self-Mobilization, and Quasi-Mobilization in Hungary, 1948–1987." *East European Politics and Societies* 3 (1): 105–52.
Hann, Chris. 1995. "Subverting Strong States: The Dialectics of Social Engineering in Hungary and Turkey." *Daedalus* 124 (2): 133–53.
Haraszti, Miklos. 1977. *A Worker in a Worker's State.* Harmondsworth: Penguin Books.
———. 1987. *The Velvet Prison.* New York: Basic Books.
Hastings, E. Hann, and P. K. Hastings, eds. 1984. *Index to International Public Opinion, 1982–1983.* Westport, Conn.: Greenwood Press.
Hausner, Jerzy. 1994. "Organizacje interesu i stosunki przemyslowe w krajach postsocjalistycznych." *Przeglad Socjologiczny* 43:9–26.
Havel, Vaclav. 1985. *The Power of the Powerless.* Armonk: M. E. Sharpe.
Hellman, Joel S. 1998. "Winners Take All: The Politics of Partial Reform in Postcommunist Transitions." *World Politics* 50 (January): 203–34.
Hemmerling, Zygmunt, and Marek Nadolski, eds. 1990. *Opozycja antykomunistyczna w Polsce, 1944–1956: Wybor dokumentow.* Warsaw: Osrodek Badan Spolecznych.
Hethy, Lajos. 1994. "Tripartism in Eastern Europe." In *New Frontiers in European Industrial Relations,* ed. Richard Hyman and Anthony Ferner, 312–36. Oxford: Basil Blackwell.
Heyns, Barbara, and Ireneusz Bialecki. 1991. "Solidarnosc: Reluctant Vanguard or Makeshift Coalition?" *American Political Science Review* 85 (2): 351–70.
Higley, John, and Richard Gunther, eds. 1992. *Elites and Democratic Consolidation in Latin America and Southern Europe.* Cambridge: Cambridge University Press.
Hillebrandt, Bogdan. 1986. *Marzec 1968.* Warsaw: Wydawnictwo Spoldzielcze.
Hofer, Tamas. 1993. "The Demonstration of March 15, 1989, in Budapest: A Struggle for Public Memory." Program on Central and Eastern Europe Working Paper Series, Center for European Studies, Harvard University.
Holzer, Jerzy. 1984. *Solidarnosc, 1980–1981: Geneza i historia.* Paris: Instytut Literacki.

————. 1991. "Kryzysy i przezwyciezanie kryzysow w panstwach komunistycznych." *Krytyka,* no. 34–35: 36–46.

Howard, A. E. Dick. 1993. "Constitutional Reform." In *Transition to Democracy in Poland,* ed. Richard F. Staar, 97–110. New York: St. Martin's Press.

Huberts, W. Leo. 1989. "The Influence of Social Movements on Government Policy." *International Social Movement Research* 2:395–426.

Hunt, Lynn. 1984. *Politics, Culture, and Class in the French Revolution.* Berkeley: University of California Press.

Huntington, Samuel. 1991. *The Third Wave: Democratization in the Late Twentieth Century.* Norman: University of Oklahoma Press.

Indraszkiewicz, Jerzy. 1994. *Democracja i gospodarka: Swiadomosc zmian ustrojowych w Polsce.* Krakow: Universitas.

Inglot, Tomasz. 1995. "The Politics of Social Policy Reform in Post-Communist Poland," *Communist and Post-Communist Studies* 28 (3): 361–73.

Instytut Literacki. 1986. *Grudzien 1970.* Paris: Instytut Literacki.

Jakubowski, Zenon. 1988. *Milicja Obywatelska, 1944–1948.* Warsaw: PWN.

Jarocki, Robert. 1990. *Tygodnik Powszechny: Czterdziesci piec lat w opozycji.* Krakow: Wydawnictwo Literackie.

Jasiewicz, Krzysztof. 1986. *Polacy '84 z poltorarocznej perspektywy: Raport wstepny z badania "Opinie Polakow—jesien '85."* Warsaw: Ewa Lewicka-Banaszak and Piotr Marciniak.

————. 1992. "Poland." *European Journal of Political Research* 22:489–504.

————. 1993a. "From Protest and Repression to the Free Elections." In *Societal Conflict and Systemic Change: The Case of Poland, 1980–1992,* ed. Wladyslaw W. Adamski, 117–40. Warsaw: IFiS Publishers.

————. 1993b. "Polish Politics on the Eve of the 1993 Elections: Towards Fragmentation or Pluralism?" *Communist and Post-Communist Studies* 26 (4): 387–411.

————. 1996. "The Enfranchised, the Re-enfranchised, and the Self-Disenfranchised: The Politics of Electoral Reforms in Post-communist Poland." Paper presented at the 92nd Annual Meeting of the American Political Science Association, San Francisco, August 20–September 1.

Jasiewicz, Krzysztof, and Wladyslaw Adamski. 1993. "Evolution of the Oppositional Consciousness." In *Societal Conflict and Systemic Change: The Case of Poland, 1980–1992,* ed. Wladyslaw W. Adamski, 35–56. Warsaw: IFiS Publishers.

Jawlowska, Aldona. 1994. "Cultural Changes in Poland in the 1990s." In *Cultural Dilemmas of Post-Communist Societies,* ed. Aldona Jawlowska and Marian Kempny, 284–99. Warsaw: IFiS Publishers.

Jawlowska, Aldona, and Marian Kempny, eds. *Cultural Dilemmas of Post-Communist Societies.* Warsaw: IFiS Publishers.

Jawor 1993. Warsaw: Civic Dialogue NGOs.

Johnston, Hank, and Bert Klandermans, eds. 1995. *Social Movements and Culture.* Minneapolis: University of Minnesota Press.

Jowitt, Ken. 1990. "Survey of Opinion on the East European Revolution." *East European Politics and Society* 4 (2): 193–97.

————. 1992. "The Leninist Legacy." In *East Europe in Revolution,* ed. Ivo Banac, 207–24. Ithaca: Cornell University Press.

Kaczynski, Jaroslaw. 1990. *Dlaczego przyspieszenie.* November 14. Cieszyn: Porozumienie Centrum.

Kaluza, Roman, ed. 1989. *Polskie wybory 1989.* Warsaw: Wydawnictwo Andrzej Bonarski.

Kaminski, Bartlomiej. 1991a. *The Collapse of State Socialism: The Case of Poland.* Princeton: Princeton University Press.

———. 1991b. "Systemic Underpinnings of the Transition in Poland: The Shadow of the Roundtable Agreement." *Studies in Comparative Communism* 24 (1): 173–90.

Karl, Terry Lynn, and Philippe C. Schmitter. 1991. "Modes of Transition in Latin America, Southern and Eastern Europe." *International Social Science Journal* 128:269–84.

———. 1995. "From an Iron Curtain to a Paper Curtain: Grounding Transitologists or Students of Postcommunism?" *Slavic Review* 54 (4): 965–78.

Karpinski, Jakub. 1982. *Count-Down.* New York: Karz-Cohl.

———. 1987. "Polish Intellectuals in Opposition." *Problems of Communism* 36 (4): 44–57.

———. 1990. *Dziwna wojna.* Paris: Instytut Literacki.

Kawalec, Stefan. 1979. *Demokratyczna opozycja w Polsce.* New York: Wydawnictwo Glos.

Keane, John. 1988. Introduction to *Civil Society and the State,* ed. John Keane, 1–31. London: Verso.

Kempny, Marian. 1993. "Between Savagery and Communism: On the Relevance of Social Anthropology to the Study of Postcommunist Culture." *Centennial Review* 37 (1): 93–103.

Kenedi, Janos. 1982. *Do It Yourself: Hungary's Hidden Economy.* London: Pluto Press.

Kennedy, Michael. 1991. *Professionals, Power, and Solidarity in Poland.* Cambridge: Cambridge University Press.

———. 1994a. "An Introduction to East European Ideology and Identity in Transformation." In *Envisioning Eastern Europe: Postcommunist Cultural Studies,* ed. Michael Kennedy, 1–45. Ann Arbor: University of Michigan Press.

———, ed. 1994b. *Envisioning Eastern Europe: Postcommunist Cultural Studies.* Ann Arbor: University of Michigan Press.

Kenney, Padraic. 1993. "Working-Class Community and Resistance in Pre-Stalinist Poland: The Poznanski Textile Strike, Lodz, September 1947." *Social History* 18 (1): 31–51.

Kershaw, Ian. 1983. *Popular Opinion and Political Dissent in the Third Reich: Bavaria, 1933–1945.* Oxford: Clarendon Press.

Kersten, Krystyna [J. Bujnowski, pseud.]. 1984. "O oporze 1944–1948 czyli o poszukiwaniu propozycji." *Krytyka* 17:163–64.

———. 1987. "Spoleczenstwo polskie wobec wladzy ustanowionej przez komunistow, 1944–1947." In *Rzeczywistosc polska i sposoby radzenia sobie z nia,* ed. Miroslawa Marody and Antoni Sulek, 9–36. Warsaw: Ewa Lewicka-Banaszak and Piotr Marciniak.

———. 1990. *Narodziny systemu wladzy: Polska, 1943–1948.* Poznan: SAWW.

———. 1993. "Rok 1956–punkt zwrotny." *Krytyka* 40: 133–45.

King, Gary, Robert Keohane, and Sidney Verba. 1994. *Designing Social Inquiry.* Princeton: Princeton University Press.

Kitschelt, Herbert. 1992a. "Comparative Historical Research and Rational Choice Theory: The Case of Transitions to Democracy." *Theory and Society* 22:413–27.

———. 1992b. "The Formation of Party Systems in East Central Europe." *Politics and Society* 20 (March): 7–50.

———. 1995. "Formation of Party Cleavages in Post-Communist Democracies." *Party Politics* 1 (4): 447–72.

Klandermans, Bert. 1989a. "Grievance Interpretation and Success Expectations: The Social Construction of Protest." *Social Behaviour* 4:113–25.

———. 1989b. "Introduction: Organizational Effectiveness." *International Social Movement Research* 2:383–94.

Kloc, Kazimierz. 1989. "Strajki w przemysle w pierwszych latach Polski Ludowej." In *Studia nad ruchami spolecznymi,* vol. 2, ed. Piotr Marciniak and Wojciech Modzelewski, 5–41. Warsaw: Instytut Socjologi, Uniwersytet Warszawski.

———. 1992. "Polish Labor in Transition (1990–1992)." *Telos* 92 (Summer): 139–48.

———. 1994. "Trade Unions and Economic Transformation in Poland." In *Parties, Trade Unions, and Society in East-Central Europe,* ed. Michael Waller and Martin Myant, 125–32. Portland: Frank Cass.

Kloc, Kazimierz, and Wladyslaw Rychlowski. 1994. *Spory zbiorowe i strajki w przemysle: Opinie pracownikow o konfliktach i ich zakladach pracy.* Warsaw: Szkola Glowna Handlowa.

Klosinska, Krystyna. 1992. "Mniejszosci narodowe w Polsce." In *Barometr Kultury,* ed. Miroslawa Grabowska, 53–63. Warsaw: Instytut Kultury.

Kochanowicz, Jacek. 1993. "The Disappearing State: Poland's Three Years of Transition." *Social Research* 60 (4): 821–34.

Kolakowski, Leszek. 1983. "The Intelligentsia." In *Poland: Genesis of a Revolution,* ed. Abraham Brumberg, 54–67. New York: Random House.

Kolankiewicz, George. 1987. "Polish Trade Unions 'Normalized.'" *Problems of Communism* 36 (6): 57–69.

Kolarska-Bobinska, Lena. 1992. "Konflikty w nowej Polsce." *Gazeta Wyborcza,* November 28–29, 11.

———. 1994. *Aspirations, Values, and Interests: Poland, 1989–1994.* Warsaw: IFiS Publishers.

Kolodko, Grzegorz. 1992. *Transformacja polskiej gospodarki.* Warsaw: BGW.

Koopmans, Ruud. 1995. *Democracy from Below: New Social Movements and the Political System in West Germany.* Boulder: Westview Press.

Koopmans, Ruud, and Hanspeter Kriesi. 1995. "Institutional Structures and Prevailing Strategies." In *New Social Movements in Western Europe: A Comparative Analysis,* by Hanspeter Kriesi, Ruud Koopmans, Jan Willem Duyvendak, and Marco G. Giugni, 26–52. Minneapolis: University of Minnesota Press.

Kopstein, Jeffrey. 1996. "Chipping Away at the State: Workers' Resistance and the Demise of East Germany." *World Politics* 48 (April): 391–423.

Kornai, Janos. 1996. "Paying the Bill for Goulash-Communism: Hungarian Development and Macro Stabilization in a Political-Economy Perspective." Discussion Paper Series, Harvard Institute of Economic Research.

Korybutowicz, Zygmunt. 1983. *Grudzien 1970.* Paris: Instytut Literacki.

Kostewicz, Tadeusz. 1996. "Terror i represje." In *Polacy wobec przemocy 1944–1956,* ed. Barbara Otwinowska and Jan Zaryn, 121–78. Warsaw: Editions Spotkania.

Kowalczyk, Roman. 1992. *Lodzki strajk studencki.* Warsaw: NOWA.

Kowalski, Sergiusz. 1990. *Krytyka solidarnosciowego rozumu.* Warsaw: PEN.

Kramer, Mark. 1995. "Polish Workers and the Post-communist Transition, 1989–1993." *Communist and Post-Communist Studies* 28 (1): 71–114.

———. 1997. "Social Protection Policies and Safety Net in East-Central Europe: Dilemmas of the Postcommunist Transformation." In *Sustaining the Transition: The Social Safety Net in Postcommunist Europe,* ed. Ethan B. Kapstein and Michael Mandelbaum, 46–123. New York: Council on Foreign Relations.

Krasnodebska, Urszula, Joanna Pucek, Grzegorz Kowalczyk, and Jan Jakub Wygnan-ski. 1996. *Podstawowe statystyki dotyczace dzialan organizacji pozarzadowych w Polsce.* Warsaw: Program PHARE-Dialog Spoleczny.

Kriesi, Hanspeter. 1995. "The Political Opportunity Structure of New Social Movements: Its Impact on Their Mobilization." In *The Politics of Social Protest: Comparative Perspectives on States and Social Movements,* ed. J. Craig Jenkins and Bert Klandermans, 169–98. Minneapolis: University of Minnesota Press.

Kriesi, Hanspeter, and Jan Willem Duyvendak. 1995. "National Cleavage Structures." In *New Social Movements in Western Europe: A Comparative Analysis,* by Hanspeter Kriesi, Ruud Koopmans, Jan Willem Duyvendak, and Marco G. Giugni, 3–25. Minneapolis: University of Minnesota Press.

Kriesi, Hanspeter, Ruud Koopmans, Jan Willem Duyvendak, and Marco G. Giugni. 1995. *New Social Movements in Western Europe: A Comparative Analysis.* Minneapolis: University of Minnesota Press.

Krzeminski, Ireneusz. 1987. *Czego chcieli, o czym mysleli? Analiza postulatow robotnikow Wybrzeza z 1970 i 1980.* Warsaw: Ewa Lewicka-Banaszak and Piotr Marciniak.

Ksiezopolski, Miroslaw. 1995. "Bezpieczenstwo spoleczne." In *Raport o rozwoju spolecznym—Polska '95,* ed. Jolanta Kucharzak, 167–85. Warsaw: Fundacja Zabezpieczenia Spolecznego.

Kubik, Jan. 1991. "Culture, Administrative Reform, and Local Politics: Overlooked Dimensions of the Post-Communist Transformation." *Anthropology of East Europe Review* 10 (2): 12–27.

———. 1994a. *The Power of Symbols against the Symbols of Power: The Rise of Solidarity and the Fall of State Socialism in Poland.* University Park: Pennsylvania State University Press.

———. 1994b. "The Role of Decentralization and Cultural Revival in Post-Communist Transformations: The Case of Cieszyn Silesia, Poland." *Communist and Post-Communist Studies* 27 (4): 331–55.

———. 1994c. "Who Done It: Workers, Intellectuals, or Someone Else? Controversy over Solidarity's Origins and Social Composition." *Theory and Society* 23:441–66.

———. 1998. "Institutionalization of Protest during Democratic Consolidations in Central Europe." In *The Social Movement Society: Contentious Politics for a New Century,* ed. David S. Meyer and Sidney Tarrow, 131–52. Lanham: Rowman and Littlefield.

Kuklinski, Ryszard. 1987. "Wojna z narodem widziana od srodka." *Kultura* 475 (April): 3–57.

Kulpinska, Jolanta, ed. 1990. "Raport PTS—Strajki 1980." In *Studia nad ruchami spolecznymi,* vol. 5, ed. Jolanta Kulpinska and Piotr Marciniak. Warsaw: Instytut Socjologi, Uniwersytet Warszawski.

Kurczewska, Joanna, Katarzyna Staszynska, and Hanna Bojar. 1993. "Blokady spoleczenstwa obywatelskiego: Slabe spoleczenstwo i slabe panstwo." In *Spoleczenstwo w transformacji,* ed. Andrzej Rychard and Michal Federowicz, 84–96. Warsaw: IFiS PAN.

Kurti, Laszlo. 1991. "Rocking the State: Youth and Rock Music Culture in Hungary, 1976–1990." *East European Politics and Societies* 5 (3): 483–513.

Laba, Roman. 1991. *The Roots of Solidarity: A Political Sociology of Poland's Working-Class Democratization.* Princeton: Princeton University Press.

Lake, Robert W., and Joanna Regulska. 1990. "Political Decentralization and Capital Mobility in Planned and Market Societies: Local Autonomy in Poland and the United States." *Policy Studies Journal* 18 (3): 702–20.

Larana, Enrique, Hank Johnston, and Joseph R. Gusfield, eds. 1994. *New Social Movements: From Ideology to Identity.* Philadelphia: Temple University Press.

Lasswell, Harold, David Lerner, and Ithiel de Sola Pool. 1952. *The Comparative Study of Symbols: An Introduction.* The Hoover Institute Studies, Series C: Symbols, no. 1. Stanford: Stanford University Press.

Lepak, Keith. 1988. *Prelude to Solidarity.* New York: Columbia University Press.

Levy, Jack. 1994. "Learning and Foreign Policy: Sweeping a Conceptual Minefield." *International Organization* 48 (2): 279–312.

Lewis, Flora. 1958. *A Case History of Hope: The Story of Poland's Peaceful Revolution.* New York: Doubleday.

Lewis, Paul G. 1979. "Potential Sources of Opposition in the East European Peasantry." In *Opposition in Eastern Europe,* ed. Rudolf Tokes, 263–91. Baltimore: Johns Hopkins University Press.

———. 1990. "Non-competitive Elections and Regime Change: Poland, 1989." *Parliamentary Affairs* 43:93–107.

———. 1994. "Civil Society and the Development of Political Parties in East-Central Europe." In *Parties, Trade Unions, and Society in East-Central Europe,* ed. Michael Waller and Martin Myant, 5–20. Portland: Frank Cass.

Lichbach, Marc I. 1996. "Where Have All the Foils Gone? Competing Theories of Social Movements and the Structure-Action Problem." Unpublished paper, October 23.

Lieberman, Ira W., Stilpon S. Nestor, and Raj M. Desai. 1997. *Between State and Market.* Washington, D.C.: EBRD/World Bank.

Lijphart, Arend. 1992. "Democratization and Constitutional Choices in Czecho-slovakia, Hungary, and Poland, 1989–91." *Journal of Theoretical Politics* 4 (2): 207–23.

Lijphart, Arend, and Carlos H. Waisman, eds. 1996. *Institutional Design in New Democracies.* Boulder: Westview Press.

Linz, Juan J. 1975. "Authoritarian and Totalitarian Regimes." In *Handbook of Political*

Science, vol. 3, ed. Fred I. Greenstein and Nelson W. Polsby, 175–411. Reading, Mass.: Addison- Wesley.

———. 1992. "Change and Continuity in the Nature of Contemporary Democracies." In *Reexamining Democracy: Essays in Honor of Seymour Martin Lipset,* ed. Gary Marks and Larry Diamond, 182–207. Newbury Park: Sage.

Linz, Juan J., and Alfred Stepan. 1992. "Political Identities and Electoral Sequences: Spain, the Soviet Union, and Yugoslavia." *Daedalus* 121 (spring): 123–39.

———. 1996. *Problems of Democratic Transition and Consolidation: Southern Europe, South America, and Post-Communist Europe.* Baltimore: Johns Hopkins University Press.

Lipka, Robert. 1992. "Nowe organizacje polskiej mlodziezy." In *Raport o mlodziezy,* ed. Barbara Fatyga and Michal Szymanczak, 200–213. Warsaw: Interpress.

Lippmann, Walter. 1956. *Public Opinion.* New York: Macmillan.

Lipset, Seymour Martin. 1960. *Political Man: The Social Bases of Politics.* Garden City, N.Y.: Doubleday.

———. 1993. "The Significance of the 1992 Election." *Political Science and Politics* 26:7.

Lipski, Jan. 1985. *KOR: A History of the Workers' Defense Committee in Poland, 1976–1981.* Trans. Olga Amsterdamska and Gene Moore. Berkeley: University of California Press.

Lipsky, Michael. 1968. "Protest as a Political Resource." *American Political Science Review* 62:1144–58.

Los, Maria, ed. 1990. *The Second Economy in Marxist States.* New York: St. Martin's Press.

Mac, Jerzy Slawomir. 1995. "Kosciol poziomy." *Wprost* 26 (June 25): 30–32.

Machcewicz, Pawel. 1993. *Polski rok 1956.* Warsaw: Mowia Wieki.

Maciejewski, Jaroslaw, and Zofia Trojanowiczowa. 1990. *Poznanski Czerwiec 1956.* 2d ed. Poznan: Wydawnictwo Poznanskie.

Maier, Charles S. 1987. Introduction to *Changing Boundaries of the Political,* ed. Charles S. Maier, 1–24. Cambridge: Cambridge University Press.

Mainwaring, Scott. 1992. "Transitions to Democracy and Democratic Consolidation: Theoretical and Comparative Issues." In *Issues in Democratic Consolidation: The New South American Democracies in Comparative Perspective,* ed. Scott Mainwaring, Guillermo O'Donnell, and J. Samuel Valenzuela, 294–341. Notre Dame: University of Notre Dame Press.

Mainwaring, Scott, Guillermo O'Donnell, and J. Samuel Valenzuela, eds. 1992. *Issues in Democratic Consolidation: The New South American Democracies in Comparative Perspective.* Notre Dame: University of Notre Dame Press.

Mann, Michael. 1984. "The Autonomous Power of the State: Its Origins, Mechanisms, and Results." *Archives Européennes de Sociologie* 25 (2): 185–213.

Manticone, Ronald. 1986. *The Catholic Church in Communist Poland.* New York: Columbia University Press.

Marat, Stanislaw, and Jacek Snopkiewicz, eds. 1990. *Ludzie bezpieki: Dokumentacja czasu bezprawia.* Warsaw: Alfa.

Marciniak, Piotr. 1989. "Horyzont programowy strajkow 1980 r." In *Studia nad ruchami spolecznymi,* vol. 2, ed. Piotr Marciniak and Wojciech Modzelewski, 131–200. Warsaw: Instytut Socjologi, Uniwersytet Warszawski.

———. 1990. "Strajki polskie lat osiemdziesiatych—ciaglosc i zmiana." In *Studia nad ruchami spolecznymi,* vol. 5, ed. Ewa Lewicka-Banaszak and Piotr Marciniak, 7–23. Warsaw: Instytut Socjologi, Uniwersytet Warszawski.

———. 1992. "Polish Labor Unions: Can They Find a Way Out." *Telos* 92 (summer): 149–57.

Margueritte, Bernard. 1995. "Post-Communist Eastern Europe: The Difficult Birth of a Free Press." Discussion Paper D-21, Joan Shorenstein Center, John F. Kennedy School of Government, Harvard University, August.

Markowski, Radoslaw. 1992. "Milczaca wiekszosc—o biernosci politycznej spoleczenstwa polskiego." In *Wybory '91 a polska scena polityczna,* ed. Stanislaw Gebethner and Jacek Raciborski, 81–107. Warsaw: Polska w Europie.

Marody, Mira. 1991. "On Polish Political Attitudes." *Telos* 89 (fall): 109–13.

———. 1995. "Three Stages of Party System Emergence in Poland." *Communist and Post-Communist Studies* 28 (2): 263–70.

Mason, David. 1987. "Poland's New Trade Unions." *Soviet Studies* 39 (3): 489–508.

———. 1992. "Attitudes Towards the Market and the State in Postcommunist Europe." Paper presented at the Annual Meeting of the American Political Science Association, Chicago, September.

Mass Privatization: An Initial Assessment. 1995. Paris: OECD.

Mazowiecki, Wojciech. 1989. *Wydarzenia 3 maja 1946.* Paris: Libella.

McAdam, Doug. 1994. "Culture and Social Movements." In *New Social Movements: From Ideology to Identity,* ed. Enrique Larana, Hank Johnston, and Joseph R. Gusfield, 36–57. Philadelphia: Temple University Press.

———. 1995. "Initiator and Spin-Off Movements: Diffusion Processes in Protest Cycles." In *Repertoires and Cycles of Collective Action,* ed. Mark Traugott, 217–39. Durham: Duke University Press, 1995.

McAdam, Doug, Sidney Tarrow, and Charles Tilly. 1997. "Toward an Integrated Perspective on Social Movements and Revolution." In *Comparative Politics: Rationality, Culture, and Structure,* ed. Mark Irving Lichbach and Alan S. Zuckerman, 142–73. Cambridge: Cambridge University Press.

McCarthy, John D. 1996. "Constraints and Opportunities in Adopting, Adapting, and Inventing." In *Comparative Perspectives on Social Movements,* ed. Doug McAdam, John D. McCarthy, and Mayer N. Zald, 141–51. Cambridge: Cambridge University Press.

McCarthy, John D., Clark McPhail, Jackie Smith, and Louis J. Crishock. 1998. "Electronic and Print Media Representations of Washington, D.C. Demonstrations, 1982 and 1991: A Demography of Description Bias." In *Acts of Dissent: New Developments in the Study of Protest,* ed. Dieter Rucht, Ruud Koopmans, and Friedhelm Neidhardt, 113–30. Berlin: Sigma.

McCarthy, John D., and Mayer N. Zald. 1987. "Resource Mobilization and Social Movements: A Partial Theory." In *Social Movements in an Organizational Society,* ed. M. N. Zald and J. D. McCarthy, 15–42. New Brunswick, N.J.: Transaction Books.

McDonough, Peter, Samuel H. Barnes, and A. Lopez Pina. 1986. "The Growth of Democratic Legitimacy in Spain." *American Political Science Review* 80 (3): 735–60.

Micewski, Andrzej. 1994. *Kosciol-Panstwo, 1945–1989.* Warsaw: Wydawnictwa Szkolne i Pedagogiczne.

Michnik, Adam. 1981. "Dziedzictwo Marca." In *Marzec '68: Sesja w Uniwersytecie Warszawskim 1981 r.* Warsaw: Studencka Oficyna Wydawnicza SOWA.

———. 1993. *The Church and the Left.* Trans. David Ost. Chicago: University of Chicago Press.

Michta, Andrew. 1993. *The Presidential-Parliamentary System.* In *Transition to Democracy in Poland,* ed. Richard F. Staar, 57–76. New York: St. Martin's Press.

———. 1997. "Democratic Consolidation in Poland after 1989." In *The Consolidation of Democracy in East-Central Europe,* ed. Karen Dawisha and Bruce Parrott, 66–108. Cambridge: Cambridge University Press.

Migdal, Joel. 1988. *Strong Societies and Weak States.* Princeton: Princeton University Press.

———. 1994. "The State in Society: An Approach to Struggles for Domination." In *State Power and Social Forces in the Third World,* ed. Joel S. Migdal, Atul Kholi, and Vivienne Shue, 7–34. Cambridge: Cambridge University Press.

Misztal, Bronislaw. 1990. "Alternative Social Movements in Contemporary Poland." *Research in Social Movements, Conflict, and Change* 12:67–88.

Mizerski, Wieslaw. 1991. *Radomski Czerwiec 1976.* Lublin: Norbertinum.

Modzelewski, Wojciech. 1989. "Symbolika Solidarnosci." In *Studia nad ruchami spolecznymi,* vol. 2, ed. Piotr Marciniak and Wojciech Modzelewski, 229–79. Warsaw: Instytut Socjologi, Uniwersytet Warszawski.

Moldawa, Tadeusz. 1991. *Ludzie wladzy 1944–1991.* Warsaw: PWN.

Myant, Martin. 1982. *Poland: A Crisis for Socialism.* London: Lawrence and Wishart.

Nalepa, Edward. 1990. *Wojsko Polskie w Grudniu 1970.* Warsaw: Bellona.

———. 1992. *Pacyfikacja zbuntowanego miasta.* Warsaw: Bellona.

Neidhardt, Friedhelm, and Dieter Rucht. 1991. "The Analysis of Social Movements: The State of the Art and Some Perspectives for Further Research." In *Research on Social Movements: The State of the Art in Western Europe and the USA,* ed. Dieter Rucht, 421–64. Frankfurt am Main and Boulder: Campus Verlag and Westview Press.

Nelson, Joan M. 1990. "Conclusions." In *Economic Crisis and Policy Choices: The Politics of Adjustment in the Third World,* ed. Joan M. Nelson, 321–61. Princeton: Princeton University Press.

Nollert, Michael. 1995. "Neocorporatism and Political Protest in the Western Democracies: A Cross-National Analysis." In *The Politics of Social Protest: Comparative Perspectives on States and Social Movements,* ed. J. Craig Jenkins and Bert Klandermans, 138–64. Minneapolis: University of Minnesota Press.

Nordlinger, Eric A. 1987. "Taking the State Seriously." In *Understanding Political Development,* ed. Myron Weiner and Samuel P. Huntington, 353–90. Boston: Little, Brown.

North, Douglass C. 1990. *Institutions, Institutional Change, and Economic Performance.* Cambridge: Cambridge University Press.

O'Brien, Kevin. 1996. "Rightful Resistance." *World Politics* 49 (October): 31–55.

O'Donnell, Guillermo. 1992. "Transitions, Continuities, and Paradoxes." In *Issues in Democratic Consolidation: The New South American Democracies in Comparative Perspective,* ed. Scott Mainwaring, Guillermo O'Donnell, and J. Samuel Valenzuela, 17–56. Notre Dame: University of Notre Dame Press.

O'Donnell, Guillermo, and Philippe Schmitter. 1986. *Transitions from Authoritarian Rule: Tentative Conclusions about Uncertain Democracies.* Baltimore: Johns Hopkins University Press.

OECD Economic Surveys, Poland 1994. 1994. Paris: OECD.

OECD Economic Surveys, Poland 1997. 1996. Paris: OECD.

Offe, Claus. 1985. *Disorganized Capitalism.* Cambridge: MIT Press.

———. 1987. "Challenging the Boundaries of Institutional Politics: Social Movements since the 1960s." In *Changing Boundaries of the Political,* ed. Charles S. Maier, 63–105. Cambridge: Cambridge University Press.

———. 1991. "Capitalism by Democratic Design? Democratic Theory Facing the Triple Transition in East Central Europe." *Social Research* 58 (4): 865–92.

Ogrodzinski, Piotr. 1991. *Piec tekstow o spoleczenstwie obywatelskim.* Warsaw: ISP PAN.

Olson, David M. 1993. "Compartmentalized Competition: The Managed Transitional Election System of Poland." *Journal of Politics* 55 (May): 415–41.

Olzak, Susan. 1989. "Analysis of Events in the Study of Collective Action." *Annual Review of Sociology* 15:119–41.

Ortner, Sherry. 1989. *High Religion: A Cultural and Political History of Sherpa Buddhism.* Princeton: Princeton University Press.

Osa, Maryjane. 1989. "Resistance, Persistence, and Change: The Transformation of the Catholic Church in Poland." *East European Politics and Societies* 3 (spring): 268–99.

———. 1997. "Creating Solidarity: The Religious Foundations of the Polish Social Movement." *East European Politics and Societies* 11 (spring): 339–65.

———. 1998. "Contention and Democracy: Labor Protest in Poland, 1989–1993." *Communist and Post-Communist Studies* 31 (March): 29–42.

Osiatynski, Wiktor. 1991. "The Round Table Negotiations in Poland." Working Paper No. 1, Center for the Study of Constitutionalism in Eastern Europe, University of Chicago, August.

Ost, David. 1990. *Solidarity and the Politics of Anti-Politics.* Philadelphia: Temple University Press.

Otwinowska, Barbara, and Jan Zaryn, eds. 1996. *Polacy wobec przemocy 1944–1956.* Warsaw: Editions Spotkania.

Oxhorn, Phillip D. 1995. *Organizing Civil Society: The Popular Sectors and the Struggle for Democracy in Chile.* University Park: Pennsylvania State University Press.

Paczkowski, Andrzej. 1991. *Stanislaw Mikolajczyk, czyli kleska realisty.* Warsaw: Omnipress.

———, ed. 1994. *Aparat bezpieczenstwa w latach 1944–1956: Taktyka, strategia, metody.* Warsaw: ISP PAN.

Parrott, Bruce. 1997. "Perspectives on Postcommunist Democratization." In *The Con-*

solidation of Democracy in East-Central Europe, ed. Karen Dawisha and Bruce Parrott, 1–39. Cambridge: Cambridge University Press.

Perez-Diaz, Victor. 1993. *The Return of Civil Society.* Cambridge: Harvard University Press.

Pernal, Marek, and Jan Skorzynski. 1990. *Kalendarium: Solidarnosc, 1980–1989.* Warsaw: Omnipress.

Perzkowski, Stanislaw, ed. 1994. *Tajne dokumenty Biura Politycznego i Sekretariatu KC: Ostatni rok wladzy 1988–1989.* London: Aneks.

Polska '93. 1992. Warsaw: Polska Agencja Informacyjna.

Pomian, Krzysztof. 1985. *Wymiary polskiego konfliktu 1956–1981.* London: Aneks.

Powell, Walter W., and Paul J. DiMaggio, eds. 1991. *The New Institutionalism in Organizational Analysis.* Chicago: University of Chicago Press.

Poznanski, Kazimierz. 1996. *Poland's Protracted Transition.* Cambridge: Cambridge University Press.

———, ed. 1993. *Stabilization and Privatization in Poland: An Economic Evaluation of the Shock Therapy.* Boston: Kluwer.

Pravda, Alex. 1979. "Industrial Workers: Patterns of Dissent, Opposition, and Accommodation." In *Opposition in Eastern Europe,* ed. Rudolf Tokes, 219–21. Baltimore: Johns Hopkins University Press.

———. 1983. "The Workers." In *Poland: Genesis of a Revolution,* ed. Abraham Brumberg, 68–91. New York: Random House.

Prawelska-Skrzypek, Grazyna. 1996. "Citizen Activism in the Life of Local Communities: Polish Experiences during the Period of Transformations." Manuscript.

Pridham, Geoffrey, ed. 1990. *Securing Democracy: Political Parties and Democratic Consolidation in Southern Europe.* London: Routledge.

Przeworski, Adam. 1991. *Democracy and the Market.* Cambridge: Cambridge University Press.

———. 1992. "The Neoliberal Fallacy." *Journal of Democracy* 3 (3): 45–59.

———. 1993. "Economic Reforms, Public Opinion, and Political Institutions: Poland in the Eastern European Perspective." In *Economic Reforms in New Democracies,* ed. Luiz Carlos Bresser Pereira, Jose Maria Maravall, and Adam Przeworski, 132–98. Cambridge: Cambridge University Press.

Przeworski, Adam, et al. 1995. *Sustainable Democracy.* Cambridge: Cambridge University Press.

Putnam, Robert D. 1971. "Studying Elite Political Culture: The Case of 'Ideology.'" *American Political Science Review* 65 (3): 651–81.

Raciborski, Jacek. 1992. "Determinanty procesu krystalizacji preferencji wyborczych." In *Wybory '91 a polska scena polityczna,* ed. Stanislaw Gebethner and Jacek Raciborski, 123–66. Warsaw: Polska w Europie.

Raina, Peter. 1981. *Independent Social Movements in Poland.* London: London School of Economics and Politics.

Rakowski, Mieczyslaw. 1981. *Przesilenie grudniowe.* Warsaw: PIW.

Ramet, Pedro. 1987. *Cross and Commissars: The Politics of Religion in Eastern Europe and USSR.* Bloomington: Indiana University Press.

Rapaczynski, Andrzej. 1993. "Constitutional Politics in Poland: A Report on the Constitutional Committee of the Polish Parliament." In *Constitution Making in Eastern Europe,* ed. A. E. Dick Howard, 93–131. Washington, D.C.: Woodrow Wilson Center Press.

Regulska, Joanna. 1993. "Self-Governance or Central Control? Rewriting Constitutions in Central and Eastern Europe." In *Constitution Making in Eastern Europe,* ed. A. E. Dick Howard, 133–61. Washington, D.C.: Woodrow Wilson Center Press.

———. 1998. "Local Government Reform." In *Transition to Democracy in Poland,* 2d ed., ed. Richard F. Staar, 113–32. New York: St. Martin's Press.

Reisinger, William M., Arthur H. Miller, Vicki L. Hesli, and Kristen Hill Maher. 1994. "Political Values in Russia, Ukraine, and Lithuania: Sources and Implications for Democracy." *British Journal of Political Science* 24:183–223.

Rev, Istvan. 1987. "The Advantages of Being Atomized: How Hungarian Peasants Cope with Collectivization." *Dissent* (summer): 335–49.

Rokkan, Stein. 1970. *Citizens, Elections, Parties.* Oslo: Universitetsforlaget.

Rose, Richard, and Christian Haerpfer. 1996a. *Change and Stability in the New Democracies Barometer: A Trend Analysis.* Studies in Public Policy No. 270. Glasgow: University of Strathclyde.

———. 1996b. *New Democracies Barometer IV: A 10-Nation Survey.* Studies in Public Policy No. 262. Glasgow: University of Strathclyde.

Roszkowski, Wojciech. 1992. "Polska." In *Raport o stanie Europy Srodkowo-Wschodniej,* 59–68. Warsaw: ISP PAN.

———. 1994. "Polska" (Chronology of Events). In *Europa Srodkowo-Wschodnia 1992,* 273–80. Warsaw: ISP PAN.

Rucht, Dieter, Ruud Koopmans, and Friedhelm Neidhardt, eds. 1998. *Acts of Dissent: New Developments in the Study of Protest.* Berlin: Sigma Press.

Rucht, Dieter, and Thomas Ohlemacher. 1992. "Protest Event Data: Collection, Uses, and Perspectives." In *Studying Collective Action,* ed. Mario Diani and Ron Eyerman, 76–106. London: Sage.

Rutkowski, Jan. 1996. "Becoming Less Equal: Wage Effects of Economic Transition in Poland." Pew Working Papers in Central and Eastern European Reform and Regionalism, Center for International Studies, Princeton University.

Ryback, Timothy. 1990. *Rock around the Bloc: A History of Rock Music in Eastern Europe.* New York: Oxford University Press.

Rychard, Andrzej. 1995. "Ludzie i instytucje: Kto tworzy nowy lad." *Studia Socjologiczne* 136–37 (1–2): 5–16.

Rykowski, Zbyslaw, and Wieslaw Wladyka. 1989. *Polska Proba: Pazdziernik '56.* Krakow: Wydawnictwo Literackie.

Sable, Charles, and David Stark. 1982. "Planning, Politics, and Shop Floor Power: Hidden Forms of Bargaining in Soviet Imposed State Socialist Societies." *Politics and Society* 2 (4): 439–75.

Sachs, Jeffrey. 1993. *Poland's Jump to the Market Economy.* Cambridge: MIT Press.

Sachs, Jeffrey, and Andrew Warner. 1996. "Achieving Rapid Growth in the Transition Economies of Central Europe." Development Discussion Paper No. 544, Harvard Institute for International Development.

Sakwa, George. 1978. "The Polish 'October': A Re-appraisal through Historiography." *Polish Review* 23 (3): 62–78.

Schama, Simon. 1989. *Citizens: A Chronicle of the French Revolution.* New York: Alfred A. Knopf.

Schmitter, Philippe. 1981. "Interest Mediation and Regime Governability in Contemporary Western Europe and North America." In *Organizing Interests in Western Europe,* ed. Susanne Berger, 287–327. Cambridge: Cambridge University Press.

———. 1992. "Interest Systems and the Consolidation of Democracies." In *Reexamining Democracy: Essays in Honor of Seymour Martin Lipset,* ed. Gary Marks and Larry Diamond, 156–81. Newbury Park: Sage.

———. 1995a. "Some Reflections about the Concept of Civil Society (in General) and Its Role in the Liberalization and Democratization of Europe in the Nineteenth Century (in Particular)." Paper presented at the conference "Civil Society before Democracy," Princeton University, October 6–7.

———. 1995b. "Transitology: The Science or Art of Democratization?" In *The Consolidation of Democracy in Latin America,* ed. Joseph Tulchin, 1–41. Boulder: Lynne Rienner.

Schmitter, Philippe, and Terry L. Karl. 1991. "What Democracy Is . . . and Is Not." *Journal of Democracy* 2 (3): 75–88.

Schopflin, George. 1983. "Poland and Eastern Europe." In *Poland: Genesis of a Revolution,* ed. Abraham Brumberg, 123–34. New York: Random House.

Scott, James. 1986. *Weapons of the Weak: Everyday Forms of Peasant Resistance.* New Haven: Yale University Press.

———. 1990. *Domination and the Arts of Resistance.* New Haven: Yale University Press.

Seleny, Anna. 1991. "Hidden Enterprise and Property Rights Reform in Hungary." *Law and Policy* 13 (2): 149–69.

Seligman, Adam. 1992. *The Idea of Civil Society.* New York: Free Press.

Sevelsberg, Joachim J. 1995. "Crime, Inequality, and Justice in Eastern Europe." In *Crime and Inequality,* ed. John Hagan and Ruth D. Peterson, 206–24. Stanford: Stanford University Press.

Sewerynski, Michal. 1994. "Dylematy i perspektywy zwiazkow zawodowych w krajach postkomunistycznych." *Przeglad Socjologiczny* 43:111—31.

Shafer, Michael D. 1994. *Winners and Losers: How Sectors Shape the Developmental Prospects of States.* Ithaca: Cornell University Press.

Shin, Doh Chull. 1994. "On the Third Wave of Democratization: A Synthesis and Evaluation of Recent Theory and Research." *World Politics* 47 (October): 135–70.

Siemienska, Renata. 1991. "Problemy demokracji w Europie Wschodniej." Raport z badan, Styczen. Warsaw: OBOP.

Skilling, Gordon. 1981. *Charter 77 and Human Rights in Czechoslovakia.* London: Allen and Unwin.

Skocpol, Theda. 1985. "Bringing the State Back In: Strategies of Analysis in Current Research." In *Bringing the State Back In,* ed. Peter Evans, Dietrich Rueschemeyer, and Theda Skocpol, 3–43. New York: Cambridge University Press.

Slay, Ben. 1994. *The Polish Economy: Crisis, Reform, and Transformation.* Princeton: Princeton University Press.

———. 1995. "The Polish Economy Six Years After." Paper presented at the 27th Annual Convention of the American Association for the Advancement of Slavic Studies, Washington, D.C., October 26–29.

Slodkowska, Inka. 1995. *Programy Partii i Ugrupowan Parlamentarnych, 1989–1991.* Warsaw: ISP PAN.

Smolar, Aleksander. 1991. "The Polish Opposition." In *Crisis and Reform in Eastern Europe,* ed. Ferenc Feher and Andrew Arato, 175–252. New Brunswick, N.J.: Transaction Books.

Smolenski, Pawel, and Wojciech Gielzynski. 1989. *Robotnicy '88.* London: Aneks.

Snow, David A., and Robert D. Benford. 1988. "Ideology, Frame Resonance, and Participant Mobilization." In *International Social Movement Research,* vol. 1, *From Structure to Action: Comparing Social Movement Research across Cultures,* ed. Bert Klandermans, Hanspeter Kriesi, and Sidney Tarrow, 197–217. Greenwich, Conn.: JAI Press.

Sokolewicz, Wojciech. 1992. "The Legal-Constitutional Bases of Democratization in Poland: Systemic and Constitutional Changes." In *Democratization in Poland, 1989–1990,* ed. George Sanford, 69-97. New York: St. Martin's Press.

Spiewak, Pawel. 1993. "Kto rzadzi w Polsce?" In *Polska 1989–1992: Fragmenty pejzazu,* ed. Miroslawa Grabowska and Antoni Sulek, 29–38. Warsaw: IFiS PAN.

Staniszkis, Jadwiga. 1981. "The Evolution of Forms of Working-Class Protest in Poland: Sociological Reflection on the Gdansk-Szczecin Case, August 1980." *Soviet Studies* 28 (2): 204–31.

———. 1984. *Poland's Self-Limiting Revolution.* Princeton: Princeton University Press.

———. 1987. "The Political Articulation of Property Rights: Some Reflections on the 'Inert Structure.'" In *Crisis and Transition: Polish Society in the 1980s,* ed. J. Koralewicz, Ireneusz Bialecki, and Margaret Watson, 53–79. Oxford: Berg.

———. 1989. *Ontologia Socjalizmu.* Warsaw: In Plus.

———. 1991. *The Dynamics of the Breakthrough in Eastern Europe: The Polish Experience.* Berkeley: University of California Press.

———. 1992. *Continuity and Change in Postcommunist Europe.* The Hague: Netherlands Institute of International Relations "Clingendael."

———. 1995. "Polityka postkomunistycznej instytucjonalizacji w perspektywie historycznej." *Studia Polityczne* 4:39–60.

Stark, David, and Laszlo Bruszt. 1998. *Postsocialist Pathways: Transforming Politics and Property in East Central Europe.* Cambridge: Cambridge University Press.

Stark, David, and Victor Nee. 1989. "Toward an Institutional Analysis of State Socialism." In *Remaking the Economic Institutions of Socialism,* ed. Victor Nee and David Stark, 1–31. Stanford: Stanford University Press.

Stefanski, Jacek. 1995. *Polska 1988–1993: Kalendarium.* Kolbuszowa: Varia Kolbuszowski.

Steinmo, Sven, Kathleen Thelen, and Frank Longstreth, eds. 1992. *Structuring Politics: Historical Institutionalism in Comparative Analysis.* Cambridge: Cambridge University Press.

Stepan, Alfred. 1985. "State Power and Civil Society in the Southern Cone of Latin America." In *Bringing the State Back In,* ed. Peter Evans, Dietrich Rueschemeyer, and Theda Skocpol, 317–43. New York: Cambridge University Press.

———. 1988. *Rethinking Military Politics.* Princeton: Princeton University Press.

Svejnar, Jan. 1995. "Economic Transformation in Central and East Europe: The Tasks

Still Ahead." Paper presented at the 1995 Meeting of the Per Jacobsson Foundation, Washington, D.C., October 8.

Swianiewicz, Pawel. n.d. "How Do Local Politics Differ? Comparison of Four East European Countries." Unpublished paper.

Swida-Ziemba, Hanna. 1994. "The Post-communist Mentality." In *Cultural Dilemmas of Post- Communist Societies,* ed. Aldona Jawlowska and Marian Kempny, 223–39. Warsaw: IFiS Publishers.

Swidler, Ann. 1986. "Culture in Action: Symbols and Strategies." *American Sociological Review* 51 (April): 273–86.

Swirska, Joanna. 1994. "Protesty pracownicze w Polsce—przeglad wydarzen w latach 1992–1994." Unpublished paper.

Syrop, Konrad. 1957. *Spring in October: The Polish Revolution of 1956.* London: Weidenfeld and Nicolson.

Szawiel, Tadeusz. 1993. "Partie polityczne w Polsce: Stan obecny szanse i zagrozenia." In *Polska 1989–1992: Fragmenty pejzazu,* ed. Miroslawa Grabowska and Antoni Sulek, 39–57. Warsaw: IFiS PAN.

Szejnert, Malgorzata, and Tomasz Zalewski. 1986. *Szczecin: Grudzien-Sierpien-Grudzien.* London: Aneks.

Szelenyi, Ivan. 1988. *Socialist Entrepreneurs: Embourgeoisement in Rural Hungary.* Madison: University of Wisconsin Press.

Szpakowski, Zdzislaw. 1996. "Zbrojne podziemie antykomunistyczne." In *Polacy wobec przemocy, 1944–1956,* ed. Barbara Otwinowska and Jan Zaryn, 34–78. Warsaw: Editions Spotkania.

Szporluk, Roman. 1990. "In Search of the Drama of History: Or, National Roads to Modernity." *East European Politics and Societies* 1 (winter): 134–50.

Sztompka, Piotr. 1991. "The Intangibles and Imponderables of the Transition to Democracy." *Studies in Comparative Communism* 14 (3): 295–311.

———. 1992. "Dilemmas of the Great Transition: A Tentative Catalogue." Program on Central and Eastern Europe Working Paper Series, Center for European Studies, Harvard University.

Taagapera, Rein, and Matthew S. Shugart. 1989. *Seats and Votes.* New Haven: Yale University Press.

Tabako, Tomasz. 1992. *Strajk 88.* Warsaw: NOWA.

Taras, Raymond. 1996. *Consolidating Democracy in Poland.* Boulder: Westview Press.

Taras, Wojciech. 1993. "Changes in Polish Public Administration, 1989–1992." *Public Administration* 71:12–32.

Tarkowska, Elzbieta. 1991. "Contemporary Polish Sociology vis a vis Cultural Anthropology or Prospects and Limitations of Anthropology in Contemporary Poland." *Polish Sociological Bulletin* 2:113–25.

———. 1993. "Temporalny wymiar przemian zachodzacych w Polsce." In *Kulturowy wymiar przemian spolecznych,* ed. Aldona Jawlowska, Marian Kempny, and Elzbieta Tarkowska, 87–100. Warsaw: Polska Akademia Nauk.

———. 1994. "The Cultural Responses to Permanent Instability." In *Cultural Dilemmas of Post- Communist Societies,* ed. Aldona Jawlowska and Marian Kempny, 268–83. Warsaw: IFiS Publishers.

Tarrow, Sidney. 1989. *Democracy and Disorder: Protest and Politics in Italy, 1965–1975*. Oxford: Clarendon Press.

———. 1991. "Aiming at a Moving Target: Social Science and the Recent Rebellions in Eastern Europe." *PS: Political Science and Politics* 24 (March): 12–20.

———. 1992a. "Costumes of Revolt: The Symbolic Politics of Social Movements." *Sisyphus: Social Studies* 8 (2): 53–71. Warsaw: IFiS/IPS Publishers.

———. 1992b. "Mentalities, Political Cultures, and Collective Action Frames: Constructing Meaning through Action." In *Frontiers in Social Movement Theory*, ed. Aldon D. Morris and Carol McClurg Mueller, 174–202. New Haven: Yale University Press.

———. 1995a. "Cycles of Collective Action: Between Moments of Madness and the Repertoire of Contention." In *Repertoires and Cycles of Collective Action*, ed. Mark Traugott, 89–115. Durham: Duke University Press.

———. 1995b. "Mass Mobilization and Regime Change: Pacts, Reform, and Popular Power in Italy (1918–1922) and Spain (1975–1978)." In *The Politics of Democratic Consolidation: Southern Europe in Comparative Perspective*, ed. Richard Gunther, Nikiforos Diamandouros, and Hans-Jurgen Puhle, 204–30. Baltimore: Johns Hopkins University Press.

Terry, Sarah Meiklejohn. 1996. "July 1976: Anatomy of an Avoidable Crisis." In *Poland's Permanent Revolution: People vs. Elites, 1956–1990*, ed. Jane Leftwich Curry and Luba Fajfer, 109–65. Washington, D.C.: American University Press.

Thirkell, John, Richard Scase, and Sarah Vickerstaff. 1995. *Labor Relations and Political Change in Eastern Europe*. Ithaca: Cornell University Press.

Tilly, Charles. 1978. *From Mobilization to Revolution*. New York: Random House.

———. 1979. "Repertoires of Contention in America and Britain, 1750–1830." In *The Dynamics of Social Movements*, ed. Mayer N. Zald and John D. McCarthy, 126–55. Cambridge: Winthrop.

———. 1984. "Social Movements and National Politics." In *Statemaking and Social Movements*, ed. Charles Bright and Susan Harding, 297–317. Ann Arbor: University of Michigan Press.

———. 1986. *The Contentious French*. Cambridge: Harvard University Press.

———. 1995a. "Contentious Repertoires in Great Britain, 1975–1834." In *Repertoires and Cycles of Collective Action*, ed. Mark Traugott, 15–42. Durham: Duke University Press.

———. 1995b. *Popular Contention in Great Britain, 1758–1834*. Cambridge: Harvard University Press.

Tilly, Charles, Louise Tilly, and Richard Tilly. 1975. *The Rebellious Century, 1830–1930*. Cambridge: Harvard University Press.

Tismaneanu, Vladimir, ed. 1990. *In Search of Civil Society: Independent Peace Movements in the Soviet Bloc*. New York: Routledge.

Touraine, Alain, et al. 1983. *Solidarity: Poland 1980–1981*. Cambridge: Cambridge University Press.

Turlejska, Maria. 1987. "Komunisci wobec spoleczenstwa polskiego: Ciaglosc i zmiana techniki wladzy." In *Rzeczywistosc polska i sposoby radzenia sobie z nia*, ed. Miroslawa Marody and Antoni Sulek, 37–63. Warsaw: IS UW.

————. 1990. *Te pokolenia zalobami czarne . . . Skazani na smierc i ich sedziowie.* Warsaw: Niezalezna Oficyna Wydawnicza.

Turner, Victor. 1978. *The Image and Pilgrimage in Christian Culture: Anthropological Perspective.* New York: Columbia University Press.

Tworzecki, Hubert. 1996. *Parties and Politics in Post-1989 Poland.* Boulder: Westview Press.

Uhlig, Anna. 1989. *W kregu symbolu: O polskiej kulturze politycznej lat osiemdziesiatych.* Warsaw: Uniwersytet Warszawski, Instytut Nauk Politycznych.

Vanshtein, Grigory. 1994. "Totalitarian Public Consciousness in Post-totalitarian Society: The Russian Case in the General Context of Post-communist Developments." *Communist and Post-Communist Studies* 27 (3): 247–59.

Valenzuela, Samuel J. 1989. "Labor Movements in Transitions to Democracy." *Comparative Politics* 21 (4): 445–72.

————. 1992. "Democratic Consolidation in Post-transitional Setting: Notion, Process, and Facilitating Conditions." In *Issues in Democratic Consolidation: The New South American Democracies in Comparative Perspective,* ed. Scott Mainwaring, Guillermo O'Donnell, and J. Samuel Valenzuela, 57–104. Notre Dame: University of Notre Dame Press.

Vanous, Jan, ed. 1994. *PlanEcon Report* 10 (February 14). Washington, D.C.: PlanEcon.

Verba, Sidney, Norman Nie, and Jae-on Kim. 1978. *Participation and Political Equality.* Cambridge: Cambridge University Press.

Verdery, Katherine. 1996. *What Was Socialism, What Comes Next?* Princeton: Princeton University Press.

Vinton, Louise. 1992. "Polish Government Proposes Pact on State Firms." *RFE/RL Research Report* 42 (1): 10–18.

————. 1993. "Poland's Social Safety Net: An Overview." *RFE/RL Research Report,* 17 (2): 3–11.

Walicki, Andrzej. 1984. "The Main Components of the Situation in Poland." *Politics* 19 (1): 4–17.

Wallace, Michael, and J. Craig Jenkins. 1995. "The New Class, Postindustrialism, and Neocorporatism: Three Images of Social Protest in the Western Democracies." In *The Politics of Social Protest: Comparative Perspectives on States and Social Movements,* ed. J. Craig Jenkins and Bert Klandermans, 96–137. Minneapolis: University of Minnesota Press.

Waller, Michael. 1994. "Political Actors and Political Roles in East Central Europe." In *Parties, Trade Unions, and Society in East-Central Europe,* ed. Michael Waller and Martin Myant, 21–36. Portland: Frank Cass.

Walton, John. 1991. "Debt, Protest, and the State in Latin America." In *Power and Popular Protest in Latin American Social Movements,* ed. Susan Eckstein, 299–328. Berkeley: University of California Press.

Walton, John, and Charles Ragin. 1990. "Global and National Sources of Political Protest: Third World Responses to the Debt Crisis." *American Sociological Review* 55 (December): 876–90.

Walton, John, and D. Seddon. 1994. *Free Markets and Food Riots: The Politics of Global Adjustment.* Oxford: Blackwell.

Walzer, Michael. 1993. "The New Political Ideologies." *Economist*, September 11–17, 50.

Wasilewski, Jacek. 1995. "The Crystallization of the Post-Communist and Post-Solidarity Political Elite." In *After Communism: A Multidisciplinary Approach to Radical Social Change*, ed. Edmund Wnuk-Lipinski, 117–33. Warsaw: ISP PAN.

———, ed. 1994. *Konsolidacja elit politycznych w Polsce, 1991–1993*. Warsaw: ISP PAN.

Wasilewski, Jacek, and Michal Pohoski. 1992. "Communist Nomenklatura in the Post-communist Poland." Paper presented at the First European Conference of Sociology, Vienna, August 26–29.

Weber, Robert Philip. 1990. *Basic Content Analysis*. Newbury Park: Sage.

Wedel, Janine. 1986. *The Private Poland*. New York: Facts on File.

Weigle, Marcia A., and Jim Butterfield. 1992. "Civil Society in Reforming Communist Regimes: The Logic of Emergence." *Comparative Politics* 25 (1): 1–23.

Wejnert, Barbara. 1988. "The Student Movement in Poland, 1980–1981." *Research in Social Movements, Conflicts, and Change* 10:173–81.

Weller, Robert, and Scott Guggenheim, eds. 1989. *Power and Protest in the Countryside*. Durham: Duke University Press.

Wertenstein-Zulawski, Jerzy, and Miroslaw Peczak, eds. 1991. *Spontaniczna kultura mlodziezowa*. Wroclaw: Wiedza o Kulturze.

Wesolowski, Wlodzimierz. 1995. "Formowanie sie partii politycznych w postkomunistycznej Polsce." *Studia Polityczne* 4:7–28.

Wiesenthal, Helmut. 1995. "Representation of Functional Interests in West and East European Democracies: Theoretical Coordinates and Empirical Assessment." Working paper. Berlin: Max-Planck-Gesellschaft, Humboldt Universitat.

Wilson, Frank L. 1994. "Political Demonstrations in France: Protest Politics or Politics of Ritual?" *French Politics and Society* 12 (Spring and Summer): 23–40.

Wilson, Richard. 1991. "Political Pathology and Moral Orientations." *Comparative Political Studies* 24 (2): 211–30.

Wladyka, Wieslaw. 1989. *Na czolowce: Prasa w Pazdzierniku 1956 roku*. Warsaw: PWN.

———. 1994. *Pazdziernik 56*. Warsaw: Wydawnictwa Szkolne i Pedagogiczne.

Wnuk-Lipinski, Edmund. 1994. "Fundamentalizm a pragmatyzm: Dwa typy reakcji na radykalna zmiane spoleczna." *Kultura i Spoleczenstwo* 38 (1): 3–12.

Wolfsfeld, Gadi. 1988. *The Politics of Provocation: Participation and Protest in Israel*. Albany: State University of New York Press.

Wozniczka, Zygmunt. 1992. *Zrzeszenie Wolnosc i Niezawislosc*. Warsaw: Novum-Semex.

Wrobel, Renata. 1994. *Cztery lata reformy*. Warsaw: Presspublica.

Wyzan, Michael. 1996. "Increased Inequality, Poverty Accompany Economic Transition." *Transition*, October 4, 24–27.

Xueguang, Zhou. 1993. "Unorganized Interests and Collective Action in Communist China." *American Sociological Review* 58 (February): 54–73.

Zagorski, Krzysztof. 1994. "Hope Factor, Inequality, and Legitimacy of Systemic Transformations: The Case of Poland." *Communist and Post-Communist Studies* 27 (4): 357–76.

Zaryn, Jan. 1996. "Ostatnia 'legalna opozycja' polityczna w Polsce, 1944–1947." In *Polacy wobec przemocy 1944–1956,* ed. Barbara Otwinowska and Jan Zaryn, 80–120. Warsaw: Editions Spotkania.

Zielonka, Jan. 1987. "Poland: The Experiment with Communist Statism." In *The Crisis Problems in Poland.* Research Project, Crises in the Soviet-Type Systems, Study 12a, 59–82. Cologne: Index.

Zinner, Paul, ed. 1956. *National Communism and Popular Revolt in Eastern Europe.* New York: Praeger.

Ziolkowski, Marek. 1993. "Two Orientations in the Post-monocentric Order in Poland." *Sisyphus: Social Studies* 9 (2): 35–43. Warsaw: IFiS/IPS PAN.

Zmigrodzki, Marek, ed. 1997. *Kierunki ewolucji systemu politycznego Rzeczypospolitej Polskiej.* Lublin: UMCS.

Zubek, Voytek. 1993. "The Fragmentation of Poland's Political Party System." *Communist and Post-Communist Studies* 26 (1): 47–71.

Zucchini, Salvatore, ed. 1997. *Lessons for the Economic Transition.* Dordrecht: Kluwer.

Index